RACE AND ETHNICITY IN CHICAGO POLITICS

Race and Ethnicity in Chicago Politics

A Reexamination of Pluralist Theory

DIANNE M. PINDERHUGHES

University of Illinois Press
URBANA AND CHICAGO

Manufactured in the United States of America
C 5 4 3 2 1

This book is printed on acid-free paper.

Library of Congress Cataloging-in-Publication Data

Pinderhughes, Dianne M. (Dianne Marie), 1947–
Race and ethnicity in Chicago politics.

Bibliography: p.
Includes index.
1. Minorities—Illinois—Chicago—Political activity—History—20th century. 2. Chicago (Ill.)—Politics and government—To 1950. I. Title.
F548.9.A1P56 1987 323.1'77311 86-19297
ISBN 0-252-01294-1 (alk. paper)

To my mother and father

Contents

Tables

Figures

Acknowledgments

The completion of this book required great generosity on the part of many people. Numerous scholars, colleagues, public policy professionals, and friends helped in its production from its genesis as a dissertation at the University of Chicago through many revisions to this book. Considerable work was accomplished during the routine demands of teaching, but substantial revisions were also completed during a sabbatical and Junior Faculty Fellowship from Dartmouth College in 1981–82. Also during that year, the Governmental Studies Program at the Brookings Institution accorded me the privileges of a Guest Scholar. Most of the prepublication revisions were completed during my last months in New Hampshire in 1984, and I am grateful to both Jim Wright, then associate dean, and Vincent Starzinger, chairman of the Government Department at Dartmouth College, for their cooperation in facilitating that process. I must also express my gratitude to the Ford Foundation Postdoctoral Fellowship for Minorities Program, the University of California at Los Angeles' Institute of American Cultures, and UCLA's Center for Afro-American Studies under Director Claudia Mitchell-Kernan for their support while I put the finishing touches on the work in late 1984.

I acknowledge the contributions of many scholars, including my original advisers, the reviewers who made careful and extensive comments, and colleagues who evaluated the book or shaped my thinking on it. They include my committee at the University of Chicago, Leonard Binder, Paul E. Peterson, and William J. Wilson; and a long but incomplete list of others to whom I am indebted—Marguerite Ross Barnett King, Michael B. Preston, Charles Henry, Lorenzo Morris, Roger Oden, Huey Perry, Robert Starks, Toni-Michelle C. Travis, Linda Williams, Ted Lowi, and Gary Orfield.

I thank my colleagues at Dartmouth in "Govy 6," Lynn Mather, Robert Nakamura, Denis Sullivan, and Richard Winters, whose intellectual stimulation and encouragement meant a great deal. With the help of Elsa Brown, Joel Levine, and Richard Winters, I learned two word processing languages, which made completion of the revisions much easier. Colleagues at Dartmouth who deserve special thanks for their personal and professional loyalty include Elsa Brown, Deborah King, Roger Masters, and Frank Smallwood.

I owe a great deal to the librarians who were helpful at various stages in the book's development. At the Chicago Municipal Reference Library, Deborah Morrow, Mary Jane Heilburger, and Gloria Huffman were patient as I requested volume after volume of city records; Alice Neff was helpful at the Brookings Institution. I owe heartfelt appreciation for all the work performed by reference librarians over the years at Dartmouth's Baker Library, including Patsy Carter, Virginia Close, Bob Jaccaud, and Lois Krieger, whom I grew to appreciate and respect as professionals and to care for as friends. Their expertise enriched my work, their personal care and concern enriched my life.

I also want to thank my copy editor at the University of Illinois Press, Barbara E. Cohen, who was meticulous in her treatment of my work, but who also took the time to talk me down from several walls I had climbed while responding to her questions. I offer many thanks and my deep appreciation.

Deborah Hodges at Dartmouth typed portions of the book several times, always with extraordinary cheerfulness and speed, often despite great personal stress. I owe her special thanks.

My research assistants included Bob Bursik, Su So Fai, and Doug Baldwin, who coded data or wrote programs for the analysis of the educational and criminal justice statistics. Charmaine Curtis researched and located recently published materials and shared her cheerful demeanor. My students at Dartmouth, including Ed Fernandez, Marsha Love, Randall Johnson, Steven Morse, Darryl Piggee, Gerald Rosenberg and Frank Wilderson, wrote papers, listened to my lectures, and asked questions that enriched the book.

I also want to thank several friends who gave freely of their trust, companionship, and love and therefore helped make this book possible: Deborah Lee Jones, Maga Jackson, Barbara and Samuel Smith, Dora Vivaz, Pat Morton Gourdine, and Dwight Lahr.

This book is dedicated to my parents—my father, D. James and my mother, Rosa—but I want to say that it is also for my sister Gayle. She tolerated my frequent visits to Boston when I needed respite from the cold New Hampshire winters, and she helps me keep things in perspective. To my family, this is for all of you.

Introduction

When I set out to research the status of blacks in Chicago politics some years ago, the city's blacks, a significant portion of the population, were subordinated within and by the Chicago machine despite the fact that they voted, held political and administrative office, and participated in the operations of the machine. No black had ever been mayor of the city, chair of the Democratic party's central committee, an elected member of the Cook County Commission after 1910, or held any citywide office; black unemployment was high, blacks were confined to exclusively black neighborhoods on the south or west sides, and academics and journalists routinely referred to Chicago as the most segregated city in America. This was a political conundrum of some magnitude that begged for an explanation. By the time this work had moved from a dissertation through several revisions into its present format, that history had rewritten itself; the deterioration and collapse of the Chicago machine simultaneous with the maturation of a political coalition within the black population led to a successful black campaign for the mayor's position.

This book explains the racial and ethnic politics of Chicago by examining the experiences of its Afro-American, Italian, and Polish citizens. My task in this book is to describe the entrance of a new racial group and two new ethnic groups into American urban politics. I examine how new groups transform themselves from immigrants and migrants into American citizens and residents of a particular urban environment such as Chicago's. In the nineteenth century large numbers of European nationalities, beginning with the Irish in the 1840s, then the Germans, Swedes, eastern Europeans, and finally in the late nineteenth and early twentieth centuries, Poles and Italians, entered Chicago and became participants in local politics.

The problem of political integration is one the United States has faced throughout its history, but during the first decades of the twentieth century this became a task of a different color as black migration from the southern cotton fields accelerated. Pushed by racist, post-

Populist southern disfranchisement and pulled by the lure of high paying, northern factory jobs going unfilled by Europeans whose immigration was blocked by the start of the First World War, blacks flooded into Detroit, New York, Cleveland, and Chicago, rapidly transforming the urban racial and political environment of these cities. This, I will argue, was a political task of considerably different magnitude.

For the first time American cities faced the task of integrating Afro-Americans, natives of the United States but of distinctive racial origins. This was to prove a considerably more serious problem than the integration of earlier waves of European nationalities, the groups from eastern and southern Europe or Mexicans, who were on occasion classified as "nonwhite" by the United States census. Race constituted a radically distinctive factor in economic, social, and ultimately political life; as Marguerite Barnett has argued, America's racial hierarchy consistently subordinates blacks politically, economically, and socially. Race, unlike ethnicity, is so distinct as to make the process of political integration considerably more difficult and different for Afro-Americans than it was for European immigrants.

When I sought some explanation for the distinct political history of blacks in the political science literature, I turned to studies of European immigrants that focused on their assimilation into the American political system, to Merton's conceptualization of political machines, and to the reports of several decades of studies of Chicago's blacks: Gosnell in the 1920s, Drake and Cayton in the 1930s, and Wilson in the 1950s. I needed to ascertain how accurately these described the events in question and whether the political life of Afro-Americans was not already sufficiently described.

All of the earlier studies examined the black population over a relatively specific period of time and, perhaps more importantly, all examined that population in isolation. In order to increase understanding of the processes of political integration, I decided to consider the economic environment within which the three groups existed and to compare the respective institutional settings in which their political growth took place. This study also compares their route and speed of entry into political participation as measured by voting, nomination, and election to political office. Because the Italians' and Poles' arrival in the United States was closest in time to the black population's maturation in Chicago, primarily during the years from 1910 to 1940, these nationalities provided a suitable basis for comparison.

To consider and accurately measure their political integration and participation, I assumed that "success" was dependent on the extent to which these groups extracted political resources and rewards from the system to which they lent their support. Two important governmental institutions for such purposes included the criminal justice and the educational systems. In the first case, recent arrivals in search of work, unemployed and unfamiliar with the rules of their new environment, were much more likely to be in frequent contact with members of the police department. Hypothetically, political integration might reduce the negative consequences of such contact. In the second, public education, largely unavailable to all three of the groups prior to their migration, was an important resource whose distribution could aid new groups seeking social as well as physical mobility. I sought to discover evidence of differences in the distribution and governance of these public goods that correlate with measures of the intensity of political participation by the groups.

These were the expectations with which I began my research, and I found the patterns of interaction much less clear than I had predicted. I expected the data to show considerable racial discrimination by the police as well as significant discrimination in the distribution of educational resources. To my consternation, I found both more discrimination and less clear patterns of it in the data than I had expected. My task in this book is to reconcile these contradictory findings with my conclusions.

This study has several specific goals. First I have the general task of explaining the apparently high degree of political integration of Chicago's black population by the 1960s and 1970s despite the relatively low degree of independent control and direct competition for citywide political leadership which it exhibited. In the process I have constructed an explanation for the extraordinary events and extraordinarily intense political period through which Chicago and its residents lived in 1982 and 1983, which resulted in the election of Harold Washington as Chicago's first black mayor.

The study's second goal addresses the theoretical explanation of black politics and black political participation in the American urban environment. The study reexamines pluralist theories of political science as they have been applied to racial and ethnic groups in the process of political integration and shows how these theories focus too narrowly on the groups, and how they fail to examine the political, economic, and social environment in which they exist. I looked for evidence of the character of the northern economic, social, and ultimately political environment for the three groups from 1910 through 1940, and I show the quite different types of "political linkages" described by Martin Kilson and Ira Katznelson created between blacks, Italians, and Poles and the native white population, which in turn affected the internal politics and organizational structures of the black, Italian, and Polish communities.

The plan of the book is as follows. The first part examines the economic, social, and political environment of twentieth century Chicago. Chapter 1 introduces Chicago of the late twentieth century, a complex multiracial, multiethnic amalgam, a city of neighborhoods, an industrial city in transition, still lovingly married to the political machine—Mayor Daley's Chicago. Chapter 2 shifts its temporal location to the city of over a half century before, during the period from 1910 to 1940, to compare the origins, institutional structures, and demographic patterns of the black population with Chicago's Polish and Italian communities. The bulk of the book will focus on this era from 1910 through the 1940s. Chapter 3 concludes the first section with an examination of the consequences of machine organization for racial and ethnic groups' political integration.

The next two chapters examine the structure of politics in the three communities, the impact of racial discrimination on the ideological belief systems of black citizens, and the character of black political participation. Chapter 4 examines the political activities of the three groups for quantitative evidence of qualitative differences in the speed of their political integration and in their political status. The chapter presents a model for analyzing ethnic and racial groups' political strength and influence and compares descriptive representation for each group. Chapter 5 discusses the concept of collective status or racial discrimination and collective benefits in a political environment that focuses on selective or economic status and divisible benefits. The chapter evaluates James Q. Wilson's model of black political philosophy and shows how it is too narrow to describe or contain accurately the full range of black political beliefs or ideologies. An alternate model of black political philosophy is proposed.

Next, two chapters analyze *substantive representation* or the extent to which public officials create public policies that respond to the interests of their constituents. When ethnic or racial groups win election to office from similar constitutenties, what Pitkin calls *descriptive* representation, without also influencing the formation of public policy in the interest of their group, *symbolic* rather than substantive representation results. I examine how the criminal justice and educational systems responded to the political participation of the three groups in question. The pluralist model predicts little variation in the regulation of the legal and educational administrations by racial or ethnic communities, especially after their political participation increases. The regular operation of the political machine should show some variation in the application of law and education based on selective rewards.

Illegal activities involving the production, distribution, and marketing of alcohol in bars and nightclubs along with concomitant activities, such as gambling and prostitution, flourished in Chicago during the years from 1910 to 1940. Two of the groups, blacks and Italians, were heavily involved in these illegal activities. Using data from the criminal justice system from 1878 through 1931, chapter 6 investigates the rates of arrests, charges, and convictions of blacks, Italians, and Poles. The quantitative and the historical evidence shows that the criminal justice administration sharply distinguished between racial and ethnic groups.

Public education prepares new generations for life, is one of the largest bureaucracies in city government, and is a very important source for employment and, therefore, for patronage. How racial and ethnic groups fared in controlling these important resources in the city as a whole, but also within their own neighborhoods, reveals a great deal about their success and their integration into the political system. Chapter 7 compares the operation of the system of public education in heavily settled black, Italian, and Polish neighborhoods, in order to determine whether differences in political participation explain any differences in educational expenditures for the three groups.

The final chapter offers analysis and conclusions. Chapter 8 matches the evidence presented in earlier chapters with the theoretical analyses about the entry of racial and ethnic groups into the Chicago political system from 1910 to 1940. Ultimately, race and ethnicity are distinguished as statuses with significantly different political meanings. In this chapter I also briefly summarize political developments in the city from 1940 through 1980 and conclude by explaining the dynamics of the mayoral primary and election of 1983.

1

The Last Days of the Chicago Machine

"I like Epton better than the other guy. . . . The other guy don't want no machine, don't want no committeemen, and don't want no Democratic Party. I'll___him on Election Day."

—Vito Marzullo on mayoral candidate Harold Washington

"We Shall See in '83"

On April 12, 1983, Harold Washington raised his arms above his head in a display of triumphant dominance and grinned at the large excited, predominantly black crowd that filled Donnelley Hall; in response to their cries of "We want Harold," he answered "You want Harold? . . . Well, you've got him!" Congressman Harold Washington had just been elected mayor of Chicago in a closely fought race with Bernard Epton. Few political observers would have predicted the outcome or even the major contenders six months before (Kleppner 1983).

A series of unexpected events characterized the 1983 mayoral campaign and made it both simultaneously possible and more difficult for Washington to win office. The Democratic primary had several entrants: incumbent mayor Jane Byrne, elected in a reform campaign in 1979; Harold Washington, congressman from the first district and former state representative; and Richard M. Daley, state's attorney and son of the late Mayor Daley. For the first time since 1931 a challenger had defeated the machine's candidate for mayor; the victor, Jane Byrne, eventually made her peace with machine politicians so that she and Daley, the prince of the city, divided leadership of important segments of the city's political elite. Against them Harold Washington was a weak challenger who was not taken seriously during most of the primary election campaign.[1]

This status gave Washington the strategic advantage because white politicians did not carefully consider how the black population's increasing turnout and independence in recent years might affect the primary. Not until late in the campaign did Byrne and Daley realize the potential of the Washington challenge. Even after Byrne and Daley perceived Washington's threat to their election, neither withdrew and high black voter turnout and loyalty gave Washington a narrow plurality.

The contest for mayor quickly moved from the phase immediately after the election, when the city was stunned by Washington's primary victory and by the prospect of a black mayor, to a determined effort to seek another outcome. Once the city's partisans realized they had a black mayoral candidate, the expected "hands-down" Democratic victory turned into a serious intra- and interparty contest for the city's highest office. Daley accepted Washington's nomination as the Democratic candidate, but Jane Byrne, who at first conceded Washington's nomination, later reneged and announced her candidacy for mayor as an independent. When she realized her efforts increased Washington's chances for election and magnified the antipathy of the city's whites toward her, she withdrew.[2]

The Republicans nominated Bernard Epton, lawyer and former state representative from the Hyde Park section of Chicago, with only 11,343 votes in his party's primary. Epton suddenly found himself the candidate of second and third generation Democratic voters, of "Democratic" aldermen (they are formally nonpartisan), and most dramatically of Democratic ward committeemen. At least eight of the fifty committeemen, including Vito Marzullo of the twenty-fifth ward and Edmund Kelly of the forty-seventh ward and superintendent of the Chicago park district, endorsed the Republican nominee for mayor (Pinderhughes 1983). Edward Vrdolyak, chairman of the Democratic Committee for Cook County, and Edward Burke of the fourteenth ward never endorsed Epton but made their disagreements with Washington public.[3]

Byrne's race for mayor four years before had produced intraparty friction but no defections from the party's central committee. In previous elections, voters affirmed machine rule, voted for, or more rarely, voted against the machine; in the Epton-Washington contest, they concentrated on "race in the race."[4] Instead of the conventional expression of Democratic identification with the Democratic party and a reassertion of the alliance that had bound Irish, Poles, Italians, blacks, Greeks, Germans, Czechs, Lithuanians, Bohemians, and Mexicans together for decades within the Democratic party, Harold Washington's nomination as mayor of the city provoked a dramatic and perhaps irreparable disturbance in the city's political status quo. It is necessary to understand why party leaders and white ethnics broke away from the Democratic party, to which they had been so loyal for over half a century, to support a Jewish Republican. What provoked them to deviate from their traditional partisan alliance? Would the 1983 electoral deviation mark a permanent realignment?

Another issue is also important in understanding the evolution of Chicago politics in this particular election. Nationally and locally Jews traditionally identify with the Democratic party. It is significant to understand how a Jewish candidate could become the 1983 mayoral nominee of the Republican party in Chicago. Prior to this time, such an occurrence would have been unthinkable. Only a few years ago Milton Rakove quoted Burke, fourteenth ward alderman and committeeman, now a Vrdolyak ally: "There is a latent anti-Semitism in Chicago and a large population that will never vote for a Jew. They would vote for anybody before a Jew" (Rakove 1979:144).

Apparently Washington's nomination so strongly affected ethnics' perception of the new political reality that they no longer behaved as nationality groups allied within the Democratic party. Instead, they responded to Washington's race rather than to his partisan affiliation. They became whites, as opposed to Americans of European descent, seeking favorable representations of their interests. In the general election, therefore, race dominated partisan identification and the only other white in the race, Bernard Epton, became the most attractive candidate despite the fact that he was a Republican.

Once the city's political leaders indicated that they would take action to block a Washington election, either by supporting and voting Republican or by challenging the Democratic and Republican candidates with an independent candidate, heightened tensions, racist events, campaign literature, and songs burst into the open. The expressions took form into which blacks and whites read racial, even racist significance. Epton's television ads ended with "Epton . . . Before It's too Late"; campaign buttons appeared on which were pictured black lips, a slice of watermelon, ribs, a can of beer, and the words "Chicongo, Po-lease"; campaign literature in police stations cautioned "No matter what anyone tells you, this election has come down to race" (Kleppner 1983:107). Finally, one Epton campaign song played with some frequency was "Bye, Bye Blackbird," to suggest Washington's defeat.

On the morning of March 27, 1983, Easter Sunday, Harold Washington and Walter Mondale attempted to attend mass at St. Pascal's Roman Catholic church, on the northwest side; they were blocked from entering by a crowd that vociferously chanted its support for Bernard Epton. This was a controversial event, as some observers charged that Washington had gone into the area to provoke violence or that it was inappropriate to bring politics into church.[5]

Partisan divisions, a wholesale decline in support for the Democratic party, racist buttons, literature, and songs among whites contrasted sharply with political activity among blacks in the city. First, black support focused on one candidate, Harold Washington. Unlike the machine's adherents who could not repress their differences about support for Byrne or Daley, the black community had decided upon and unified behind Harold Washington by late 1982. After the choice was made, in a process which will be described in the concluding chapter, there were no challenges to Washington's candidacy by blacks in either the primary or the general elections (McWorter et al. 1984).

Approximately 84.7 percent of blacks voted and 64.2 percent of the black population of voting age turned out to participate in the primary. In the general election 73 percent of voting age blacks turned out and 99.7 percent voted for Washington (Kleppner 1983: 70, 84, 98). Over the last decades, national voter registration and turnout figures for whites over blacks have shown a 5 percent or greater surplus, but for the 1983 primary in Chicago 82.2 percent of whites, 87.2 percent of blacks, but only 37.7 percent of Hispanics were registered to vote. By the general election the figures reached 83.2 percent, 89.1 percent and 37 percent for whites, blacks, and Hispanics respectively. Black voter turnout equalled or exceeded white voter turnout in the 1983 primary and general election. Sixty-four and six-tenths percent of the white, 64.2 percent of the black, and 23.9 percent of the Hispanic voting age population turned out for the primary; for the general election, blacks surpassed whites as 73 percent of the total black, 67.2 percent of the white, and 24.3 percent of the Hispanic voting age population voted. The sharp contrast between national patterns of voter registration and the Chicago percentages in the 1983 primary represents another puzzle. There must be an explanation for this sharp divergence from "normal" black voting behavior, assuming that we can establish what is normal for black voters. The literature on black voters poses a number of explanations and offers markedly different explanations for their behavior. I believe the sharp rise in turnout in this and other local and congressional elections requires a reexamination of existing explanations of political participation by blacks (see Jennings 1983:v–viii; Nie et al. 1976: chaps. 13–14; Pinderhughes 1984; Verba and Nie 1972).

The Daley Machine

On April 2, 1975, only eight years before Washington's victory, Richard J. Daley stood before a crowd of party workers and acknowledged their support for his election to an unprecedented sixth term of office. Although three opponents had challenged Daley in the Democratic primary, he defeated them soundly, winning 57.8 percent of the vote; he took the general election with 79.6 percent of the vote (Zikmund 1982:36, 42). Mayor Daley, whom columnist Mike Royko reported was known by some of the city's children as having the first name of Mayor, was known fondly to journalists and political observers by a number of names, among them "Hizzoner," Da Mayor, and Dick Daley.[6]

Famous for his malapropisms, such as "the policeman isn't there to create disorder, the policeman is there to preserve disorder" (Rakove 1975:46), Daley was nevertheless a formidably talented political leader, the most talented since mayor Anton Cermak, who died in 1933. Elected in 1955, Daley held not only the mayor's position but also chaired the Democratic party's Cook County Central Committee, which put him in charge of the city's administrative as well as its political apparatus. No other mayor had held the party leadership alone before Daley; none has held it since.[7] Milton Rakove explained this concentration of power: "He used his power as mayor to strengthen his role as party chairman, and he used his power as party chairman to strengthen his role as mayor" (Rakove 1982:219).

"Hizzoner" was a restrained, disciplined, and oddly charismatic mayor; he was educated in Chicago's Catholic schools, including De Paul University Law School, which he attended at night. He came from a working class Irish family and lived all his life in Bridgeport, in the eleventh ward near the stockyards and industrial areas of the inner city. Yet he took control of the city and the machine decisively and managed them in a way that is best summarized by the late Milton Rakove:

Daley significantly altered the Chicago political machine and the government of the city. First, the power balance within the machine was changed. Daley strengthened the role of the mayor, improved the quality of the bureaucracy and city services, took control of the city council and public policy away from the ward committeemen and worked out a partnership built on mutual self-interest with the powerful business and labor elites who provided the major economic underpinnings of the city. He created in Chicago a sophisticated political/governmental/private interest group system of relationships and collaboration based on a pragmatic assessment of the realities of power in a body politic (Rakove 1982:222).

A powerful mayor and party leader, Daley's political organization had a reputation for overwhelming, if not precluding, all challenges and avoiding losers. William Singer, Richard Newhouse, and Edward Hanrahan challenged the machine in the 1975 primary, but they were unable to win even a majority of the citywide vote. Singer was a north shore, independent alderman, Newhouse a state senator from the independent Hyde Park-University of Chicago section of Chicago, and Hanrahan, a former machine state's attorney turned dissident. Singer won nearly thirty percent of the total vote in the primary, but his strongest support came from the neighborhoods of high socioeconomic status and independent political identification along the lake shore. Newhouse won only 7.9 percent of the vote in the primary, suggesting he fared poorly with black voters, but Zikmund's analysis shows that the three challengers polled more votes together than Daley in twelve wards, nine of which were predominantly black. Electoral turnout for the 1975 primary was very low at 48.5 percent for white voters, 34.1 percent among black voters, and a dismal 23.6 percent in the black wards of the late William Dawson (the second, third, fourth, sixth and twentieth wards). Machines generally prefer winning an election with lower voter turnout to losing it with massive voter mobilization (Kemp and Lineberry 1982:16; Kleppner 1983:70; Wilson 1960a; Zikmund 1982:42).

On the other hand in 1975, the Daley machine's strongest support came in the industrial and outer city wards where the European ethnic population was most heavily concentrated (Grimshaw 1982: 71–75; Zikmund 1982:40–42). None of the challengers made any serious inroads into the mayor's strongest base of Democratic support. In 1975 Daley governed the machine and the machine governed the city with undivided white ethnic support and an unmobilized and divided black electorate represented by "controlled" or "administration" political officials.[8]

If black voters were not unanimous in their support of the administration in 1975, they at least behaved consistently with some of the theories of political behavior. Citizens of lower socioeconomic status typically register and vote at significantly lower rates than those of higher status; black voters fall into lower socioeconomic categories more frequently. In recent decades black turnout in Chicago has been low; as recently as the 1977 mayoral primary, only 27.4 percent of the black population of voting age voted. Chicago's political observers predicted no significant changes in the political behavior of blacks; some argued that their absence of leadership, failure to vote, and lower socioeconomic status itself limited the potential for black voting (Kleppner 1983:70; Peterson 1976; Preston 1982b).

The 1975 and 1983 elections thus represented two radically different periods in Chicago politics, so different that it is difficult to believe they were separated by only eight years. The death of the mayor certainly brought about significant changes, but how and more importantly why did such dramatic reorderings of the city's political structure occur so quickly after his death? While Chicago had only four mayors (Cermak, Kelly, Kennelley, and Daley) in the forty-five years between 1931 and 1976, Harold Washington is the third mayor (after Bilandic and Byrne) in only eight years. While the machine faced three challengers in the 1975 primary, it successfully defeated them. The low vote totals in that year might be explained as one of the goals of political machines because low turnout elections are more easily controllable.

From time to time other independent challengers arose, such as Edward Vrdolyak, Charles Chew, or Fred Hubbard, who just as quickly made their peace or arranged their price with the machine.[9] Chew ran as an independent candidate for alderman in 1963 and moved to the state senate in 1966, while Vrdolyak contested the machine's candidate for Cook County assessor in 1974, but each later rejoined the machine. Hubbard was elected alderman of the second ward, but later disappeared along with close to $100,000 in cash from the Chicago Plan, a program he directed to develop jobs for blacks in the construction industry (O'Connor 1975:220–21; Rakove 1979:134–35).

While party identification is strongest among those individuals who live through a critical electoral period, as did the parents and grandparents of Chicago's voters, there was no erosion of votes to the Republicans in the 1970s among these younger ethnic Democrats; there was a perceptible increase of independent voting among blacks and upper middle class whites in the city. While black voters had gradually decreased their turnout and loyalty to the Democratic machine, the party leaders expected no serious challenge to their continued control, and black observers predicted no dramatic changes in black political behavior. Where do we look, therefore, for an explanation for the unexpected changes that have occurred since 1980? What happened to destroy the last of the big city political machines?

Characteristics of Machines

In order to see how the Chicago political machine operated and then failed, the simplest strategy is to turn briefly to an examination of the characteristics of that machine and its methods of operation, all of which are discussed in greater detail in chapter 3. Rakove summarized Daley's strategy for satisfying voters and winning elections:

> pick a slate of candidates who represent the racial, cultural, religious, and social biases of the polyglot constitutencies that make up the city's body politic. Second, take care of the basic private needs of the voters. Third, get the voters you represent out on election day. If you did those three things well . . . elections would be won . . . [based on] votes in return for emotions appeased, services rendered, and a disciplined organization maintained (1982:220).

How well had the machine achieved these goals of descriptive representation, private substantive representation, and electoral mobilization? Identifying a broad coalition is never difficult in Chicago, but picking one that represents the heterogeneous views within each community is a delicate task. The job of satisfying the private needs of one's constituents is considerably more problematic. Machines focus on tangible and divisible benefits, which they distribute selectively to each constituent in exchange for a vote. The machine just as selectively denies or withdraws the benefit if the constituent fails to support the machine's slate of candidates.

There are several problems in this framework; first, does the machine distribute these benefits proportionately? If a group's size wanes over time, but it refuses to relinquish its hold on the benefits tendered by the machine, new or expanding groups face delayed political rewards. Second, private demands of groups sometimes conflict; one group may oppose property ownership, employment, and other goals of another group, particularly when benefits are scarce. When such conflicts occur, providing benefits to one or another group satisfies neither. Third, machines provide tangible, selective incentives when some groups demand intangible, collective benefits, such as the desire of blacks to end society's discrimination against them as a group. Solving problems of discrimination in public or private employment, pay, or housing rewards groups as a whole. Fourth, private demands frequently have public as well as private consequences. Certain private demands, such as collective benefits, are inherently public. There is no way to limit the consequences of such demands to one segment of the society. In politics, the private is public. Fifth, benefits that reward private demands at one point in time might prove thoroughly unsatisfactory at another. Blacks accepted or perhaps tolerated lower status machine jobs from 1931 through the 1970s, but no longer found them sufficiently rewarding afterwards.

All of these possibilities accumulated to the situation that characterized the operation of the Chicago machine in the late 1970s. Although descriptive representation suggests political equality as well as a certain amount of flexibility and competition, this was not the case in Chicago. The Chicago machine was a static hierarchy ruled by the Irish, managed at the intermediate levels by loyal but restive European ethnics, such as the Poles, Germans, and other eastern Europeans. At the bottom of that hierarchy, blacks controlled black areas but competed for leadership in no other neighborhoods of the city. Their subordinate status within the machine grew out of their late coerced entry into it, while their national status, which subjected blacks to discrimination in law and in custom, reinforced their status at the local level.[10]

The national pattern of racial subordination created private demands among blacks that exceeded the bounds of the selective tangible benefits provided by the machine. Thus the creation of the machine involved an inherent tension between what it provided and what blacks wanted. As long as national politics subordinated blacks firmly, strongly, and the machine itself was also strong, that tension was only theoretical. But when blacks rejected racial discrimination and demanded their citizenship rights, along both the political and economic dimensions (discussed in chapter 5), and when national subordination of the black population eroded, then the tension between the selective benefits provided by the machine and the collective racial status goals of the black population in Chicago became more intense if not intolerable.[11] Once the black population acknowledged the significance of racial discrimination as a factor in its political status, it could think about challenging the operations and the existence of the machine, but as long as national subordination continued and the machine was strong among its other constituent groups, the tension was more potential than actual.

Yet for Chicago's political leaders to acknowledge the existence of past differences in political and economic status between blacks and European ethnics created considerable tension among its white supporters. Those at the top and intermediate levels of the fifty-year-old hierarchy did not willingly accept a change in status or in controlling the rewards that machine loyalists distributed to themselves.

The remainder of this study demonstrates how the machine bound European ethnics and blacks together in the static political hierarchy that distributed selective benefits to whites as well as to blacks, although a bit more selectively to the latter. I demonstrate that blacks won some benefits from the machine, but it did not protect them from the consequences of discrimination because of its focus on specific selective benefits rather than on broader collective goals.

To address issues of racial discrimination in Chicago, blacks had several options; they could reform discriminatory structures at the national level, they could reform the machine by competing directly for its leadership with white ethnics and forcing them to share power, or they could destroy it altogether, directly addressing the issue of race and making racial discrimination into a substantive issue on the local political agenda. The conventional form of the machine between 1921 and the late 1970s permitted none of these options. Because society recognized blacks collectively rather than individually and discriminated against them because of their membership in a group rather than because of their individual characteristics, to mitigate racial discrimination blacks had to reform or to move outside the political system that recognized and rewarded them individually. Until blacks used the political system to address the issue of racial discrimination, they would be unable to eliminate racial discrimination in politics, in the economy, and in the law.

From 1976 through 1982, when blacks raised the issue of race, the machine faced the most serious threat to its existence since 1931. White and black machine leaders who were unwilling or unable to respond to these demands lost the contest to retain the machine in an explosion of political turmoil, violent and vituperative racism the likes of which had not been seen in a political campaign in Chicago since 1931.

Endings and Beginnings

The stunningly different political scenes with which this chapter opened present an irresistible puzzle to a political scientist interested in the specifics of one city and in the generality of political theory. How does a political organization, particularly one which has survived for nearly fifty years, which has undergone several crises and regenerations, and which has socialized generations of citizens, collapse, erode, and disintegrate within eight years? How does a political center which held for fifty years, fail to hold? How does a group which accepted selective benefits for fifty years, and which failed to concentrate on race, suddenly focus on the collective and demand its place within the political system, as a group?

The surge and complexity of emotions generated by the Washington campaign suggests years and decades of political repression among Chicago's blacks and political domination by whites. The explosive 1983 mayoral campaign in Chicago represented public recognition by all the participants that the political machine as they had known it in some form for fifty years was dying, was indeed already dead. The election let loose all the economic, racial, and ethnic conflicts which that structure had contained and mediated for five decades. Yet, if so much energy was contained by the machine's organization, why and how did it come into existence? Why did it survive for so long, and why did blacks and the subordinated ethnics accept its legitimacy for so long?

To understand the machine's demise, it is necessary to examine the entrance of blacks and of two European ethnic groups, Italians and Poles, into the disorganized, disorderly political system that was Chicago in the early decades of the twentieth century, and to examine how they and all the other groups joined together in political agreement to govern their city. To understand the two radically different electoral victories with which the chapter began requires an understanding of how these groups entered into Chicago politics and into the larger American political experience. To explain the machine's ending, the book now turns toward its beginning.

2

Racial and Ethnic Economic Life: The Case For a Pluralist Interpretation

Introduction: The Pluralist Model

Pluralist assumptions have dominated political scientists' explanations of racial and ethnic groups' integration into American politics. In this chapter I examine the economic status of blacks, Italians, and Poles in order to lay the foundation for a radically different interpretation, explained in succeeding chapters, of their political status and of the processes by which they were assimilated into the American political system. Brief summaries of pluralist theory and its application to racial and ethnic groups set the stage for the chapter's analysis of the economic lives of the groups in early twentieth-century Chicago. Three basic assumptions are abstracted from the work of pluralist theorists and examined in relation to their economic lives, including labor market participation, the formation of businesses, and residential and home ownership patterns. The chapter begins with a discussion of pluralism.

Pluralism and Political Integration

Pluralism has as many meanings as there are authors on the subject. Three different uses are identified here, with the first and last more closely related. Pluralism has a long history in the study of politics. European in origin, pluralism "refers to specific institutional arrangements for distributing and sharing governmental power, to the doctrinal defense of these arrangements and to an approach for gaining understanding of political behavior" (Kariel 1968:164).

Critics and proponents alike cite Robert Dahl perhaps most frequently as a propounder of pluralism. John Manley summarizes Dahl's pluralism as "multiple centers of power and limited popular sovereignty" (1983:369); William Connolly describes it as "a balance of power in which each group constrains and is constrained . . . and share[s] a broad system of beliefs and values which encourages conflict to proceed within established channels and allows initial disagreements to dissolve into compromise solutions" (1969:3). Andrew McFarland summarizes pluralism as follows: "decentralized power structures, fragmented causation and complex systems . . . characterize pluralist findings" (1969:3). According to William Kelso, pluralism means that "political power is and ought to be wielded by a number of groups rather than any single set of interests" (1978:34). Dahl stated pluralism's fundamental axiom: "Instead of a single center of sovereign power there must be multiple centers of power, none of which is or can be wholly sovereign" (1967:24).[1]

Although Harry Kariel declared that "political pluralism as an ideology has lost most of its explicit apologists and only lingers quietly as a submerged, inarticulate ingredient of western liberalism" (1968: 164), political scientists do not necessarily agree with him. In recent work by Dahl and Charles Lindblom, as well as by Manley, it is clear these theoretical issues remain unresolved. As Manley comments in a recent article, "there is little doubt that pluralism is the dominant theory or paradigm of power among American social scientists" (Manley 1983:368). Dahl and Lindblom have separately and together acknowledged weaknesses in earlier formulations of pluralist theory. As Lindblom commented, "The conventional theory creaks" (1982). Yet on balance, their recent comments have addressed this first definition of pluralism, which concerns itself primarily with the interactional characteristics, formal or informal, of political life.[2]

The second meaning links sociological language with vernacular usage of the term and is perhaps the least theoretical. Milton Gordon writes that "with respect to racial and ethnic relations, America now faces a *new dilemma,* a dilemma which is oriented toward a choice of the *kind of group pluralism* which American governmental action and the attitudes of the American people will foster and encourage" (1981:182–83). Gordon differentiates liberal from corporate pluralism; in the former, government neither recognizes, rewards, nor penalizes race, ethnicity, or religion, while in the latter, government formally recognizes the rights of racial and ethnic groups. This use derives from a popular rejection of the melting pot image, from the interest group strain of pluralist theory associated with Truman and Bentley, and from the evolution of judicial law on civil rights policy (McFarland 1969:33). It should be sharply distinguished from the first meaning, which describes political processes and political interactions within political science. This second meaning and its implications will be reexamined in the conclusion to the study.

So far this discussion of pluralism has emphasized its structural-interactional characteristics and its group-based meanings. Now the analysis turns toward the third definition, more closely related to the first: the question of racial and ethnic political integration. How do new groups enter a political system, specifically, a pluralist political system? If new groups assimilate according to the major axioms of pluralist theory, they require relatively undifferentiated responses from their environment. According to Parsons "generalized rules . . . [show a] cognitive as opposed to an expressive interest. . . . Goal achievement and instrumental actions" rarely lead to "the promotion of the welfare of a collectivity" (1951:182–83). Theories that emphasized ethnic and racial assimilation thus fit compatibly with larger pluralist notions that dominated the profession. In these areas, many pluralist-derived explanations remain unrevised.

The following three principles summarize the processes by which racial and ethnic groups find ready entrance into the American urban political system according to pluralist theory: interest diversification, interest incorporation/integration, and racial-ethnic democracy.

Interest Diversification. According to this concept, racial and ethnic groups have little or declining necessity for group formulation of political interests. To the extent it occurs, such conceptualization is limited to the first or proletarian stage of residence. Groups move rapidly away from ethnic homogeneity and experience increased social, economic, and political diversification. Race and ethnicity blur as other issues take precedence.[3]

Interest Incorporation. Once groups realize their subjective interests, the members achieve political incorporation through bargaining. Isaac Balbus (1971) identifies two types of interest: subjective, in which the individual is aware of an issue which has personal impact, and objective, which affects a person even though he or she is unaware of it. Balbus argues that the pluralist model focuses solely upon the subjective or self-actualized form of interest, namely, the active interest group. By so doing, the model ignores the problem of representation for those who are affected but unaware of an issue. Both models accept the notion that the realization of an interest, its self-actualization, is an important variable in explaining political influence. Once a group recognizes its interest in the political process, political organization of that interest leads naturally to political representation and incorporation. Martin Kilson, for example, applies the colonial modernization model to Afro-American politics (1971:171–77). In effect blacks have passed through the stage of "clientage" politics and will gradually articulate their own interests, reaching a status comparable to the already "modernized" citizens.[4]

Racial and Ethnic Democracy. Finally, in the absence of persistent group identity and with political representation dependent upon the realization of interests, theorists predict little political hierarchy or inequality based on group status. James Q. Wilson, for example, introduced his *Negro Politics* with the following words: "The bulk of the book, then, will concern the factors conditioning Negro life internal to the Negro community. . . . It will be argued here that the ghetto has a life and a logic of its own, apart from whatever whites might do to create and maintain the outer walls of it" (1960:7). Wilson has little interest in how those external forces shape and influence internal politics. Kilson, Wilson, and Dahl thus locate the black population and black politics in a pluralist political environment. Wilson ignores forces external to the ghetto, Dahl predicts "full assimilation" of blacks in the north and slow integration even in the south, while Kilson expects eventual integration into the political system through modernization.

Recent examinations of black political participation at the national level sharply distinguish themselves from these works. Studies by Mathew Holden, Milton Morris, Lucius Barker, and Jesse McCorry not only fail to use the pluralist model, but also to varying degrees presume important political separations between Afro-Americans and the rest of the American polity. Holden, for example, speculates: "If any two groups differ significantly as to physical places of residence, cultural styles and outlooks, levels of capital and income, political habits, legal rights, and habits of communication and exchange, then it may be quite reasonable to describe them as separate 'nations'. . . . In this light, it is sensible to speak of blacks as constituting a separate socio-economic 'nation'" (1973:1).

Milton Morris introduces his study of black politics with "the image of a democratic polity committed to the principles of justice and equality for all could not tolerate the reality of inequality and systematic oppression that has been the experience of blacks" (1975:4). Barker and McCorry state that "how black people fare in the American political system . . . allows us to see quite vividly that some of our most cherished political values do not necessarily operate to the benefit of all Americans" (1976:vii). Charles V. Hamilton's *Black Power* (1967), coauthored with black activist Stokeley Carmichael, was clearly antipluralist; more recently Hamilton commented, "The political situation of black Americans always posed a special problem for the pluralist system" (1981:168).

This chapter shows how external and internal forces interact and how the external factors dominated the internal affairs of the black population. If American urban politics matches the pluralist model, the historical record of the groups' economic lives should show a diversification in economic status, the integration of economic interest in business, and group democracy in the labor market (see Dahl 1956: 138–39). Next in the chapter, I examine labor markets and labor organizations, business enterprises, housing ownership, and residential patterns for the three groups in Chicago under examination here.

The Labor and Business Markets

All three groups—blacks, Italians, and Poles—moved to Chicago for similar reasons. Overcrowded agricultural areas in rural Poland, small agricultural towns of southern Italy, and the rural American south scourged by the boll weevil and by Reconstruction were especially responsive to the increased demands for wage labor in the midwestern American industrial cities in the early twentieth century. Whereas all left rural agricultural environments, their arrival in Chicago thrust them into the urban labyrinth of small shops, businesses, and large factories with its concomitant competition for jobs, economic independence, and housing.[5]

Labor Force and Labor Unions

Poles and Italians arrived in large numbers from the late 1800s until the beginning of the First World War, but they moved into industrial positions at very different rates. Italian population centers tended to be located in areas where manufacturing positions were available, but few Italians took such positions in the steel or meatpacking industries. One study evaluated industry's estimation of workers:

> To how great an extent these attitudes represent observation of actual race and nationality characteristics . . . and to how great an extent they represent various biases . . . it is impossible to say. There can be

no doubt that some of them, at least, reflect *perfectly objective observations of fact,* such as the seemingly endurable preference of the Italian for outdoor work as opposed to foundry or machine-shop work. But whether these attitudes represent objective facts or subjective feelings, their significance to the workers is the same. The employment policies of the various employing authorities are inevitably influenced by these attitudes, and the economic fortunes of thousands of individuals are influenced by them (Carpenter 1927:110–11, quoted in Feldman 1931:151).

Paul Taylor's survey of the nationalities in the basic industries in the Chicago and Calumet region showed only 493 Italians, or one percent of the work force. Poles, on the other hand, constituted over a quarter of the work force in the meat-packing and steel industries before the First World War and twenty percent of the work force in the stockyards in 1904 (Taylor 1931:40, 43n, 46, 60). They entered the industry first as strikebreakers, but after a short period moved into production jobs as part of the regular work force. Poles and other eastern Europeans were for a time attractive to employers because they worked for lower wages and were immune, at least initially, to unionization due to language and cultural differences. The 1904 meatcutter's strike, however, moved the Poles toward unionization and reintroduced blacks to strikebreaking (Herbst 1932:15–22; Kantowicz 1975:28–29).

Labor increased its bargaining power with management due to a combination of factors, including the war and 1921 legislation ending massive immigration. Unions used this rare occasion of labor scarcity to bolster their membership and to strike for increased wages. Poles were strong supporters of the unions, but the cessation of Polish immigration reduced the entry of Poles into the work force to those eligible through natural maturation. Before the war, Poles equalled about one-quarter of the work force in meat-packing and steel, but by the end of the 1920s foreign-born Poles had yielded their dominant position in the meat-packing and steel industries to blacks and native-born whites (Newell 1961:68–70; Tuttle 1972:134–37). In meat-packing this represented a two-thirds drop in real numbers of Polish workers, while their numbers declined by only one-third in steel (see table 2.1). By the end of the 1920s, Poles and other Europeans' participation in industry had declined because "the war . . . had accelerated the tendency for northern European workers to move into higher occupational levels" (Cayton and Mitchell 1939:231). The war also

Table 2.1
Racial and Ethnic Employment in the Steel and Meat-Packing Industries in the Chicago Region, 1909–1928

	Meat-Packing		Steel	
	1909	1928	1912	1928
Blacks	3.0%	29.5%	1.5%	12.3%
Poles	27.7%	11.9%	25.7%	14.1%
Italians	.5%	.8%	1.2%	1.0%
Native-Born Whites	18.9%	27.3%	25.5%	33.8%
Other Foreign-Born	49.9%	30.5%	46.1%	38.8%
Total	100.0%	100.0%	100.0%	100.0%
N	15,489	13,194	17,441	22,061

Source: Taylor 1931: tables 5–6, pp. 40, 42.

stimulated the migration and importation of Mexican labor into Chicago for the first time; their numbers equalled or surpassed the increase of black workers, and Mexicans suggest a provocative comparison group with blacks (see especially Taylor 1931).

Horace Cayton and George Mitchell argue that the cycle of black employment and unemployment shifted in response to at least three major variables: the economic cycle, the availability and the cost of white labor, and the possibility of strikes (Cayton and Mitchell 1931: chap. 1). If the demand for labor was based on nondiscriminatory criteria, black employment would vary only with the economic cycle and with the possibility of strikes. When the cycle was on the upswing, the demand for labor would increase apart from racial distinctions; when on the downswing, presumably layoffs would occur in heterogeneous fashion.[6]

Instead, the black labor force changed in ways that cannot be explained solely by changes in the economic cycle. The remainder of the discussion is divided into two parts: factors encouraging and those discouraging black employment.

Increasing Black Employment. Black employment increased rather substantially when political or economic events required increased production and when few whites were available to fill the demand. On the other hand, if the northern labor market had operated according to strict racial dominance "the Negro need never have been employed after 1923" (Herbst 1932:103). Since factories hired black workers, the urban model is clearly not characterized by perfect racial domination. An examination of the significant points of entry reveals a mixed system. Industry used blacks extensively as strikebreakers during the period of industrial warfare, in the Pullman strike of 1894, and in many other industrial conflicts. In the 1894 Pullman strike, for example, when blacks "became cognizant of the fact that the American Railway Union barred the Negro from union membership . . . [they] retaliated by forming the Anti-Strikers Railroad Union" (Herbst 1931:18n.1).[7]

This characterized the position of blacks in the industrial work force in Chicago: blacks, excluded from the labor force on a normal basis by industry and from union membership by written constitution, by ritual, or by practice, used the unusual circumstances of industrial strife to gain access to the labor market. "Through many experiences Negroes came to believe that the only way they could get into a unionized industry was through strike breaking" (Harris and Spero 1969: 261). Herbst notes that previous waves of immigrants suffered similar barriers to entry, but these impediments fell within a limited period. Blacks were involved in strikebreaking in the railroads in 1894, in meat-packing in 1901, 1904, and 1919, in the steel strikes of 1904 and 1919, and in strikes in the corn-refining and garment industries in 1919 and 1917 respectively. Blacks continued to be available for strikebreaking because they were discharged after a strike was settled and replaced by whites or by unionized blacks. When the next strike occurred, blacks remained marginal surplus labor available for work.[8]

By 1910 when the average Chicagoan worked in manufacturing, transportation, or trade, 60 percent of the black work force was concentrated in lower paying positions in domestic and personal service. A somewhat higher percentage of the black than white population was employed in 1910 and 1920, but this was accounted for by the unusual concentration of the black population in the young adult years. By 1920 and 1930 the total and employed black population had more than doubled, and blacks had begun to move into heavy industry and manufacturing (see table 2.1), but they remained disproportionately concentrated in the service and domestic areas. By 1930 not only were blacks unemployed at very high rates, but they also had fewer numbers and positions relative to whites. About thirty-four percent of all blacks were on relief as compared to ten percent of all Chicago's whites. Even with this shift in occupational distribution, blacks held a smaller share of manufacturing positions than any group except native whites, and between 1920 and 1940 their hold on service jobs actually increased. When the depression arrived in full force, it reduced the size of the black work force by nearly forty percent (Bureau of the Census 1914: table 8, 544–47; 1922: vol. 3:261, 273–76; 1932: vol. 3:628, 640–42; 1943: vol. 2:639, 642; Chicago Commission on Race Relations 1922:359; Federal Emergency Relief Administration 1933:8).

This brings us to the second and third major variables necessary for increased black participation in the work force: a shortage of white workers and a prosperous economy in which there was increased demand. Only in rare instances between 1910 and 1950 did both of these factors occur simultaneously. World War I precipitated both factors, since it increased production and the demand for labor, while shutting off the influx of European immigrants. The 1920s were characterized by gradually declining economic demand, followed by the decade-long depression in the 1930s and a sharp rise in demand during World War II.

Congress legislated the close of European immigration in 1921 so that industrial labor demand was satisfied primarily by North American continental migration. The black population of Chicago grew from 44,103 in 1910 to 509,437 in 1950, with the first surge of growth set off by the start of World War I (Bureau of the Census 1914: vol. 4:544–47; 1952: vol. 2(1):140). The Urban League, the *Chicago Defender,* and large industrial firms publicized the need for labor throughout the south in 1915 (Strickland 1966: chap. 3). *The Negro in Chicago* recorded the number of blacks in manufacturing positions in 1920 as ten times the number it had been only five years before, with most of the growth concentrated in the production of food products, iron, and steel.[9]

This rapid increase in the industrial work force was not maintained; as war-related production declined after World War I and soldiers were released from service, "normal" market factors began to reduce the number of jobs available to blacks: "Blacks were usually the first to feel the effect of the immediate post-war unemployment that spring. Black women were the first to be discharged; black men and white women soon followed. Sometimes there was even a hierarchy of color; those of black skin were fired first, then those of brown and lighter brown" (Tuttle 1972:130).

During the war the shortage of white labor and increased industrial production encouraged labor union organization. With blacks in demand, both the unions and packers actively recruited them, the former to guarantee a monopoly on the labor market, the latter to ensure its division. Spero and Harris argue that Swift and Armour weakened efforts at unionization by discharging organizers and hiring blacks: "The packers were banking on the traditional difficulty of organizing Negro workers as well as upon the fact that many of the organizations having jurisdiction over crafts represented in the yards did not accept Negro members" (Harris and Spero 1969:269).[10]

Alma Herbst studied the meat-packing industry in the early 1920s and found that the percentage of blacks hired by the packers varied with the economy and the proportion of whites in the labor pool. In 1923 and 1924 about the same number of blacks, but larger numbers of whites, applied for work in the latter year because of slack economic conditions. Thus when whites were scarce, blacks equalled 64.7 percent of the applicants and 45.2 percent of those hired; when whites were plentiful, the respective figure fell to 45.1 percent and 20.6 percent. The ratio of hired to applicants fell from 70 percent to 46 percent in just one year. In each case, whites and blacks were hired in higher and lower proportions to those in which they had applied (Herbst 1932:107).[11]

Restrictions on Black Labor Market Participation. What were the impediments to black entry into the labor market? Labor organizations and industry discriminated against blacks in creating the industrial work force. Institutional hiring procedures reflected a preference for white workers. William Wilson, in a recent s udy, compared the roles of labor and industry in creating a split labor market, one in which the work force is divided along fundamental lines (such as race or religion) and is, therefore, unable to oppose industrial capitalists in unified fashion; although Wilson concluded that while workers and unions were unable to restrict black entry completely, "efforts to restrict black advancement [between 1890 and 1940] were almost exclusively associated with the white working class" (Wilson 1978:83).

The evidence reveals a more complex picture. In the 1890's strike, the Chicago packers initially avoided black strikebreakers because "it was not necessary or advisable policy to antagonize the whites" (Harris and Spero 1969:268). According to Wilson and Bonacich, economic factors explain employers' use of blacks as strikebreakers; employers sought to reduce costs rather than to exacerbate racial tension. If this was true, blacks should have entered the industrial work force by the turn of the century, since they were in some cases willing to work for less than whites when there were no strikes. Instead, black entry was delayed until more expensive organized white workers struck and less expensive white labor was otherwise unavailable for strikebreaking or for regular employment. Wilson, on the other hand, argues that American labor history confounds Marxist theory because the white working class supported and encouraged racial exclusion: "There is little indication that this represented management's efforts to divide the working class by developing a white labor aristocracy; rather, the data suggest that management wanted to cut costs by allowing blacks to compete more or less freely in the open market and by discouraging black participation in labor unions" (Wilson 1978:84).

Both labor and industry excluded black workers whenever whites were available and relatively inexpensive. Labor unions played a major role in excluding blacks from the work force by the greater organizational success of craft as compared to industrial unions. To maximize their control of the more valuable skilled trades, craft unions rejected blacks, whom they viewed as threats to high wage rates. The American Federation of Labor (AFL) included many federated unions whose constitutions, rituals, and informal practices barred blacks; when blacks were members of unions, it was because they were admitted through separate, segregated locals or local "federal unions" directly affiliated with the AFL. In some cases these "independent" all-black unions were under the direct supervision of the group that had excluded them.[12]

Only a small proportion of blacks were in skilled trades when union organizing began in the 1890s; those who practiced a trade were frequently driven out of the profession by white unions. Industrial unions, specifically the Congress of Industrial Organizations (CIO), emphasized union strength by opening their ranks to all workers regardless of race, ethnicity, or job type. In the mining and garment industries, where mechanical specialization limited specialized divisions of the labor force, the CIO was more successful and more likely to target black as well as white workers in unionization drives. The AFL and craft unions that had traditionally excluded blacks were unable to overcome the anti-union sentiment among black workers, especially those newly arrived from the south. This sentiment, born of union opposition to black membership and reinforced by anti-union positions taken by black ministers and interest groups, precipitated industrial conflict and was an important basis for the Chicago riot of 1919 (Strickland 1966:48, 56–82; Tuttle 1972:108–58).

Mancur Olson argues that small homogeneous groups with coercive incentives organize more effectively than large heterogeneous associations (1971:66–91). In practice a large union composed of smaller federated units of single-skilled workers of one racial or ethnic group, which operates in a closed shop, would be more successful than large industrial unions organized on a plantwide basis to include workers of a variety of racial and ethnic groups. Race and ethnicity determined economic entry.[13] There were measurable differences in black economic status as a result of these practices. Restricted competition and entry meant that blacks were concentrated in unskilled and semiskilled jobs and were paid (as an artifact of job category) at lower rates than whites. Because of their marginal economic status, blacks more willingly accepted unskilled or semiskilled jobs at lower pay than did whites.[14]

After blacks entered the industrial work force in large numbers during World War I, they assumed subordinate positions relative to other whites. Blacks were concentrated in lower-paying positions requiring little skill. Only one percent of the blacks in manufacturing surveyed by the Chicago Commission on Race Relations were in skilled or semiskilled positions. Herbst reported that the average minimum earnings were higher for whites than blacks in the stockyards (Herbst 1932:86). In a study of the income and standard of living of

Table 2.2
Chief Wage Earner by Race

	White*	Black
Above $2,000	2.1%	—
$1,800–$1,999	3.8%	—
$1,600–$1,799	10.7%	8.8%
$1,400–$1,599	32.4%	18.7%
$1,200–$1,399	31.5%	22.5%
$1,000–$1,199	16.0%	43.7%
$ 800–$ 999	3.5%	6.3%
Total	100.0%	100.0%
N	343	80

*About two-thirds of the white workers were foreign-born. They included 138 Poles and 72 Italians (Houghteling 1927:21).
Source: Houghteling 1927: based on table 7, p. 24.

unskilled laborers, Leila Houghteling found black workers' (chief wage earners) incomes concentrated to a much greater extent at the bottom of the earnings scale. Fifty percent of black versus 19.5 percent of white workers earned less than $1,200. No black workers earned above $1,800, while two percent of the whites did (see table 2.2). About half of the black female population worked, as compared to 22 percent of Polish and 10 percent of Italian females (Houghteling 1927:24, 57); black women equalled 20 percent of the women surveyed and 38 percent of the women employed.

Thus fundamental racial differentiation pervaded the native, migrant, and immigrant sectors of the labor force. Blacks found access to jobs barred both by industrial hiring practices and by trade union exclusivity. Jobs opened intermittently during labor strife and when a permanent shortage of white labor and increased economic demand occurred simultaneously. Once in the industrial work force, blacks frequently remained in semiskilled and unskilled positions and, therefore, received lower wages. Their European predecessors made their way into the labor force through similar patterns, but they found the market more permeable and with fewer restrictions.

Business Enterprise

The simplest measure of economic prosperity for each community is the number of businesses operated by members of the Italian, Polish, and black communities. In the early 1930s Cipriani's directory of Italian commerce listed "4500 stores, firms and professional men" (Cipriani 1933, cited in Nelli 1970:142). The *Dziennik Zjednoczenia* reported that by 1928 there were some 10,247 Polish-owned businesses in Chicago valued at $16.2 million, which employed over 16,000 people (Wargin 1948:54, table 1). Chicago ranked first among cities in the number of black-owned stores and stores with stocks on hand and second in net sales per capita of the black population in 1929 (Bureau of the Census, 1935:519, table 16; also table 10, 510 and 520, 521).

Yet this "large" number of black businesses amounted to only 815 black-owned stores in Chicago. Using 1930 as a population base, there were 39.16 Poles, 40.41 Italians, and 287 blacks per store. The black stores employed only 723 people, of whom 286 (or 40 percent) worked in restaurants and food stores of various types. In the south, blacks lived in rural areas, so that there were few black-owned stores in comparison to their size in the population. Overall the largest numbers of businesses were located in the south, but businesses in northern or southern border states had higher net sales. In all states the majority of these businesses were grocery stores, restaurants, and cafeterias.[15] Two black-owned banks were founded in Chicago during the 1920s, but neither survived the depression. More importantly, neither Jesse Binga nor Anthony Overton, who owned the Binga and Douglass national banks respectively, participated in politics. Gosnell reported that Binga had been a barber, Pullman porter, huckster, and real estate agent, while Overton founded the Overton Hygienic Company, a cosmetics firm, and Victory Life Insurance Company. Undertakers, such as Dan Jackson, real estate agents, such as Oscar DePriest, and lawyers, such as Edward Wright, were the most prominent businessmen-politicians, but white rather than black leaders financed second ward political activities (Gosnell 1967:106–7).

Thus the black community's commercial and economic resources compared unfavorably to those of Polish and Italian immigrants. Blacks also frequently relied on white philanthropists for aid. Blacks organized Provident Hospital, the Wabash Avenue YMCA, and the Wendell Phillips Settlement, but Julius Rosenwald, the Pullmans, and the Armours helped fund them.[16]

Prosperity also eluded black and ethnic newspapers; most based their finances on subscriptions rather than advertising. Robert E. Park's study of the immigrant press showed that it was vulnerable to commercial manipulation because of the marginal returns from subscriptions. The relationship between newspaper circulation and advertising was critical; the papers were unable to survive on their subscriptions, and there were too few and too narrow a range of black businessmen to make black advertising profitable. Even the ethnic presses, with much larger commercial bases, were marginal operations. Low-cost newspapers increased the number of readers, increased the overall proportions of funds from advertisers (because the paper cost less), and increased the possibility of external controls (Park 1922:384–90). The United Brewers Association, which was opposed to prohibition, provided indirect funding for the Association of Foreign Language Newspapers (which also opposed prohibition) through Louis N. Hammerling. The connections between interest and policy were quite clear in this case, but the tastes of the reader and advertiser happened to be in agreement.

In the black community, the *Chicago Defender* among other papers opposed the unionizing campaign of the Brotherhood of Sleeping

Car Porters in 1926. There were suggestions that the paper was influenced by its long association with the Pullman Company, but because the porters were in a position to have a devastating effect on the paper's distribution, sales plummeted and Abbott changed the paper's position in short order. The *Chicago Whip* was a much smaller and more radical paper until bought out by Daniel Schuyler, a representative for both Pullman and Insull interests in Chicago. The *Whip* changed its policy from support for to opposition toward the Sleeping Car Porters Union after its purchase.[17]

Economic enterprises flourished in the ethnic and racial communities of Chicago, but the industrial giants of the age, the Pullmans, the Armours, and the Sears, many of which were located in Chicago, dwarfed firms founded by blacks, Italians, and Poles. Economic activity and intermediate organizations such as labor unions and newspapers in the black community were especially weak.

Housing Patterns

Physical Location and Concentration

Social scientists and historians have described immigrant neighborhoods as locations where one group—Poles, Irish, or Italians—dominate cultural and social life.[18] Over time the dominant ethnic group disperses into other neighborhoods less identified with a specific group and another dominant ethnic group takes its place. Presumably a highly concentrated black ghetto offers no unusual settlement patterns under the pluralist model, since it is simply a replication of the usual pattern of ethnic concentration in the initial stages of the group's urban life, which would eventually be followed by gradual decentralization.

Ethnic Patterns of Settlement. Chicago has a number of neighborhoods identified as the old Polish, Italian, Greek, and Jewish areas, but examination of census data on these areas suggests a reconsideration of the assumption of concentrated ethnic settlements. Thomas Lee Philpott, Ernest Burgess, and Charles Newcomb have defined several important characteristics of Chicago's ethnic neighborhoods: they were composed of multiple locations, usually near a Catholic church (in the case of Jewish neighborhoods, a synagogue), and the level of ethnic concentration was rarely greater than 50 percent. Polonia, on the northwest side of the city, was the most important Polish neighborhood with two large active churches, with shops, stores, businesses,

Polish fraternal organizations, and newspapers. While 95 percent of the ten-block area was Polish, Philpott notes, "At no time did more than six to twelve percent of the city's . . . Poles live in such concentrations" (Philpott 1978:139). Poles and other ethnics lived in numerous settlements "all over the city, but a minority of the group's population was located within such areas, and many other groups resided within the same neighborhoods" (Philpott 1978:141; see also Burgess and Newcomb 1931, 1933).

Kantowicz reported that none of the areas had Polish populations greater than 50 percent (1975:18, table 2). In the St. Stanislaus district, where the largest portion of the Polish population settled, Poles constituted 47 percent of the entire population of the area in 1910, and 45 percent of the city's Polish population. The Polish population in other concentrated areas was much smaller. By the early 1930s, Burgess and Newcomb's study of Chicago census data showed the concentration of foreign-born Poles below 35 percent in the most heavily concentrated areas. Thus large numbers of other nationalities also resided in areas designated as Polish (1933:682–83).[19]

Another example of ethnic concentration was the neighborhood around Hull House, described around the turn of the century as Greek and Italian. A survey conducted by the settlement house itself and reexamined by Philpott revealed that the "Greek and Italian" ghetto was inhabited by representatives of twenty-six nationalities, mixed in an unpatterned stew, with one notable exception. The Hull House sample ran east from Halsted, crossed the railroad and warehouse areas, over the south branch of the river, and extended to State Street. There the heterogeneity ceased in a black area. As early as 1895 blacks lived in concentrated, territorially defined, predominantly black areas, but because their numbers were still relatively small they did not dominate neighborhoods as they would later in the twentieth century.

Philpott reconsiders census data and earlier studies and rather effectively lays to rest the notion of the immigrant ghetto. Although an area might be called "Little Italy," as the Hull House area was in 1910, it was "by no means exclusively Italian." Italians settled in a number of different areas in Chicago also. By 1900 there were settlements on the near south side, both east and west of the river, south to Twelfth Street, and further south between Twelfth and Thirty-Ninth, State and Halsted. "In none of the Little Italys was there an all-Italian block; in fact, in the whole period 1890–1930, not even one single square block was ever 100 percent Italian" (1978:137; see also Nelli 1970a:chap. 2; *Hull House Maps and Papers* 1895: esp. maps; Kantowicz 1975:14; Vecoli 1963:chaps. 1–2).

Polish arrivals settled originally near Noble Street and Milwaukee Avenue, and they built St. Stanislaus Kostka Church, around which grew the first and most important settlement in the city (Kantowicz 1975:14). After Holy Trinity, Poles established another Polish-language Catholic church in 1872, and the Milwaukee, Division, and Ashland intersection just north of Noble Street quickly became the cultural and economic heart of the Polish community. Over time Poles moved outward along the Milwaukee Avenue artery. Still other major Polish areas developed in Bridgeport, in South Chicago north of the steel plants, and south of the curve of the lake. The Polish "community" in Chicago was actually composed of several geographically separate neighborhoods that developed in differing ways, since they had their own churches, differing working conditions, and were separated by distances that were not easily covered at the time.

Thus for many of the immigrants the expanding American economy provided outward physical mobility if not upward social mobility. Inner-city neighborhoods served as ports of entry for many immigrants, but were only temporary locations until non-ethnic neighborhoods opened up. In contemporary Chicago the skeletons of these previous immigrant generations remain, but they are patronized by newer immigrants or suburban commuters.

Racial Patterns of Settlements. A number of studies have suggested that large concentrated black ghettoes appeared only in the early twentieth century, after the years of heavy migration during World War I. Both Allan Spear and Stanley Lieberson examined the origins of black residential concentration, and both concluded that residential segregation was significant only around World War I. The black population was neither concentrated in one area nor segregated within its area of residence prior to that time, and it suffered increasing residential concentration afterward (Lieberson 1963:chaps. 3–4; Osofsky 1966:pt. 2; Spear 1967:126–34).

Spear's and Lieberson's conclusions result from two problems. They based their comparisons on large statistical units, and relatively small numbers of blacks resided in these wards in 1900 and 1910. A Hull House study showed a very high degree of concentration by race as early as 1895. The city council redrew ward lines after each census so that there is little comparison over time in either the neighborhoods included within the wards or in the relative size of the wards. Between 1910 and 1940 the city council increased the number of wards, thereby decreasing their size, which artificially magnified the proportion of blacks in each ward from 35 to 50 percent over time. Redistricting in Chicago generally took place immediately after each census (in 1901, 1911, 1921, and 1931) to gerrymander political boundaries. Officially, the changes were intended to equalize ward population, but in practice the changes gerrymandered population increases to meet the needs of those holding political office. More important, the changes increased the chances for ethnic groups to win political representation (see chapters 3 and 4 for further discussion).[20]

Spear and Lieberson suggested that segregation increased along with the black population, but Philpott argues that segregation is a characteristic of black residence in Chicago regardless of the size of that population (1978:121–31).[21] By the 1930s, 92 percent of the black population lived in "black areas" and blacks constituted over 80 percent of the ghetto population. The upper limits of European and ethnic segregation would have been, for blacks, a relatively integrated neighborhood. Racial segregation increased between 1920 and 1930, but significant segregation existed before 1930.

Methodological difficulties thus masked the substantial black residential concentration that existed before 1920 and understated the dominant segregation afterward. As Philpott states:

> The use of smaller units [in 1930] uncovers a degree of segregation for 1920 which remained hidden [using the larger 1920 census tracts]. . . . The percentage of blacks living in areas more than 50 percent Negro turns out to be not 51 but 60, and the percentages of those in tracts more than 75 percent black goes up from 36 to 45. Ten years later 90 percent of the black population lived in tracts over 75 percent black. In 1920 no black people had lived in tracts that were 90 percent Negro. In 1930 *two out of three* black Chicagoans were packed into tracts where the population was 90 percent black or more (1978: 127).

In figure 2.1, Philpott's two measures of concentration (percentage of groups ghettoized and group's percentage of ghetto population: the total percentage of the group in the ethnic or racial neighborhood and the proportion of the neighborhood that the group

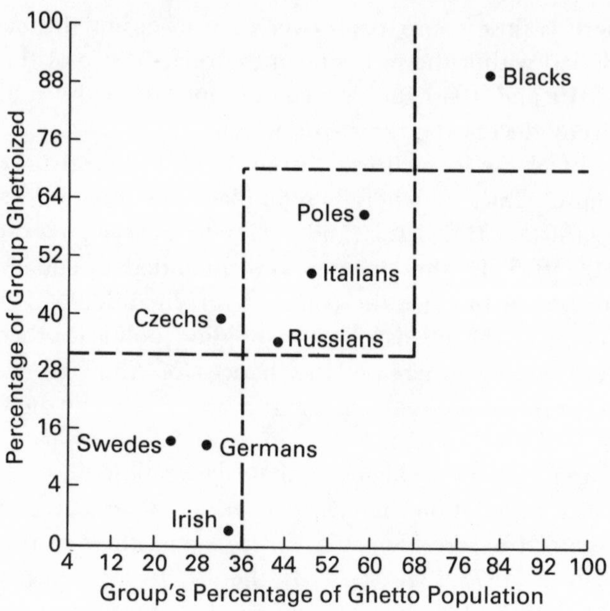

Source: Philpott 1978: table 7, p. 141.

Figure 2.1 Racial and Ethnic Residential Concentration, Chicago, 1930

constituted) are used to plot the character of each group's residential patterns. Of course none of the groups are perfectly segregated or integrated, but the communities clearly fall into distinctive categories. Groups of northern Europeans, such as Irish, Germans, and Swedes, fall into the relatively integrated sector and show the lowest levels of concentration. In the intermediate category, Czechs and Russians appear to have lived in less concentrated settlements, and eastern and southern Europeans (such as the Italians and the Poles) lived in more ethnically concentrated areas. Blacks, however, outstripped them all; nearly all lived in areas that were close to perfectly segregated.

Burgess and Newcomb's work on Chicago census data for 1920 and 1930 shows somewhat lower degrees of ethnic concentration and higher degrees of racial concentration (1933:681).[22] The 1900 data might, therefore, show higher levels of ethnic concentration, but all studies point to rapid population dispersion after 1930. Diagrammed, this development would appear as a single peaked curve; on the other hand, considerable evidence suggests that the black population would be represented by an upwardly sloped line located well above and beyond other groups in such a diagram. Northern Europeans, followed by the southern and eastern Europeans, established moderately heterogeneous residential settlement patterns that became increasingly heterogeneous over time. The residential patterns of the black population, on the other hand, moved perilously close to perfect segregation over time. In the next section of this chapter, the forces that contributed to these patterns of residential settlement are examined.

Market Forces. Economic cycles influenced the production of new dwelling units. Chicago's population grew rapidly from its founding in the 1830s until the 1930s, often doubling in the years between census counts. Yet housing construction lagged behind this growth. As measured by the issuance of building permits, housing boomed only in the eight years before and immediately after World War I. A slight rally at the end of the 1930s and the beginning of the 1940s was cut short by the Second World War. Very few houses or apartments were constructed between 1929 and 1946, at which time permits again reached the level of construction at the end of the 1920s (see figure 2.2).

This was of great significance to the groups in question. Most of the immigration by the Italians and Poles occurred betwen 1880 and 1915, a period during which construction levels were "normal"; they were thus able to move into established areas of housing or to create new ones. Despite the ethnic heterogeneity in neighborhoods, high density and poor, absolutely wretched housing conditions made life miserable for many Poles and Italians (Philpott 1978:29–33).

Housing construction and immigration declined and black migration increased as the war began. From 1915 to 1921 housing construction was seriously limited, so competition for existing housing necessarily increased. In the immediate postwar years the housing shortage was aggravated by the concentration of construction along the outer rim of the city, away from the older black and ethnic neighborhoods. Between 1919 and 1922 only 238 new apartments and houses were built in the inner sectors where the black, Italian, and Polish population was concentrated.[23] Ten times as many dwellings were built in ward eight, which covered the southeasternmost part of the city and which included Polish and Italian settlements. The absence of new construction within established ethnic communities was less critical, since immigration-driven population expansion had ceased and areas of new construction were open to ethnic penetration.

Blacks and whites faced the problem of accommodating a rapidly

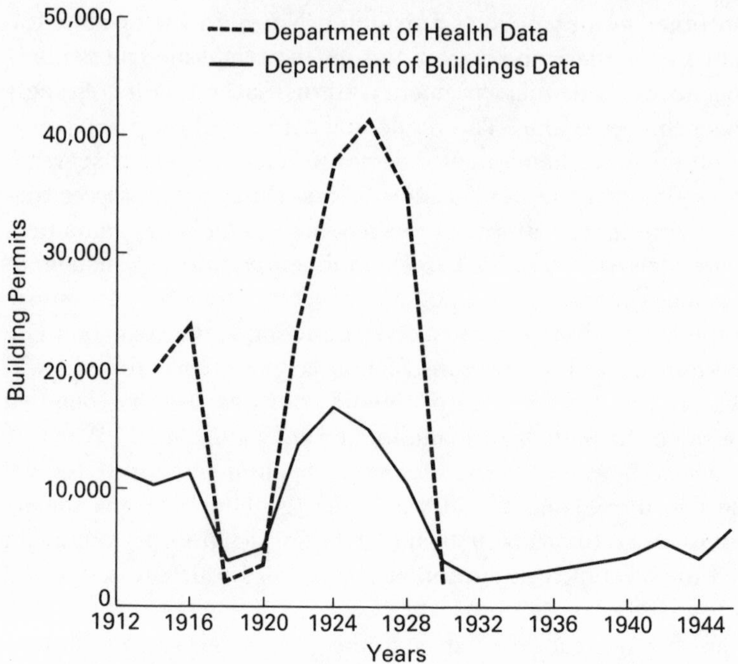

Source: *Annual Reports,* Department of Health and Buildings, City of Chicago.

Figure 2.2 Housing Construction in Chicago 1912–1946

expanding black population within a stable housing market. Blacks could be housed in a number of ways represented on a continuum. At one end is a pluralist alternative: a heterogeneous pattern of residential settlement in which the rapidly expanding black population settled wherever vacancies occurred; at the other end, a nonpluralist alternative: a homogeneous pattern in which all blacks were confined within the boundaries of the black area. As Philpott demonstrated, no perfectly heterogeneous communities existed; so there were "natural social" forces encouraging some degree of ethnic and racial concentration for all groups. Some neighborhood character is explained by a search for cultural and associational supports. St. Stanislaus Kostka, for example, was the geographical focus for culture and politics in the Polish community, around which large numbers of Poles settled. Over time, however, St. Stanislaus and Milwaukee Avenue became the route out of which the Polish population migrated to outlying residential single-family areas (Kantowicz 1975:chap. 3).[24]

These associational factors do not explain the high degree of residential concentration that existed on the black south side. Numerous, comprehensive, profound types of restraint had to be employed in the face of a population explosion that increased the number of black Chicagoans by more than nine times between 1900 and 1940. A number of private and public institutions participated in these restraints.

When the black population pressure increased, real estate agents and private owners in Chicago protected their property from racial invasion (Martin 1941) by a mix of legal and violent tactics. Philpott and Long and Johnson discussed the creation of the restrictive covenant, an agreement among property owners in a neighborhood to the effect that they would not sell or rent to blacks. Between 1927 and 1929, eighty-eight covenants were established and their continued certification throughout the 1930s and 1940s helped halt the southward and eastward migration of the black population until after World War II. Banks, insurance companies, and other financial institutions rarely granted loans to blacks; when they did, "Negroes had to put down a larger down payment, pay higher interest on the balance, and pay higher insurance premiums than anyone else. Families who would have been able to afford a conventional purchase arrangement if they were white often had to buy on contract or not at all" (Philpott 1978:159; see also Long and Johnson 1947:92n.1).

This imposed a number of constraints on the black population besides physical containment. The "black belt" overlapped with the city's vice district; because whites rejected racial integration, blacks shared their living space with the only other citizens of Chicago who would tolerate them, the saloons, gambling halls, and houses of prostitution of the vice district. As blacks moved south, these areas tended to expand with them (Chicago Commission on Race Relations 1922: maps after p. 342).

Second, the competition for housing within the segregated, overcrowded black belt pushed the price of rental housing above that in most of the city. In 1920, 1930, and 1934 surveys by Edith Abbott showed that blacks spent more on rent than Jews, foreign-born whites, Bohemians, or Poles (1936:296–97). Because the housing market within black areas was constantly tight, higher rental prices than any other area in the city could be sustained regardless of the condition of the housing (Adams 1926:39, 63; Cayton 1940:16–17;

Hughes 1925). Houghteling found that only 5.6 percent of white wage earners but 33.4 percent of black wage earners spent more than a third of their income for rent. Seventy percent of white workers but only 18.7 percent of black workers spent less than 20 percent of their income for rent (Houghteling 1927:table 65). Figure 2.3 shows the concentration of white workers at the lower proportions of income and the more even distribution of blacks toward the upper end.

Violence and terror also helped contain the black community. A number of studies have examined the measures employed against black families that dared to move from the overcrowded, overpriced belt to contiguous white neighborhoods (Chicago Commission on Race Relations 1922:33–40; Hirsch 1973, 1983:chaps. 2–3; Martin

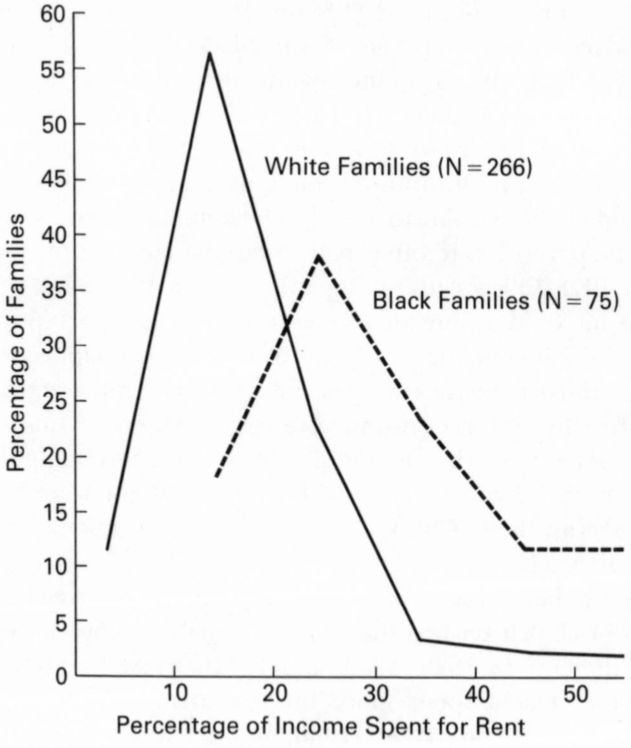

Source: Houghteling 1927: table 65, p. 113.

Figure 2.3 Percentage of Earnings of Chief Wage Earners, Chicago, 1924

1941; Philpott 1978:chaps. 7–8; Tuttle 1972:chap. 4). Fire-bombing, gang attacks, riots, and individual and organized campaigns of terror maintained the territorial borders of the black belt. The antiblockbusting bombing campaign of 1919 in Hyde Park, the riots of 1919, and a long series of violent acts sought to discourage large-scale black migration.[25] There were persistent patterns of violent attacks by whites against blacks who violated territorial boundaries. Hirsch (1983) showed that the violence continued into the period after World War II (see also Helper 1969:chap. 3). More importantly, legal institutions took little or no protective action to defend blacks. These factors meant that racial integration was a passing characteristic that coincided with the short period during which a neighborhood changed swiftly from white to black. Thus blacks were highly segregated, restricted from home ownership, overcrowded, economically disadvantaged, overcharged for housing, and subject to violent attacks if they sought to escape.[26]

The Pluralist Model Evaluated

The focus now returns to the theoretical interpretations of racial and ethnic politics. Using the richly detailed historical evidence of racial and ethnic social and economic life in Chicago, how should pluralist theory be reevaluated; what are the political implications for the three groups? I earlier identified three characteristics of American politics that allowed swift assimilation of racial and ethnic groups. These three principles—interest diversification, interest incorporation, and ethnic and racial group democracy—will structure the evaluation of the pluralist model.

Interest Diversification. The housing and labor markets provide different clues for the three groups considered in this study. The labor market offered numerous examples of the use of discrimination in distributing unemployment disproportionately to blacks or in determining the distribution of skilled and unskilled employment. All the groups experienced some job restrictions and the historical record suggests that employers continually related the quality of job performance to racial or ethnic criteria. In the most extreme case, employers seemed to exclude Italians altogether; Poles, for a short time, and blacks, for a long time, found persistent impediments to industrial employment. Blacks entered the market only when there was a shortage of inexpensive white labor. The black business sector was clearly the weakest of the three examined, but even the more active Italian and Polish businesses were dwarfed by the national firms that made Chicago their home base.

In the housing markets, Italians experienced the fewest restrictions, evidenced by the fact that they had the lowest degrees of concentration of the groups examined; Poles gathered in a number of important settlement areas, but only blacks suffered persistent, severe, informal and formal, de jure and de facto, as well as legal and violent restrictions aimed at limiting their settlement to one or two areas in the city.

Under these conditions, the diversification of political interest in the black community was highly improbable; with strong racial restrictions operating in two important economic sectors, the formation of political interests was more likely to focus on racial issues. Political concerns and demands were more likely to address issues of collective racial status. Political interests were not diversified to any great extent, since great efforts were taken to restrict spatial and economic diversification.

Poles and Italians, though more group-oriented in the 1920s than northern Europeans, were subject only to inconsistent and low-key restrictions on economic participation and to few limitations on their residential mobility. Philpott comments, "Briefly in 1922 and 1923, immigrants came under the attack of disgruntled natives and diverted attention from the blacks. The nativist effort was abortive, *utterly failing to hold white ethnics in check.* This is significant because of the contrast it provides to the subsequent campaign to control the movement of blacks. The latter effort, in which *ethnic and native whites collaborated, was successful*" (1978:185, emphasis added). Such groups would experience some, possibly significant, diversification, as their economic and physical locations diverged. In chapter 5, racial political philosophy will be analyzed in greater detail.

Interest Incorporation. Theorists assume that a subjective interest, one which is realized and articulated, attains some level of systemic incorporation. The pluralist model requires few rules of entry and places high values on goal achievement. Earlier in the chapter I described discriminatory employment and housing patterns for blacks in Chicago, amounting to formidable barriers to entry. In such an environment, the representation of political views by various ethnic groups and social classes reflects some of the qualities of other sectors of the society.

Neighborhood improvement associations and the Chicago Real Estate Board formed the organizational base for the creation of a network of racially restrictive covenants in Chicago (Philpott 1978: 185). Labor unions excluded blacks through their constitutions, rituals, and organizational construction. The political demands formulated by these and other economic institutions reflected their concerns about race. The political interests formulated within these organizations did not seek to accommodate, even in incremental fashion, political interests developed by blacks. In a heterogeneous community governed by discriminatory principles, all political interests are not easily incorporated or amenable to bargaining.

The political interests of labor unions and neighborhood improvement associations were in conflict with blacks, who primarily sought more and better jobs and housing. These were issues which were difficult, even explosive, but which ultimately, might not be amenable to bargaining. In the economic slowdown of the 1920s and the depression of the 1930s, competition over these increasingly scarce items spiraled upwards. The discriminatory character of the economic sector certainly influenced the political sector. As the last of the immigrants, Poles and Italians initially alienated their northern European predecessors, but moved through the barriers to ethnic entry in a short time. They did not suffer the distinctive set of economic and group restrictions applied to blacks.

Racial-Ethnic Democracy. There is varying evidence of racial-ethnic democracy. The Italian and Polish population settled in a number of areas identified with their respective nationalities. Abbott noted some nativist dissatisfaction with new Polish and Italian neighbors, but there was no evidence of consistent or formal attempts to limit their free entry to the housing market, either through restrictive covenants or prohibitively high rents. In the labor market, Poles and Italians formed their own national locals and were also integrated into nonethnic locals. Blacks, on the other hand, were decisively subordinated by economic organizations. They were either excluded from or subordinated within labor unions, and they found their housing concerns subordinate to the interests of a whole range of other ethnic and economic interests in Chicago. The concerns of the groups with which blacks were in contact and in conflict were more likely to win acceptance. In short, the concerns of native white and European immigrant interests had a powerfully constraining impact on the black community.

So far I have tried to show the existence of a pattern of racial interaction that not only contradicts the principles of the pluralist model, but that also conforms rather closely to the elegantly simple but very effective theoretical analysis on the status of blacks developed by Marguerite Ross Barnett. She argues first that racial status is characterized not by diversity, incorporation, and democracy, but by hierarchy and collectivism (Barnett 1976; Barnett and Vera 1980). Blacks are in all locations within the country subordinate to whites as a race, regardless of the ethnic status of whites. Second, blacks are treated as a group; no individual achievement ameliorates the status of an individual or elevates the position of the group as a whole.[27]

In conclusion, historical data on racial and ethnic life in Chicago suggests considerable caution in the use of the pluralist model of political participation. Many rather subtle distinctions were applied to the three groups within the housing, labor markets, and business world. The profiles of the groups' participation within the two economic sectors were strikingly different; their participation across sectors was also different, with the exception of the black population. In comparison to blacks, Poles and Italians experienced minor discrimination, although the evidence shows that distinctive criteria were also applied, though less systematically, to both. Black economic life supported politics of a very different character than that proposed by the pluralist theorists. In the next chapter, I examine Chicago's general political environment as a prelude to an examination of black, Italian, and Polish politics.

3

From Competition to Monopoly: The Formation of the Chicago Democratic Machine

> The machine has its origin in the slum areas of the industrial city, where immigrant populations exist in their initial stages of transiency and social disorganization. Ward bosses exercise control by a combination of coercion and control of unskilled private and public jobs. The illiterate new Americans, unused to Democratic ways, are easily manipulated into voting as the unscrupulous bosses direct. However, the effectiveness of this low-level patronage system works gradually along with other factors to raise the immigrant community's level of living and its ability to sustain an organized style of life. The "ethnic village" emerges, protected and represented by formally constituted ethnic associations and an exquisite network of familial, religious, and neighborhood ties.
>
> —Thomas H. Guterbock, *Machine Politics in Transition* (1980)

American social scientists have frequently articulated a mythical view of early twentieth-century urban immigrant life, based on pluralist theories, in which a patriarchal political leader governs an urban village; under his tutelage the upwardly mobile immigrant community is integrated into American political and economic life. According to these theories, the lower political and economic status of the European immigrants and black migrants in the early twentieth century was transitory. Machine politics helped the groups move out of their lower status, helped divest them of their narrow national or racial orientations, and helped them accept mainstream American goals and values.[1]

In Chicago a system of wildly competitive party factions evolved into a mature, stable, and monopolistic machine in the early 1930s. The formation of the Democratic machine imposed fundamentally different patterns of political organization, increased the capacity of party leaders to control and manipulate goods and services, and affected ethnic and racial group relations. The dramatically different party systems in operation before and after 1930 offer naturally comparative settings against which the assimilative power of machines can be evaluated.

Physical Structure: From Machine Politics to Political Machine

The year 1931 was the watershed mayoral election demarcating the end of the era of Chicago's "machine politics," a period of intense interparty and intraparty rivalry, and the beginning of the increasingly centralized, dominant one-party Democratic machine. Raymond Wolfinger distinguishes between machine politics and political machines in this way:

> "Machine politics" is the manipulation of certain *incentives* to partisan political participation: favoritism based on political criteria in personnel decisions, contracting and administration of the laws. A "political machine" is an organization that practices machine politics, i.e., that attracts and directs its members primarily by means of these incentives . . . [and also] is a united and hierarchical party organization in a state, city or county (1972:374–75).

Before 1930 Chicago politics had little partisan coherence or consistency. Partisan conflicts arose from several factors. Economic, ethnic, racial, and linguistic differences between immigrant groups clashed in cacophonous disarray and were transmitted into the complex partisan interaction of the 1920s. First, Chicago was an industrial city composed of a population sharply demarcated by positions of employment, management, or ownership. Second, many European nationality groups with many languages shared the city's living, working, and political territory along with blacks, Chinese, and Mexicans. Acting in addition to the economic, ethnic, racial, and linguistic differences were the competing Democratic and Republican parties. In practice the multitude of constituencies made the two-party system unstable, leading to constant intraparty factionalism and complicated interparty rivalry. Factions in opposing parties frequently became allies in order to defeat their respective party rivals, as well as to limit their competitors' access to political patronage. More often than not in the period prior to 1930, party unity was subordinated to personal and factional competition. Nearly every major political figure was the focus for a small coterie of followers and patronage. With a complex environment created by the strongly defined economic groups in the city and cross-cut by linguistic, ethnic, racial, and religious differences, each aspiring political leader could transform a small following into a strategic balance in a city primary or election.[2] Factions were composed by means of temporary alliances between these leaders. Each party had workers at precinct, ward, and county levels and patronage workers in city agencies, but neither party was sufficiently disciplined to support a united ticket during or after primary competition. As Lowi has noted, "A primary fight indicates the breakdown of bargaining techniques inside the party" (1964:19).

Chicago city and county governments also facilitated partisan fragmentation by acting as sources of patronage for the multiple subparty factions. Independent city and county school boards, civil service commissions, and independent taxing authorities provided locations from which ambitious political leaders might bargain for votes and power. With separate sources of patronage, a defeat at the polls need not mean political oblivion; a party faction could still retain control of resources by being in control of an independent park or school district.[3] In the short run intraparty competition and rivalry advantaged party leaders skillful and daring enough to conceive and execute aggressive strategies. If the feint were successful, the candidate won increased access to political patronage; if not, the faction still had a political or bureaucratic base from which to operate and to plan new forays.

The Democratic and Republican parties were divided into groups roughly designated reformers and regulars. Between 1910 and 1920 bosses Roger Sullivan and George Brennan, reform-oriented former mayor Carter Harrison, and Governor Edward T. Dunne led factions in the Democratic party. After Sullivan died in April 1920, Brennan and the increasingly powerful Czech Anton Cermak opposed the Dunne-Harrison faction. After Brennan's death in 1928, Cermak emerged as a strong candidate for party leadership. Loosely aligned with Democrats such as Harrison, Dunne, William O'Connell, and James Igoe, Cermak was opposed by Brennan's Irish supporters, Michael Igoe, Ed Kelly, J. J. Crowe, and Martin J. O'Brien. Republican alliances radiated around Thompson and Deneen, although realignments were frequent (Gottfried 1962:chap. 10; Stuart 1936:163; Wendt and Kogan 1953:191–251).[4]

With so much conflict, a variety of competitive strategies were employed. Intervention in the opposing party's activities might increase a faction's standing within its own party by drawing stronger competition against intraparty opponents. In 1915, for example, Carter Harrison, a weak Democratic party leader, supported Republican William Hale Thompson, an untested candidate for mayor. Thompson had served as alderman of the increasingly black second ward in 1900 and as a member of the Cook County Commission in 1902. Harrison's Democratic competitors, Roger Sullivan and George Brennan, controlled the party apparatus and engineered Robert Sweitzer's nomination over Harrison. Harrison would have lost nothing if Thompson had been defeated; when he won, Harrison controlled Democratic access to the new Republican administration and simultaneously weakened Sullivan and Brennan by denying them the city's patronage (Stuart 1936:114–15).[5]

In 1923 George Brennan felt that the Democrats should nominate an honest mayoral candidate and should avoid the factional struggles that had doomed their chances in previous mayoral elections. Thompson won the mayor's office in 1915 and 1919. Brennan therefore secured agreements from Dunne, Harrison, and William O'Connell, but after Democrat William Dever's election, Brennan refused to share the patronage.[6]

Why a Democratic Machine?

The formation of a Democratic machine is based on several developments. Identifiable and self-conscious ethnic voting patterns emerged for the first time in the late 1920s. Ethnic political coalescence, an issue to be discussed later in this chapter, played a crucial role in the creation of the machine. Second, Democrat Anton Cermak and Republican "Big Bill" Thompson assumed sharply divergent leadership roles for their parties prior to 1930. Cermak gradually restructured the system of Democratic partisan interaction from conflict and competition into a unified and disciplined organization, and he linked party leadership with control of city and county governments. Thompson discouraged coalition building and cooperation in favor of one-man erratic, charismatic rule, which resulted in the gradual disintegration of the Republican party.

Republican Disintegration. The Democrats established competing but relatively stable leadership factions, but by contrast there were no continuing Republican patterns of association other than the Deneen-Olson alliance and the long-term Thompson-Deneen rivalry. The Republican party's 1931 mayoral defeat was preceded by over a decade of internecine warfare. Thompson was first targeted for mayor in 1915 by Fred Lundin, former U.S. Senator William Lorimer, and Len

Small, who was later elected governor in 1920 (MacDonald 1962:254–56). After Thompson's 1919 mayoral relection and a 1920 electoral victory in which several of his candidates won election, Thompson and Lundin felt strong enough to attempt to undermine their Republican rival, Senator Charles Deneen. They nominated only four incumbents for the June 1921 elections for the circuit and superior courts, the rest being patronage appointees with little legal experience (Wendt and Kogan 1953:195–97). The Democrats took advantage of the public indignation this aroused and nominated a coalition slate of incumbent Republicans, Deneen and Brundage, and a few Democrats (Bright 1930:179; Stuart 1936:135–36). The Thompson slate was completely defeated.

Immediately after Governor Small's second inauguration in 1925, Thompson proposed Attorney General Oscar Carlstrom for governor in 1928. Offended, Small stripped Thompson of all power and state patronage in Cook County and replaced him with Fred Lundin (Stuart 1936:book 13; Wendt and Kogan 1953:219–20). Lundin had parted company from Thompson in 1922 after his and others' indictments for misuse of school funds by a Thompson-appointed school board (Stuart 1935:138). Thompson's original coterie completely disintegrated.

Thompson and Crowe attempted to eliminate Senator Deneen from political competition by challenging his candidate for state's attorney, John Swanson, in the 1928 primary. Deneen's and Swanson's houses were bombed, and "Diamond Joe" Esposito, a Deneen candidate for reelection as twentieth ward committeeman, was murdered (Nelli 1970a:226; Stuart 1936:362–63; Wendt and Kogan 1953:303–4). Afterwards, Robert E. Crowe, state's attorney and Swanson's Democratic primary opponent for reelection, assured Chicagoans that "I am satisfied that these two bombings are the result of a conspiracy upon the part of a few Deneen leaders to win the primary election April 10 (1928)" (Stuart 1936:362). Most of the meager evidence suggested the reverse. So many bombs were tossed that the election was nicknamed the Pineapple Primary, and the public, repelled by the Republican tactics, rejected Thompson's candidate for the Cook County Board of (Tax) Review and his candidate Crowe for state's attorney.

Thompson and other Republicans kept up a dizzying pace of conflict. In 1915 Lundin, Thompson, and Small were opposed by Olson, Deneen, and Edward Brundage, later Illinois attorney general. By 1925 Lundin had broken with Thompson, who attacked Small, who in turn reassociated himself with Lundin. Brundage had supported Thompson for mayor in 1915, indicted Thompson's ally Lundin in 1922, and aligned himself with Thompson again in 1926 (Wooddy 1926:287). State's Attorney Crowe had helped indict Lundin in 1922 also, but by 1928 he was Thompson's candidate for the same post.

In 1930 Ruth Hanna McCormick, the daughter of Republican Mark Hanna and the widow of Medill McCormick, the coowner of the *Chicago Tribune,* denied Thompson's claims that he had contributed to her nomination to the U.S. Senate over Deneen, since she had led the Republican mayoral ticket by 200,000 votes (Stuart 1936:410). Thompson responded by supporting her Democratic opponent, J. Hamilton Lewis, who offended many of Thompson's black supporters and allies with the statement "This is a White Man's country" (quoted in Gosnell 1967:44–46). DePriest responded "No sane mind, unless ill-advised or sick, would ask the colored people to vote for a Democrat" (quoted in Wendt and Kogan 1953:319).

By the time of the 1931 mayoral primary, the Republican party was so divided that Thompson had to fight two strong competitors for the party's nomination. The Deneen faction nominated Arthur F. Albert, but even Thompson's long-time ally George F. Harding favored Judge John Lyle (Lyle 1960:258–62). The depth of the party divisions can be measured in the fact that Thompson's opponents outpolled him by 30,000 votes in the primary (according to the Municipal Reference Library, Chicago City Hall, microfilm records of the Feb. 1931 primary, Thompson received 296,204 votes, Lyle 227,986, and Albert 99,137). After the primary the party disintegrated completely, with Thompson's former comptroller Samuel Ettelson and other former allies such as Harding, Lundin, and most of the Cook County Republican Committee supporting the Democratic nominee Cermak (Gottfried 1962:206–14, chap. 8).

Democratic Unification. The Democrats combined luck with the leadership of Anton Cermak. Cermak was elected president of the Cook County Board of Commissioners in 1922, but only seven of the fifteen commissioners were Democratic, so he began to try to win control of the board by giving the Republicans access to patronage. Because the tactic was successful, Cermak used the same strategy to maximize his position within the Democratic party. This was possible in part because as president of the board of Cook County, he was also president of the Board of Forest Preserve Commissioners, a source of patronage. The Republicans and their candidates were frequently hurt by the ties that Democrats such as Brennan and Cermak made throughout the 1920s. Republican State's Attorney Robert E. Crowe and Attorney General Brundage indicted Thompson's patronage chief Fred Lundin and other members of the Thompson-appointed Board of Education in sufficient time prior to the mayoral primaries for the 1923 election to force Thompson to drop out of that race (Herrick 1971:142–43).

Cermak also undermined Democrats when it was in his interest; he suppressed the Democratic vote for the incumbent Democratic mayor, William Dever, in 1927. Cermak took such action for strategic as well as substantive reasons. Dever enforced the prohibition laws, while Cermak, reflecting his ethnic constituents' views, had always opposed prohibition and its enforcement (Gottfried 1962:150–51). For example, in 1905 Cermak had helped found and lead the United Societies for Local Self-Government, an antiprohibition organization. Thompson's position in 1927 also appealed to Cermak since "Big Bill" claimed that he was "wetter than the Atlantic ocean" (Allswang 1977:101–16). Cermak rewarded his Republican allies on the Cook County board and strengthened his prestige with the non-Irish and rebellious Irish factions in the Democratic party. Finally, and perhaps most significantly, he laid the groundwork for reinforcing his own position within the Democratic party by denying Brennan, who died shortly afterwards in August 1928, and his faction the substantial patronage accessible to the mayor.[7]

By the time of the 1931 mayoral election the Republicans and Democrats presented clear political alternatives. Bloody gang warfare, financial bankruptcy of the school system, and recurring tax scandals during the Thompson administration from 1927 to 1931 helped propel the electorate toward the Democratic party as it became clear that the Republicans could not govern.[8] Cermak's Republican and Democratic allies helped administer the coup de grace to his Republican opponent Thompson. In the 1931 mayoral election, Deneen's and Cermak's ally, Republican State's Attorney Swanson, raided the office of Thompson's city sealer, Daniel Serritella, and indicted him for shorting city weights and measures. Serritella was later convicted, with the decision reversed on appeal, but the charges were directed at influencing the election returns in the Democrats' favor (Gottfried 1962:235). State's Attorney Swanson indicted Cermak's Irish Democratic enemies T. J. Crowe and Martin J. O'Brien because of their mishandling of the administration of the sanitary districts in 1931, which neutralized them as potentially active opponents of Cermak (Gottfried 1962:chap. 11; Stuart 1936:book 24). These indictments were highly selective and aimed at gaining politcal advantage for one party or party faction at the expense of the other. Sullivan's and Brennan's deaths in 1920 and 1928 and Cermak's successful manipulation of the system of party conflict made him the dominant figure in the Democratic party by 1930. With Crowe and O'Brien neutralized in 1931, Cermak won over ninety-five percent of the vote in the Democratic primary (see microfilm records, Municipal Reference Library, Chicago City Hall; Wooddy 1926:286–87).[9]

Thompson was a brilliant strategist, but in the long run his brilliance turned back upon itself. In the 1922 judicial elections and in the 1928 Pineapple Primary, he pushed too hard and used unacceptable tactics so that the usually dormant reformist impulses of Chicago's voters were aroused. In the Small debacle in 1925, Thompson announced his intention to eliminate Small, even though Thompson was no longer mayor and was still dependent on Small's gubernatorial patronage and political support. Thompson thus frequently alienated those who were in a position to help him. In contrast Cermak minimized his vulnerabilities by making close ties with those who were of use to him. When he wanted to attack his enemies, he did so in ways that engendered public support or that attracted little adverse notice to himself.

By the early 1930s Anton Cermak's Democratic machine replaced the partisan machine politics of the 1920s. In 1928, for the first time during a Republican administration, a Democrat, John Traeger, was elected sheriff of Cook County (Peterson 1952:373). In 1930 J. Hamilton Lewis's Democratic senatorial victory was accompanied by Cermak's impressive reelection as president of the Cook County board with 60 percent of the vote (Stuart 1936:453). After he won the mayoral election in 1931, he remained president of the board until February 1932, at which time he appointed a Democratic ally, Emmet Whealan, to fill the position, but he did not relinquish his seat.

Another ally, Pat Nash, became chairman of the Cook County Democratic Central Committee; in 1932 Cermak slated and successfully engineered the election of Henry Horner as governor. Within ten years of his election as president of the Cook County Board of Commissioners in 1922, Cermak was able to consolidate most of the "scattered fragments of power" in Chicago and Cook County into a centralized, hierarchical Democratic machine that manipulated incentives to encourage political participation (Gottfried 1962:chap. 13).[10] Chicago's mayoral election of 1931 was clearly a local version of a critical election, one in which voters turned out in large numbers, in which there were significant reorganizations of existing electoral coalitions and partisan associations, and in which the issues in the election mobilized significant numbers of new participants. This new political realignment was a powerful one, lasting for half a century.

The New Machine

The supportive integrative machine described by Merton (1949, 1961), Kilson (1971a, 1971b), and others required a political structure with flexibility and considerable slack. Chicago's pre-1931 system of machine politics, while complex, disorganized, and frenetic, was for those very reasons much more like Merton's model than the Democratic machine. Formally, the emergence of the machine reduced rather than enhanced the bargaining opportunities for political and ethnic groups. Bureaucratic decision making was no longer located in administrative bureaucracies controlled by competing associations of parties and factions; decisions were made by a centralized unified party hierarchy with few administrative agencies outside its jurisdiction.

Unified political control of bureaucracies also certified universal access to governmental resources, goods and services, jobs, and political influence. Wolfinger (1972) distinguishes between machine politics and political machines. In the former case, decentralized competitive parties "manipulate incentives," material or otherwise, to capture a large enough portion of the voters to win office. In the latter instance, political machines practice machine politics, and in cases such as the Chicago Democratic party they faced no serious political competitors after 1931. With all formerly warring Democrats and Republicans allied behind Cermak, with Nash and Cermak heading the Democratic party, with Cermak in control of the mayor's office, with Cermak a member and de facto head of the Cook County Board of Commissioners, and with Democratic officials in place throughout the city, county, state, and the presidency by 1932, Chicago's political apparatus was highly centralized and powerful. Partisan politics was dominated by one party, which also exercised control over the city and county administrative apparatus.

Having defeated his partisan opposition and having established political control over the region's bureaucracy, a highly lucrative source of patronage, Cermak and the Democrats established greater control over individuals and groups that attempted to transform electoral resources into political power. As McConnell notes, large complex political constituencies afford greater opportunities for diverse political representation than small homogeneous ones (1966:91–118; see also Sullivan et al. 1980:19–43). Although the focus of political interaction shifted from small factions to a citywide coalition, machine politics offered multiple competing constituencies before 1931 and a monopoly afterwards. The formation of the machine vastly simplified the process of coalition building for party leaders but minimized the bargaining powers of the many ethnic groups in the city by the reduction in the number of partisan groupings around and in which such interests might find representation. Under the hierarchical, centralized machine, small groups seeking political influence had far less leverage than they had in the past and had access to far fewer resources with which they could bargain.

The Manipulation of Incentives: Selective Benefits in a Collective World

Merton asked social scientists to consider the role of machines in a different framework than the pejorative one which reformers had used for nearly half a century. Because "we should *ordinarily* (not invariably) expect persistent social patterns and social structures to perform positive functions *which are at the time not adequately fulfilled by other existing patterns and structures,* the thought occurs that perhaps this publicly maligned organization is, under present conditions, satisfying basic latent functions" (1949:71–72).[11]

In his effort to shed new light on the role of the machine, Merton adopted a structural-functional interpretation of the machine, arguing that it was a positive substitute for inadequate political institutions. In order to differentiate himself from the reformers, Merton took a position opposite theirs, although he might have criticized the machine from a different vantage point. Next I will establish the grounds for that alternate criticism as it relates to three of the four functions Merton identifies: aid and support for the voter, economic support for legitimate business, and economic support for illegitimate business. I argue that the persistence of political institutions and their support of various sectors in society does not necessarily lead us to the conclusion that their roles are positive. Merton's fourth function, upward mobility, will be discussed later in the chapter and again in chapter 4.

The form and substance of public goods bind the voter and the political machine in an intimate embrace. Substantively, political incentives fall into the same broad categories as those outlined by Merton. They are the kinds of public goods that Downs (1967) and Olson (1971, 1973:355) identify as motivating voters and interest groups; when political organizations distribute them selectively, voters have much greater incentive to lend their support to political regimes. Downs argues that the costs of intelligent voting are higher than any individual is ordinarily willing to pay and that collective benefits are often bestowed independently of voting behavior. Citizens, therefore, typically vote or pay attention to policymakers when a decision or vote has a powerful, especially a selective, and an economic impact upon them. Individual voters, small and large businessmen, proprietors of gambling houses, and houses of ill-repute thus all found it important to lend their political support to the political system in Chicago because it had the potential to significantly influence their economic livelihoods. Many benefits were administrative favors, but the bulk (such as jobs, ticket-fixing, political influence, contracts, toleration of numbers running, gambling, liquor, and prostitution, enforcement or lax enforcement of housing, health, or safety codes, and zoning laws) had important economic consequences for the beneficiaries (Gosnell 1968:69–90).

Economic concerns also dominate Olson's analysis of the logic of collective action (1971). Groups that influence policymaking are more likely to be composed of individuals whose economic and therefore political interests are similar. He argues that organization for economic self-regulation precedes the entry of the group into the political sector and that political action is a by-product or consequence of economic organization. The one element that unites voting, political lobbies, and political organizations is economic interest. Lobbying and bargaining would be carried out by members of special interest groups.

Merton and Guterbock have emphasized the affectual character of the interaction between the voter and party organization. According to Merton, machines humanize and personalize social welfare and other personal assistance for immigrant groups. Lincoln Steffens quoted Lomasny of Boston on this issue: "There's got to be in every ward somebody that any bloke can come to—no matter what he's done—and get help. Help, you understand; none of your law and your justice, but help" (1931:618).[12] Writing a generation later, Guterbock has asserted that voters' commitment to the machine is no longer established or compelled by the exchange of goods and services; voters' moral commitment to the local political system precedes and is independent of any exchange of services. Services exist because "they facilitate social processes growing out of the interaction that enhances the organization's effectiveness" (Guterbock 1980:212).

Both Guterbock and Merton have emphasized the affectual nature of machine-voter relations, but an economic exchange creates and sustains the relationship. Both parties must adhere to their portion of the bargain; Guterbock's description of moral commitment for the voter from the machine and Merton's concern with "aid and support" for the voter from the machine suggest an asymmetrical rather than a symmetrical exchange. Without the cooperation of both voters and machine in the exchange, the relationship would not exist. The sentimental portrait of altruistic political leadership capable of humanizing and distributing the services provided by an otherwise cold bureaucracy has nothing to do with political reality.

Partisan incentives bind voters to the machine on a formal as well as a substantive basis. Many of the goods, services, and favors provided by the machine are divisible; they can be broken down into individualized components and distributed to or retrieved from a voter on a personal basis. Here the machine's use of the goods and services of the type Merton has described substantially enhances its control of the population. Strategically, the benefits are provided so that they can be distributed or withdrawn selectively, thereby acting to establish an even firmer commitment by the voter to the political organization. The economic nature of the goods and services is also complemented by their manner of distribution. First, patronage is divisible so that the voter might be influenced selectively. More often than not benefits are also material—a job, a streetlight, a relative freed from jail, a bribe—so that the exchange is clearly defined in the minds of both parties.

Services are provided to voters in order to encourage political participation, which enhances a faction's hold on political office. Machines distribute divisible and material incentives in order to bind the voter more effectively to the source of patronage; failure to perform as expected results in the separation of the voter from the patronage. In the competitive system, where no faction controls a majority or even a plurality of the votes, winning the support of one additional ethnic, interest, or business group could make the difference between electoral victory and defeat. Small groups take on disproportionate status and become the targets for patronage bidding wars.

Selective economic benefits encourage voter participation, but with the formation of the machine the political leverage of party leaders increases; with one centralized source of patronage, voters lose considerable discretion in making political choices, in encouraging ideological conflict, in supporting alternate policies, or in reinforcing patronage bidding wars. The selective nature of benefits is clearest for individual voters; businessmen, either legitimate or illegitimate, received not only goods and services but also benefits not always apparent to the naked eye. Thus the economic nature of the relationship dominates whatever affectual elements may have accompanied it, and the efficiency with which incentives compel political participation is vastly enhanced by the maturation of the political machine. For the maturing Democratic machine this was certainly true.

Under what circumstances does this system of benefits distribution necessarily result in the transformation in status that Merton attributes to it. The machine and its directors have to meet certain requirements. The aggregate results of selective distribution of goods, services, and policies would at worst avoid increased group differentiation and at best eliminate group differentiation. On the aggregate, a group would have to be better off; or one might assume that only minimal inequalities already existed and that the machine would reduce these. Thus the machine should increasingly redistribute public goods and services, as ethnic, racial, or class groups participate in the political system (Lowi 1964). Only if a political setting includes minimal inequalities should goods and services be dispensed in a selective fashion.

Are there any inherent impediments to a political machine or the use of selective material benefits having an ameliorative and integrative political effect? A full answer requires, first, examination and discussion of the types of benefits distributed to other beneficiaries and supporters of the political machine and, second, an analysis of the strength of the collective status of ethnic or racial groups in the society.

Are there any groups that might oppose redistributive or regulatory policies and whose interests would also be represented by the machine; are there any groups for which redistributive policies might be necessary? An affirmative answer for both questions would force acknowledgment of the problematical nature of selective benefits, since they are not in and of themselves redistributive, and of the political context in which they are distributed.

Individual voters represent only one of the groups with which machines deal. Merton has also identified services to legitimate and illegitimate business as two of the four functions of machines. Business groups frequently request lax enforcement of laws governing their conduct or operations. In Chicago legitimate businesses preferred underassessment of taxes, liberal terms for utilities or transportation franchises (by means of regulatory policy), tacit acceptance of shaky or clearly illegitimate business deals and contracts with the city school board or city hall, and a favorable business climate.

Gottfried reported that business groups, civic organizations, newspapers, and Chicago's "silk-stocking" elements "had investments in the impending World's Fair, and there were real fears that the unfavorable international press caused by the Thompson regime [caused by the gang wars of the late 1920s] would jeopardize the success of these investments. The same bad press was causing deleterious effects upon the value of city securities in which many of these persons had considerable holdings" (1962:228).

Illegitimate business required lax enforcement of laws against prohibition, prostitution, and gambling. Failure to acknowledge or prosecute illegal activities was widespread throughout Chicago's city government, from the tax collector, city inspector, police and fire departments to public utilities responsible for billing after-hours clubs. Where laws restricted certain activities, the Chicago political machine facilitated the conduct of business by failing to regulate them closely. In other cases the city failed to regulate business at all.

Max Weber reported on one example of lax or limited regulation:

> After their work, the workers often have to travel for hours in order to reach their homes. The tramway company has been bankrupt for years . . . [and] new tram cars are not purchased. The old cars constantly break down, and about four hundred people a year are thus killed or crippled. According to the law, each death costs the company about $5,000, which is paid to the widow or heirs, and each cripple costs $10,000, paid to the casualty himself. These compensations are due so long as the company does not introduce certain precautionary measures. But they have calculated that the four hundred casualties a year cost less than would the necessary precautions. The company therefore does not introduce them (Gerth and Mills 1946:16).[13]

While loose enforcement of regulatory policy was a prime concern of Chicago's business interests, the possibility of enforcement, or more accurately of the formation and implementation of redistributive policy, was also a matter of great concern for the business community. First, the costs of city government in direct social welfare expenditures were considerably lower in Chicago than other cities on a comparable basis. Education and other health and welfare costs that would have reduced or minimized social and economic inequalities were sharply lower (Pinderhughes 1977b:402).

Secondly, as I have already noted in chapter 2, sharp ethnic and racial differentiation was observed in both the housing and labor markets in Chicago. The fluctuations in employment of racial and ethnic groups observed was the result of selective and differential recruitment, training, promotion, and discharge both by management and labor.

In the previous chapter I showed how industries attempted to divide the labor force along racial and ethnic lines in order to minimize their bargaining power with management and, therefore, to reduce their overall labor costs. In chapter 2 I also showed how white labor often cooperated in creating racial divisions within the work force. The political concerns of industries that manipulated ethnic and racial divisions to minimize labor unity and class conflict within factories were relatively simple. They required a city government with limited powers of intervention in the economic sector. Intervention to reform industrial hiring and promotion practices in the stockyards, meat-packing industries, steel mills, and Sears mail-order business and to minimize discrimination in many other large and small firms in the city would have required an aggressive city government with the power and authority to regulate the behavior of some of the nation's largest corporations; this would have been a redistributive policy that promoted upward social mobility.

The Chicago city government would have had to adjudge that the distribution of goods and services by itself, as well as the distribution of economic resources in the private sector, was not only *not* equal but that it ought *to be* equal. In the housing market, where there was strong evidence of racial discrimination in the location, sale, rental, and purchase of homes, the city would have had to invade the private domain of the real estate and banking industries, which had developed their own discriminatory criteria to maintain and preserve the values of homes, property, and neighborhoods (Helper 1969). The city would have had to legislate a change in those values in order to produce a racially heterogeneous distribution of population and to promote an equitable pattern of home ownership.

Evidence presented in chapter 2 established the presence of a pattern of racial differentiation in housing and employment in Chicago; remedying these practices required redistributive public policies. For political participation to have had at least the consequences (since they did not have the characteristics) described by Kilson, Merton, Dahl, and Wilson, political benefits and public goods and services should have been dispensed in a radically redistributive fashion.

Because racial differentiation existed in Chicago, those groups that incorporated racial discrimination into their economic practices would probably have opposed attempts to form and implement redistributive policy. Because there were groups that would have benefitted from redistributive policies and groups that would have suffered from them, public goods and policies that attempted to address the concerns of voters on a collective basis would have been highly controversial. Given the larger political and economic setting, the character of political exchange, the difficulty of maintenance of political control in a contentious city, and the selective distribution of goods, the redistributive character of Chicago politics was unlikely.

The Missing Policy Dimension

The larger economic environment recognized some sectors of the population on what Barnett and Dorn call a "collective basis." Racial discrimination in hiring and employment involved recognition and demarcation of blacks as a group rather than as individuals differentiated by economic status, education, or personality. Political structures and public policy benefits, however, organized and distributed on a selective and individual basis were intended to stimulate the participation and loyalty of voters rather than to alter the behavior of economic actors in the private sector or to redistribute public goods and services within society (Barnett 1976:30).

For Lowi, "the political machine, by its very entrepreneurial essence, is a neutral apparatus" (1964:233), while for James Scott it is a "non-ideological organization interested less in political principle than in securing and holding office for its leaders and distributing income to those who run it and work for it" (Scott 1969:1155). Though it is called neutral and nonideological, it is formally based on selective benefits; such a system is structurally incapable of recognizing or redressing the collective status of a racial or economic group. Selective benefits used in a system that differentiates groups are neutral in the sense that they have no ameliorative impact on collective status. A system in which benefits are distributed selectively can be compared to equal opportunity in which "bias across races has been neutralized or eliminated. A rule of weak equal opportunity will lead to racial equality only under one condition: that the races are substantively equal at the time the rule is imposed. Failing that condition, the rule will produce ambiguous change" (Dorn 1979:139).

Failure to influence collective status in an organization that also reduces political competition has the effect of reinforcing collective status. This is not to say that the machine reinforces racial status while other political forms do not, but that a centralized political hierarchy strengthens the ability of political interests to control and resist demands of economically disfranchised group, such as blacks. Selective goods need not prohibit a change in status, but for change to occur public officials or party leaders must reallocate jobs and patronage in favor of groups with lesser economic standing. To do so, however, requires them to rank redistributive goals above the organizational ones of political control and reelection. Thus the collective status of portions of Chicago's population, although an economic and a political reality, was not explicitly recognized within the organizational responsibilities of the machine.

In figure 3.1, the theoretical alternatives of public action are outlined in the diagram. The vertical dimension represents the quality of the goods and services dispensed by the machine. Tangible goods include material benefits, jobs, petty favors, ticket-fixing, and Christmas baskets, for which machines are best known. The other end of the continuum represents intangibles, stated or unstated political agreements on the rules of the game (Bachrach and Baratz 1962). The rules of the game are also public policy for the major economic interests in the community, which also include the relationships between the public and private sectors. Intangible goods and services are public policies that certify how business will be conducted in the city.

The horizontal dimension represents the manner or form in which the goods and services are distributed by the political organization in power. In the selective category the focus of attention is the individual. Such a system is an extremely effective one for controlling and mobilizing voters' individual behavior when material goods and services are at the disposal of a political organization. In the absence

Quality of Goods and Services	Political Organization, Public Policy and the Distribution of Goods and Services Form of Organizational Recognition: Selective	Collective
Tangible Goods and Services	1 Equal Opportunity Aid and Support for Voter Legitimate and Illegitimate Business Bans	3 Compensatory Inequality Goods and Services Redistributed Increased Inequality Increasing/Decreasing Concentration
	Distributive	Redistributive
Intangible Rules of the Game	2 No Rules, Prohibitions on Racial Status/Citizenship Protection Organizational Maintenance Free Market Policy—General Specific Collective Status Racial Hierarchy	4 Reformist: Downward and Upward Mobility Anti-Discrimination Policy Regulatory Discriminatory Policy

Figure 3.1 Public Policy Orientations

of a consensus for collective reforms dealing with race, ethnicity, sex, or economic redistribution, politicians impose few political or legal restraints on business. Gambling houses need not fret about police interference or harassment, real estate operators escape stringent implementation of zoning and housing regulations, while large corporations avoid the costs of rules and regulations governing safety conditions in the plant and hiring and promotion practices. Ethnic and racial groups enjoy differing status based on formal and informal law. Voters focus only on their individual benefits rather than on their collective difficulties.

In the collective category the organization recognizes social or economic status. It redistributes goods and services through "compensatory inequality" to ease or to reinforce the cumulative consequences of historical collective inequality. The interaction of collective recognition with intangible goods and services regulates the public sector through efforts to end or to increase racial discrimination, to reduce or to expand economic differentiation, and other means.

Each of the categories matches a specific type of policy dimension or arena such as that described by Lowi. Selective dispensation of material goods and services is distributive, while the type of policy that supports it is free market or organizational maintenance. Lax policy enforcement for legitimate and illegitimate business falls into the selective intangible category, while tax rebates are selectively tangible. Distribution of goods and services on a selective basis is aimed at political control of the voters. In this category the machine does not regulate behavior or redistribute wealth and status in the public or private sector.

Unless a "compensatory inequality" goods redistribution policy is formulated to compensate for the accumulation of past collective status, machines can not have the impact the pluralists predict. The third category (collective tangibles) redistributes material goods, services, and jobs while the fourth category (collective intangibles) regulates discrimination (regulatory policy) and affects political status, leading to upward political mobility for some groups and downward mobility for others. Collective reallocation of goods and services is redistributive, while policies formed to implement it are regulatory.

For a political machine to be successful in the real world, however, it must address all of the significant interests in its environment that help maintain it. It parcels out selective benefits to lower status social and economic groups, provides a regulation-free environment for large businesses, and distinguishes whites from blacks through the creation and maintenance of a variety of "white-skin privileges," including better jobs, housing, and psychological status.

Ethnic Hierarchy

In this chapter I have emphasized the selective nature of the benefits of political participation, but Merton asserted that the machine "more or less satisfied [ethnic groups'] culturally induced needs"; and the "sheer existence and operation of the political machine" helped fulfill the function of upward mobility. The machine "no longer appears as merely a means of self-aggrandizement for profit-hungry and power-hungry individuals, but as an organized provision for subgroups otherwise excluded from or handicapped in the race for 'getting ahead'" (1949:78).

For Merton the machine not only recognizes but also resolves the collective status of ethnic groups. Yet the earliest gains in ethnic and racial political participation and representation occurred in Chicago before the development of the Democratic machine. If political machines encourage upward social mobility, how can pre-1931 ethnic participation be explained? Merton's claim might be vitiated either by a competitive or by a monopolistic use of partisan incentives, with the latter having an even greater positive mobilizing effect. In this section I present a comparison of ethnic mobility under these two types of political organization.

The competitive system supported many political factions that competed for the votes of the different ethnic and social groups. Small party factions seeking to accumulate enough votes to win city or county elections courted ethnic and racial groups with increased patronage offers. Conversely, small ethnic or racial groups increased their leverage to the degree that they concentrated their votes on one candidate or party. Blacks and ethnic groups in Chicago elected representatives to city or county and state government long before their counterparts in other cities were able to do so. Competitive politics arising out of numerous ethnic groups and small wards increased black electoral success. (See chapter 4 for a discussion of the impact of district elections on black representation.) For example, black politicians such as the Reverend Archibald Carey allied with Republican William Hale Thompson when he ran for alderman in 1900 and for mayor in 1915, 1919, and 1923. Carey also supported Democrats, such as Carter Harrison in 1911 when he ran for mayor and Edward Dunne for governor in 1912. Although black politicians took a flexible approach to partisan alliances, they supported Republicans most consistently (Branham 1977; Gosnell 1967:37–60).

The Republican alliance with black voters was based on several contrasting elements. Because the Republican party led the nation during the Civil War and implemented Radical Reconstruction, blacks identified with the Republican party when they had the freedom to be politically active. In Chicago Thompson's hearty, audacious political style and political appeals were directed at the black population. Although Ferdinand L. Barnett, a black lawyer and assistant state's attorney under State's Attorney Deneen, and Ida B. Wells-Barnett, a newspaper publisher, clubwoman, inveterate activist, and Barnett's wife, supported Charles Deneen for senator, the bulk of other black politicians supported the Thompson Republicans. A few blacks, including Earl B. Dickerson, were Democrats as early as the 1920s, but on only two occasions before 1931 did more than sixty percent of the black vote go to local Democratic candidates. The Democrats, however, drew largely upon working-class and ethnic voters, such as the Irish, Swedes, and older European groups whose interests were frequently at odds with those of blacks.

Alliances between political leaders from competing nationalities were no easier than those between party members. Political competition was a reality, but even before the political realignment of 1931 there was some partisan consistency across groups. Several black, Italian, and Polish aldermen and city officials were elected and appointed before 1931. The Irish, however, dominated the city's politics by the early twentieth century, controlling both factions of the Democratic party and making serious inroads into the Republican. Gottfried reported that "not only had the top [Democratic] party leadership been exclusively Irish since 1915 . . . but at least thirty-three of the fifty city ward committeemen in 1926 had been Irish. . . . Wooddy's analysis of the 1926 Brennan county slate revealed twenty-five Irish candidates for a total of forty-two" (1962:175).

If Merton's and Kilson's analyses have some validity, if the Irish, Poles, and Italians participated in political life to an increasing degree under machine politics, then the formation of the centralized machine and the manipulation of partisan incentives that had greater control over the entire political environment ought to have broadened the ethnic and racial political base, creating a heterogeneous political organization. In short, why should not increased political coordination maximize ethnic and racial political integration and political participation?

As the formation of the Democratic machine affected the city's political structure and the manipulation of goods and services, it also had powerful and far-reaching effects on ethnic and racial group power and status. In cities such as New York, ethnic mobility into upper-level political positions occurred with two limitations. In his examination of the cabinet appointments of the mayors of New York, Lowi concluded: "It has been the role of the minority party in New

York to provide a channel of mobility for new ethnic groups." The political party out of power absorbed ethnic groups at the bottom of the status hierarchy, and appointees from new ethnic groups were well established economically before they were named to political office (Lowi 1964:37).

In Chicago the Democratic and Republican parties roughly divided the Irish, Poles, Czechs, Jews, and Germans from the old English, blacks, and Italians, respectively. As the disintegration of the Republicans and the centralization of the Democrats proceeded, the Democratic party gradually attracted most of the city's ethnic voters. The Italians contributed an overwhelming majority of their vote to Thompson in 1927; they deviated from the rest of the city's ethnic population in the 1931 mayoral election, giving 57 percent of their vote to the Republican, Thompson. Leaders of the Republican party were drawn largely from the native white population. Italians and blacks, such as Bernard Barasa, Oscar DePriest, and Edward Wright, served the Republicans as ethnic leaders, but none of them competed with Thompson, Deneen, Small, or Lundin for citywide leadership of the Chicago party. By the mid-1920s, as the second generation southern and eastern Europeans reached political maturity, the Republican party was led by Thompson, who courted these groups but failed to understand them or take them seriously as an increasingly significant force in Chicago and American politics (Allswang 1977:100, 110). He grasped the importance of issues of concern to ethnic groups in the 1927 mayoral election when he advocated lax enforcement of prohibition, but he failed to realize the symbolic political significance of ethnic candidates in 1931, which contributed to his defeat (Kantowicz 1975:151–61; Nelli 1970a:231–34; Thurner 1971).

Thompson taunted Cermak during the 1931 mayoral campaign with a derogatory slogan that shocked large numbers of southern and eastern Europeans just reaching political maturity. The words to the song were as follows:

> Tony, Tony, where's your pushcart at?
> Can you picture a World's Fair mayor
> With a name like that?
> What a job you're holding!
>
> And now you're trying for two.
> [To be mayor, in addition to his chairmanship of the Cook County board]

Better start thinking of one for me.
Instead of two for you!
(Wendt and Kogan 1953:329–30).

Thompson's long-time alliance with black voters also heightened many ethnic groups' distaste for him.

Cermak had none of these difficulties. He used his Czech nationality as a political counterpoint to the Irish Democrats led by the Sullivans, Brennans, and Dunnes. Gottfried reports that many eastern European groups disliked Irish dominance of Democratic leadership and patronage, and the combined Jewish, German, Polish, and Czech voting strength far surpassed the Irish. "All of the above except the Czechs were more numerous than the privileged Irish. The Poles were more than double and the Germans and Jews almost reached this figure. These numerically superior groups had become more and more restive. They clustered around Cermak, who symbolized both their fears and aggressions and their hope" (1962:175).

By the late 1930s Cermak's non-Irish ethnic expansiveness, superior organizational skills, ethnic issue orientation, and the gift of an insensitive opponent in Mayor Thompson propelled Cermak into the mayor's office with the support of nearly every group in the city. Cermak won even traditionally Republican middle-class groups such as Swedes and old stock English. Blacks and Italians were the only exceptions (Allswang 1977:104).

What changes occurred in ethnic descriptive representation as Cermak established control of the city? Hanna Pitkin describes three major types of representation. In "formalistic" the representative is authorized to speak for the voter without specifications as to the kinds of characteristics that individual should have or as to the obligations of the person. "Descriptive" representation broadens the definition to specify that the representative should resemble his or her constituency but makes no attempt to describe the representative's obligations toward the constituency. "Substantive" representation emphasizes the substantive qualities of the elected's actions for his or her constituency while in office (Pitkin 1967:chaps. 3, 4, and 6).[14]

Upward mobility or increased descriptive representation occurred on a limited scale in Chicago. The initial formation of the Democratic machine introduced more heterogeneous representation of newer immigrant groups into government, with some of the explanation structural, some historical. Structurally, multiple political hierarchies offered a greater number of opportunities for ethnic competition. Irish dominance of both factions of the Democratic party blocked non-Irish political leadership. The Thompson Republican wing based its political strength on strong black support. Although eastern European and black voters were not courted with equal fervor by all factions, the competitive system provided them with viable options. The formation of the machine also centralized all ethnic political competition within one party hierarchy. The new system expanded the jurisdiction and cemented the control of the mayor throughout metropolitan Chicago for the first time in the twentieth century. With a single route to power and with newly stabilized partisan administrative relationships, the political machine reduced rather than increased upward mobility.

An example of the increasingly stable patterns of operation can be seen in the turnover of mayors and chiefs of police from 1907 through 1951. Between 1907 and 1931 each mayor typically appointed two chiefs for the four years he served, while after 1930 the average dropped below one. In the twenty-three years from 1907 through 1930, four mayors appointed twelve different police chiefs. In the twenty years from 1931 through 1951, three different mayors appointed three police chiefs. Even that is exaggerated, since Kelly governed for fourteen of those years but appointed only one chief. The change from a competitive personalized system of appointments to a bureaucratic one meant that the mayors no longer needed to appoint their "own" chief of police, since loyalty to mayor and machine was synonymous (Peterson 1952:370–74; Pinderhughes 1977b: 146).

With access to the unified hierarchy centralized, competition for jobs would also intensify, since every aspiring politician in the city would focus on that single party hierarchy. Even with stabilized relationships and patronage, the winning ethnic coalition's hold over leadership positions should have expanded. Instead, Irish dominance of city government continued because of historical accident. Cermak was assassinated in 1933 while riding in a car with President Franklin D. Roosevelt. Along with the eastern Europeans, Cermak's wing of the Democratic party included fringe Irish such as Pat Nash, Ed Kelly, and Emmet Whealan. After Cermak's death, Nash suggested and the city council confirmed Kelly's appointment as mayor and Whealan's as county board president. In this way the Southside Irish came to rule a united Chicago. The competitive system afforded the Irish the opportunity to move up to leadership positions in the Democratic party.

The political machine enabled the Irish to step into a consolidated political hierarchy with power over other ethnic groups (Gosnell 1968:15).

What became of the groups that opposed Cermak in 1931? The Democratic monopoly over patronage forced the Italians and especially the blacks, with few economic resources, into the party. Since these groups included a large enough number of voters, leaders of the political machine wanted to foreclose the possibility of the group's becoming a base for political competition.

If blacks were averse to Democratic candidate Cermak, how did individual black voters and black politicians become part of the Democratic machine? A number of observers credited Cermak's gambling raids with the transition. John Leonard East, long-time Republican committeeman in the fifth ward, reported that Cermak arrested large numbers of blacks for gambling, but East described the alleged gambling as friendly games of whist. When the jails overflowed with blacks and requests were made for their release, Cermak let it be known that he could not do anything until "your people are Democrats" (John Leonard East, interview, Jan. 26, 1974; see also Gosnell 1967:200–201, 232–33). Cermak also discharged large numbers of black job holders. By the late 1930s Cermak's and later Kelly's encouragement, along with the depression and the stabilization of national and local Democratic control, helped encourage more and more of the black electorate into the Democratic party.

Oscar DePriest stayed in the Republican party out of loyalty to its record of facilitating black political participation and representation. Others, such as William Dawson, moved into the Democratic party to take the second ward committeeman post and in 1942 to assume a seat in Congress.[15] Earl B. Dickerson reported that by the late 1930s Dawson decided that his future lay with the Democratic party and he made plans to form a coalition with the Democratic faction led by Dickerson. Dickerson was critical to Dawson's success because Dickerson had been affiliated with the party before the formation of the machine. Most of the city's patronage was controlled by the Democrats, but substantial numbers of blacks still voted for the Republican party. A coalition would bring the voters and the patronage together and make its leaders powerful. Dawson, a Republican, was second ward alderman by 1933, but his former opponent, ward committeeman William King, opposed him again. Dickerson reported that Dawson asked him to intercede with Kelly to appoint him Democratic committeeman of the second ward in place of Joseph Tittinger. Dickerson decided he should trust Dawson; the black south side might become very powerful or, at worst, somewhat more influential.

After gaining Kelly's agreement, Dickerson explained the arrangement to a meeting of the second ward Democratic organization, using explicitly collective and redistributive appeals: "if we put the minority Republican group with us we'll be in charge. . . . Then we will be able to control our ward and make demands on the dominant downtown people so that we will get the same kind of accommodation, the same kind of treatment and services that the whites in other sections are getting, and we'd get more political appointments and so on. I want you men to be independent to make these demands and I'll be the person to take them forward for you." The next morning Dawson visited Dickerson at his office at the Supreme Life Insurance Company at 35th and South Park and told him: "Earl, that speech of yours was wonderful last night; you surely had them going, but you can *never* make a speech like that again in *my* organization because the decisions are made *downtown.* We have to do what we can to change those decisions down there, but they're made downtown and they cannot be initiated in this ward" (Earl B. Dickerson, interview, Sept. 11, 1975; emphasis added).

This clearly illustrates the difference in the operation of the old and new political systems. Before 1931 Dickerson might have packed up his organization and sought support from another faction or party. After 1931 there was literally nowhere else to go; the second and third ward Republicans retained control of patronageless party structures. Dawson led this acceptance of the new Democratic reality of a centralized party and decision-making structure. To gain the leverage to bargain for rewards required the consistent delivery of Democratic votes regardless of candidate or issue. A DePriest or an Edward Wright (black second ward committeeman in the 1920s) bargained and opposed Republican nominees before 1930, but there was no political base for competitive bargaining in the new organization. Collective politics, debate over the intangible rules of the game, or redistributive questions were no longer valid under the political machine.

James Q. Wilson's comparison of Dawson and Adam Clayton Powell captures the substantive differences that arise from the two different political organizations. Powell was a highly charismatic leader who emphasized racial and social welfare issues; his political base was the politically independent Abyssinian Baptist Church where he and his father were ministers. Dawson was a low-key individual who emphasized selective benefits at home and nonracial noncontroversial issues in Congress. In 1928 as an up-and-coming politician he challenged Congressman William Madden's (of the increasingly black First Congressional District) position in Congress: "By *birth,* training and experience *I am better fitted to represent* the district at Washington than any of the candidates now in the field. . . . The present congressman . . . is a white man. Therefore, for those two reasons, if no others he can hardly voice the *hopes, ideals and sentiment* of the majority of the district" (*Chicago Daily News,* March 2, 1928; cited in Gosnell 1967:79, emphasis added).

Before 1931 William Dawson challenged the highest ranking Republican official on the south side on the issue of descriptive representation, because the party system was so divided and decentralized that he knew his political future could not be influenced irrevocably. After 1931, as Democratic ward committeeman, Dawson refused to consider a challenge on the substantive grounds of race, since he knew Mayor Kelly could transfer patronage from him just as easily as he had bestowed it. William Dawson and the black south side had just joined the political machine (Gosnell 1968:234; Wilson 1960a:78–83).[16]

By 1931 Chicago had shifted from a competitive political system of machine politics into a more stable monopoly, a racial and ethnic political hierarchy known as the Democratic machine. The success of the machine demanded political incorporation of diverse groups, but on a descriptive rather than a substantive basis. Moreover, in exchange for full control none of the subordinate ethnic or racial groups controlled the political process. Chicago's political machine no more facilitated ethnic assimilation that it did racial assimilation. Instead, it captured all those groups at one point in time and held them, except for very slow or very slight adjustments, in stasis until the machine collapsed decades later.

4

Hierarchy and Political Ethnicity

> The Poles, the Jews and all the other nationalities are insisting on adequate representation in public affairs. The colored Republicans comprise fully one half of the Republican voters of the second ward and are entitled to one alderman.
>
> —*Chicago Defender*, Feb. 3, 1912

Hierarchy is a problematic issue. What is its proof in politics: attacks, name-calling, and rejection of any black officials, or acceptance of blacks in only the lowest, least important political offices? In a society in which European immigrants were generally subject to disapprobation, how should ethnicity be distinguished from racial discrimination and be assigned different weights? Does difference equal hierarchy; is it necessarily evidence of racial discrimination? Should it be attributed to the differing talents and capabilities of blacks, Italians, and Poles, that is, to internal factors specific to each community, to demographic factors such as ethnic group size, ethnic heterogeneity, residential settlement, or to external factors, such as political or economic variables? Because comparison of internal and demographic factors with the groups' electoral participation and descriptive representation does not fully explain the variation, I consider how external forces have helped to create and reinforce different political outcomes.

A full investigation of the issues requires examination of both external as well as internal factors. James Q. Wilson's analyses focused on internal variables, while Ira Katznelson concentrated on external political linkages but failed to relate them to internal forces. One of the earliest students of black politics, Harold Gosnell, acknowledged the force of race: "In the last analysis the peculiar difficulties which confronted the Negroes in their struggle for political power can in some way be related to the factors of color" (Gosnell 1967:358). This chapter contains an examination of internal, external, and demographic variables and an evaluation of their combined influence on racial and ethnic political hierarchy in political representation.

The Literature on Ethnic and Racial Politics

Two schools of political science study the political behavior of new groups in American society. One, which fits more comfortably into urban politics, considers how groups assimilate into the political process. The second, linked to national studies of voting behavior, investigates the partisan identification of specific racial and ethnic voters.

The urban ethnicity literature concentrates on the problem of political assimilation. Theorists apply a single model to racial and ethnic groups with little sensitivity to their varying histories, cultural institutions, or economic backgrounds (see Banfield 1965; Banfield and Wilson 1963, 1964; Dahl 1961; Parenti 1970; Rakove 1975). In the introduction to his classic *Who Governs?* Robert Dahl asked how a "democratic system work[s] amid inequality of resources?" Dahl assumed that ethnic immigrants assimilated gradually into the socioeconomic and therefore the political systems, which were transformed from "a 'democratic' system of cumulative inequality of political resources into a system of dispersed inequalities." Ethnic politics equalled assimilationist politics, which "emphasized the divisive rather than the unifying characteristics of voters and yet played upon the yearnings for assimilation and acceptance" (Dahl 1961:3, 34, 33). Dahl described assimilation as a three-stage process, accomplished in little more than a century. Economic homogeneity, cultural identity, and national identity encouraged close physical and political association in the initial years of the group's residence in the new society, but over time the group diversified its economic occupations and its political alliances in a second stage. By the third stage, education, new jobs, and new neighborhoods reduced the significance of the old ethnic identity, and new social and political patterns looked more like a random sampling of average Americans.

Raymond Wolfinger (1970) found that ethnic voting in New Haven persisted rather than declined over time. Where Dahl identified homogeneous partisanship among ethnic groups with lower-class status, Wolfinger held that new groups actually developed self-conscious political identity. This required some kind of group identity and depended upon two factors, the "intensity of ethnic identification and the level of ethnic relevance in the election" (Wolfinger 1970: 117). Ethnic relevance means having an identifiably ethnic name at the head of the ticket, while ethnic mobilization occurs when a group has developed a middle class from which it nominates a political candidate. The entire group need not have reached middle-class status, only a certain segment of it.

Wolfinger accepted Dahl's proposition that social and economic differentiation increased in the respective communities over time, but he suggested that this facilitated ethnic group consciousness and ethnic voting rather than prompted their decline. Although Wolfinger did not specify the requirements for group identity, the group either brings some sense of itself with it, creates an identity through its experiences in the new land, or develops a new American identity unrelated to the old. By separating ethnic voting from socioeconomic status and relating it to symbolic descriptive representation, Wolfinger also weakened the case for a substantive economically-based ethnic politics. He replaced Dahl's social, economic, and political assimilation with a pattern midway between assimilation and ethnic acculturation.[1]

Michael Parenti moved the debate further from Dahl's original position. He maintained that dress, language, and residence no longer distinguished ethnics, but traditional patterns of social interaction sustained the associational boundaries of ethnic communities. Parenti concluded that American society is composed of vertically segregated, class conscious ethnic groups, and that ethnicity and ethnic identification explain substantial portions of the variation in ethnic political participation and provide politicians with "economical" appeals to ethnic voters (1970:63–68).

For all their disagreements on ethnicity, Dahl, Wolfinger, and Parenti treated racial differences as a minor issue. For Dahl blacks were an exception: "By 1950 all ethnic groups in New Haven except the Negroes were rapidly approaching, if they were not already well into, the third stage of political, social and economic assimilation" (Dahl 1961:59), or a success: "full assimilation of Negroes into the normal system already has occurred in many northern states and now seems to be slowly taking place even in the South" (Dahl 1956:138–39). He estimated that each ethnic group spent between forty and fifty years in the first stage of assimilation. Although Dahl reported that blacks entered stage two in 1950 (166 years after their arrival in this country), he had no alternative explanation for their status (Dahl 1961:36).

Dahl's model also fails for blacks on the concept of diversified voting patterns. In Chicago in the 1920s, when blacks might have been classified as first stage, Gosnell found black voting even more strongly homogeneous and Republican than usual in a city dominated by first- and second-generation European ethnics (Gosnell 1967:35, 51n). Although New Haven's blacks shifted their votes to the Democrats in the early 1930s and continued that support through 1959, Dahl concluded that "if our guiding hypothesis . . . is correct, in the long run ethnic influences must decline and socio-economic factors must correspondingly increase" (1961:59). Wolfinger found that black politicians' political demands resembled their ethnic predecessors'. Is this an accurate formulation of ethnic and black voting and patterns of political participation?

The theoretical debate on political assimilation centered on two issues: (1) the generation and dissolution of homogenous ethnic partisanship and (2) the patterns of ethnic association and integration into the society.[2] Wolfinger showed that Dahl ignored ethnicity's independent influence upon political identity and that political ethnicity correlated with low socioeconomic status. Parenti concluded that social interaction continued to be based upon ethnic rather than socioeconomic factors.

How do Dahl's model and Parenti's and Wolfinger's critiques compare to the second school that studies ethnic and racial voting patterns and party identification? Electoral studies show strong ethnic Democratic party identification and voting beginning in the 1930s with the 1932 Roosevelt realignment. The critical question that validates or challenges assimilationist theory is, what happened prior to 1932 and after 1965? How do the theories explain the creation of ethnic Democratic partisanship during the critical electoral period in the late 1920s and the decline in Democratic partisanship during the 1960s and 1970s?

Conversion in the 1920s from Republican identification or mixed partisanship to strong Democratic identification from the 1930s through the 1960s, followed by declining Democratic identification, would tend to confirm parts of Dahl's and Wolfinger's propositions. If Poles, Italians, and blacks behaved as Dahl suggested, then assuming that they had just become Democratic in the late 1920s and that they had been voting before the late 1920s, they had to have been strongly Republican prior to their strong identification with the Democratic party. They converted to strong Democratic identifiers late in the 1920s through the 1960s and detached themselves from the party in the 1960s. *Socioeconomic status* would then determine political behavior. If Poles, Italians, and blacks behaved as Wolfinger suggested, they would have converted from mixed partisanship to strong and stable Democratic party identification. Wolfinger's ethnic groups would have had distinctive voting patterns. *Ethnicity* or *race* would strongly influence political behavior.

Critical election theory suggests that voters change their identification with a political party. V. O. Key and MacRae and Meldrum identified changing voting patterns in a number of New England towns and cities, beginning with the Smith candidacy in 1928 and continuing through the Roosevelt elections in the 1930s. Their implication was that Catholics, union members, European ethnics, and northern blacks who had been heavily committed to one party or who had split their vote between parties were converted to the Democratic party in large numbers by the ethnic appeal of Catholic Al Smith and by the policies of the national Democratic party led by Roosevelt. Short-term forces strengthened or weakened the actual electoral support for the Democratic party in 1936 and 1948, and even permitted the election of Republicans in 1952 and 1956, but the underlying commitment to the party remained strong and unwavering. Over time, as specific issues disturbed the electoral coalition, long-term allies splintered from and eventually abandoned the weakened party. Democratic identifiers gradually became independents or, in some cases, Republicans (Burnham 1970; Campbell et al. 1960; Key 1955; MacRae and Meldrum 1960; Nie et al. 1976).

But this pattern is not entirely invulnerable to reinterpretation of the beginning and the ending of the cycle, as Kristi Andersen's reexamination of the genesis of the Democratic coalition shows. Instead of conversion, mutual switching, mutual exchange, or a combination of these, Andersen argues that mobilization of large numbers of previously politically uninvolved young ethnics explains the creation of the Democratic majority at the national level. She shows that a percentage of partisan votes shifted from the Republicans to the Democrats, but that the total number of Democratic voters expanded while the Republican contribution remained the same. The Republicans retained a stable core of electoral support throughout the critical period, while the Democratic vote was unstable but drawn from previously nonvoting sectors of the population. The Democratic party mobilized first- and second-generation ethnics more successfully than the Republicans did, and most of its increase in political support came from the newly mobilized rather than the converted (Andersen 1979: 103).

Ethnic political participation and homogeneous partisanship came only after the groups had become politically acculturated and a significant portion of the group had been mobilized and had developed group identity. Homogeneous ethnic support for the Democratic party developed from political mobilization of the immigrant population rather than from conversion. This was the case because European countries, especially Italy and Poland, were not fully formed, mass based, representative, politically organized nations at the time of emigration. Citizen participation structures were minimal, and the rural peasantry, from among which most of the American immigrants derived, lived furthest from the few political institutions that existed. Transplanting these political innocents into the comparatively complex American political system was not the simple process Dahl suggests it was. Time passed before these groups developed a sense of their own identity relative to the new nation to which they had migrated, a process that involved mutual adjustment, perception, and understanding by the groups and by American citizens. Secondly, these groups had to become socialized to the norms, values, political structures, and processes of their new nation and locale. Wolfinger also suggests that the degree of ethnic participation was also related to the degree of ethnic relevance. Voting, Downs argues, is a rational act requiring some incentives for the participants (Downs 1967; Thomas and Znaniecki 1918:vol. 4). Without a sensible combination of such incentives, whether economic (the 1932 national Democratic program) or symbolic (Al Smith's 1928 candidacy), participation rarely occurred. Only after these factors created politically relevant incentives did the homogeneous partisanship and mass voting described by Dahl emerge among ethnic voters.

Dahl correctly identified a period of strong ethnic partisanship but misunderstood the reasons for its genesis, thereby hastening its demise in his model. Dahl based his analysis on social and political behavior specific to New Haven's Italians and Irish. With a local Democratic party dominated by the Irish, Republican recruitment of an Italian mayoral candidate encouraged Italian alliance with the Republican party during an era of national Democratic realignment. New Haven's Italians contributed slim majorities of their votes to the Democratic party during the national realigning period from 1928 through 1948, but Eisenhower's elections in the 1950s drew them back toward the national Republican party (Andersen 1979:19; Dahl 1961:49; Wolfinger 1970:112–13).

Critical election research suggests that political identification persists, but in recent decades a period of dealignment has reduced but not eliminated ethnic and Catholic identification with the Democratic party. Andersen argues that ethnics have decreased their Democratic identification but they have not become Republicans (Andersen 1979:229). Their Democratic allegiance has decreased less than other groups, so that they remain more Democratic (relative to other groups) than they have been in the past (Andersen 1979:229; Sullivan et al. 1980).

Black voters exhibit extremely high partisan loyalty. From the Civil War through the 1930s, whenever local conditions permitted electoral participation, blacks tendered consistently high support for the Republican party. In the early 1930s the combined impact of the depression, a liberal national Democratic administration, and the increasing antipathy of the Republican party for the black vote lured some northern black voters into the Democratic party. Whereas the bulk of the increase in ethnic Democratic support was based on mobilization, Andersen notes that the increase in support for the Democratic party among black voters between 1932 and 1936, probably was "a real change in preferences" (Andersen 1979:103–6; see also Bunche 1973; Walton 1972). Black voters were already highly mobilized in the 1920s and 1930s in Chicago; in fact, Andersen's data show that black turnout in presidential years was higher or equivalent to *both* ethnic and native white voters. Any expansion in black Democratic support resulted from conversion rather than mobilization. In the 1960s and 1970s, when according to Dahl blacks should have divided their votes between the Republican and Democratic parties and as other voters decreased their partisan identification, black voters instead consolidated their support for the Democratic party. Southern blacks increased their Democratic identification; northern blacks' identification did not increase as much, but still remained considerably higher than that of other groups (Nie et al. 1976:228–34).

On a broad national level, then, the data support Wolfinger's and Parenti's assertions of the strength of race and nationality as an explanation for partisan identification and political participation. What does examination of Chicago's mayoral election data from 1915 through 1939 reveal?

The data in table 4.1 supports Andersen's position of ethnic mobilization. Selection of heavily black and ethnic wards and precincts shows the mayoral choices of black, Italian, and Polish voters from

Table 4.1
Black, Italian, and Polish Partisanship in Mayoral Elections, 1915–1939

	1915	1919	1923	1927	1931	1935	1939
Italian							
Democ	4,915 (56%)	4,257 (64%)	4,766 (78%)	2,739 (42%)	2,485 (40%)	94,372 (90%)	
Repub	3,616 (41%)	1,557 (23%)	1,059 (17%)	3,437 (53%)	3,831 (61%)	4,227 (7%)	
Total	8,822	6,654	6,088	6,490	6,286	60,221	
Polish							
Democ	5,880 (53%)	3,970 (63%)	8,786 (84%)	5,510 (55%)	9,178 (77%)		
Repub	4,888 (44%)	1,468 (23%)	1,335 (13%)	4,641 (47%)	2,742 (23%)		
Total	11,108	6,345	10,517	9,947	11,920		
Black							
Democ	14,036 (30%)	10,489 (24%)	17,353 (60%)	8,639 (16%)	8,285 (18%)	33,225 (78%)	37,934 (57%)
Repub	31,024 (67%)	25,929 (60%)	10,761 (37%)	44,276 (82%)	37,866 (82%)	8,452 (20%)	27,580 (43%)
Total	46,242	43,183	29,086	53,879	46,111	42,336	66,869

See appendix for ward and precinct selections. Democratic and Republican votes do not add to totals because of third-party candidates. Voting results from *Chicago Daily News Almanac* for respective years; 1935 Italian results and all of black results are ward totals.

1915 through 1935. The Italian voters, clustered in the nineteenth ward, supported Democratic mayoral candidates in the early 1920s, Republicans such as Republican William Thompson in 1927 and 1931, but they turned overwhelmingly Democratic by 1935. The figures represent a very small portion of the Italian population, so they are not a good barometer of that group's voting behavior. Blacks and Poles were more concentrated; over fifty percent of each group lived in predominantly Polish or black neighborhoods, although black Chicagoans were even more physically unified.[3] Polish voters in Polish precincts supported Democratic mayoral candidates before the formation of the machine; they voted more strongly Democratic than their neighbors in other precincts within the same wards that supported or split their votes for Thompson in 1915 and 1927. When the wards went Democratic, Polish voters gave 60, 70, even 80 percent of their vote to Democratic candidates. The total number of votes for mayor in these years was lower than for presidential elections, but the 1931 election drew out more voters in Polish precincts than had come to the polls in fifteen years. Poles voted strongly Democratic in the 1920s, but turned out poorly. In 1931 turnout increased by 20 percent; following Andersen's analysis, if it is assumed that the same people voted in 1931 as went to the polls in 1927, approximately 23 percent of that group switched from the Republican to the Democratic candidate. Another 20 percent of the 1931 voters had not participated in 1927; of this group of 1927 nonparticipants, half had not voted in 1923. These data suggest that the formation of the Democratic machine at the local level was accompanied by both mobilization and partisan switching (Andersen 1979:53–72).

The black wards revealed very different voting patterns. Except for 1923, they voted for Republican mayoral candidates by 60 percent or more of the vote. The 1915 and 1919 ward totals conceal an even more intensely committed core of voters in all black precincts. Gosnell reported that Thompson's mayoral nominations rested on the overwhelming support given to him by black voters in the second ward. In 1923 Thompson withdrew from the race because the corruption in his administration had grown too difficult to hide. Thompson and other Republicans encouraged blacks to vote for the Democratic candidate, William Dever, in order to limit the political future of Thompson's Republican opponent, Lueder, who reportedly treated blacks unfairly in the post office (Gosnell 1967:26, 41–44, 306–7). Although they voted Democratic, the 33 percent drop in turnout revealed the black community's ambivalence. Thompson's return to the mayoral race in 1927 nearly doubled the black turnout over 1923 and increased it by 25 percent over his previous campaign of 1919. In 1931 Thompson won 82 percent of the vote in the second and third wards, as he had in 1927, but his overall support declined, with a 14 percent dropoff in the total vote.

Cermak's victory in 1931 marked the formation of the Democratic machine, but black voters neither switched nor increased their turnout. As Andersen found in national elections, blacks switched their political support to the Democratic party, but the change occurred a full term after Cermak's election (Andersen 1979:105–6). Blacks voted 82 percent Republican in 1931 and nearly 78 percent Democratic by 1935, but unlike the Poles in Chicago or ethnic voters at the national level, black turnout declined significantly. By 1939, when former Republican William Dawson's alliance with long-time Democrat Earl Dickerson had begun to shape the Negro submachine, turnout increased by 58 percent but the Republican party captured the bulk of it. The Democratic machine converted blacks to Democrats, but the conversion was a tenuous one requiring constant attention. Black turnout and registered voters in the second and third wards declined relative to the total numbers of black adults in Chicago in the 1940s.

The local and national data show that homogeneous partisanship occurred only after ethnic groups had resided in the country for two generations. Blacks' partisan identification relates inversely to other groups of comparable economic status, unless they have no other political alternative. Dahl projected that ethnic and racial groups become politically and economically homogeneous over time. In fact, a variety of historical factors particular to each group more successfully explains their voting behavior.

A summary of the findings on ethnic and racial voting behavior shows the following. Table 4.2 is a list of average partisan voting percentages for the three groups in Chicago mayoral elections from 1915 through 1931. By the twentieth century, Poles contributed fluctuating majorities of their votes to the Democratic party. The Italians voted heavily Democratic until 1920, when the nineteenth ward was redistricted and freed from Irish Democratic rule. After 1924 the Italians supported Republican mayoral candidates; they increased their support for Democratic national and state candidates, but not to as great a degree as other southern and eastern European immi-

Table 4.2
Summary of Racial and Ethnic Partisanship, 1915–1931

	Percentage of Vote	
	Democratic	Republican
Mayoral Primaries 1915, 1927, 1931[a]		
Blacks	20%	80%
Italians[b] 1915	87%	13%
1927	25%	75%
Poles	65%	35%
Mayoral Elections 1915–1931[c]		
Blacks	25%	75%
Italians	58%	42%
Poles	62%	38%

a. Based on the averages of percentages in mayoral primaries. For results, see Pinderhughes 1977b: tables 17 (p. 224) and 69–73. Exclusion of the 1923 primary depresses the Democratic average for all groups. Thompson was not a candidate, and the Democrats won a higher portion of the vote.
b. The percentages would have suggested a divided vote for the Italians rather than a change in electoral support. Italian wards based on selections made by Humbert Nelli. See Pinderhughes 1977b: table 72, for wards and precincts he selected.
c. Based on Table III.1, p. 42, and Table A.2 (Appendix), pp. 218–19, in Allswang 1971.

grants. They were somewhat less Democratic in national and state elections in the early 1920s, but in 1928 they shifted toward the Democrats. The Poles, on the other hand, contributed overwhelmingly Democratic support for the national, state, and local elections after the early 1930s (Allswang 1971:42; Andersen 1979:103–5).

Blacks became Democratic more slowly and with considerably more reluctance than other groups. Only blacks and Italians contributed less than fifty percent of their vote to the Democratic mayoral candidate in 1931 (the Italians only marginally less); only blacks remained out of the Democratic coalition in the 1932 national and state elections. According to Andersen, Democratic mobilization of ethnic voters hit its peak by 1936, while conversion of black voters had just begun. At the local level blacks supported Republican mayoral candidates through 1931, but in a nearly complete turnaround they shifted

Table 4.3
Turnout in Presidential Elections

	1924	1928	1932	1936	1940
Black	52%	57%	69%	71%	62%
Native	65%	50%	61%	72%	45%
Ethnic	31%	44%	51%	54%	54%

Source: Andersen 1979: 103–5.

their support more decisively toward the Democratic party by the 1935 mayoral elections, when 75 percent of the black voters supported the Democrats, though to a lesser degree than the general electorate. In successive years, smaller proportions but still majorities of the black voters supported Democratic candidates, an important and highly significant change given their previous voting behavior.

Andersen's work also identifies nonvoting as a measure of citizens' evaluation of political participation. Ethnics participated in presidential elections in large numbers only when the Democratic party used substantive issues and symbolic appeals. Table 4.3 summarizes Andersen's turnout measures in black, ethnic, and native wards in Chicago and shows significant increases respectively for ethnic (23 percent) and black (19 percent), but mixed changes for the native wards. Only the ethnic wards sustained sharp increases for the national election. Critical elections marked ethnics' initial political mobilization and black voters' conversion. Although blacks were not strong or consistent Democrats by 1940, the party organization within the black community had been reconstructed and few Republican leaders controlled patronage (see figure 4.1).

What prompted the change in black voting in the 1930s if blacks had maintained close and loyal relations with the Republican party during the previous decades? Political scientists and historians argue that Roosevelt's New Deal programs encouraged blacks to become Democratic. Rita Werner Gordon and Elmer Henderson suggested that the creation of the Roosevelt administration's relief programs and social welfare state, as well as the absence of a Republican program, motivated black voters. What explains black Democratic conversion: the shift in Republican racial interest or the Democratic welfare state (Gordon 1969; Henderson 1939:34)? Gordon pointed to the Republican party's increasing disaffection for black voters as Hoover

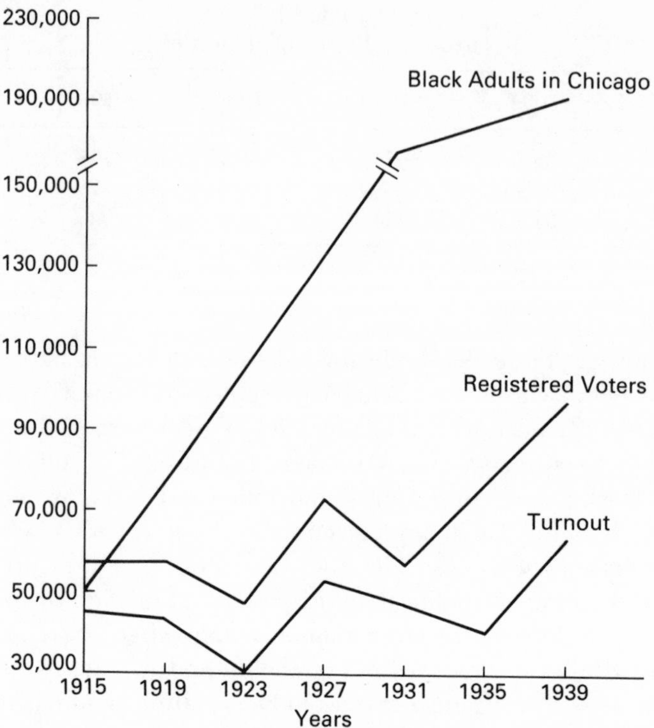

Sources: *Chicago Daily News Almanac,* 1916, 1920, 1924, 1928, 1932; Skogan 1926.

Figure 4.1 Black Citizens and Electoral Participation in Wards 2 and 3, 1915–1939

sought to split the solid south. Black Chicagoans, such as Alderman Louis B. Anderson, noted the shift in racial sentiment within the party as early as the 1928 convention: "The Republican party has shown us the gate. Now let all the colored people walk out" (*Chicago Defender* Oct. 20, 1928; quoted in Gosnell 1967:30).

The Chicago Democratic party was not friendly to black voters' substantive concerns, but it recruited blacks for their strategic significance. The national Republican party had come to see blacks as a substantive and electoral liability; they could not court the Democratic south for its votes with black allies. The national Democratic party felt free to incorporate ideologically contradictory regional factions; it sought and actually won the support of black voters in national contests in northern areas and ignored the plight of black voters in southern states. Pushed out of the national Republican party, blacks found that the national liberal Democrats welcomed their support. Locally, blacks and a few native whites guarded the remaining remnants of the Republican party, but the consolidation of patronage, political office, and electoral support in the new machine left them with no alternative but to move into the Democratic party, which they did by the 1935 mayoral elections. Strategic, national, and local issues and racial concerns thus transformed black Republicans of the party of Lincoln into Rooseveltian Democrats. The conversion was not fully completed at the national level until the early 1960s, but crucial shifts began in the 1930s (Walton 1972).

A Model of Racial and Ethnic Political Participation

Having surveyed and evaluated the theoretical literature on assimilation and effectively weakened the case for a pluralist model of political participation and assimilation, I now propose a new political participation model, one which explains and assesses electoral participation and the relative success of groups in winning office. This section examines how external, internal, and demographic variables interact in order to compare how they affect black, Italian, and Polish electoral participation. The relative differences in the three groups on these variables should reveal which set of factors is important in their success.

External Variables

External variables are those that fall outside of the specific characteristics of racial or ethnic groups, and which are not random. They include economic and political variables. For example, in chapter 2, I described the pervasive anti-black racism present in the housing and labor markets and the varying but less restrictive patterns of discrimination against European ethnics. Political variables include the character of political interaction, the political structure, and partisan competition. For example, in chapter 3, I described the character of political interaction in Chicago. Noncompetitive one-party politics replaced fierce inter- and intraparty rivalry by the 1930s. The differences in the character of these two eras profoundly influenced the political success of the three groups. Ethnic and especially racial discrimination dominated life in Chicago before 1931, but the machine established a system of political interaction that reinforced rather than challenged that hierarchy of values.

Geographic concentration is the result of external as well as internal factors, but on balance the external forces prevail. More importantly, how does geographic concentration or dispersal affect descriptive representation? To elect officials who describe the group, each needs a large enough voting population and turnout within an electoral district or ward to dominate an election. Might not the group control events more consistently if it constituted the electoral balance in a ward split between two other groups? Alternatively, might not scattered populations produce more elected representatives?

There are two ways of evaluating geographic concentration: (1) by the percentage ethnic or racial groups constitute within a neighborhood, and (2) by the total proportion of the ethnic or racial population of the city that resides in homogeneous areas. Figure 4.1 shows the possibilities between the two types of measures. Only a small proportion of Italians lived in identifiably Italian neighborhoods, and scarcely one of these was dominated by Italians. A significant portion, though not a majority, of Poles lived in ethnic settlement areas. The Polish downtown on the northwest side was an important population, institutional, cultural, and economic center that was more than fifty percent Polish. Blacks, on the other hand, settled almost exclusively within one major area and that one area was almost exclusively black. Blacks lived in extremely highly concentrated settlements; by 1920 they lived in the first, second, and third wards in a densely concentrated, narrow, slowly expanding area that was almost completely black. Eighty to ninety percent of the black population lived in this area (see table 4.4).

Partisan competition indicates whether the respective parties compete for ethnic and racial votes. Partisan competition enhances the bargaining power of groups accepted by the parties; when even one of the parties ignores the substantive concerns of a group, that racial or ethnic group has no choice but to cooperate with the other party. Such exclusion reduces political influence. In chapter 3, I showed how only the Republican party aggressively recruited black votes, while both parties courted Italian and Polish voters.

The political structure indicates the rules and procedures by which elections occur. Chicago elected its city council and the state elected its legislatures by the district systems. Over time, city officials reduced the size of the districts, known as aldermanic wards. The smaller the constituency, the greater the chance that the largest group within the district will dominate the elections. Recent research suggests that district systems more descriptively represent a constituency than an at-large system, in which candidates compete for office from the city as a whole, and that small groups have more opportunity for electoral success in the former.

A second factor, cumulative voting for the state legislature, was also found to advantage smaller groups. Each voter held three votes, and a state representative needed only one-third of the total to win election. Smaller groups concentrated their ballots and elected members of their group to office.[4]

Demographic Factors

Demographic factors have a significant impact upon political behavior, although they are not necessarily related to internal factors. Group size, for example, affects the number of votes available to the party or the machine, but the proportion of adult citizens is a more important determinant of eligible voters. Ethnic heterogeneity increases the potential political influence of any one group (Pitkin 1967:chaps. 3, 4, and 6).

Chicago had perhaps the most racially and ethnically heterogeneous population of an American city in the early twentieth century. As the major transportation, commercial, cultural, and industrial center for the Midwest, it attracted and absorbed workers from many European countries and from the American south for several generations. Poles, Italians, Irish, Germans, Swedes, Lithuanians, Greeks, Czechs, Slovaks, Bohemians, Chinese, and blacks constituted groups of significant size. During most of its first century, immigrants and their children constituted the bulk of its population, as high as 80 percent in 1890.

Group size is positively correlated with potential political influence. In a competitive political system, parties generally minimize cost and maximize return; they appeal to groups that have large numbers of voters and that turn out in large numbers. Larger groups with high rates of participation exercise greater influence because of their potential and actual electoral resources.

Table 4.5 is a list of the number and percentage of Poles, Italians, and blacks in Chicago from 1880 through 1940. The three communities grew unevenly, with the Poles outdistancing the others in the first third of the century, but by 1940 the blacks equalled the Poles and

Table 4.4
Percentage of Black, Italian, and Polish Population in Wards of High Black, Italian, and Polish Residential Concentration, 1910–1940

Wards by Group	1910		1920[c]		1930		1940	
	Total Ward Population	Group as % of Ward	Total Ward Population	Group as % of Ward	Total Ward Population	Group as % of Ward	Total Ward Population	Group as % of Ward
Black								
2	42,801[a]	25.0%	68,572	69.5%	47,027	100.0%	87,530[f]	92.1%
3	46,135	24.0%	79,068	24.7%	69,255[e]	65.4%[d]	75,028	98.2%
Italian								
19	58,023[a]	40.3%	49,372	30.8%				
20					32,802[e]	69.0%	55,043	
21							57,312	
25					45,346	19.2%	49,018	
26					45,833	19.4%		
27					44,013	21.6%	59,869	

Polish							
12					77,323[e]	38.0%	69,174
13					40,284	25.2%	
16	65,223	50.3%[b]	52,298	28.7%			
17	70,099	24.3%	57,142	29.4%			
26					45,833	91.5%	57,144
28	68,183	11.8%	69,238	.09%	54,927	15.5%	
29	81,985	11.4%	113,941	.09%			
31					39,576	47.3%	
32					46,996	75.2%	64,338
33					46,400	52.5%	62,279
38					55,338	17.9%	

a. Bureau of the Census 1913, vol. 2:512–14. All ward totals and black and Italian foreign stock based on this source.
b. Chicago Board of Education, *School Census,* 1908. U.S. Census did not list Poles as a separate national group in 1910. Cited in *Chicago Daily News Almanac,* 1909: 467. Percent equals foreign stock.
c. Bureau of the Census 1922, vol. 3:274–76. Foreign-born only.
d. Gosnell Papers, Chicago Historical Society, Box 1, "Notes and Reading Folder." Black percentage.
e. "Compiled by Frederick Rex, Librarian" (Chicago: Municipal Reference Library, City Hall, 1942). Ward totals and Italian and Polish foreign stock based on this source.
f. Bureau of the Census 1943, vol. 1:314. Ward totals and black population.
g. Bureau of the Census (1943) did not list foreign-born or foreign-stock information by wards.

Table 4.5
Black, Italian, and Polish Population as a Percentage of the Chicago Population, 1880–1940

Census Year	Chicago Total	Black	Polish	Italian
1880[a]	508,185	1.2%	1.1%	.26%
1890[b]	1,099,850	1.3%	2.2%	.51%
1900[c]	1,698,575	1.8%	6.3%	1.60%
1910[d]	2,185,283	2.0%	10.5%	3.44%
1920[e]	2,701,705	4.0%	11.8%	4.60%
1930[f]	3,376,438	6.9%	11.9%	5.40%
1940	3,396,808[g]	8.2%	8.8%[h]	4.30%

a. Bureau of the Census 1883, vol. 1: 417, 541. Poles and Italians represent foreign-born population.
b. Bureau of the Census 1895: part 1, pp. 454, 672. Poles and Italians represent foreign-born populations.
c. Bureau of the Census 1902, vol. 1: 613, 879. The figures represent Polish foreign white stock, composed of foreign-born and the children of the foreign-born.
d. Bureau of the Census 1913, vol. 1: 946. The figures represent Italian foreign white stock. Total and black population for 1910, vol. 1: 208. Polish population is foreign white stock which spoke Polish, vol. 1: 989.
e. Bureau of the Census 1922, vol. 3: 261, vol. 2: 1007. The figures represent foreign white stock which spoke Polish, vol. 2: 958. The figures represent Italian foreign white stock.
f. Bureau of the Census 1932, vol. 3: 628, vol. 2: 316. The figures represent Polish and Italian mother tongue of foreign white stock.
g. Bureau of the Census 1943b, vol. 2: 639. For total and black population figures.
h. Bureau of the Census, 1943a, *Nativity and Parentage of Native Population, Mother Tongue,* 1943, p. 33. For Polish and Italian population figures.

were twice the number of Italians. Did the potential electorate grow in proportion to the respective populations of each group? About seventy percent of the total black population was eligible to vote because most of the migrants were young adults who had come north in search of jobs. By 1940 the imbalance had diminished somewhat, but continued migration from the south kept the percentage high. Gosnell estimated that 70 percent of the black population of the second ward was registered to vote in 1930; applying this proportion to the entire city produced about 120,000 registered black voters (Gosnell 1967: 36n). The Italian and Polish voting potential is more difficult to calculate. The census identified white Americans by national origin for two generations, unless they were also foreign-language speakers. By

Table 4.6
Italian, Polish, and Black Voting-Age Population in Chicago, 1920–1940

Year	Italians	Percent Foreign Stock	Poles	Percent Foreign Stock	Blacks	Percent Total Populat
1920	39,791[a]	32.0%	103,479	32.5%	81,872[b]	74.8%
1930	67,500	37.0%	163,326	41.0%	165,959[c]	70.9%
1940	71,500	49.0%	139,072	47.0%	191,242[d]	68.8%

a. 1930 and 1940 Polish and Italian estimates are conservative. See appendix for full explanation of procedures used to generate estimates.
b. Bureau of the Census 1922, vol. 3: 274, 512–14.
c. Bureau of the Census 1932, vol. 3: 67.
d. Bureau of the Census 1943b, vol. 2: 640.

1940 large numbers of Italians, Poles, Germans, and Irish were statistically "lost." Only the foreign-born and natives of foreign parentage (altogether, foreign stock) were identified. Moreover, the census identified nationality, citizenship, and age, but these were rarely crosstabulated on the ward level, so that there are no reliable counts of ethnic voters.

Nelli (1970a:119) and Kantowicz (1975) listed wards and precincts with high numbers of Italian and Polish voters but avoided estimates of total voters. Nelli, for example, identified only 1,695 Italian registrants in 1920 because there were few densely-settled Italian neighborhoods. Sixty-four percent of foreign-born Italians lived outside of the nineteenth ward, which Nelli identified as heavily Italian. Through a complicated procedure the potential Italian and Polish vote was calculated for this study. Table 4.6 is a summary of the estimates of Polish and Italian voting-age population, with totals for the black population.[5]

Poles equalled a larger proportion of the population of Chicago than blacks, but naturalization requirements slowed their electoral participation. This is clearest when the population of voting age of the three groups is calculated as a percentage of their foreign-stock and total populations. Poles and Italians eligible to vote ranged from one-third to less than one-half of their foreign stock, while eligible blacks never fell below 60 percent of their total. This is confirmed by the data in table 4.7, which compares each group's voters with the city's voters. Only in 1920 did either immigrant group's percentage exceed that of

Table 4.7
Black and Ethnic Voters as Proportions of Total Adult Citizens, 1920–1940

Year	Chicago	Black	Italian	Polish
1920	1,703,123[a]	4.8%[c]	3.1%	8.2%
1930	2,209,514[b]	7.5%	3.0%	7.3%
1940	2,397,392[b]	8.6%	3.2%	6.3%

a. Bureau of the Census 1922, vol. 3: 274.
b. Bureau of the Census 1943b, vol. 2: 640.
c. Percentages based on figures from Table 4.5.

black voters, and that was by a smaller margin than their proportions in the general population.

Blacks only needed to satisfy residency requirements of one year for the state, ninety days for the county, and thirty days for the precinct. Naturalization, on the other hand, took over ten years, although the minimum residency requirement for immigrants was five years and three months. Other factors tended to exaggerate the differences between the groups. Southern states strongly, violently discouraged black voting; in the absence of explicit racial restrictions, blacks voted in disproportionate numbers as an affirmation of their newly acquired political citizenship. Polish and Italian electoral participation also lagged behind that of blacks because fewer immigrant women were naturalized. The black electorate was potentially much more significant than the Italian or the much larger Polish voting population.[6]

Internal Variables

Internal variables include leadership institutions, political socialization, partisan identification, and political issues. This section examines these variables for each of the three groups.

Polonian Politics. In the Polish community, the Catholic church played the most important role in shaping and influencing politics and political participation within the Polish community. The church defined and structured the significant issues, created and supported mediating organizations, identified and encouraged political leaders, invented communications media, as well as established economic, religious, physical, social welfare, cultural, and political frameworks within which Poles became Americans. The church socialized its parishioners, affected their partisan identification, and identified important political issues. Polish Catholics self-consciously organized the process of assimilation: "We are building here a Poland where a Pole born on American soil will not be a European Pole, but we wish him to believe in Catholicism, to speak Polish, to know the history and traditions of Poland, otherwise let him be a yankee" (Kuziniewski 1975:24; Parot 1981).

The schismatic Polish National Catholic church emphasized the church's organic relationship with the Polish people and the existence of a Polish nation and criticized the Roman Catholic church's Irish and German hierarchy. The pastor of St. Stanislaus Kostka (the center of Polish downtown), Father Vincent Barzynski, member of the Resurrectionist order, acknowledged the authority of the American Catholic hierarchy, which was largely Irish and German, but the order was founded "to unite Catholicism with the cause of Polish national rebirth" (Kantowicz 1975:31). Pastors in both churches assumed paramount leadership roles in religious and secular affairs (Andrews 1953:12–13; Zuziniewski 1974:30–34; Przudzik 1947:897). The church played a crucial political role before 1900 when Poles were new arrivals, spoke little English, and were unfamiliar with American norms and politics. In the 1890s the Democrats sought Father Barzynski's help in gaining Polish support for John Altgeld's gubernatorial candidacy. They opposed the Edwards Law, which required attendance at schools that taught certain subjects in English and would have undermined Polish-language parochial schools. "Just before election day in 1892, thousands of copies of the Edwards law were distributed to the parishioners of St. Stanislaus and Father Barzynski personally urged a mass meeting in the parish hall to oppose the law by voting for Altgeld" (Kantowicz 1975:52). Democrats Carter Harrison I and Carter Harrison II also appealed to the St. Stanislaus hierarchy during their mayoral campaigns. The elder Harrison donated $1,500 to the Polish National Hospital, while the younger Harrison spent an evening with the priests of St. Stanislaus familiarizing them with his knowledge of Polish history and culture.

Barzynski and other Resurrectionist clergy also established indirect institutional links to encourage political and religious development. Barzynski founded the Polish Roman Catholic Union (PRCU) to preserve the Catholic faith and Polish heritage among immigrants. The Polish National Alliance (PNA) had secular, nationalistic concerns that pitted it against the PRCU. The alliance's publication, the *Zgoda,* described Peter Kiolbassa, president of the PRCU and candidate in 1888 for sixteenth-ward alderman, as the handpicked choice of the "manager," Father Barzynski. After the PNA's Kowalski defeated him, Kiolbassa accepted the Democratic party's nomination for city treasurer at Barzynski's encouragement. The *Chicagoski,* on the other hand, founded by the secular alliance, was politically neutral, although it occasionally endorsed Democrats (Allswang 1971:51). The PRCU tended to support Democratic candidates, while the alliance supported Republicans more frequently. One Polish faction was religious, strongly supportive of the Democratic party, and more likely to be conservative. The other was anticlerical, extremely nationalistic, somewhat less interested in narrowly-defined partisan politics, and made up of social reformists. Some of the conflict declined by the 1930s, since a number of Polish politicians, such as August Kowalski and Joseph Rostenkowski, joined both organizations (Allswang 1971:51, table 3.3; Busyn 1950:13–20; Busyn 1951; Wytrwal 1961: 227).[7]

Polish factionalism invaded the electoral arena. Poles voted Democratic, but intraparty and community factionalism limited their attempts to gain office. Although the PNA proclaimed Kowalski's election a victory for the Polish community, Kantowicz reported that there were too few Polish voters in the electoral district to have elected Kowalski; on the other hand, Kiolbassa won his greatest support in the three precincts where Polish voters were in the majority (Kantowicz 1975:45). Germans and Scandinavians elected Polonia's first Polish alderman.

The Politics of Italian Provincialism. The Italian institutional framework, or more precisely the lack of one, generated a different type of politics. Whereas the Polish Catholic church dominated all aspects of community life, the Italian church confined its interests to religion. It had opposed national unification in Italy in order to protect the Vatican, and so it assumed no role in generating national unity in the old world or the new. While a cultural, economic, institutional, and demographic Polish downtown literally centered around the parish church St. Stanislaus Kostka, the Italian community had little of this church-fostered coherence.

Northern Italians viewed the church as a conservative opponent, while southerners felt it an expensive burden after the Risorgimento (1815–70), when its material and land holdings had been substantially reduced (Covello 1967:453). The Irish Catholic church resisted Polish and Italian demands for national language and ethnically oriented parishes, but Polish priests and Polish nationalists overrode these objections more successfully than those of the Italians. By 1940 one parish existed for every 9,100 Poles in Chicago, but the Italians maintained only one per 15,155 Italians. More dispersed residential settlements and the smaller number of Italians explain some of the differences in the two groups, but weak Italian identification, antipathy to the Catholic church, and strong regional, local, and familial bonds also explain the absence of persistent and complex cultural, economic, and institutional centers. Italian clergy were thus not a major force in the creation of institutional and political Italian life in Chicago (Kantowicz 1975:17; Nelli 1970a:195; Pinderhughes 1977b: 76).

Southern Italy, from which most of Chicago's Italians had migrated, had little public life. With a weak, almost nonexistent business sector, a poor landless peasantry, and a wealthy and defensive Catholic church, only labor, fraternal, and criminal organizations such as the Unione Siciliana (which combined all three) offered any base for political leadership in the United States. The combination of a weak socioeconomic network and a small, widely dispersed population reduced the Italians' impact on American electoral politics.

The Black Belt.[8] Two major forces structured black politics, the first institutional (the black church) and the second ideological. The black church was the most important institution within the black community. It was not as aggressive or as inventive as the Polish Catholic church in creating a complex set of interrelated organizations to satisfy a variety of needs so that the immigrant never needed to leave Catholic associations. On the other hand, unlike the Catholic church, it was an organization with few economic resources apart from the contributions of its poorly paid congregation. The Polish organizations were established as satellites to the parish and other Catholic associations, while the black churches served as umbrellas under which a complex variety of church organizations were gathered. Black churches did not establish newspapers, publishing houses, or other types of organizations with separate secular identities. They had, however, a highly complex but more insular religious life. Finally, while the church as an institution played a critical role, no single denomination dominated religious life; the church was thus a label for a variety of religious organizations that responded in different ways to political and social issues (Drake and Cayton 1940, 1970:chap. 15; DuBois 1968; Hamilton 1972; Woodson 1921).

Black churches developed political roles because they were simple and efficient ways to reach large numbers of voters quickly. Moreover, there were few other organizations for mobilizing political support. Clubs, fraternal organizations, professional associations, and unions were never especially successful in the political arena. With a weak business sector and only slightly stronger political groups, black churches functioned as important social and political networks. In the 1930s the Abyssinian Baptist Church in Harlem and Adam Clayton Powell, Jr., led bus boycotts and protests against discriminatory commerical hiring practices. Abyssinian Baptist was distinguished from Chicago's churches by its financial independence. When Powell's father assumed leadership of the church in the early twentieth century, it was located in New York's tenderloin district on the Lower East Side. As the commercial and financial district expanded, blacks began to move north and settle in Harlem. With land values on the rise, black congregations built new structures with little or no indebtedness (Powell 1938; Powell 1945, 1971). In Chicago black migration out of the Loop was unrelated to commercial expansion, and most black churches operated with large mortgages. Politics was thus an economic opportunity for debt reduction, and ministers rarely challenged racial discrimation publicly. Black ministers were either politically neutral, hoping to bid up the return for political support, or were strong advocates of the inevitable winner.

The minister J. C. Austin was a case in point. In the 1939 mayoral election, Democratic candidate Edward Kelly visited the morning service at what was described as the second largest black church at the time and left the minister fifty dollars. Only eight years before Gosnell had described Austin's extravagant praise for Republican mayor Thompson: "We saw Big Bill go down out of the confidence of the people. . . . The *Tribune* wrote an obituary. I went back again and looked upon the grave. . . . But thank God before the primary I heard the grave crack, the tombstone fall and saw William Hale Thompson rise (applause) and stand over his enemies and say 'I am on the side of truth, of right, of justice' (big applause)" (Gosnell 1967:52; see also 53–54, 94–100; Drake and Cayton 1970:428).[9]

"Clerico-politicians" such as Archibald Carey preferred long-term alliances with Republican William Hale Thompson. The municipal playground built in the second ward during Thompson's aldermanic years was located across the street from Carey's Institutional Church. Carey and Thompson maintained a long association, culminating in

Thompson's appointment of Carey to the Civil Service Commission in 1928. Black churches were unprepared, for economic reasons, to deal with politics differently than any other organization in Chicago, and they frequently became contacts for politicians seeking votes (Drake and Cayton 1970:412–19, 428).

The second factor in the structure of black politics is ideological and links political socialization with concerns about goals and identification with the group. The Urban League and National Assocation for the Advancement of Colored People (NAACP) divided responsibility between improving the economic and the political status of blacks. Status goals, according to James Q. Wilson, attempted to eliminate racial discrimination; since whites resisted this type of goal, blacks who advocated it risked losing their objective with little else to show for it. Welfare goals ignored the issue of segregation and focused on economic benefits for the black community. The division between economic and political goals, reflected in the disagreement on strategy and goals between the NAACP and the Urban League, limited institutional cooperation. In chapter 5 I discuss these issues more extensively.

Racial discrimination in the south shaped northern black voting patterns. Southern Democratic control over national racial policy reached its maturity in the 1920s. As southern Democrats reached the peak of the congressional seniority system, they proscribed national consideration of the legal and political, as well as the economic, dimensions of racial status. Northern race relations were adjusted to the urban industrial capitalist setting, where discussion of redistributive economic issues was strongly resisted. Black voters and politicians therefore focused on race as a symbolic issue (Bunche 1973; Key 1949; Martin 1979).

Racially polarized elections and ones in which one of the candidates had a highly defined position on racial issues turned out extraordinarily high proportions of black voters for the candidate with the most liberal racial policies. In Chicago in the 1920s, this meant blacks voted most frequently for the Republican candidate. Even in elections where race was not always explicit, black voters supported the Republican party with exceptional consistency until the mid-1930s. The Thompson Republican faction based its success upon the black vote, but few of the other Republican factions made more than half-hearted attempts to woo black voters.[10]

Racial and Ethnic Politics

Political participation varies by racial and ethnic group. Society responds to each group somewhat differently, each group has distinctive internal characteristics, and factors unrelated to either the group or to the urban political environment influence the group's political experiences. In this section I describe black, Italian, and Polish political participation and descriptive representation.

By the 1890s most Poles were aligned with the Democratic party under Barzynski's encouragement/direction. The Carter Harrisons and other Democrats supported parochial schools, backed antiprohibition referenda, and helped establish a solid base in the Polish community, while Republican anti-Catholicism and opposition to Sunday drinking alienated the Poles. Numerous Poles were elected to political office. Kiolbassa and Stanley Kunz served in the state legislature in 1877 and 1888, and Kiolbassa was reelected city treasurer in 1891 on the Democratic slate in an otherwise Republican year. Kunz was elected sixteenth ward alderman in 1891 and began serving concurrently as state senator in 1902. Ethnic groups elected descriptive representatives when electoral districts and community boundaries matched and when community and party factionalism were low.[11]

Among the Polish politicians active before 1900, only Kunz became involved in the rough and tumble of the city's factional politics. Kunz had the dubious distinction of being a member of the city council's "Gray Wolves," along with "Foxy Ed" Cullerton and John Powers (Wendt and Kogan 1953). Kunz slugged his way through a series of bitter conflicts with Democrats, Republicans, and even Polish opponents as he sought aldermanic and congressional seats. Kunz and Polish nationalism fell victim to a complicated series of factors, including ward boundaries and strong partisan conflicts. German candidates, whom Poles identified with German overlords in Poland, generated strong support among Poles for opponents, such as Republican mayoral candidate Thompson in 1915 and Democratic mayoral candidate William Dever in 1923 (Kantowicz 1975:79–83, 170–78). Kunz fought and was defeated in a series of conflicts with the Harrison faction from 1904 through 1920.

The Poles fared moderately well in electoral politics, but they were hindered by institutional and religious divisions in the Polish community, which affected their success at mobilizing political support around one party or even a single candidate. These internal divisions were reinforced and exacerbated by the system of party factionalism, so there was as much competition among Poles within the Democratic party as there was between Polish Democrats and Polish Republicans. Ideological divisions between Polish factions did not help Polish voters decide how to cast their votes; when offered two Polish candidates, they (most often) divided their support, so that a third, non-Polish candidate frequently won. The Polish voter was not certain of the most desirable characteristic for a Polish candidate, other than his Polishness.

For those Italians who lived in close proximity to one another in the nineteenth ward, winning election to office and ending political control by the Democratic party became crucial issues. Italians lived in greatest numbers in the west side's nineteenth ward, but they had to contend with strong Irish resistance to Italian political representation. Irish Gray Wolf John Powers won the ward's aldermanic seat in 1888 and held it until 1923, when the city redistricted (or more appropriately gerrymandered) the Italian voting bloc out of existence. His lieutenant, James Bowler, was elected to the ward's other aldermanic seat in 1906 and served until 1923. For twenty-five years, Italian and other reform groups mounted unsuccessful attacks on Powers' domination of the ward. Powers' reaction to the efforts of Jane Addams, the Municipal Voters' League, Oscar Durante (editor and publisher of *L'Italia*), and Allessandro Mastro-Valerio of *La Tribuna Italiana (Transatlantica) La Parola dei Socialisti* was printed in *L'Italia:* "I can buy the Italian vote with a glass of beer and a compliment" (Nelli 1970a: 98; 1970b). The Irishman John Powers became Johnny DePow or Gianni Pauli to hold his growing Italian constituency, and as late as 1921 he defeated Anthony D'Andrea, president of the Hod Carriers Union, Sewer and Tunnel Miners' Union, and the Unione Siciliana. Shortly after the election, D'Andrea received death threats that persuaded him to sever "all connections with Nineteenth Ward politics" (Peterson 1952:116), but he was permanently retired on May 11, 1921, by a sawed-off shotgun.[12]

Powers dominated the ward so successfully because he also chaired both the powerful finance committee on the City Council, as well as the Cook County Democratic Committee. Powers served as alderman and committeeman of the twenty-fifth ward until 1927. Bowler served as alderman (there were two per ward), shared the committeeman's job with Powers until 1927, and led the ward in both positions until 1953. Vito Marzullo was elected as alderman in 1953 and remains in office as alderman and ward committeeman in 1985.

Allswang used the nineteenth ward as his measure of Italian partisanship and, therefore, identified consistent Italian Democratic partisanship between 1890 and 1916, followed by a surge in Republican partisanship. Irish Democratic dominance of the ward and city skewed Italian voting patterns between 1890 and 1920. After ward redistricting in 1922 and the nomination of an antiprohibition Republican (Thompson) in 1927, the Italian Democratic vote for mayor dropped below 50 percent for the first time in over thirty years (Allswang 1971:215–40).

Because of Powers' dominance, the first Italian aldermanic victories appeared in areas where there were not enough Italian votes to have decided the election. Republican Stephen R. Revere was elected to the city council from the tenth ward in 1885 and from the seventeenth in 1897. Democrat Frank Gazzolo was elected from the eleventh ward in the 1890s and from the eighteenth in 1913 (Nelli 1970a: 113–16). Italians voted Republican in Thompson's 1931 mayoral election, when blacks were his only other major supporters. Italians leaned toward the Republicans but they were not strongly committed to them, and they were not intimately involved in factional politics. The Italians fielded political candidates under both Republican and Democratic labels, but there were too few Italians to elect any one candidate.

Italians fared poorly in comparison to Polish descriptive representation on the ward level. Hampered by the absence of strong, centralized, politically oriented community institutions, the physical dispersal of the Italian population, and dominance by Irish Democrats of the one locale where they were concentrated, Italian politicians often found it difficult to win elections. Although there were negative reactions to Italian immigrants, Italian public life was too thoroughly private and their collective identity was too weak to define the concerns of the Italian "community" or to mount a public political response.

Democratic party bosses Roger Sullivan and George Brennan rejected the participation of black voters (Allswang 1971:147, 153). Ferdinand Barnett, publisher of the Chicago *Conservator,* lawyer, and later assistant corporation counsel, won election to the municipal court on the Republican ticket in 1906. Barnett lost a recount demanded by the Democrats, who controlled city hall. Because the Democrats had submitted only one objection and that to the only black Republican, black leaders assumed the Democrats had sent them a clear message. As late as the 1927 elections, the Democrats attacked William Thompson because he had appointed a large number of blacks (Allswang 1971:42; Gosnell 1967:85, 214, 224, 406).

The Democrats sometimes courted blacks. Spear reported that the Harrison-Dunne faction intermittently attempted to enlarge its base of black supporters. Dunne named Archibald Carey and R. R. Jackson to posts on the state commission charged with planning the 1915 celebration of the Emancipation Proclamation. The Carter Harrisons appointed blacks to municipal jobs but never nominated them to elective office (Spear 1967:64).

Blacks voted strongly Republican because they felt most at ease in that party. William Hale Thompson explains much of the affinity between blacks and the Republican party between 1900 and 1930. Thompson's support from Ida B. Wells, his alliances with Oscar DePriest and Archibald Carey, and his extravagant public support for blacks made him the overwhelming favorite of black voters. He said, "I'll give your people jobs. And if any of you want to shoot craps go ahead and do it. When I'm mayor the police will have something better to do than break up a little friendly crap game" (Wendt and Kogan 1953:103–4). Thompson, George Harding, and Samuel Ettelson built their political careers in the second ward by creating close ties with the black community. Thompson was elected alderman of the second ward in 1900 on a reform platform which promised to clean up the vice district.[13] Blacks debated the wisdom of their commitment to the Republican party, but in most cases the issue was moot. Allswang surveyed black partisanship from 1918 through 1932; except for the 1923 mayoral election when Thompson was not a candidate, blacks gave 66 percent or more of their votes to the Republicans. Charles Deneen, a Republican reform-oriented leader, slated blacks for primaries and appointed them to political office, but after he lost the 1912 gubernatorial election and his candidate, Olson, lost the 1915 mayoral primary, Deneen's patronage and attractiveness to black voters dwindled (Gosnell 1967:38).

Strong racial self-identification and high residential concentration minimized the extent to which intraracial conflicts invaded electoral politics. With increasingly large numbers of black Republican voters concentrated in southside city council and state legislative districts, there were few head-to-head contests that divided the black vote and allowed a white candidate to win. Gosnell described the 1918 legislative primary in which Thompson Republicans offered a black and white candidate and the Deneen faction nominated one black candidate. Although blacks liked Thompson, they obviously liked the idea of two black state representatives more, since they concentrated their votes on both black candidates. When blacks competed against each other and another white candidate in the 1928 state legislative race, Oscar DePriest helped organized blacks to concentrate their ballots on only one of the black candidates to prevent the white candidate from winning.[14]

Descriptive Representation

Representation in Heterogeneous Areas. Next I want to assess descriptive representation systematically; citywide representation is discussed first. Ethnic or racial representation outside of their areas of heaviest residence is the type of representation that most decisively demonstrates political assimilation and acceptance. A European ethnic or an Afro-American elected to represent other ethnics and native whites indicates the group has some measure of the legitimacy of its leadership for others and of its acceptance in the larger community.

In spite of the difficulties of minimizing intraparty and interparty factionalism in ward politics, Democratic and Republican administrations appointed Polish officials to citywide office. Kiolbassa and Smulski had served under Deneen as city treasurer, city attorney, and state treasurer by 1910. Carter Harrison's last term as mayor, from 1911 to 1915, was "something of a springtime for Polish politicians" because of the Democratic dominance of city, county, and state governments (Kantowicz 1975:83; see also 54–56, 60, 64). Harrison appointed Julius Smietanka and Stephen Pietrowicz[15] to the school board; between 1894 and 1937 eleven Poles were appointed to the board. During his years on the school board, 1909 to 1927, Smietanka served as its president and was also appointed Collector of Internal Revenue by Woodrow Wilson. Joseph LaBuy was elected municipal court judge in 1912 and was a Cook County commissioner in the 1930s, while Edmund Jarecki was elected to the post of county judge from 1922 through 1954; his duties included supervision of the county election machinery. Poles served on the Board of Assessors, Board of Tax Appeals, as Collector of Customs, and as superintendent of the Municipal Tuberculosis Sanitarium (*Poles of Chicago, 1837–1937* 1937: 23–27, 124–27).

Few Italians were elected to office from the late nineteenth through the mid-twentieth century, although not for lack of trying; Nelli listed twenty-four candidates for alderman, fourteen for the Board of County Commissioners, seven for state senator, twenty-one for the state legislature, eight for municipal court judgeships, and one each for lieutenant governor and state's attorney between 1896 and 1920. One Italian won a post in the state senate, four in the house, four were elected state representatives, and one was elected to the city council, while Italians were appointed to the state's attorney's office and to the Board of Local Improvements (Nelli 1970a:113–16; Schiavo 1928:103–5). Electoral office was typically so elusive that Italian publications usually stressed the choice of any Italian candidate over non-Italian opponents of any party. The Italians had one alderman and committeeman outside of their areas of heaviest residence before 1940. Daniel Serritella was elected Republican committeeman of the first ward in the late 1920s and early 1930s as a representative of the Capone organization to the Thompson administration (Rather 1972:116).

Blacks fared poorly in citywide electoral offices. Democratic mayor Dever nominated Albert B. George, who was the first black elected to the municipal court. George lost his reelection campaign in 1930, victim of the Democratic landslide and the organization's disapproval of his political behavior. The next black judge was elected in 1939 (Lyle 1960). Mayor Thompson appointed Archibald Carey chairman of the Civil Service Commission in 1928, but he died in 1931, and no black was appointed to fill his position. Governor Small appointed Edward Wright and Dan Jackson to serve on the Illinois Commerce Commission during the 1920s, with Jackson filling out Wright's unexpired term on the former's resignation (Gosnell 1967: 215). Black elected officials were concentrated in areas of heaviest black population. Blacks won election to state office regularly after the 1870s. The cumulative voting system provided each voter with three votes, which could be concentrated or split as the person desired. John W. E. Thomas won office in 1876 and 1882, after which as Gosnell wrote in the early 1930s "there has never been a session of the Illinois General Assembly which lacked a colored representative" (1967:66). Two blacks went to the state legislature in 1914, three in

1918, and five in 1929. Adelbert H. Roberts won a seat in the state senate in 1924, and in 1928 Oscar DePriest won the Republican nomination and election to the first congressional district in Illinois after the incumbent William Madden died between the primary and the general election. DePriest served from 1928 to 1934, the first black congressman in the House since G. H. White of North Carolina's term ended in 1901 (Walton 1972:172).

Blacks were rarely nominated for city office and were elected even more rarely, with one exception. Before 1910 blacks served frequently on the Cook County Commission. John Jones won a seat on the commission in 1871 and 1872, Theodore W. Jones in 1894, and Edward Wright, who had withdrawn his candidacy for the county board in 1894 to end a division among the black delegates at the county convention, was nominated and elected to the board in 1896 and 1898 (Robb 1929). Oscar DePriest followed him to membership on the commission in 1904 and 1906, and Frank Leland in 1908. These were countywide elections, when fewer than three percent of the city's population was black.

How can these successful cases before 1910 and the absence of nominations after 1910 be accounted for? Prior to 1910, party conventions nominated candidates for county and city offices. Voters selected commissioners from party slates of fifteen candidates including, in addition to the Republican and Democratic, the Prohibition, National (Gold) Democrats, the Socialist-Labor, and the "Middle of the Road" parties (*Chicago Daily News Almanac* 1897: 392). Most voters cast their ballots on the basis of party slates rather than individual candidates. The November 1896 election results showed each of the ten Republicans and Democrats with 195,500 and 142,500 votes, respectively.

The party constructed balanced tickets at conventions to appeal to voters from the entire metropolitan area. John Leonard (Bunnie) East, fifth-ward committeeman from 1931 until recent years, felt that the convention system was fairer because representation was more heterogeneous. In 1910 reformers introduced the nomination of county commissioners by party primaries. Reverend Archibald Carey and others "protest[ed] against the passage of the so-called Primary Election Law. . . . We feel that the passage of this bill will completely eliminate from the politics of the state the colored voters and take from them all opportunity of any member of their race being nominated to office" (Branham 1977:253). The proof of Carey's allegation is that after 1908 no blacks won election to office, though a few were nominated. Between 1910 and 1980 only four blacks served on the county commission, all by appointment (John Leonard East, interview, March 11, 1974).

Black Chicago's strongest political ally, Thompson, concentrated black patronage in the law department. In his first administration, he named Edward Wright and Louis B. Anderson, later second-ward alderman, assistant corporation counsels and Archibald Carey investigator, and he increased appointments to 14 percent after reelection in 1927 (Gosnell 1967:199, 201). Even under Thompson's administration, Gosnell noted that blacks "have not yet won the headship of a city department and at no time have they received in the patronage positions as a whole, rewards which were commensurate with their voting strength. Even Mayor Thompson failed to name a colored man to the Board of Education, the Board of Local Improvements, or a city cabinet position" (1967:201–2). Blacks fared poorly in citywide positions in contrast to Poles and even to Italians. How do the three groups compare on their own territory?

Descriptive Representation in Homogeneous Areas. Demographic factors, political structure, and internal factors were integrated in early twentieth-century Chicago to the advantage of the black population. Large numbers of black adults migrated to Chicago and were forced into a few southside neighborhoods where the city's ward and the state's legislative district system enhanced rather than reduced their political influence. Although the same structural factors applied to Italians and Poles, neither group was so large nor so geographically constrained in its place of residence as to be forced into potential political dominance. Racial political issues, although complex and volatile in the city as a whole, were so much more dominant among black voters than ethnic concerns that Republican politicians such as Oscar DePriest and William Hale Thompson, who were willing to use them for political appeals, found a stronger and more predictable response.

All things being equal, black voters should have been most successful in gaining descriptive representation at the ward level. This section begins with an examination of ward-based descriptive representation when the population was homogeneous. Descriptive representation can be measured by comparing the number of aldermen elected from a district in toto to the number that describes the majority of the population in an electoral district. Longitudinal measurement of descriptive representation is also appropriate, since high turnover of descriptive officials serving single rather than repeated terms tends to exaggerate their political impact. A second measure of years in service will also be examined for ward aldermen and committeemen.

Turnover is an important issue for numerical as well as longitudinal representation. The number of occasions when elections were held between 1910 and 1940 indicates political stability within the wards and serves as a base of representatives against which to compare officials who fit descriptive characteristics. Since the city held twenty-one aldermanic elections between 1910 and 1940, twenty-one different individuals could have won office from each ward. Next, the number of officials actually elected was percentaged against the number of elections held, as a simple measure of turnover in each of the ethnic and racial group's wards. Then the black, Italian, and Polish aldermen elected from their respective wards were percentaged against the total number of aldermen elected from 1910 to 1940 as a measure of descriptive representation. See table 4.8 for a listing of wards.

Table 4.8 is a summary of these two measures. Turnover, the percentage of elections in which different individuals won office, reveals the degree of accessibility in the organization of the wards in question. The least accessible organization, not surprisingly, was in the Italian nineteenth ward (33 percent), while the black wards were most accessible, at 52 percent. Poles scored highest on descriptive representation, at 61 percent, while the black wards elected representatives at a rate of 32 percent, and the Italians at 20 percent. Measuring descriptive representation by years in service produces marked changes only for blacks. Their score jumps from 32 percent to 57 percent.

Ward committeemen positions were the most coveted within Chicago wards because of their control over political patronage. Because committeemen wield such power, the positions are and were much more difficult to win. Under these circumstances, ethnic and racial representation might have been lower, but that was not the case (see table 4.9). In the Democratic party the black wards had the highest and the Italian wards the lowest turnover; in the Republican party, turnover was approximately equal (40 percent). Descriptive representation was highest among Polish Democrats (48 percent) and black Republicans (62.5 percent), lowest among Polish Republicans (17.5 percent) and black Democrats (20 percent). Italians won only marginally more

Table 4.8
Black, Italian, and Polish Aldermen, 1910–1940

Wards by Nationality	Total Elections	Number of Different Individuals Elected		Number of Aldermen Who Fit Descriptive Characteristics	Percentage of Descriptive Aldermen
Black[a]	42	22	(52%)	7	32%
Italian[b]	46	15	(33%)	3	20%
Polish[c]	84	41	(49%)	25	61%

Sources: Rollheiser 1975; Stratton 1930b, 1932b; Hughes 1934–35a, 1936–37a, 1938–39a, 1940–41a; *Chicago Daily News Almanac,* 1913, 1914, 1917, 1919, 1920, 1921, 1922, 1926.

a. Wards 2 and 3.

b. Wards 19, 20, 21, 25, 26, 27.

c. Wards 12, 13, 16, 17, 26, 29, 31, 32, 33, 38. See Table 4.4, for wards by nationality by years.

Table 4.9
Black, Italian, and Polish Ward Committeemen, 1910–1940

Wards by Nationality	Democratic Party				Republican Party			
	Total Elections	# and % Individuals Elected	Number Who Fit Descr Characterists	% Descr Comm'men*	Total Elections	# and % Individuals Elected	Number Who Fit Descr Characterists	% Descr Comm'men*
Blacks	20	10 (50%)	2	20.0%	20	8 (40%)	5	62.5%
Italians	29	12 (39%)	2	15.0%	26	11 (39%)	3	33.0%
Poles	40	29 (43%)	14	48.0%	40	17 (43%)	3	12.5%

Sources: Rollheiser, 1975; Stratton 1930b, 1932b; Hughes 1934–35a, 1936–37a, 1938–39a, 1940–41a; *Chicago Daily News Almanac,* 1913, 1914, 1916, 1917, 1919, 1920, 1921, 1922, 1925, 1926.
*Committeemen percentaged using total number of individuals elected as a base.

Table 4.10
Black, Italian, and Polish Ward Committeemen by Years, 1910–1940

	Democratic Party			Republican Party		
Wards by Nationality	Total Years Served	Descriptive Years Served	Percent of Total	Total Years Served	Descriptive Years Served	Percent of Total
Black	52	11	21.0%	52	30	57.7%
Italian	68	10	14.7%	64	20	32.0%
Polish	104	60	57.6%	104	20	19.2%

Sources: Hughes 1934–35a, 1934–35b, 1936–37a, 1936–37b, 1938–39a, 1938–39b, 1940–41a, 1940–41b; Stratton 1930a, 1930b, 1932a, 1932b; *Chicago Daily News Almanac* 1913, 1914, 1916, 1917, 1919, 1920, 1921, 1922, 1925, 1926.

ward posts among the Republicans (three) than the Democrats (two), but given their low population that was significant. When descriptive representation among ward committeemen is calculated by years, the Polish Democrats were underrepresented and black Republicans over-represented by their numbers (see table 4.10). Poles were more successful in electing aldermen than blacks and slightly less successful in electing ward committeemen (see table 4.11). Blacks were more effective than Poles in reelecting representatives to the city council, but they were less effective in extending their ward committeemen's terms of office. Black partisan commitment to the Republican party produced a much higher level of representation in black areas, while Polish partisan conflict and factionalism reduced Polish representation in ward committee slots. A simple standardization measure confirms this.

Table 4.11
Aldermanic Representation by Years, 1910–1940

Nationality	Total Years Served	Years Served by Descriptive Representative	Percentage of Total
Black	88	49	55.7%
Italian	93	14	15.0%
Polish	172	107	62.2%

Source: Rollheiser 1975.

Table 4.12
Ratio of Descriptive Representation

	Aldermen	Committeemen	
		Republican	Democratic
Black	.6	1.08	.95
Italian	1.3	1.03	1.0
Polish	1.0	.65	.83

Ratio derived from percentage of descriptive aldermen divided by percentage of descriptive years served.

A ratio constructed of the percentage of descriptive alderman divided by the percentage of years descriptive aldermen served shows that Italian and Polish descriptive representation compared equally across both types, while blacks were slightly underrepresented in the first type. The ratio for ward committeemen shows that blacks and Italians representation was about equal in both categories with Poles underrepresented in the first type (see table 4.12).

Finally, table 4.13 compares representatives from each group that held aldermanic and ward committee seats. Politicians in Polish wards held the two positions most frequently (nine) in the Polish wards, with politicians from the Italian wards (five) and incumbent politicians from the black wards (two) much less often. Polish descriptive representatives ranked first with five, followed by the black and Italian populations with one each. Poles increased their representation because they competed for posts in a large number of wards with substantial Polish populations.

Table 4.13
Correlation Between Aldermen and Ward Committeemen by Race and Nationality

Wards by Nationality	Aldermen Who Were Also Ward Committeemen	
	Descriptive	Nondescriptive
Black	1	1
Italian	1	4
Polish	5	4

The examination of demographic, external, and internal variables suggests that black citizens held an electoral advantage over the Poles and Italians, the first because they were more unevenly distributed throughout the metropolitan area and the third because of their small size and wide dispersion. An examination of descriptive representation, however, shows that despite these advantages blacks were considerably less likely to elect descriptive representatives numerically but were relatively, though not absolutely, more successful at reelection. The black population was concentrated in a highly constrained area on the south side; once blacks were elected (Oscar DePriest, second-ward alderman in 1915, and R. R. Jackson in 1923 in the third ward), these offices became "black" but turnover was higher. Geographic concentration seems to have reduced the number of aldermen-ward committeemen. Italian and Polish politicians held both positions in wards where they resided more often than blacks held them in the black wards. Despite their intragroup conflicts and partisan divisions, Poles were relatively and actually more successful than blacks, who held the advantages of ideological homogeneity, partisan unity, racial identity, and geographic concentration.

Conclusion: External Forces and Political Hierarchy

Blacks dominated electoral representation in the districts in which they were highly concentrated, but unlike the other groups, their representation was confined to those areas. Black partisan representation was confined to the Republican party, based on voluntary identification and involuntary rejection, until the party's collapse in the 1930s precluded any other alternatives. Similarly, blacks dominated their segment of the Republican party, but even that was highly restricted; the Democratic party at both the grass-roots and leadership levels rejected black support and participation. This evidence suggests hierarchical electoral and representative systems in which black representation was significantly more restricted than ethnic representation. The Irish Democrats combined efforts at maintaining political control in a city with a rapidly rising tide of non-Irish immigrants, requiring gerrymandering and comparable strategies. Black participation was limited and confined even by its allies to a degree unmatched by other groups.

Political hierarchy founded on black subordination was based on strong bipartisan grass-roots ideological resistance, Republican efforts at containment, and ethnic territorial defensiveness. Both the Republican and Democratic parties limited their public support for and association with blacks, the latter more than the former. Democratic party leaders and followers rejected black support and participation. The Carter Harrisons were two exceptions, winning majorities of black voters' support (Allswang 1971:218–21) in three of their five races, but Charles Branham notes, "The Chicago Democracy was unable to shake the racial conservatism that dominated the party throughout the first third of the century. They ignored the requests of their few black supporters and never nominated a single black for even the most minor elective office" (1977:261).

In 1927 Democratic boss George Brennan attacked Thompson's mayoral candidacy based on his alliance with the black community; the Democratic campaign literature got down to the point: "Do You Want Negroes or White Men to Run Chicago?" (Allswang 1971:147; Wendt and Kogan 1943:256). The Democratic leadership's racist opposition was political as well as personal. Their followers included immigrant and working-class voters who competed directly with blacks for jobs and housing, and therefore for political status. The Chicago riot of 1919, the lengthy bombing campaigns against blacks in Hyde Park in 1919, juvenile gang wars, and other hostile acts against blacks who "invaded" or lived on the borders of white neighborhoods were visible, violent evidence of the long-term conflict (Philpott 1978; Tuttle 1972).

Opposite the Democratic leadership was the Republican, more consistently representative of the city's native white upper class or upwardly mobile citizenry. This group was not in direct economic or physical competition with blacks for jobs or housing. Moreover, they were typical of the Republicans with whom blacks had allied against the working classes in the Democratic party since the Civil War. One example was Mayor William Hale Thompson; after he fared poorly at Yale, his parents supported him while he played cowboy for several years in the remains of the Wild West. George Harding, Samuel Ettelson, and others, wealthy businessmen or their representatives, were also active in politics on the south side of Chicago (Gosnell 1967:53–54; Wendt and Kogan 1953:30 and photograph opposite).

The racial hostility between blacks and the new ethnic groups established the black-white upper middle class Republican alliance but also eliminated the possibility of class politics. The upper class-black Republican alliance was not entirely free of racial problems, however.

Thompson appointed few blacks to citywide office and none as department heads. The Republican party welcomed blacks, but it made every effort to control the terms of their entry and participation in the party. Branham reports that the white Republican incumbent Martin Madden narrowly defeated William Cowan, a black real estate dealer and an ally of Edward Wright, in 1914. DePriest won the nomination in 1915 because he had supported the party organization, while Wright was establishing the feasibility of a black alderman by challenging the Republican party organization (Branham 1977:248; Gosnell 1967:74).

Charles Deneen headed another reform-oriented faction of the Republican party that was supported by black attorney and newspaper publisher Ferdinand Barnett and social worker, journalist, and wife of Ferdinand, Ida B. Wells-Barnett. Even Barnett's alliance with Deneen did not guarantee his support. Deneen had been elected state's attorney after promising Edward Wright he would name a black assistant state's attorney. Wright requested that Barnett be appointed, but Deneen took no action. He named Barnett only after County Commissioner Wright held up appropriations for Wright's office (Branham 1977:243; Gosnell 1967:154–55).

Southside Republicans conceded the second and third wards to black voters and elected black officials, but in 1931 they literally drew the line at the fourth ward. By 1930 the fourth ward's population was 20 percent black, and as it was clear that the black population would increase, city officials redrew the ward boundaries to maximize black population within the second and third wards (Gosnell 1967:76–77). Even so, the fourth ward's black population rose to 33 percent by 1940, but a black alderman was not elected until 1955 (Rollheiser 1975:14).

By the 1920s Wright had become ward committeeman, but Gosnell reported that Wright's very inventiveness and personal strength in political bargaining drew the jealousy and opposition of white politicians, including Mayor Thompson (Gosnell 1967:153–62). Wright fell victim to the Republican fratricidal warfare between his patron, Governor Len Small, and former mayor Thompson in the mid-1920s. Small supported John Dill Robertson as Republican mayoral nominee over Thompson; forced to choose, Wright decided to remain loyal to his patron. Thompson allotted patronage to his new second-ward committeeman, Dan Jackson, an undertaker, who soon attracted Wright's followers.

Gosnell reported that Wright was a victim of miscalculation rather than racism, but the party's choice of a replacement was most instructive. Jackson was the antithesis of Wright; a handsome, easy-going man, he preferred to leave political interaction to his allies. John Leonard East reported that Jackson was uninterested in party politics and allowed Thompson to handle much of the ward's political affairs. Gosnell confirms this approach: when Oscar DePriest sought the Republican nomination for Madden's seat in the House of Representatives, Jackson's only comment to Mayor Thompson was "I'm with you, Mr. Mayor" (Gosnell 1967:182).

Finally, there were dangerous consequences for the person who entered politics outside of black territory. The 1922 redistricting gerrymandered the Italian community of the nineteenth ward into the twentieth, twenty-fifth, twenty-sixth, and twenty-seventh wards. A serious problem of succession confounded the choice of the next ward committeeman. The Republicans postponed the problem by retaining the old formula until 1928.[16] Octavius Granady, a black attorney and war veteran, opposed Morris Elder for the Post; Elder was a Thompson ally, in the "Bloody Twentieth" ward. Deneen reported that Granady had pleaded for protection at noon on election day, but that evening he was fired upon as he stood near a polling place: "He jumped into his automobile and sped away. The assassins and another car with three men pursued him. More shots were fired. Granady's car crashed into a tree. When the police arrived they found a dozen shotgun slugs in his body" (Stuart 1936:375; Wendt and Kogan 1953:308; see also *Illinois Crime Survey* 1929:956).

Do the patterns described in this chapter amount to political hierarchy? Individual examples compare to events in both the Italian and Polish communities, but the combined impact of the segregation of electoral competition, the virtual exclusion of blacks from leadership roles in city and state administration, the comprehensive hostility to black politicians outside of their neighborhoods, along with organizational resistance, certainly placed blacks at the bottom of the Chicago political hierarchy.

5

The Philosophical Labyrinth of Race and Political Beliefs

"You folks just ain't ready for integration."
—An anonymous black man

Black politicians faced a paradox: to serve their constituents' interests, they had to treat race as a political issue, but in so doing they generated strong, even dangerous, resistance from those organized groups that benefitted most from racial discrimination.[1] The philosophical problems inherent in constructing a political agenda within a political system characterized by hierarchy and collectivism are the subject of this chapter.

Nancy Hartsock and Irene Diamond argue that women's physical and social experiences of the world differ so radically from men's that analyses of the elements of political interaction rest on only a partial or male account:

> The reduction of all human emotion to interests and interests to the rational search for gain reduces the human community to an instrumental, arbitrary and deeply unstable alliance, one which rests on the private desires of isolated individuals. . . . Certainly a mother's characteristically nurturing relationship to her child is difficult to describe in terms of instrumental interests in individual gain. . . . Perhaps the best way to determine whether a public issue is concerned with advancing the representation of women is to establish whether it merely advocates extending to women rights established for men, or whether the discussion moves into new territory (Hartsock and Diamond 1981: 719).

The underlying distinctions in political interest and philosophy between blacks and whites arise from differences other than biological ones. The American political context functionally differentiated black and white roles. Recent political changes have slightly eroded but have not altered white dominance over blacks in income, wealth, and job status. The political differences these economic differences make parallel but surpass the type of problem Hartsock and Diamond identity for women. Did an extension of the same rights or, in Chicago, the same goods and services solve blacks' problems, or did the particular political and economic status of blacks so differentiate them from whites that qualitative rather than quantitative reforms needed to be agreed upon and implemented to remedy their political differentiation?[2]

The economic, political, and social experiences particular to blacks imprinted them in two contradictory ways, as I will show in this chapter. Discrimination, whether legal, formal, or informal, so constrained black American economic, political, and social life that those subject to it developed a measurably different type of political philosophy, one substantially more complex and more critical of the status quo than that of non-blacks. At the same time, the public presentation of black political interests by blacks was highly constrained by the responsiveness of the white public and white-controlled political, economic, and social institutions and organizations. This created a complex and subtle form of black political philosophy and action. The model presented in this chapter proposes a difficult and subtle proposition. Whites constrained but did not control black political behavior. Whites very effectively set the boundaries in electoral politics, but blacks remained active in nonelectoral areas. White political attitudes and behavior compose a dominant, but not an independent variable to black political attitudes' subordinate but not dependent variable. Black political behavior is related to white political behavior, but it is hardly dependent upon or controlled by it.

Black Political Attitudes

Groups that suffer sharp political and economic restraints react to them in a variety of ways. Strengthened or weakened barriers to political participation produce quantitative changes in voting.[3] In specific cases, restrictions might conceivably result in an increase in turnout or participation because the groups upon whom the restraints are imposed might wish to challenge the attempt to change the status quo. On the other hand, a group may decide that the penalties for violating the newly introduced political limits are too high to risk. In any case, measurable differences in political variables, such as participation, political attitudes, and socialization among those individuals or groups newly subject to political exclusion, should appear.

Political science studies of black political participation have focused on these quantitative changes in electoral politics, but groups subject to political restraints react qualitatively as well as quantitatively. That is, such groups react not only by increasing or decreasing their participation in electoral or institutional politics, but also by broadening the range of alternatives available to them within electoral politics and by developing a counterelectoral focus in which they consider different, more satisfactory alternatives (Axelrod 1972, 1978; Danigelis 1977, 1978).

A subordinate group's reaction to political change is thus not predictable based on the actions of the superordinate group alone. In chapter 2, I noted that analyses of blacks' political behavior should not treat blacks as if their political decisions occurred independently of external white forces. In this chapter I continue to argue that while the white society clearly exerted political dominance over blacks, that does not allow for prediction of black political behavior either quantitatively or qualitatively. Models based only on an examination of variables associated with the superordinate group miss the impact of the subordinate group upon the political process.

In the next section I examine how political belief systems have been measured and considered by means of four concepts in the literature: political socialization, partisan identity or loyalty, location by ideological position, and political participation, and I summarize the research on blacks in each of these areas. The section shows how blacks view American political institutions and authority figures.

The Case for Black Political Integration

Political Socialization. Black political socialization varies substantially from that of whites. Black children, for example, develop different expectations of the role of political authorities than white children of the same age. As they reach ten years of age, black children's positive affect toward authority symbols, such as the president, policemen, and the American flag, declines sharply and recovers only slightly as they reach puberty. Edward Greenberg showed that there were some similarities but also some very significant differences between black and white children's socialization in Philadelphia. In the 1960s black children regarded the government as significantly less benevolent than whites did; they also diverged from white children in their increasingly negative evaluations of the national, state, and municipal governments, although the first suffered the least. Even after controlling for class, black children were less likely to conclude that political leaders are selected by "whoever the most people want." Finally, black children of all classes defined democracy more frequently as a setting "where leaders do what they think is best for people," rather than one "where government does what the most people want" (Greenberg 1970a:268).[4] As black children reach the age of reason, they respond to their social and political environment by a lack of confidence in government in general and state and local governments in particular. This difference in political socialization continues with political maturity.

Partisan Loyalty. As a group, blacks display consistently high levels of partisan identification and loyalty. Nie et al. (1976) showed that blacks identified with the Democratic party more than all other groups except for white southerners and Jews until the Johnson administration facilitated passage of civil rights and voting rights laws. Afterwards, black identification with the Democratic party surpassed all other groups. Blacks' increasing Democratic identification in the 1950s and 1960s mirrored their previously high allegiance with the Republican party from 1860 through the critical electoral period of 1930. Whenever and wherever blacks voted during this period, they had identified almost exclusively with the Republican party (Bunche 1975; Campbell 1977; Gosnell 1967:24–39; Walton 1972).

While black partisan identification has been relatively consistent, black partisan loyalty has reached extraordinary heights. Presidential voting returns from 1952 through 1976 show that the lowest levels of black loyalty fell just below the highest levels of loyalty among other groups of voters. Moreover, in any given election, black loyalty was surpassed only once, by Catholics voting for John F. Kennedy in 1960.[5]

Before the start of the transition from Republican to Democratic party dominance, Gosnell reported somewhat sardonically that:

> A comparison of the voting behavior of Negroes in Chicago with that of citizens in other parts of the city shows that the Negroes are atypical in a number of respects. . . . The districts inhabited largely by Negroes have a larger percentage of Republican votes, a larger ratio of straight Republican ballots, and a higher percentage of favorable votes on bond issues and on prohibition repeal measures than any other part of the city. Until recently [the 1932 election] this attachment of the Negro voters to the Republican party has not been affected by landslides, economic depressions, or by other influences that seem to sway the voters in other parts of the city (Gosnell 1967:35).

Gosnell noted further that "the nineteen units in which the Negro population was twenty percent or more of the total *were so atypical* that they *destroyed the normality* of many of the distributions" (Gosnell 1967: 35n; emphasis added).

This unusually high partisan identification and loyalty occurs among black voters because they consistently, almost uniformly, commit themselves to the party, faction, or individual candidate that is most supportive of racial reform. Many studies have shown that this pattern repeats itself in the north and the south, in urban and in rural areas, before and after the transition to the Democratic party, which began in the 1930s and ended in the 1960s (Andersen 1979; Barker and McCorry 1976; Campbell 1960; Keech 1968; Ladd 1969:285–302; Mathews and Prothro 1966; Verba and Nie 1976; Walton 1972).

A second factor that explains this peculiar pattern is that the American political parties rarely if ever compete on the basis of racial issues for the black vote on the national or local levels. Consequently the national Republican party dominated the black vote for nearly seventy years because of its antislavery position during the Civil War and because of the Democratic party's strong support from European ethnics and working-class voters in the north and from the plantation owners and poor white farmers in the south, who all displayed a strong antipathy toward blacks. Black voters moved into a period of increased interest and support for the Democratic party in the 1930s when the Roosevelt administration initiated social welfare programs, such as social security, the Wagner Act, farm programs, and aid to families with dependent children, programs that benefited blacks as well as whites. When the party sponsored national civil and voting rights legislation in 1964 and 1965 respectively, thereby ending de jure discrimination in the south, as well as a strong antipoverty program for the nation as a whole, black identification with and loyalty to the Democratic party reached the previous levels of association with the Republican party (Pinderhughes 1984; Walton 1972:84–120).

Ideological Location. Blacks also differentiate themselves from whites in their philosophical location. As Nie et al. said of black political views in the 1970s, "no other group in American society is as distinctively liberal as American blacks" (1976:255). Their comparison of black attitudes on economic welfare, size of government, black welfare, school integration, and foreign policy to the attitudes of the American population as a whole showed a majority of blacks in the most extreme liberal position by the 1970s. The American population as a whole, on the other hand, was clustered toward the center of a liberal-conservative continuum, with smaller proportions trailing off toward the extremes. While a majority of blacks do not always support policies generally identified as liberal, a higher proportion support such policies than any other group except Jews (Pinderhughes 1984).

In very recent data, 29 percent of blacks questioned in the Gallup Poll in December 1980 agreed that women and minorities should be given preferential treatment, an awkward and incorrectly phrased description for affirmative action, while only seven percent of whites agreed with the affirmative action position. In September of 1982, 70 percent of nonwhites and only 59 percent of whites favored the Equal Rights Amendment; 61 percent of nonwhites favored a nuclear freeze compared to only 42 percent of whites.[6]

Finally, blacks place greater distance between their expectations of and the actual outcome of political behavior of political officials than whites. Aberbach and Walker (1970, 1973) showed that blacks held significantly lower levels of trust than whites in Detroit in 1967 and 1971. Baxter and Lansing's more recent analysis of contemporary research found that black men and especially black women have lower and declining levels of trust in government than whites (1981:92). Bruce Campbell showed that while trust relates inversely to socioeconomic status among black adults (that is, the higher the status the lower the trust) although political efficacy is positively correlated, trust is uniformly low among younger blacks regardless of status (1980:651–56).

Political Participation. Until the early 1980s numerous authors reported that blacks voted less than whites on average. Several factors explain these low levels of participation. The major research on voting explains that citizenship correlates positively with socioeconomic status. The higher one's income, education, and occupation, the more likely a citizen votes to affirm his or her membership in the political community. Black voters typically rank at the lower end of all socioeconomic scales and therefore should, according to this theory, participate less than whites. Also, higher status blacks should vote more often than lower status blacks. National voting patterns in the 1950s and 1960s confirm this. Axelrod (1972, 1978) showed that blacks turned out in mediocre numbers at best in presidential elections from 1948 through the 1970s. Other studies have concluded similarly or explained, as did the original studies, that low socioeconomic status reduced the overall levels of black political participation (see, for example, Campbell 1960).

Several sets of facts pose problems for this theory. From the 1950s through the 1960s, black electoral participation increased sharply as legislative reforms, federal administrative support, and community mobilization, which was also fueled by the civil rights movement, reorganized the political environment in the south and spilled over to influence northern political participation as well (Cassell 1979:910; Morse 1981; Pinderhughes 1984; Walton 1972:44; Wirt 1970).

Second, after 1964 northern black voter registration and turnout declined, so that a significant gap between black and white voting participation persisted. A number of studies have shown, however, that when political participation is more broadly defined, levels of participation by race shift. When Verba and Nie (1972) divided participation into electoral and nonelectoral types of activity, with the latter subdivided into institutionally (governmentally) versus non-institutionally oriented politics, black participation increased, in fact surpassed, that of whites.

Verba and Nie, Shingles (1981), and others have shown that, on average, blacks participate less than whites, but when they control for other factors, black participation exceeds white. They argue that by controlling for racial group consciousness and social class, blacks campaign and participate in cooperative politics (collectively oriented community activity) at higher rates than whites do, vote at the same rate as whites do, but contact public officials at a rate considerably below whites. When Verba and Nie controlled for social class, they found that for specific types of politics, blacks "participate in politics somewhat more than we would expect given [their] level of education, income, and occupation and more than . . . white[s] of similar status" (Verba and Nie 1972:157).[7] Moreover, the stimulus for this high level of participation is group consciousness; the greater the consciousness of race (by frequency of voluntary citation), the higher the participation.

Toni-Michelle C. Travis argues that group consciousness is too general a concept to fully explain either the type of participation or the content of the participation. Mention of race may well stimulate activity, as Verba and Nie suggest, but to what end? Does a Booker T. Washington, a Malcolm X, or an Adam Clayton Powell emerge? (interview, Jan. 16, 1982; see also Travis 1983). Richard Shingles makes a similar argument, but Verba and Nie avoid the mistake into which Shingles stumbles: that social class combined with mistrust have the net effect of race or by implication that race and high social status reduce cynicism: "the transition from blaming oneself to blaming the system for one's plight does not pertain to economically successful blacks. Those who have not failed have no need for blame and therefore have nothing to transfer [from self to system]" (Shingles 1981: 82). Verba and Nie concluded that "we have not eliminated the effects of race by taking into account social class" (1972:157). Even Shingles also notes that blacks express high levels of mistrust across all class lines. The black middle class is efficacious but cynical; still Shingles's data show considerable attitudinal similarity between low- and middle-income blacks. Mistrust and political efficacy link black consciousness to particular types of political participation, especially among lower-class blacks. On the other hand middle-class blacks, though successful and efficacious, remain cynical regardless of their level of consciousness of race (Shingles 1981:84–87).

Danigelis attempted a global explanation for quantitative changes in black participation by replacing three separate models with a political climate model. In the first model, blacks vote less than whites because they are disproportionately lower-class, so that socioeconomic status or indirect effects explain the racial differences in participation. Second, whites obstruct black political participation with social and structural barriers that produce social alienation and political isolation. Finally, social and structural barriers produce a sense of social cohesion and political community and higher levels of political participation, which he calls the ethnic community model (Danigelis 1978:757).

Danigelis treats the ethnic community model as if it applied primarily or only to voting behavior, when it is more convincingly linked to Verba and Nie's cooperative activity. Black voting patterns are explained less by the existence of a cohesive ethnic community than by a specific set of historical circumstances. Black voter participation exceeded white participation in 1964 because President Lyndon Johnson had deeply impressed the racial sensitivities of Afro-Americans by supporting passage of a civil rights bill. As if that were not sufficient, his Republican opponent Goldwater was widely viewed by blacks as a racist. As early as four months before the election, in August 1964, 94 percent of non-whites polled by the Gallup organization supported Lyndon Johnson (*The Gallup Poll* 1972:1901).

Danigelis's political climate model assumes that the determining factor that explains black voting is white political behavior toward blacks. There is, in short, a direct relationship between white political intolerance, neutrality, or support and low, medium, and high electoral participation among blacks (Danigelis 1977:39). In fact this model might reasonably be named the "white political climate model" since Danigelis excludes the possibility of any variation by and among blacks except as related to the behavior and attitudes of whites. Unless the political analyst acknowledges that whites independently attempt to constrain but do not determine black political behavior, he or she creates an asymmetrical model lacking sufficient variability. Moreover, the analyst also incorporates a theoretical puzzle. Unless Danigelis also allows black citizens to participate or not to participate independent of white political attitudes, he creates a regime that not only restricts black participation on some occasions but also coerces it on others. In fact, blacks do not lend their full support to electoral politics unless they discern significant benefits, normative as well as material, from that participation. They do not participate just because of or to win the approval of whites. Shingles, Verba and Nie, and Aberbach and Walker note multiple political responses to changing racial climate.

But there is a third set of facts that poses a problem for the conventional socioeconomic status explanation of black political participation. Black voting is not now nor has it consistently been low. Urban black voters' turnout surpassed white voters in the early twentieth century, and black voters increased their electoral participation in the south and in Chicago without any significant changes in socioeconomic status. In chapter 4, I analyzed black electoral participation in Chicago in detail and showed that an average of seventy percent of the adult black population registered and that a high percentage of the population turned out to vote in national and, more interestingly, in local elections through the 1920s. In the previous chapter I showed that black voting and turnout declined from 1931 through the 1970s in Chicago as a percentage of all eligible voters.

Black voting increased significantly in the American south from the 1950s through the 1970s, increased precipitously in Chicago in the late 1970s and early 1980s, and has increased among urban blacks in a series of local elections and in national off-year and congressional elections since 1980. What explains these changes in participation that challenge the socioeconomic status explanation of voting?

The research on which the following conclusions were based, as well as the socializing experiences of the children and black adults studied in this and the following three sections, occurred after the time period that is the focus of this study of Chicago politics. This analysis might be accused of projecting more contemporary attitudes backward in time onto a differently socialized population. The analysis in this section does not presume identical socialization, partisan loyalties, ideologies, or political participation for black citizens of the early and mid-twentieth century. However, racial discrimination pervaded American life even more strongly between 1910 and 1940 than it did in the years after World War II when research on political attitudes, partisan identification, and socialization was conducted. One might, therefore, accurately assume that any views on the political attitudes of black adults and authority figures expressed by black children in the 1960s would certainly be as strongly articulated in earlier, more difficult years.

Prescriptive Alternatives

Just as political, social, and economic discrimination impressed upon black children differential political socialization, black adults express their political sensitivities about race in a number of striking ways. They are highly committed and loyal to the political party that they judge to be supportive of racial reform. They are strikingly, dramatically more liberal than nearly every other group in the society because their concern for race is interwoven with economic issues and with high levels of political suspicion and mistrust. The pressure of racial discrimination forces black political views leftward from the ideological center of American politics.

Nonelectoral and noninstitutionally oriented politics typically attract much higher levels of political interest and support among blacks (Verba and Nie 1972). Differential political socialization, consistently high partisan loyalty, liberal political ideology, avoidance of institutional political contact in favor of campaigning, and cooperative activity suggest that blacks develop alternative political prescriptions for political change as well as norms and values that buttress these recommendations, which have a more limited value within the electoral system.

Decreased voting may be one of the responses to an increasingly hostile, isolationist political climate, as Danigelis suggests, but only one. Nonelectoral activity directed toward institutional change may be another, as well as increased attention to qualitative issues. Constrained from full participation in political and economic life, blacks may shift their political concerns from the limited range of options offered by the electoral system to theoretical examination and prescription of recommendations for political change. They may withdraw through a variety of strategies, including genuine, tactical, or value withdrawal as Holden denotes them (Holden 1973:42–44; Salomon and Van Evera 1973:1291).

A number of studies have discussed models of black political goals and attitudes, but James Q. Wilson's analysis has been most widely adopted. His analysis of black political goals and beliefs serves as a starting point for this discussion. Wilson developed his typology of political goals based on Chicago's black politics of the 1950s: " 'Status' ends are those which seek the integration of the Negro into all phases of community on the principle of equality . . . on the basis of principles other than race. . . . 'Welfare' ends are those which look to the tangible improvement of the community or some individual in it through the provision of better services, living conditions or positions" (1960:185). Status ends exclude segregation on either a de jure or de facto basis; they are concerned with the resolution of inequalities in the relationship between blacks and whites; that is, they address the issue of racial status. Welfare ends focus on material welfare or economic well-being; what kinds of and how much of certain goods and services should blacks have? The two types of goals are not necessarily mutually exclusive according to Wilson: "in many issues, it is possible to obtain some of both benefits and the problem is how to reach an optimum balance. But the choice exists, and in many cases it is a hard one" (1960:186). One concludes that material well-being is emphasized only at the peril of racial integration and only by foregoing the elimination of collective status.

Wilson treats the goals as if they were at the ends of a one-dimensional set of policy choices that are, for the most part, mutually exclusive. In fact, they tap two interrelated, but very different, dimensions of interest. Status and welfare goals interconnect rather than separate because membership in the black race represents a peculiar identity in American society. According to Katznelson, "ethnic groups . . . are socially defined on the basis of their cultural characteristics (religion, language, etc.) while racial groups are socially defined by their immutable physical characteristics" (1976:18). But blacks are not simply a nationality group whose status varies by degree from other ethnic or nationality groups; they are a distinctive racial group upon whom political, social, and in the American context, economic restraints were applied. Blacks participated in the economy in highly limited and specific ways that sharply restrained their ability to become independent entrepreneurs or to accumulate wealth (Becker 1971; Berry 1971; Greenberg 1980; Higginbotham 1980; Kain 1969; Reich 1981).

Black life in America incorporates limitation along racial-political as well as economic dimensions. These restrictions pervade all sectors of Afro-American life and have led to the development of political beliefs that reflect these constraints. The subordinate status of blacks in the United States is most apparently based upon that which is easily observable—racial identity—but discrimination incorporates both economic restrictions and racial components. These two aspects of discrimination, racial and economic, can be considered separately, but they are often mixed and confused as if they were only one, racial type. In the American context they interrelate, fold back upon each other, and interact in complex and unpredictable ways. This is best represented by a long-term controversy over the economic or racial explanation for the origins of racial slavery. The racial proponents argue that Europeans enslaved Africans in order to encourage their conversion to Christianity, because they wanted to "civilize" blacks. Their first encounters with Africans automatically provoked Europeans to behave in racist ways and to structure their interaction along hierarchical lines.[8] The economic proponents hold that race became a superficial justification for economic enslavement; this excluded blacks from direct competition with whites in the labor force and from the acquisition of property or wealth. They argue that racial slavery was an institution whose most significant functions were economic. Race and racism used ideology and psychology to mask the economic origins of slavery; the economic dimension was, therefore, difficult to distinguish in the labyrinth of racist ideology that had developed as early as the eighteenth century.[9]

In fact, the status of Afro-Americans is based on economic *and* racial components that have combined to create an extremely complex, intractable status hierarchy. Dorn makes the point that "blacks were a sizable minority in the United States a full two centuries before the hordes of white ethnics began to arrive. Why are blacks now in the position of having to catch up with groups that arrived much later?

The answer is clear: by law and social practice, whites have been treated far more generously than blacks" (1979:139). As Barnett explains, blacks relate to whites as a collectivity located at the bottom of a hierarchy of European ethnic groups rather than on the basis of egalitarian individualism (1976:9–13; MacPherson 1966).

The collective hierarchical character of racial status crosses political, economic, and social spheres in the United States. A survey of ethnic interaction in a number of ethnically heterogeneous societies shows the indigenous, usually more numerous, population controls the politics, while a secondary ethnic group exerts greater or disproportionate control over the economy. Examples include Guyana and Kenya, where East Asians controlled entrepreneurial activities or contributed a major portion of the agricultural work force and labor unions. Malaysian Chinese and Indians in Uganda exercised disproportionate influence over the economic sector. In the American case, whites dominate in the political, economic, and social spheres (Katznelson 1976:19).

Ethnicity has been a much softer, more permeable category by contrast. In small towns or socially defined settings, ethnic status might retain its power of political, social, and economic constraints, but continued economic, demographic, and geographic (in large cities) change reduced the capacity for social reinforcement and reproduction of the status. More importantly, though European ethnics might compete as groups with each other, none had to face the complete expropriation of wealth and property, the destruction of social and familial networks, the legal restrictions, coerced immigration, or bondage in the United States. In fact, European ethnics competed for the less attractive jobs upon arrival, which meant that they displaced blacks downward in the economic marketplace.

But let us return to Wilson's analysis of the status and welfare ends, which reflects these two dimensions. Universal discrimination, which dominated all sectors of Afro-American life, created political belief systems among blacks that reflected these constraints. The extreme pressure of discrimination in effect pushed blacks away from the ideological center of American political beliefs. Yet racial status and the resolution of that status is interpreted differently by blacks. Some focus on the less apparent economic component and its resolution, others on the racial aspect and its resolution through political means. Others mix the two in a variety of unpredictable ways. According to Wilson, status goals emphasize an end to "externally imposed collectivism," or racial segregation and discrimination on the basis of race carried out by whites, and they aim for racial integration. Yet black political views show a broader, more complicated set of political positions. Black political activists and politicians searched broadly for resolution of the status of blacks relative to whites. By the 1950s many had moved beyond the accommodationist position to argue for an end to segregation and discrimination, but once past that point agreement declined. Conservative "accommodationists," for example, accepted segregation, incremental integration, or a series of erosions of the status quo, while integrationists argued for an end to any recognition of collective identity. Whereas integrationsists felt that all collective recognition ought to be eliminated because it was racist, black nationalists, a highly significant third strain, emphasized "internally based collectivism" (Barnett 1976:40).[10]

The integrationist and nationalist views are important, traditionally held philosophical positions within black political history. They emerged as early as 1830, when David Walker's "Appeal" argued the importance of ending racial hierarchy and externally imposed collectivism while maintaining positive racial identity and internally based collectivism (in Aptheker 1963:93, 113–14, 126–32; see also Walker, in Bracey et al. 1970:29–34).[11] In the mid- and late 1800s, Martin Delaney and Frederick Douglass debated the creation of the Liberian Colony and the Back to Africa movement; Booker T. Washington's and W. E. B. DuBois's early twentieth-century conflicts contained elements of this tension, as did DuBois's and A. Philip Randolph's opposition to Marcus Garvey.[12] After Garvey, Elijah Muhammad created the Nation of Islam in Detroit and Chicago. The nation grew slowly on the nationalist strains of northern black cities until Malcolm X helped bring it into prominence in the 1960s (Essien-Udom 1962). In Chicago Edward Wright and Oscar DePriest were known as Race Men, because they never feared opposing their white allies if they disagreed over a racial issue (Gosnell 1967:162, 195). Numerous other political conflicts over black nationalism have occurred between older black organizations, such as the NAACP and the Urban League, and successive younger generations, including the Black Power–oriented cohorts of the Student Nonviolent Coordinating Committee (SNCC) and the Congress of Racial Equality.[13]

While Wilson's identification of status goals accurately tapped an important ideological strain in Afro-American or in nationalist politics of any type, his presentation of black politicians' views radically truncated and simplified what is in fact a much more complicated perspective. Wilson allowed black politicians' limited discussion of status goals to obscure the existence of a more complicated set of sharply differing alternative positions within the black community on the status of blacks in relation to whites.

If status goals symbolize an ideological dimension in themselves, are welfare goals equally complicated? Wilson's choice of language is appropriate since, by his definition, welfare benefits take on the character of public goods and services available at the behest of whites rather than on the basis of full political citizenship and economic independence of blacks. According to Wilson, Chicago's black politicians expressed a limited range of political alternatives; in fact, they addressed economic questions more forthrightly and more broadly than his analysis suggests. Just as the status dimension considered a variety of options for black-white relations, the welfare dimension illuminated blacks' political concern about their relationship to the economic system, or more precisely, about what that relationship ought to be.

Blacks such as Booker T. Washington emphasized private enterprise capitalism and allied with captains of industry such as Julius Rosenwald. Both the Chicago and the Detroit Urban Leagues organized programs to train black migrants in the social behavior that would increase their marketability with white employers and managers. DuBois emphasized the racial-political dimension and integrationist and elitist goals in the early twentieth century, but by the 1930s, as the depression weakened the already poor economic condition of the black community, he shifted his concern to the economic. Since DuBois was founder and editor of the *Crisis*, the NAACP's monthly periodical, this change provoked a policy battle with the NAACP board that ended with DuBois's departure and return to Atlanta University, where he resumed his scholarly research (Harlan 1972; Strickland 1966; Thomas 1981; Washington 1970).

Black political activists debated the nature of economic programs: should they be privately initiated or publicly redistributive? Supporters of the redistributive side ventured into socialist and Marxist theory in the 1920s.[14] A. Philip Randolph and Chandler Owen organized the Brotherhood of Sleeping Car Porters, linking both the social and economic dimensions, and they published the black socialist journal, the *Messenger* (Brazeal 1946; Harris 1977; Harris and Spero 1969). Blacks responded most favorably to the Communist party during the depression when the party mounted specific issue-oriented campaigns against evictions, in support of increased income, and better working conditions, and least favorably when the party organized membership drives. Marcus Garvey's Universal Negro Improvement Association and Elijah Muhammad's Nation of Islam stressed racial identity through independent, private self-help.[15]

The Logical Fallacy: Links Between Leadership Style and Ends and Means

Wilson related the status-welfare dichotomy to a militant-moderate leadership typology in which the militants sought status goals through protest and mass action and moderates aimed for welfare goals through bargaining by elected or appointed leaders. Wilson's model captured one philosophical moment in time. In the 1950s political observers associated militance with status goals, but by the 1960s militants rejected the integrationist aspects of status goals. Because Wilson's model telescoped the status and welfare dimensions into one and allowed the nationalist section of the status dimension and the complexity of the economic to go undetected, a simple reversal of militant and moderate stances does not accommodate or accurately represent the ideological positions of the black activists (Wilson 1960: 214–54). See figures 5.1 and 5.2.

Wilson's model of political leadership subordinates ends and means to leadership styles; he links particular status and welfare ends and means to the militant or the moderate style. There is a certain logic to the identification of leadership styles with political means. Militants of any ideological type are more likely to employ protest and mass mobilization as a means to attain specific ends, while moderates or conservatives prefer personal contact and bargaining. There was

Leadership Style	Militant	Moderate
Ends	Status Collective	Welfare Tangible/Selective
Means	Protest Mass	Bargaining Elite

Based on Wilson 1960a.

Figure 5.1 The Wilson Model

Welfare Dimension (Economic Issues) (E)	Status Dimension (R) (Racial - Political Issues)		
	Noncollective Status	Collective Status	
		Externally Imposed	Internally Generated
	Integrationist (I)	Accommodationist (A)	Nationalist (N)
Capitalist (C)	NAACP ------------------------ Roy Wilkins Urban League LeRoi Jones (1962)	------NAACP, Wilkins	Marcus Garvey Nation of Islam Malcolm X (1963) Booker T. Washington Imamu Amiri Baraka (1969)
Marxist (M)	Du Bois (1955)		Malcolm X (1965) Amiri Baraka (1974) Black Panthers

Figure 5.2 Racial Policy Orientations

considerable conflict within the integrationist-oriented civil rights movement, for example, over the use of protest as a bargaining tactic.[16] Yet militants can be integrationists or nationalists, capitalists or Marxists, if they emphasize protest and mass mobilization.

But this has mixed the definition of militants. Militance is a concept that has had powerful significance in black political ideology and that assumes the person is less closely associated with white norms and values. Whites apply the same criteria as blacks to identify militant blacks, but they reverse the values associated with the roles (Campbell 1971). Gary Marx identified 26 percent of the blacks he studied as militants in the early 1960s. For blacks who are militants, such an identity is highly valued. Although Marx classified a minority of blacks as militant, a majority of blacks approved of mass demonstrations, while a majority of whites disapproved or expected them to hurt blacks' attempts to gain racial equality (Marx 1969:54, table 31).[17]

Robert Smith notes that "in the literature [black] leaders are more or less militant to the extent [that] their goals, methods and rhetoric diverge from the conventional goals, methods and rhetoric deemed appropriate by [the] dominant class [of] whites" (Smith 1981:21). Thus Marcus Garvey, a man who aroused the black masses with explicitly nationalist, anti-integrationist, capitalist, specifically anticommunist appeals and whose political philosophy would not fall into Wilson's definition of status goals, was viewed with such trepidation by the American government that he was indicted and jailed for mail fraud. Garvey, who was uninterested in integration, fell into the militant category for the 1920s (Cruse 1967:46; Martin 1976).

The relationships between political means and leadership style are consistent over time, but they are not necessarily correlated with political ends. Wilson notes that: "Race can be kept independent of one's other values, such as one's attitude toward labor unions, free enterprise, communism and so on." But he also assumes that: "This independence can and often does lead to suspicion between militants and moderates. . . . [One person commented] 'I kept finding myself surrounded by Communists. . . . On that bill to outlaw segregation in public housing. . . . Boy I stayed out of things after that. I don't want no part of those reds.'" Liberal reformers commented: "'I have never been convinced that labor organizations have a particular advantage. . . . They are an unstable foundation on which to do any constructive work'" (Wilson 1960:234).

Suspicion develops less from the militant-moderate division than from disagreement on a number of other factors that Wilson's model fails to distinguish. Figure 5.2 shows that blacks might agree on both the racial and economic matters; they might disagree on racial or economic and agree on the economic or racial goals; or they might disagree on both. Moreover, the model distinguishes three racial positions from two economic ones. The following equation summarizes the thirty-one possible combinations of theoretical positions. Let R = racial issues and let E = economic issues. Let each have the following alternatives: I = Integrationist; A = Accommodationist; N = Nationalist; C = Capitalist; M = Marxist. The sum of possible alternative positions is as follows:

[R(+)E(+)][CI + MI + CA + MA + CN + MN] +
[R(+)E(−)][I + (CI + M) + A + (CA + MA)+ N + (CA + MN)] +
[R(−)E(+)][C + (CI + CA + CN) + M + (M + MA + MN)] +
[R(−)E(−)][CI + MI + CA + MA + CN + MN] + Universe =
C + M + A + N + I.

Does one political leader support an integrationist position and the other accommodationist goals, while agreeing on their support for private, government, or socialist economic programs? Do they disagree on programs for economic reform, but agree that progressive economic redistribution is a necessary alternative? Do they have some differences on racial and economic questions, but attempt to subordinate them in favor of national black unity? All these differences served as the basis for conflict or occasional unity among blacks rather than the simple division between militants and moderates identified by Wilson.

Political means of protest or bargaining are employed by each political category rather than by one or by the other. Integrationists and nationalists can be either militants or moderates, but militant accommodationism is presumably logically impossible. Roy Wilkins and Martin Luther King represented moderate and militant leaders fervently committed to status or to integrationist goals. Malcolm X and Elijah Muhammad were both nationalists interested in private enterprise, but they were distinguishable by their disagreements on political means. Muhammad expelled Malcolm X when he made a specific condemnation of John F. Kennedy after his assassination (Haley 1966).

In short, the militant and moderate positions are meaningless designations outside of their particular time frames. A more appropriate model must be based on the fundamental ideological elements that define the belief systems of the actors in question. It would then be possible to identify a militant position at Time A, but to show that that position might be outdistanced by a *more* militant stance at Time B or C. Ladd, for example, discusses repeated ideological eclipses of positions previously defined as militant that took place as the civil rights movement accelerated pressure for political and social reform (1969: 134).

Thus, the six-category figure (figure 5.2) expands status and welfare goals into two more complex continua. Studies of black politics have identified conservatives, accommodationist black leaders who accepted segregation or, as black protest gathered strength, conservative reforms. Such leaders argued that the status of blacks would best be served if they identified goals least antagonistic to whites and worked to minimize rather than to maximize racial change. Those who opposed racial segregation and worked to change it could not agree on what black-white relations ought to be when the externally imposed sanctions were lifted. Integrationists worked to end all collective identification, while nationalists urged blacks to organize among themselves for their own interests. Black leaders have also considered a wide variety of economic alternatives for dealing with the economic status of the black population. Thus the model divides the welfare continuum into private enterprise or capitalist and Marxist goals, but the capitalist block is again subdivided at the upper end into "welfare," distributive, and redistributive goals (Burgess 1973; Katznelson 1976; Ladd 1969; Mathews and Prothro 1966; Myrdal 1964; Thompson 1963; Walton 1972).

Are there any data that support the existence of these differing perspectives? A large number of studies identify integrationist and accommodationist leadership positions, but there are fewer studies on black nationalism (Essien-Udom 1962; Lincoln 1973). Marx and Aberbach and Walker found very strong support for "integrationist" political views in their surveys of blacks in the 1960s. Marx found very low levels of support for his "index of black nationalism," with only 24 percent of his sample identifying with even the weakest position on the scale. He identified less than one percent of his sample as strong and consistent supporters of black nationalism and only four percent as moderates.[18] Somewhat higher proportions of support were found in urban areas such as New York and Chicago, but not by any significant amount. Aberbach and Walker surveyed black support in Detroit on a number of issues, including black nationalism, from 1967 through 1971 and found a sharp increase in support for the Nation of Islam and SNCC during this time. About 42 percent of blacks supported black power in Aberbach and Walker's survey in 1967 and 53 percent in 1971. While support for black nationalism was on the increase, Aberbach and Walker found a decline in support for integration in housing and schools among blacks (Aberbach and Walker 1973:39, 66; Essien-Udom 1962; Marx 1969).

Black nationalists are distinctive. Although Marx found very few black nationalists in his survey, they held sharply differing views from militants or conservatives. Twenty-seven percent felt civil rights demonstrations helped; a higher proportion felt things were getting worse, held less faith in whites, and felt that violence and riots did some good (Marx 1969:111–17). They were also demographically distinctive: 72 percent were men, while only 54 percent of militants and 31 percent of conservatives were so identified; 70 percent were under forty-four years of age, with fewer of the other groups so identified; and a full 26 percent of the nationalists were unemployed, while only one-tenth of the militants and conservatives were out of work. Why would a black nationalist feel that civil rights demonstrations helped? Presumably a demonstration was appropriate, but the integrationsist goal would be antithetical to theirs. In fact, most blacks support an end to collectivism externally imposed by whites. At the same time, they want to maintain their right and privilege to internally generated collectivism, that is black nationalism (Aberbach and Walker 1970, 1973:109; Barnett 1976:36–40; Pinderhughes 1977a).

How can the model explain the rapid emergence of such a distinctive group, one that was almost nonexistent previously? Because even black nationalists support "integrationist goals," that is, an end to "externally imposed collectivism," a significant proportion were previously identified as integrationists. Black nationalists urged an end to externally imposed collectivism so that they could pursue internally generated collectivism with impunity. Second, Marx used a specific group to define the limits of black nationalism, creating a highly sectarian index. When Aberbach and Walker tested blacks in Detroit on Black Power (a more general concept), the levels of support increased sharply. Whites, on the other hand, expressed strong disapproval for both views. As blacks participated in mass demonstrations, white support and approval fell from 24 percent in 1963 to 10 percent in 1964, which precipitated an increase in black mistrust and alienation and triggered increased interest in internal identification (*Gallup Poll* 1972:1723–24, 1828–29, 1884; Aberbach and Walker 1973:chap. 6).

Finally, how do these positions relate to each other over time? The militant, moderate, or (in this analysis) accommodationist positions are relative both to whites and to each other. How can this be represented in relation to figure 5.2? Think of the integrationist and nationalist portions of the horizontal continuum as progressively militant the further outward and downward from the accommodationist position one moves. Movement occurs in two ways. Individuals may shift position within the integrationist category, becoming more or less supportive, moving through the welfare away from the formal capitalist toward redistributive or Marxist positions. Individuals may change category altogether, moving from militant capitalist integrationist to militant redistributive nationalist to a Marxist nationalist.

Fantastic as these changes might seem, Amiri Baraka (né LeRoi Jones), Eldridge Cleaver, and others have already passed through them. Second, black perceptions of the relative militance of specific political positions shift over time so that the entire continuum contracts inward. Thus a militant integrationist in 1947 would have been considered an accommodationist by 1963. What had been considered beyond the bounds of political acceptability in 1947 had shifted to only slightly left or right of accommodationism by the mid-1960s. Ladd (1969) discusses the swift changes in political definition of militance in Winston-Salem and Greenville in the 1940s and 1950s.

The inward movement of the continuum occurs asymmetrically, since the major ideological focus may rest on either end. At any one time, the integrationist segment moved more swiftly from 1950 through 1965. Despite the 1964 Civil Rights Act and the 1965 Voting Rights Act, whites continued to view the elimination of collective status as militant, while black political activists decided the issue was an accommodationist, irrelevant question. Their concerns shifted to internally generated collectivism and economic issues, Black Power, and pan-Africanism.

On the welfare dimension, black politicians are more likely to end up at the capitalist end of the continuum than all other black political activists, but black politicians are as a whole more likely to emphasize redistributive perspectives than are other non-black politicians. At the same time, Wilson's and Ladd's "welfare" goals are not formally capitalist, since they emphasize publicly distributed rather than privately generated goods and services (Dorn 1979). Other variables have been excluded for the sake of simplicity. One important facet, for example, is an emphasis on African or Afro-American culture that appeared as part of the resurgence of interest in black nationalism in the late 1960s. An accurate presentation of this variable with the others requires a third dimension that would run from front to back on a flat plane through the present two-dimensionally represented model.

Racial subordination and capitalism involve some contradictions, since an entire sector of the population is subjected to unequal economic treatment, is restrained from acquisition of property and the accumulation of wealth, and in general participates in the economy in restricted fashion. Equitable distribution of property, capital, and enterprise requires some downward mobility by whites and the recognition of blacks as higher status by whites (Dorn 1979:chap. 4).

Once the collective externally imposed bars to economic participation are removed, there is underlying agreement on its meaning among black activists: the freedom to receive the full economic fruits of one's labors and to eliminate all restrictions to participation in upper-status and financially rewarding occupations. At this point, the politicians and political activists diverge, because they disagree on the form of the economic system that would remove residual economic differentiation based on race and class.

In summary, American racial politics is riddled with unforeseen complications and ideological puzzles because the racial issues mask the equally important economic basis of the problem. Each dimension contains a series of positions that interact with the other and expand the range of political alternatives far beyond what can be developed from the Wilson typology. The racial dimension is perhaps the most difficult to settle philosophically because it reflects a psychological as well as political ambivalence that saps the energy that can be applied toward a solution. Since whites have radically and rapidly changed their sentiments from time to time on racial policy, blacks have been uncertain how much energy they ought to devote to changing political institutions and, having changed them, how to respond when whites' sentiments change again.[19]

Conflicting Dimensions

How do blacks resolve the coexistence of these two ideological dimensions? Does that resolution correlate within the black population with any identifiable factors, such as class or socioeconomic status? An important, continuing philosophical debate within the black community has raged for over a century over which of the two dimensions is primary. How one answers the questions explains the strategy used to resolve the problem.

Those who emphasize status or argue that it is primary focus on the racial or the political dimension. They support adjustment or elimination of collective status in such examples as DuBois's talented tenth, Garvey's Back to Africa movement, the civil rights movement, and the Republic of New Africa. Those who feel the basis is economic argue that the development of material welfare or economic resources is primary and the elimination of political or racial restrictions is unimportant. They focus on the economic dimension. Booker T. Washington argued for separate economic development in his Atlanta Exposition speech; Marcus Garvey emphasized economic independence; and W. E. B. DuBois shifted his concern from the political to the economic dimension in the 1930s. The Nation of Islam and the Nixon-era black capitalists focused on the economic dimension. These individuals and groups played on one or another end of their dominant dimension and placed less but nevertheless significant emphasis on the minor level.

There has not been nor will there be an authoritative resolution of the two-dimensional conflict. These two dimensions interact constantly, with fault lines at a number of points. Many of those who focus on the status dimension cluster at the far integrationist end, since they strongly oppose any institution or policy that would allow the survival of racially identifiable groupings, whether internally generated or externally imposed. In effect, they have a strong, even phobic, aversion to racially distinguishable groupings as a result of the psychological residues of segregation. The NAACP under Walter White's and Roy Wilkins's leadership consistently resisted external and internal pressures to incorporate nationalist and economic philosophy, thus the break with DuBois; but both the NAACP and the Urban League have consistently emphasized public-sector activities and public-private cooperation. The Urban League traditionally worked in close touch with big business and in the early 1920s set as its mission reshaping the styles, habits, speech, bearing, and work habits of black migrants so they would fit into the urban industrial work force (Strickland 1966).

At the other end of the status continuum, nationalists are as phobic about coalitions with whites as integrationists are about any residual collective recognition. Stokeley Carmichael worked in civil rights organizations that were actively engaged in formal coalitions with whites and that integrated whites into predominantly black organizations. He developed a critique of those portions of the black leadership willing to make coalitions and specified the terms on which they were possible. He argued that successful coalitions stem from mutual self-interest, independent power bases, and specific goals, in short, from a more coherently black perspective (Barbour 1968; Carmichael and Hamilton 1967:79–80; Pouissant and Ladner 1968).

But Carmichael and Hamilton were latecomers to nationalism. Others, such as Marcus Garvey, Elijah Muhammad, and later the Chicago and California nationalists of the post 1960s (poet Don Lee and political activist and political scientist Maulauna Karenga), excluded any alliances with whites, even to the point of opposing Marxism. Karenga later moved to the left, along with Amiri Baraka and many others, but Haki Madbhuti (Don Lee) continued to emphasize black nationalism. Manning Marable quotes Shawna Maglangbayan: "Marxism-Leninism [is] a reactionary and white supremacist ideology whose chief aim is to maintain Aryan world hegemony once capitalism is overthrown" (Marable 1980:85).

Despite the integrationist concerns of major black organizations such as the NAACP, the nationalist impulse has found broad mass response in the Afro-American population from time to time. Marcus Garvey's 1920s campaign, the Nation of Islam, and Black Power galvanized and restructured the political ideas of large portions of the black population. On two occasions black political leadership has attempted to solve its disagreements on collective questions. In 1936, 585 black organizations formed the National Negro Congress. The congress eventually collapsed under the combined weight of numerous broad and complex philosophies that attempted to crowd all their varied economic and political considerations onto the rather vague platform of racial identity. The Communist party also held an ideological repugnance for the nationalist implications of the organization and the party's political manipulation of the congress, which destroyed the collective confidence and trust of the participants.[20]

Just as Carmichael's commitment to black nationalism developed out of his reaction to efforts to integrate the civil rights movement, blacks who integrated white institutions during the 1960s and early 1970s created a new generation of black professional, academic, and social organizations.[21]

Black leadership again mobilized around nationalist goals in 1972 in the National Black Political Convention, in which a vast array of black groups including Amiri Baraka's New Ark, labor organizations, and the Congressional Black Caucus (CBC) attempted to form a coherent political alliance.[22] The CBC grew faint at the combined nationalist and socialist impulses that emerged from the leadership and mass level during the convention. Poor or nonexistent funding and organizational structure and the complex process of coordinating hundreds of groups confounded the broad range of philosophical views represented in the organization and aborted its full emergence by the mid-1970s (Barnett 1975:34–50, 1977:17–26, 1982; Henry 1987; Marable 1980).

A second question is whether black political beliefs and goals correlate in any consistent way with socioeconomic status? By the 1940s and 1960s black political activists had begun to criticize the black upper class represented by the NAACP and the Urban League, because they emphasized the integrationist end of the status dimension and the capitalist end of the welfare dimension. The NAACP included members more likely to be middle- and upper-class blacks and who were more likely to be philosophical conservatives and capitalists (Garfinkel 1969; Marx 1969:112–21; Pinderhughes 1983).

However, the black middle class faces contradictions if it emphasizes integrationist goals. Robert Smith explains that before 1965 the black middle and upper class was based on private professional activity, such as law, medicine, religion, and undertaking—professions in which economic livelihood was based on a highly concentrated, segregated black population. Full implementation of an integrationist position would have eliminated their economic base (Smith 1981). Wilson reported, "Some Negro doctors felt they might lose Negro patients to white doctors if integration were a fact, but a Negro militant, presumably not an MD, discounted the importance of their fears[:] . . . 'you have to be prepared to accept a temporary period of suffering if you are going to gain anything in the longrun'" (1960a: 219).

After 1965, the public sector expanded and, in the process, supported the growth of a new black middle class. Dahl might have predicted that such a group would be ideologically conservative or at least more heterogeneous, but Hamilton found that this group "does not move to the right. . . . In fact, tentative data . . . show they tend to move further toward the liberal progressive pole" (1976:244).

Thomas Sowell, Walter Williams, and other black conservatives fear that liberal black leaders and political organizations misrepresent the political beliefs of the black masses, which are fundamentally conservative. While economic issues subtracted of racial content elicit "conservative" (opposition to public-sector intervention) responses from blacks, the same issues linked to racial questions produce heavy support for government action. Banfield and Wilson found unpredictably high levels of support for public-regarding values among blacks in the 1960s. Gallup polls show black approval of educational vouchers by a substantial margin, but when asked to vote on tuition tax credits (in effect, a delayed voucher), Washington, D.C.'s largely black electorate rejected the plan by an overwhelming margin of approximately 8 to 1. Although the ideological sources of their cynicism and political liberalism differed, Shingles showed that black lower- and middle-class political attitudes were very similar (Banfield and Wilson 1964:883–84, 1971:1058).[23]

Just as race obscured the economic origins of racial slavery, the racial dimension overpowers the consistent expression of differing economic interests within the black population. Predictions of political position based on race are more accurate than those based on class. Marcus Garvey and Elijah Muhammad appealed to the "black masses" using black nationalism and black capitalism with Christian and Islamic undertones; Martin Luther King moved the same groups with nonviolent and integrationist appeals. The Black Panthers won a positive response from Oakland's black working poor using black nationalist and mildly Marxist appeals. Although economic issues are more intractable, serious questions for the working and nonworking poor, this group has not been particularly responsive to the Communist party's mobilizing efforts because of the party's ideological commitment to avoiding such philosophical contradictions as nationalism. In failing to manipulate racial issues, however, the party has also failed to win the support of the black population.

Conflict between those with philosophical views arising out of the status dimension as opposed to the welfare dimension also played a role in the recent debates over William J. Wilson's analysis of changing economic status within the black population in *The Declining Significance of Race* (1978). Many of Wilson's critics argued that he ignored or undervalued the importance of race. The conflict erupted because Wilson attempted to readjust perceptions of the relative primacy of the status or racial dimension downward in favor of the welfare dimension. Wilson drew criticism from all along the status dimension when he suggested that:

> [While] the previous barriers were usually designed to control and restrict the entire black population, the new barriers create hardships essentially for the black underclass; whereas the old barriers were based explicitly on racial motivations derived from intergroup contact, the new barriers have racial significance only in their consequences, not in their origins. In short, whereas the old barriers bore the pervasive features of racial oppression, the new barriers indicate an important and emerging form of class subordination (1978:1–2).

Wilson did not abandon the significance of the racial dimension; he simply argued that race was no longer as consistently restrictive for all blacks as it had been in the past.

Conclusion: The Case Against Black Political Integration

The racial dimension and the economic dimension each offer powerful interpretations for the experience of blacks in the United States, but neither is sufficient in and of itself. Yet black political activists tend to prefer one or the other, or to prefer that one dominate the other, rather than that they function with equal weight.

Ideology and organization also tend to fall into two different patterns. The simplest, least complicated strategy for mounting a successful political appeal to the black population is an emphasis on racial ideology, since racism operates collectively, against the group as a whole, regardless of economic status. Before 1965 segregation in the north and the south meant there was very little differentiation by socioeconomic status within the black population. Blacks of all economic backgrounds and color respond viscerally to a racial appeal. Several patterns, therefore, have occurred. Blacks intermittently attempted to organize themselves into one overarching organization, but those organizations consistently failed. Organizations that drew from upper-, middle-, and lower-status blacks, such as the NAACP, emphasized general racial and political concerns that apply to nearly all blacks rather than economic issues that affect some blacks differently and about which there is little agreement.

Thus, even though there are two dimensions, the racial issues offer some generally stronger bases for political unity. When black politicians and organizations manipulate material from the racial dimension, they are more stable and more successful because the opportunities for agreement are greater.

Earlier, I noted that black voting participation is sometimes quite high. The explanation for increased voting among blacks is as follows. Since race is the single most important factor that affects the economic, political, and social status of the black population (and as Verba and Nie and Shingles have shown, racial self-consciousness increases black cooperative activity), then racial self-consciousness or awareness, generated either by positive ideological incentives (that is, those which tap the dimension of race), offered by a white or especially by a black candidate, or negative incentives which heighten black voters' awareness of continued or increased racial domination, increase black voter turnout to unusual levels (Pinderhughes 1985).

Moreover the model of political beliefs that initially applied only to nonelectoral politics also easily incorporates electoral politics by subsuming it within the left end of the status continuum and the upper end of the economic continuum. After all, recommendations for civil rights and integration logically include participation in political institutions.

In general, however, organizations are more effective in attracting and controlling their membership when they focus on specific economic issues and employ divisible material incentives. In effect, the philosophical and organizational logics conflict, putting disorganizing pressures on each. To maintain organizational membership and order, one emphasizes economic selective incentives, but these cut through the theoretical logic of race which, as this chapter has already shown, is an extremely powerful motivation for black political and organizational participation (Downs 1967; Olson 1968; Pinderhughes 1983).

If black political beliefs and theories are so complex, why was James Q. Wilson's analysis so limited? Charles Branham's observations on Chicago's black politicians provide some insight: "Pre-migration black politics was formed from the confluence of post–Civil War black middle-class ideology and black acceptance of established conventions of urban ethnic politics. . . . Black middle-class politics [sought] individual or status rewards from politics [and it was] generally conservative." Branham concedes the accuracy of Wilson's and Katznelson's analyses, upon which the preceding quote is based, but concludes: "What is missing in these generally admirable observations is the particular historical context of black political development. Morris, Wright and DePriest did not spring full-blown from the head of Zeus. The generally conservative and essentially individualistic pattern of black politics emerged from a specific tradition of black and Chicago politics" (Branham 1977:249–52).

Wilson's simpler ideological analysis arose from the powerful constraints imposed upon black politicians and black electoral politics. On economic issues, the Roosevelt and Cermak administrations eliminated the consideration of radical Marxist alternatives. Even in Wilson's study, divisible welfare benefits were not strictly capitalist since the city distributed them in exchange for black political support. Roosevelt also implemented symbolic reforms; he consulted his black kitchen "cabinet" and used his wife Eleanor as an informal ambassador to the black population. In the face of the Democratic party's historical position on race, Roosevelt's sympathetic posture was a dramatic improvement. Allswang reports that Cermak sought black support, but he did not run on a platform of racial reform. In fact the Democrats allegedly used racist materials in the 1931 mayoral campaign (1971: 159).

Status goals, on the other hand, were generally unattainable. Policy decisions were rarely made apart from racist considerations. In the few instances when Chicago officials decided to distribute benefits on a nondiscriminatory basis, the policy was opposed with such brute force and violence at the grass-roots level that the decision was either overturned or implemented in a highly incremental fashion (Banfield 1965; Hirsch 1983; Philpott 1978).

Black politicians thus faced three problems: how to minimize the articulation of the dizzying philosophical combinations available to black activists; how to hold and maintain a substantial portion of black political activists' interest; and how to express political interests that appealed to the average black voter and black political activist, while also fitting into the organizational and ideological structures of Chicago in the 1920s and 1930s?

In chapter 3, I showed that competitive partisanship broadened the range of political benefits that could be offered and increased the possibilities, though not necessarily the probabilities, of substantive policy implementation. Monopolized partisanship streamlined these attempts and strengthened the control of the machine over relationships and interaction with the voter, but they minimized the substantive political issues with which the machine had to deal and stabilized the operations of the political system as a whole. In the electoral arena, blacks turned from a competitive political system of the 1920s to the highly limited electoral alternatives of the 1930s. They also faced the austerity of the electoral arena as a whole, relative to the rich complexity of their political belief system. In chapter 4, I showed how the existence of racial hierarchy constricted black electoral alternatives in comparison to Italian and Polish opportunities for descriptive representation and for political control.

DuBois, Baraka, and Malcolm X (Cruse 1967:126) are men who exemplify the philosophical journeys possible while searching for an appropriate combination of the racial and economic dimensions. The result is something that applies directly to social life, but which has relevance to political ideas: "As members of the Negro slum culture grow older, there is the depressive strategy in which goals are increasingly constricted to the bare necessities for survival (not as a social being but simply as an organism). This is the strategy of 'I don't bother anybody and I hope nobody's gonna bother me: I am simply going through the motions to keep body (but not soul) together'" (Rainwater 1966:206–7, quoted in Marx 1969:88). The audacious dramatic variety of black politicians of the 1920s, Edward Wright, Dan Jackson, and Oscar DePriest, faded to the more restrained leadership of William Dawson, the organization's man.[24]

Fundamentally, Wilson, Kilson, Dahl, and others equate black and European groups' interests as ethnically equal. This means it should have been philosophically and organizationally possible to integrate black political demands in coherent fashion into the existing political order. But for this to have been the case, black political interests would have had to focus on the tangible or welfare side of the dimensions at the upper, nonredistributive, capitalist end and to ignore any adjustments on the status dimension, since the machine ignored collective issues except for the formulation of symbolic descriptive representation, in other words, the balanced ticket. Wilson states, "The chief consequence of the use of material incentives is that the organization and its executive pay relatively little attention to stated purposes even to the substantive goals implied by their activities" (1973:37).

Black politicians faced complex philosophical and strategic problems, given the range of interests to which they had to appeal. With a variety of positions about which there was more disagreement than agreement, black politicians were more likely to express views that reflected the lowest common denominator and upon which the most agreement could be generated. Race was thus more likely to be emphasized than economic issues, but by 1931 the machine foreclosed that policy option. Black politicians were left with selective, divisible material incentives to political participation and with political office itself as a reward. Racial status was raised only by injudicious, naive politicians or by activists uninterested in electoral politics. The following chapters pursue these political restraints.

In this chapter I have shown how black political attitudes and beliefs sharply reject the legitimacy of conventional American political institutions and authority symbols. Blacks have created a complex system of political alternatives to those offered within the framework of American politics, one considerably more diverse and multidimensional than the system of status and welfare goals proposed by Wilson over two decades ago. Black political integration by the pluralist model thus faces theoretical problems from a second direction. The first problem, outlined in chapters 2 and 3, arose from the high degree of racial discrimination inherent in American society, which posed serious barriers to black political integration. In chapter 4, I described the limitations that were directly applied to expansion in black representation or to metropolitan representation.

The second problem arises from the political philosophy of black citizens, who expect to find integrationist as well as nationalist values within the polity; this is perhaps most daringly and wryly summarized by the title of a recent work by Charles Henry and Lorenzo Morris, *The Chit'lin Controversy* (1978), and by a story recounted therein. Upon seating himself in a newly integrated restaurant in Washington, D.C., a Negro was perplexed after being told by a waiter that there were no chitterlings, turnip greens, ham hocks, black-eyed peas, or hog jowl on the menu: "The Negro put his glasses back in their case, pushed his chair back and rose slowly. 'You folks,' he observed thoughtfully, 'You folks just ain't ready for integration'" (Morris and Henry 1978:2).

6

Crime and Punishment in Chicago

> "Sure we have crime here. We will always have crime. Chicago is just like any other big city. You can get a man's arm broken for so much, a leg for so much or beaten up for so much. Just like New York, excepting we print our crime and they don't."
>
> —Mayor William "Big Bill" Hale Thompson

> "I'm for Big Bill hook, line and sinker."
>
> —Vincent "the Schemer" Drucci

The influence of blacks, Italians, and Poles on the administration of criminal justice is the subject of this chapter. Since illegitimate businesses played an important role in economic life in the black and Italian communities, restrictive enforcement of the law would have limited their abilities to prosper. As these groups increased their political participation and descriptive representation in elective and appointive positions in city government, they should also have been able to increase their impact on the formation and implementation of substantive public policies such as criminal justice.

According to the pluralist model, blacks and Italians would have sought to minimize any differences in the administration of criminal justice since their economic profiles become more heterogeneous rather than more homogeneous over time. According to the model of the political machine, racial and ethnic groups sought to maximize the differential response of the political system through selective benefits. They sought to protect offenses associated with business, illegitimate or otherwise, from prosecution. Prosecution of ethnic or racial groups should, therefore, relate inversely to political participation. As political influence increases, susceptibility to political prosecution should decline, which should be reflected in the statistics of arrests and prosecution.

Racial and Ethnic Groups and the Underworld of Business

The Volstead Act and the National Prohibition Act of October 28, 1919, created opportunities for illegitimate business on a vast scale. The demand for drinkable alcohol, to some extent actively generated by underworld organizations, made an expanding, highly profitable new market available to those who had no scruples about violating the law. Blacks, Italians, and Poles participated in different types of crime in different ways. Ogburn and Tibbitts's study of nationality groups in organized crime showed that Italian, Irish, and Jewish "owners and managers" accounted for three-quarters of that entire group, although Italian managers were a slightly larger percentage than the other two (1930). Blacks equalled about 12 percent, which meant that all of these groups were involved in organized crime to a much higher degree than their proportions in the population.[1]

As a group, Italians concentrated on the production and distribution of illegal alcohol and on the development and management of a citywide criminal organization. Blacks worked in the gambling and prostitution houses and cabarets on the south side and in the development and operation of the southside policy wheels. A few Poles were involved in criminal activities, but as a group they were the least active of the three. Blacks, Poles, and Italians, then, participated in different sectors of the underworld. Italian organization was based on closely knit, familial and ethnically organized fraternal associations or gangs. The Genna brothers brewed alcohol on Chicago's west side, while Capone's brothers—Ralph, Frank, Albert, and James—were involved in his illegitimate business (Nelli 1970a:218–19; Pasley 1930:174). The Irish frequently organized athletic clubs, open public associations incorporating large numbers of people, which provided the infrastructure and supplied the manpower for illegal activities. The Ragen Colts were active for over thirty years and at one time counted over two thousand members on the south side. The Hamburgers continue to hold parades and support candidates today. Blacks organized juvenile gangs less frequently than Italians or Irish, and they were rarely stable or wealthy enough to support clubhouses. The Jones brothers, sons of an Evanston Baptist minister, operated the most important black policy wheels (a form of lottery, called "the numbers" in eastern cities) in the 1930s and 1940s.[2]

The Irish created, but the Italians quickly captured, control of the organization of crime in Chicago. In the late 1880s, Irish first ward aldermen "Bathhouse" John Coughlin and "Hinky Dink" Michael Kenna allied with the vice dealers in the levee district around Clark and Taylor Streets to provide protection from the police in exchange for votes. When Jim Colosimo organized a group of streetsweepers in the first ward, he caught Kenna's and Coughlin's attention, and they made him a precinct captain. Between 1900 and 1920 he became well known as the operator of a legitimate business, Colosimo's Cafe, which attracted a locally and nationally known clientele. Colosimo also joined illegal saloons and houses of prostitution into the largest syndicate in the city by 1914, but his reign ended in May 1920 when he was murdered by "unknown" assailants. Colosimo's nephew, John Torrio, assumed leadership of the syndicate and evidence suggests he took his position by force. Torrio faced the same situation a few years later but survived the attack and retired from the business. This led the way for his agent, Al Capone, whom Torrio had imported from New York as a bodyguard (in the same way the Colosimo had brought him), to take control (Peterson 1952:107–8; 1963).[3]

Colosimo and Torrio specialized in brothels, although Torrio also pioneered in the new market to produce bootleg liquor. During the period between 1920 and 1928, the Colosimo-Torrio-Capone syndicate incorporated prostitution, bootlegging, and gambling within its jurisdiction, which was an important innovation and organizational expansion; until 1920 gambling had been controlled by Mont Tennes of the north side, who had allowed lesser figures in other parts of the city to operate betting parlors and bookie joints in which he controlled all the apparatus that communicated information about racing results (see Lashley 1929:chap. 19).

Prohibition and Mayor William Dever's administration so altered the political and economic environment that they produced the heyday of Chicago's underworld. Prohibition created a huge new market for illegal business and made any organization involved in the production and distribution of alcohol a target for competition or takeover. Simultaneously, the reform-oriented Dever administration ended conventional arrangements between gangsters and law enforcement agents, which resulted in intense and open competition for control of territory. Two major conflicts erupted in the 1920s. Italian and Irish gangs fought for control of crime at the metropolitan level and Italians fought each other for control of the Unione Siciliana, which was an umbrella organization for a variety of economic and fraternal activities among Italians, including the organization of westside alcohol producers.[4]

The struggle for control of the Unione erupted in 1924 when the president of the Board of Directors of the Unione, Mike Merlo, died. The Genna family, which operated a large number of small stills on the west side and was allied with the Deneen Republicans, wanted to appoint the next head of the Unione, as did Capone. The Unione was important because alcohol production had been decentralized after the increased pressure of the Dever administration was augmented by active federal enforcement of prohibition. This meant that groups such as the Gennas, who had obtained government licenses to operate an alcohol distillery, actually produced for the illegitimate market. U.S. District Attorney Edwin Olson reported to Senate judiciary committee hearings in 1926 that there was virtually no effective enforcement of prohibition before 1923.[5]

Merlo's death encouraged the Gennas to seek control of the Unione for money, for prestige, and because it would give them a near monopoly over the manufacture of alcohol in the entire Chicago region. Capone won control by the end of 1925 by killing as many of the Genna brothers and their successors as chose to name themselves head of the organization. When Capone's gunners had murdered Angelo, Mike, and Antonio Genna in less than two months, the remaining three brothers decided to move to Sicily for their health (Lashley 1929: 1035; Lyle 1960:145–46, 209; Peterson 1952:109–11).

One of their lieutenants, Sam "Samoots" Amatuna, lasted about four months as head of the Unione before being killed, after which Capone named as head his original designee, Antonio Lombardo, in December 1925. He served until 1928, when Capone installed a friend, Pasqualino Lolardo, who served until his murder in January 1929 by the Moran-Aiello alliance. This prompted the famous St. Valentine's Day Massacre a month later, in which Capone's forces murdered most of the Moran group, although Moran escaped injury (Lyle 1960:204; Pasley 1930:109–11).

In the second major conflict, Italian and Irish gangs fought for control of the citywide syndicate; the Colosimo-Torrio-Capone leadership group faced a number of contenders in the 1920s, but its strongest opposition came from the O'Banion-Moran group based in the forty-second and forty-third wards on the near north side. Torrio attempted to neutralize O'Banion in 1924 by inviting him to share the profits in the free and unpoliced western Cook County town of Cicero. O'Banion alienated the syndicate and its allies by refusing to share his profits in the Cicero enterprises and by supporting Republican Robert Crowe for state's attorney over the Democratic candidate, Michael Igoe, Torrio's lawyer.[6] The Gennas were reportedly responsible for O'Banion's murder in his flower shop near Holy Name Cathedral in November 1924, which sent the O'Banionites, led by "Bugs" Moran, into a murderous rage.[7] They attacked both Torrio and Capone. Torrio retired to Europe with a serious injury, while Capone escaped unscathed to lead the syndicate. George Moran allied with the Aiellos, and Hymie Weiss, a member of the Moran group, clandestinely joined with the Saltis and Oberta southside groups in an effort to undermine Capone. Some killed each other, but Capone triumphed because he consolidated control of all these groups; he competed and organized without hesitation, fear, or distaste for violence. Capone outmaneuvered all of his underworld opponents and outweighed them all in sophistication, in organizational ability, but most importantly in ruthlessness (Pasley 1930:54).[8]

After William Hale Thompson's return to the mayor's office in 1927, a period of relaxation ensued in which the transparently friendly relations between the world of illegitimate business and the world of politics shocked even normally callous Chicago. After Cermak's election and assassination, Capone's imprisonment for tax evasion in 1932, and the end of prohibition, Frank Nitti and then Tony Accardo assumed control of the syndicate, and the underworld's conflicts receded from the public eye. By the time prohibition was repealed in 1933, Capone had already begun to move into legitimate business, government bureaucracy, and labor unions. Organized crime passed through the same stages as legitimate operations: jurisdictional competition, expansion to monopolize if possible, and coexistence and price fixing otherwise.

Only one Polish gang engaged in high-level competition for control of criminal activities, but it was located on the southwest side near the stockyards and outside the institutional center of Polish Chicago. Poles such as Hymie Weiss were involved in organized crime, but all of the literature suggests they were scarce in numbers and weak in organization.

Gosnell and Drake and Cayton identified black owners of gambling houses as "policy kings,"[9] but their operations were relatively small and all were circumscribed by the boundaries of black neighborhoods (Drake and Cayton 1970:chap. 6; Gosnell 1967:127). In the early 1920s Mushmouth Johnson and Robert Motts owned cafes and gambling spots. Johnson allied with Kenna and Coughlin of the first ward for protection. Motts subsidized voter registration and get-out-the-vote drives, in return for which he demanded political jobs. At the turn of the century Henry Teenan Jones operated a club at Fifty-sixth and Lake Park in predominantly white Hyde Park. The club was patronized by black servants from the area, but according to Jones, "the real foundation of my business was whites. . . . The leading lawyer in the hotel used to say to white visitors and gay slummers, 'Go to Teenan'" (Gosnell 1967:129n.51). After racial antagonism forced Jones and other blacks out of Hyde Park in 1910, he moved into the predominantly black second ward and opened the Elite No. 1 at Thirty-third and State and the No. 2 at Thirty-fifth and State.[10] Gosnell reported that Jones "confessed . . . he had been head of a gambling syndicate" in a trial in which he, Oscar DePriest, and Captain Stephen K. Healy of the Chicago police were charged with conspiring to allow gambling houses and houses of prostitution to operate, and with bribing the police. Jones and Healy turned state's evidence but DePriest was found innocent (Gosnell 1967:130, 172–74). There is no evidence that his syndicate was linked with a citywide organization.

After Jones, Daniel Jackson became the next head of the gambling and policy operations within the black community. Jackson was an undertaker, a political activist (for example, he was a Republican candidate for the county commission in 1900), and head of several gambling halls. Gosnell described him as "head of a great syndicate," controlling vice, bootlegging, and gambling (Gosnell 1967:131). Lyle reported that Jackson, with the help of black alderman Louis B. Anderson, sold one of his clubs, the Pekin Inn, to the city. It later became the site of the city courthouse and police station (Lyle 1960:137–39). Although he controlled operations within the black belt, he was an associate of Capone and Capone's gambling representative, Jimmy Mondi. He did not compete for control of activities in other areas.[11]

By the 1930s gambling and policy operations provided lucrative and increasing income for their owners. The Jones brothers' (Edward, George, and McKissock) daily income grew from $2,000 in 1930 to $10,000 in 1938, during the heart of the depression. Drake and Cayton reported that three policy companies operating in the city grossed $18 million per year. Between 1939 and 1950 the two companies owned by the Jones brothers alone netted over $8 million, or an average of $700,000 per year. Between 1945 and 1950 the various policy companies took in over $150 million. Policy operations were organized in 1931 into a syndicate formed to provide political protection to independent operators. Seven black and three white men contributed $7,500 per week for political protection.[12]

Some of Capone's allies were members of this syndicate. A Cook County grand jury indicted seven black and three white policy men in 1942: Iley Kelly, Jim Knight, Julian Black, James "Big Jim" Martin, Edward Jones, George Jones, McKissock Jones, Julius Benvenuti, Pat Manno, and Pete Tremont. Gosnell identified Benvenuti as a policy figure and a member of the second ward Democratic organization in 1935. Manno and Tremont had operated the Standard Golden Gate (policy) Company since 1929. The Kefauver investigation of the early 1950s listed all of the above as still operating in the city (Gosnell 1967:134n; Truman Gibson, Jr., interview, Aug. 27, 1975).[13]

The Internal Revenue Service prosecuted George Jones and sent him to jail in 1940, "(reputedly) taking the rap for the family's alleged collective evasion of income tax payments" (Drake and Cayton 1970: 490). While in the federal penitentiary in Terre Haute, Indiana, Jones boasted to Sam Giancana, a Capone associate, about the profits of his policy wheels, about cash in twenty-five banks, and the brothers' net worth, which exceeded $1 million. In 1946, when both had been released from jail, Edward Jones was kidnapped and later released for $100,000 ransom; that amount was listed under the receipts of Jake Guzik, a long-time Capone ally, that same year. Edward and George moved to Mexico after this and continued to receive income from their wheels, although in lesser amounts than in previous years (De Maris 1969:chap 1; Peterson 1952:292; Special Committee to Investigate Crime in Interstate Commerce 1951:1163–75).

Drake and Cayton emphasized black control of policy and gambling, citing an explicit agreement with Capone that blacks controlled gambling in return for their noninterference in the liquor trade (1970:485). The general attitude in the black belt was that policy was a black-owned and operated "honest" business that provided jobs and money for investment. In fact, most of the profits from policy were "pouring into the pockets of the Capone syndicate . . . notwithstanding the efforts of both Negro and white politicians to perpetuate a myth that the policy racket was operated and controlled exclusively by Negroes" (Peterson 1952:195).[14] Landesco reported that Capone's gambling representative, Jimmy Mondi, required 25 percent of the earnings of gambling establishments in return for operating and protection privileges.

Black underworld activities were permitted at the behest of more powerful forces in the city. Black policy kings did not attempt to compete for the larger stakes available, but accepted the operational limits set by the Chicago syndicate.[15] With revenues from liquor production and sales and other operations estimated at $105 million in 1927, the syndicate leadership was content to allow policy to operate in black neighborhoods without any direct interference on their part. But as the profits from policy wheels increased, as prohibition ended, and as criminal activities in the city became more organized in the 1930s, policy operations became an ever more attractive object for external control (Lashley 1929:chap. 20; Pasley 1930:61–62).

Black participation in the underworld was as segregated as it was in the rest of Chicago's economy. Capone, O'Banion, and others restricted black operations by function and geography; neither Jackson nor the Jones brothers attempted to set up operations in Cicero, nor were they invited to move in with Dion O'Banion on the north side.[16] During prohibition Capone competed with the Gennas to control the production and distribution of alcohol and, when federal officials closed the breweries, to handle the importation and distribution of alcohol from the Canadian border and the East Coast. Blacks were completely excluded from these most profitable of the illegal activities; they were relatively free to operate only in the area of policy, and that only through the 1920s (Chicago Commission on Race Relations 1922; Gosnell 1967:118–21; Lashley 1929:912–19; Reckless 1933:25–31, chaps. 1 and 4).

Organized crime welcomed blacks most frequently by providing employment for them in many of the saloons, houses of prostitution, and black and tan cafes as maids, porters, prostitutes, waiters, and servants. Thus, although organized crime complimented Irish political success and supplemented Italian difficulties in economics and politics, it reinforced the barriers blacks faced in housing, in industry, and in politics. If they found it difficult to be hired in the steel mills or stockyards, there was always work in the bordellos and gambling houses of the underworld. On the whole, blacks worked at lowest-level jobs or patronized the businesses in the underworld. Black policy kings were important figures within the black belt because of the funds they supplied to black politicians, churches, and organizations, but the color line barred them from citywide competition for leadership of the underworld (Drake and Cayton 1970:488–89). Italians organized crime or produced illegal products but were rarely directly involved in street-level public violations of the law. Blacks operated gambling and prostitution houses with or without syndicate protection and staffed their operations in the black belt. The higher the level of organization and the less public the activity, the more effective the protection between the violator and the criminal justice system.

Organizational ties paid off in the day-to-day business operations of the underworld. When Dion O'Banion was killed, Police Chief Morgan Collins noted that he was responsible for the deaths of twenty-five people, yet he had served only twelve months in jail. Landesco's study of Illinois crime showed that the police knew few of the most well known of underworld figures officially, with no recorded arrests or convictions in the Police Identification Bureau despite the fact that their participation in these illegal activities was well known. Torrio was indicted for robbing the Sieben brewery only because Police Chief Morgan Collins handed his prisoners over to U.S. District Attorney Olson rather than to Republican State's Attorney Crowe (Lashley 1929:914–916; Peterson 1952:125).

Protection for blacks involved in organized crime was highly inconsistent. Teenan Jones, Oscar DePriest, and Dan Jackson and all the gambling houses in the black belt operated with police protection. The police raided those businesses unwilling to pay and pressed them into cooperation. On the other hand, Teenan Jones and Oscar De Priest were indicted in 1917 by Democratic State's Attorney Maclay Hoyne for gambling offenses.[17] Daniel Jackson and Oscar DePriest were indicted in 1928 by a special grand jury for southside vice and gambling. Newspaper accounts noted the ties between crime and politics: "Disclosures regarding conditions in the second and third wards of this city show that these conditions could have existed only through police protection" (*New York Times,* Sept. 30, 1928; see also *Chicago Daily News Almanac* 1926:821). The 1917 indictments were brought by a Democratic state's attorney who wished to wound a Republican opponent, Mayor Thompson. Oscar DePriest was forced to withdraw from his aldermanic race for reelection. The 1928 indictments were brought by a grand jury and First Special Assistant Attorney General David Stansbury, under the direction of Oscar E. Carlstrom, attorney general under Governor Len Small, Republican opponent of Thompson. They sought to punish Jackson for his alliance with Thompson because Jackson had replaced Deneen's ally Wright as a Thompson ward committeeman. The charges against Jackson remained in force when he died in 1929 (John Leonard East, interview, 1974; Gosnell 1967:133). The partisan interpretation of the latter incident is substantiated by the fact that Stansbury was reported by the *Chicago Tribune* to have been attempting to "show that these two men made large contributions to the recent primary campaign in behalf of State's Attorney Robert E. Crowe, and that in return they were permitted to influence the policemen in their territory" (*Chicago Tribune,* Aug. 17, 1928). Illinois Attorney General William Harrison's declared "opposition" to gangster leadership could hardly have been more closely linked to political considerations.

Thus, while black underworld figures paid for and received protection for their day-to-day activities, they were not always immune from criminal prosecution, while Torrio, Capone, and others served time only after federal charges and prosecution.[18]

Racial and Ethnic Violations of Law

Statistical reports of criminal activity in Chicago show that there were radical variations in arrest and prosecution by race and ethnicity. The Chicago police recorded arrests by nationality from 1878 through 1931, charges, felonies, and misdemeanors by nationality from 1905 through 1931, and convictions from 1913 through 1931.[19] The data show surges and declines in citywide and in group arrests, charges, and convictions. The number of arrests increased sharply from 1889 through the late 1890s, steadily in the years before World War I, and surged upward in the mid-1920s. Charges and convictions show similar changes (see figures 6.1, 6.2, and 6.3); these variations correlate with the long bloody Pullman strike and the economic depression of the early 1890s and the prewar years of high immigration. The increased levels of arrests, charges, and convictions in the mid-1920s correlate with the reform administration of Mayor William Dever, who discarded the traditional alliances between the city's policitical leaders and illegitimate business, which set off notorious Chicago gang wars for control of the production and distribution of liquor, for the control of gambling joints, and for control of territory.

But how do blacks, Italians, and Poles compare over time and with each other? Although blacks equalled more than four percent of the population before 1920 and only 8.2 percent by 1940, they were arrested and charged with crimes more often than Italians (at 4.6

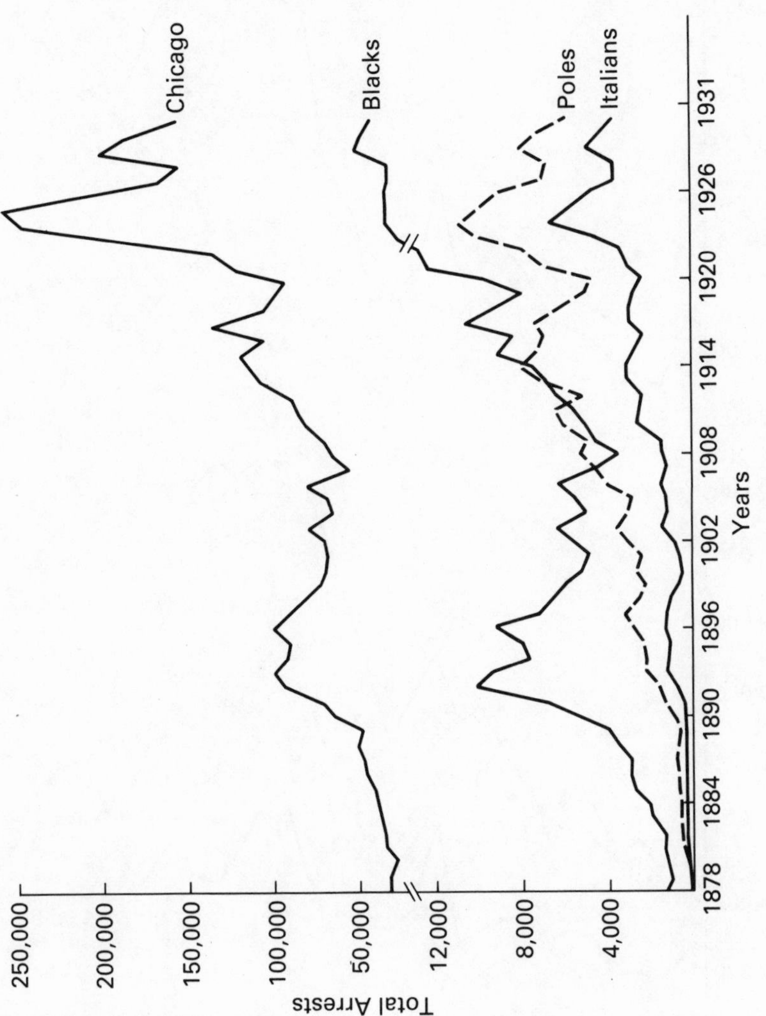

Figure 6.1 Arrests by Nationality, 1878–1931

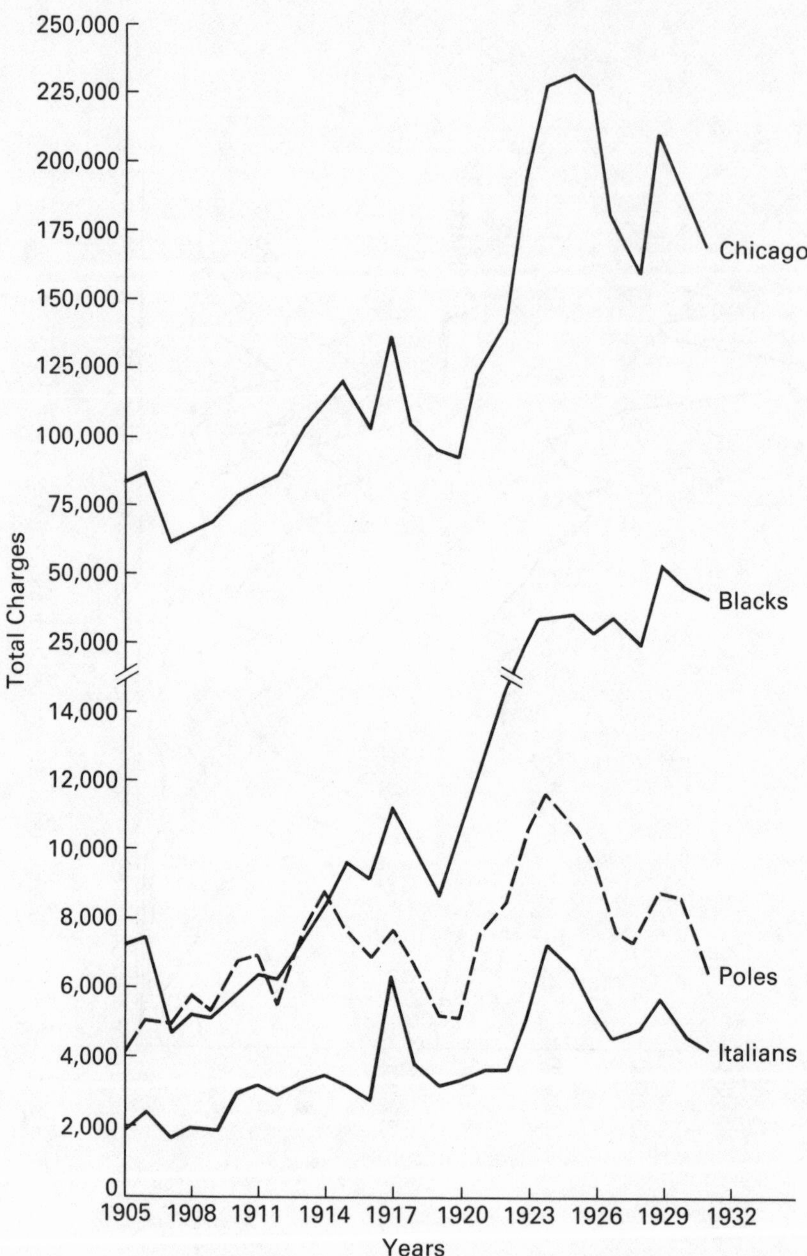

Figure 6.2 Felony and Misdemeanor Charges by Nationality, 1905–1931

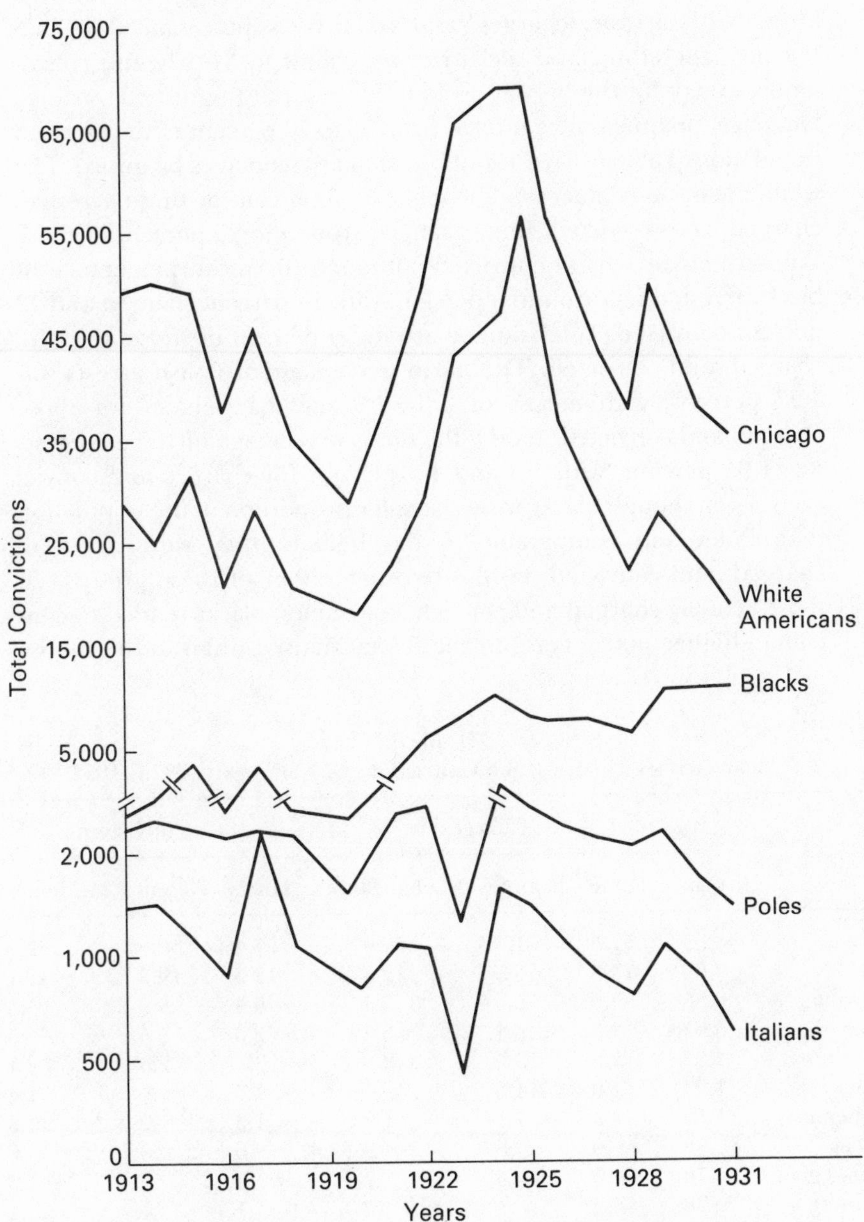

Figure 6.3 Total Convictions by Nationality, 1913–1931

percent and 4.3 percent of the population) or Poles (at 11.8 percent and 8.8 percent) for all the years of the survey except 1907 through 1914. With arrests, charges, and convictions percentaged by nationality, the ethnic and racial rankings show up clearly and consistently, except for the prewar period. Whites undistinguished by dress, language, or appearance ranged from 50 to 70 percent of the arrested population. Table 6.1 is a list of the mean percentages by group. The white mean percentages equal about 57.5 percent of those arrested, charged, and convicted. Blacks ranged from 5 to 25 percent of those arrested, charged, and convicted, although the mean percentage of blacks arrested was around 9 percent, with 13 percent charged and 12 percent convicted. Poles ranged around 5 percent of those arrested, charged, and convicted. The mean percentage of Polish arrests was 4.27 percent, with means of only 2.8 and 2.1 percent for those charged and convicted. Lastly, the mean percentage of Italian arrests was 1.95 percent, with 1.9 and 1.3 percent for charges and convictions. Even though blacks were a smaller proportion in the population than Poles and comparable to the Italians, they were arrested, charged, and convicted more often than either of these groups. Of those actually charged and convicted of crimes, blacks tended to contribute higher percentages to the felony statistics than to the misde-

Table 6.1
Mean Arrests, Charges, and Convictions by Nationality, 1878–1931

		Charges			Convictions		
	Arrests	Totals	Felonies	Misdemeanors	Totals	Felonies	Misdemeanors
White	58.35%	57.5%	61.4%	57.4%	57.4%	56.8%	57.7%
Black	9.69	13.3	16.5	12.8	12.5	19.3	12.1
German	6.86	5.6	5.5	5.7	5.4	5.9	5.3
Irish	5.97	3.3	3.1	3.4	2.3	2.5	2.5
Polish	4.27	2.8	3.3	2.8	2.1	2.5	2.1
Italian	1.93	1.9	1.0	2.1	1.3	.6	1.4
Bohemian	1.10	1.6	1.1	1.5	1.3	.9	1.3
Greek	.98	.9	.8	.9	.6	.8	.6
Norwegian	.79	.6	.3	.7	.6	.4	.6
Chinese	.28	.2	.1	.2	.1	.1	.1
Other	9.78						
Chicago	100.00%	100.0%	100.0%	100.0%	100.0%	100.0%	100.0%

meanors. In twenty-four of the twenty-seven years for which there is data, blacks contributed a higher percentage to those charged with felonies; white and European ethnics contributed more often to misdemeanors (based on Pinderhughes 1977b:tables 26, 31, 34, 41, and 43).

To increase legibility, only the three main groups appear in the figures, but Germans and the Irish contributed higher percentages to the arrested population than blacks from 1878 through 1891. From 1891 through the early 1900s, black and German percentages approximated each other, while the Irish percentages fell rapidly. Over the years Germans and the Irish shifted from relatively large to relatively small proportions of the violators, while Norwegians, Bohemians, Greeks, and Chinese equalled small proportions of the population of violators. Blacks contributed a significant proportion overall, but their percentage rose from a relatively high level to much higher levels in the 1920s and presumably in the 1930s. After 1908 blacks were the second largest group arrested after white Americans, while for charges and convictions they scored highest (see figures 6.4 6.5, and 6.6; Pinderhughes 1977b:tables 75, 77 and 79).

The relationship between number or percentage of violations and population size is unclear. Calculating the number of violations per thousand of the population standardizes the data across time and group. Figure 6.6 shows that the groups' ranking shifts once population size is accounted for. Using census years as a population base against which to compare violations, blacks ranked higher than all the other groups. Arrest rates in figure 6.6 show a high peak at the beginning of the reporting period, with a gradually declining curve through 1920, followed by a marked upturn. Poles' rates were least responsive to economic or political shifts. Italians were arrested at relatively high rates in 1887 (98.7 per thousand), but the rate dropped slightly in 1890; black and whites rates rose precipitously in 1890. By 1900 Italian rates fell along with most of the other groups, which brought Poles and Italians into comparable levels.[20]

The Italian and Polish rates were, therefore, lowest at the end of the period. Black rates began at a level over four times the rate of whites, nearly doubled to 1890, fell just below that rate in 1900, continued downward until they compared with white Americans in 1910 and 1920, but jumped upward to close to 200 per thousand in 1930. Standardizing violations by population shows that blacks ranked high, if not highest, across the sixty year period. Although exceeded by

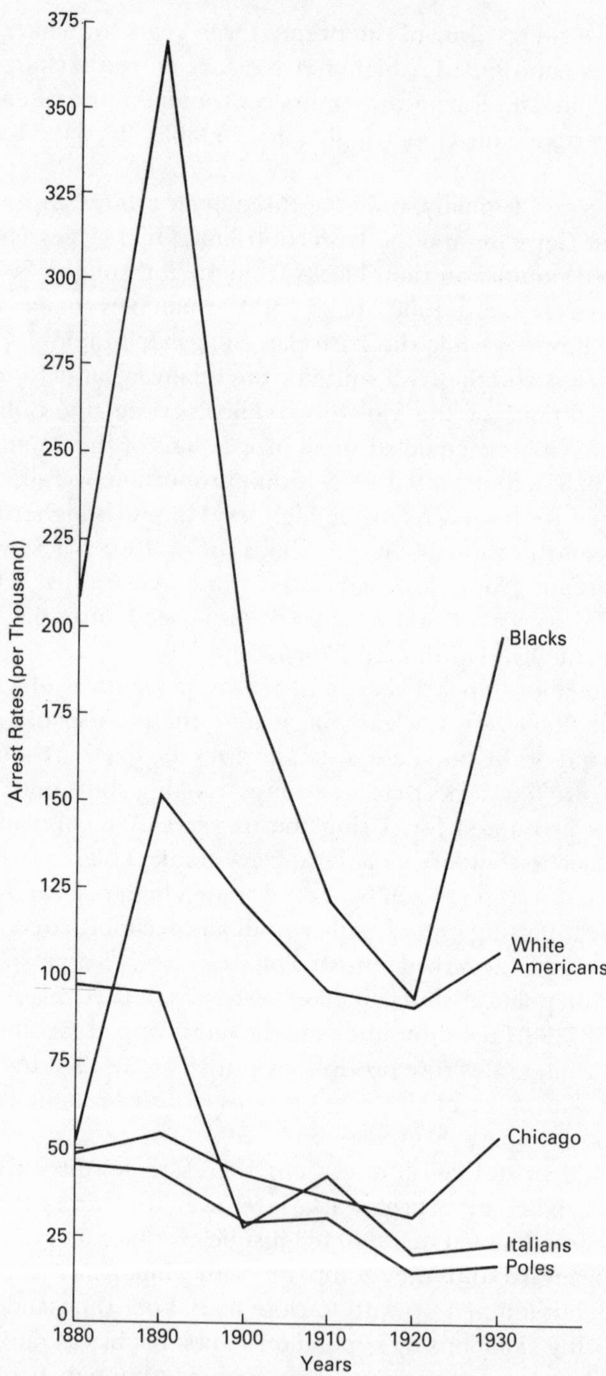

Figure 6.4 Arrest Rates (per Thousand) by Nationality, 1880–1930

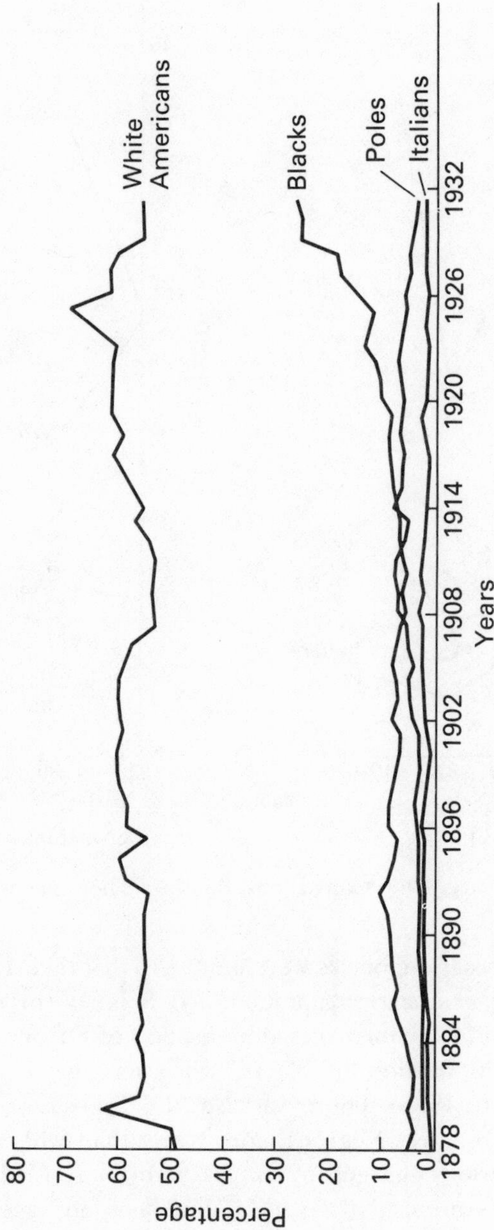

Figure 6.5 Arrest Percentages by Nationality, 1878–1931

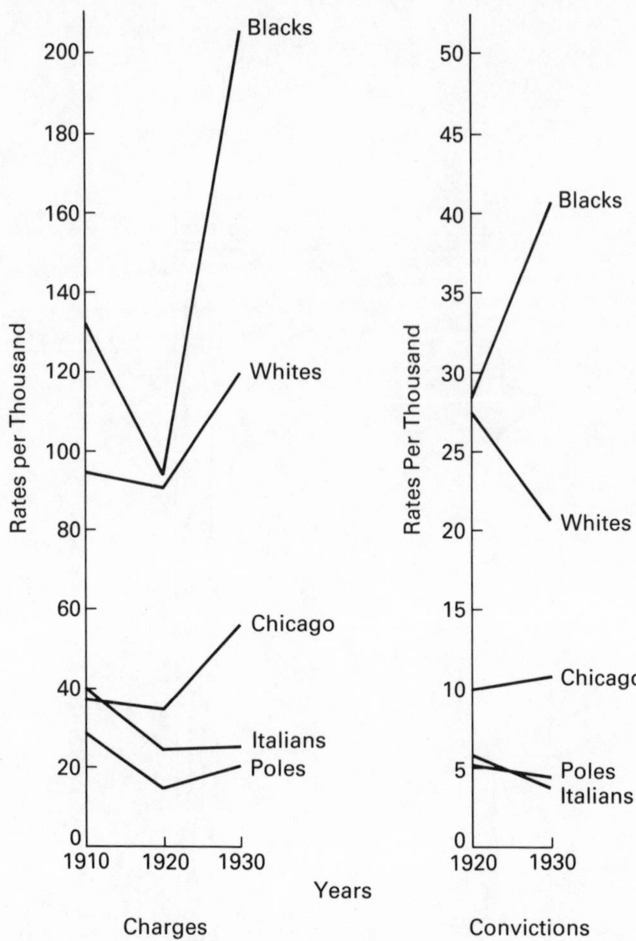

Figure 6.6 Charges and Convictions, Rate per Thousand, 1910–1930

some groups on occasion, blacks were unique in that their rates failed to decline *relative to any other groups* identified. Some of this difference may be accounted for by incorrect identification of European ethnics and accurate identification of blacks, who were more easily distinguishable (Curtis 1926). There was also "the disposition, conscious or unconscious, to arrest Negroes more freely than whites, to book them on more serious charges, to convict them more readily and to give them longer sentences" (Chicago Commission on Race Relations 1922:328–30). The Chicago Crime Commission (1953) commented on the unreliable and inconsistent reporting of crimes in general.

A second method of standardization is the index of representation, which divides the percentage of each group in the arrested population by their percentage in the total Chicago population (Mathews 1960:273). A score of 1 indicates that the two populations are proportionately equal; a score lower than 1 indicates their representation in the arrested population is lower than their proportion for the city. A number higher than 1 indicates overrepresentation. Figure 6.7 demonstrates that blacks were consistently overrepresented by 3.5 times their proportion of the city's population among those arrested, charged, and convicted, while Poles and Italians were almost as consistently underrepresented. More importantly, the chart shows a high degree of consistency; the rate of overrepresentation is nearly identical in all three measures of black violations, but much less similarity is apparent among Poles and Italians. The high level of violations in the early years of the data declines until 1920, when it again increases.

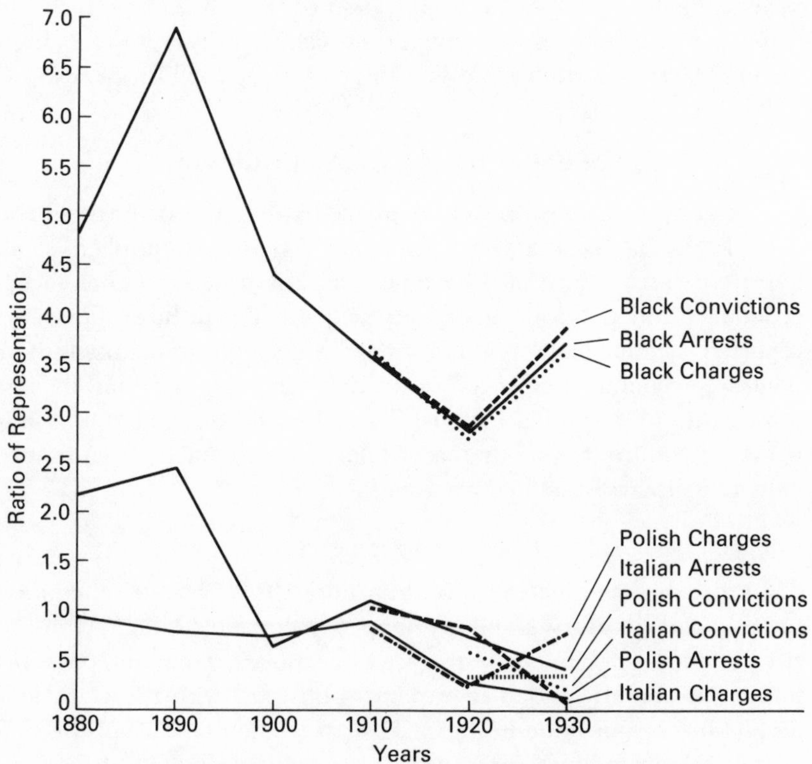

Figure 6.7 Index of Overrepresentation

Italians reflect some of this but, like the Poles, decline rather than increase after 1920.

Figure 6.8 shows the mean charges and convictions plotted separately according to felonies and misdemeanors. Most of the groups reported appear in order to show the pattern of violations in the data. European groups, especially northern and western Europeans, had relatively low rates of violations. Southern and eastern European rates, although low, were higher than those for their northern counterparts. The rates for the city and for Chinese were higher still, surmounted only by otherwise undifferentiated whites and by blacks.

The conclusion is clear: groups were arrested, charged, and convicted of crimes in a rather orderly hierarchy, with blacks and whites at the top, southern and eastern Europeans in the middle of all groups in the city but at the top of white ethnic groups, with northern and western Europeans at the bottom. Except for blacks, violation rates declined over time. These are simply descriptions; the patterns must be explained. What was the composition of the crimes for which the respective groups were arrested and punished? Why were rates high among blacks and whites and low among immigrant Europeans?

The Patterns of Crime in Chicago

There are several possible explanations for the patterns in the data. First, the law may have been more rigorously applied in all lower-class areas. Race may have been a mask for class. Other social, economic, and political factors may explain the differing levels of reported criminal activity. Whites may have sought to maintain their political, economic, and social status through more rigorous law enforcement policies in black areas. Blacks may have engaged in criminal activity more frequently than whites, thereby making them more vulnerable to arrest and conviction.

Geography

From the late nineteenth century until 1912, Chicago sanctioned a segregated vice district that overlapped with the black belt. After the city fathers decided to end segregated vice, policy, gambling, prostitution, and cabarets tended to expand southward with the black belt despite black opposition in the early years to the presence of the vice district. Unlicensed cabarets were also concentrated in the Loop, which ran east of the Chicago River in an arc along the north shore.

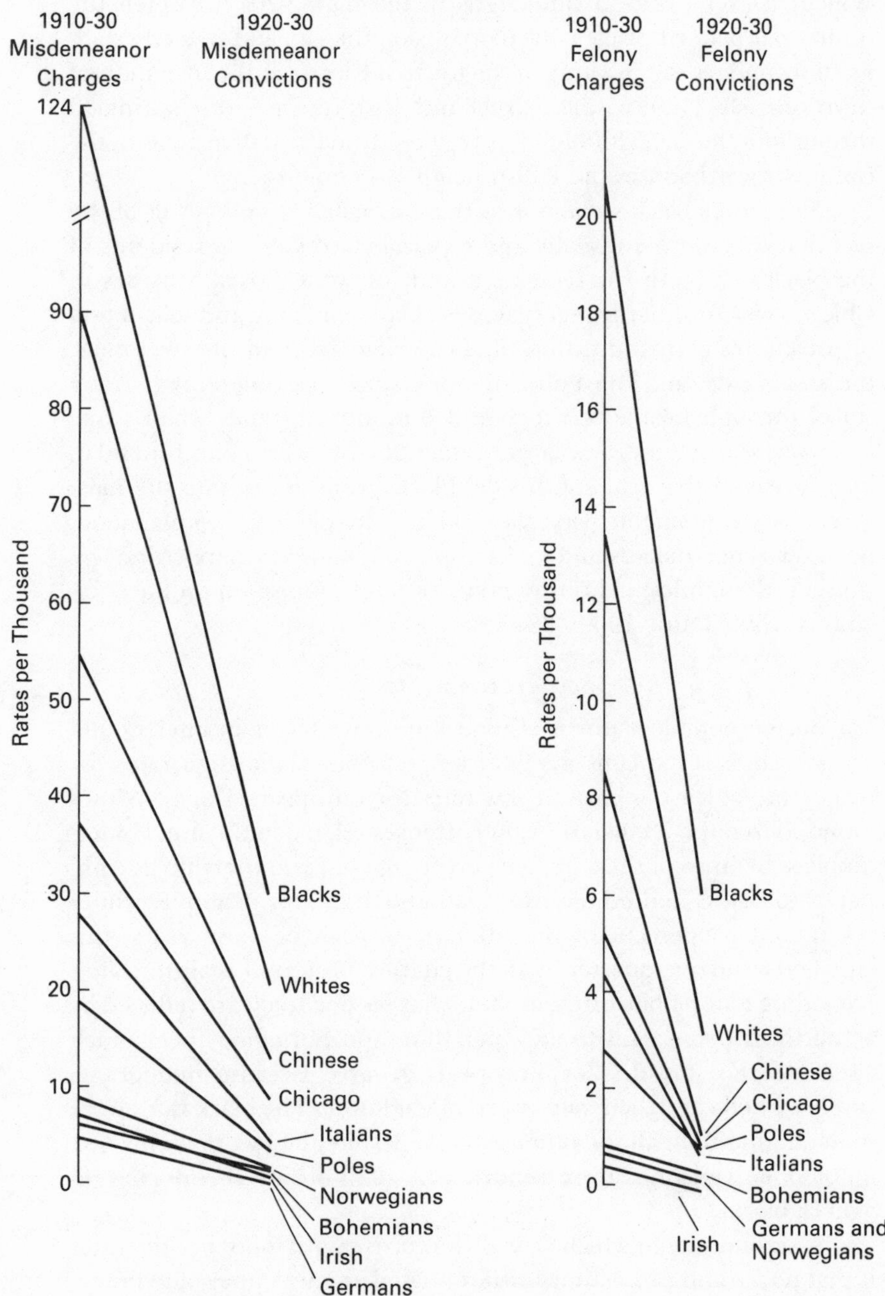

Figure 6.8 Ranked Mean Rates for Charges and Convictions

William Dever's reform campaigns in the mid-1920s disrupted the traditional pattern of illegal activity inside the city and helped establish a secondary staging area in the town of Cicero, at the invitation of town officials. Otherwise, cabarets and "vice resorts" were sprinkled throughout the city, although less frequently in the Italian areas of the twentieth ward and in the Polish neighborhoods.[21]

Numerous black violations in these activities were a result of the fact that they were unusually and especially accessible to residents of the black belt, both for recreation and for work. Social activities in Chicago were ordinarily segregated, so black gambling and solicitation of prostitutes occurred within the black belt. Work in the steel mills, the stockyards, and the Pullman works was accessible only by long travel through hostile territory and only during times when white labor was scarce. Since few large-scale industries were concentrated in black areas of the near south side, blacks were drawn into the most accessible economic activity, vice. This is hardly a full explanation, however, since Italians and Poles also lived in areas where crime was present, though less concentrated (Chicago Commission on Race Relations 1922; Tuttle 1969:408–32).

Socioeconomic Status

Socioeconomic status is also an important factor in interpreting the statistics. It explains a significant portion of the high rates for whites and at least in part the low rates for European ethnics. Whites monopolized the 18,000 to 19,000 offenses related to the use of automobiles, because of their higher percentage of car ownership as compared to blacks and ethnics. In 1916 and 1920, for example, whites committed 88 percent of the offenses in each of those years; this equalled a full one-quarter of all the charges preferred against whites. Excluding automobile offenses their charges per 1,000 are reduced by a full third (from 94.2 to 68.7 per thousand), bringing them much closer to the statistics for European groups. Because immigrants rarely owned cars, their rates were much lower. The black rates were much higher than all the other groups, despite the fact that only 381 automobile violations were reported in 1920 out of 10,750 charges against blacks.

A second way in which class differences might influence the rates is that police and prosecutors differentiated among upper- and lower-class violators. After the Chicago Riot of 1919, the Chicago Commission on Race Relations reported that most of the blacks arrested had little education or money and that they were unable to meet bail or hire a lawyer. In short, they were members of the lower class. Merriam reported that 52 percent of the prisoners in the Cook County Jail were laborers or unskilled workers, that only 1.5 percent were professionals and another 4.2 percent merchants and tradesmen, and that poor or petty criminals were punished more heavily than the wealthy or representatives of organized crime. Despite this recognition of class discrimination within the criminal justice system, Poles, Italians, and other immigrant groups, who were of comparable socioeconomic status to blacks, had lower rates of arrest, as well as lower rates of charges and convictions, than blacks (Chicago Commission on Race Relations 1922:chap. 7, 331; Merriam 1915).

Social Structure

Black, Italian, and Polish communities represented three different types of family and social structure. Southern Italians developed tight, unyielding, family-centered units. Any individual, especially an unmarried daughter who lived within that social grouping, had little contact with activities outside the family system. Italian women were less likely to engage in individual behavior of any type, let alone such activities as prostitution or attendance at vice resorts. Clearly this pattern underwent some deterioration in the crowded urban river ward slums of Chicago, but the social costs of maintaining an inwardly focused family were low. Italians regarded externally or governmentally defined crime as morally neutral, so that there were no sanctions against male participation in family-centered, profitable, although illegal, enterprises such as bootlegging and gambling. Italian social structure might actually have been strengthened by transplantation to the United States. The family's control over women seems to have been increased, at least in the short run. Moral prohibitions against sexual relations outside of marriage were used to regulate women's behavior more rigorously, while men were free to approach non-Italian women without threat to family stability or honor (Covello 1967).[22]

Although Polish life was not dominated by family activities, the Catholic church attempted to create a structure of religious, social, and community activities to preserve its members from involvement in non-Catholic, non-Polish secular activities. There were relatively few arrests of Poles.

Black family structure was neither as exclusionary as the Italian nor as church-dominated as the Polish (Billingsley 1968; Gutman 1976; Moynihan 1965). It easily accommodated neighbors, distant relatives, and acquaintances. Relationships between family members were flexible; behavior and range of interaction were not as completely defined by tradition or family.[23] Black, Italian, and Polish commemorative books reflect the difference in the type of family patterns. No women were pictured in the Italian yearbook, four in the Polish, and many in the black book (Cipriani 1933; *Poles of Chicago, 1837–1937* 1937; Robb 1927).

Finally, community life varied according to the concentration of family units. Nearly three-quarters of the black population was composed of adults, mostly young people who had migrated from the south. One-third to one-half of the Polish and Italian population in the 1920s and 1930s was over twenty-one during those years. Adolescents and young adults traditionally have higher crime rates; in this case, single black adults, freed of the moral, conservative, religious, and racial strictures of the rural south, attended the cabarets that were universally accessible in order to have a good time. Other Chicagoans behaved in similar fashion, but differences in socioeconomic status, geographical location, age, and social structure may not fully explain the differences in levels of arrests, particularly since Chicagoans in general took a lackadaisical attitude toward crime and punishment (Pinderhughes 1977b:162–70, 508; Rather 1972; Robb 1927; Schiavo 1928).

Types of Criminal Involvement

Another explanation for the statistical variation rests with the types of criminal activity surveyed. Which groups were involved in organized crime and what was their level of involvement? Although all of the groups in question committed murder, burglary, and other offenses that made local headlines, such crimes composed only a small portion of the totals. This section focuses on the violations that accounted for an important segment of criminal activity and that therefore had an important impact within the respective communities in question. Offenses associated with organized crime, such as gambling and prostitution, and disorderly conduct accounted for an average of 50 percent of the misdemeanor charges. Liquor violations, from which many of the others arose, were federal offenses.[24]

Figure 6.9 is a summary of gambling offenses. Blacks accounted for 12.5 percent of gambling offenses in 1912; their rates rose to

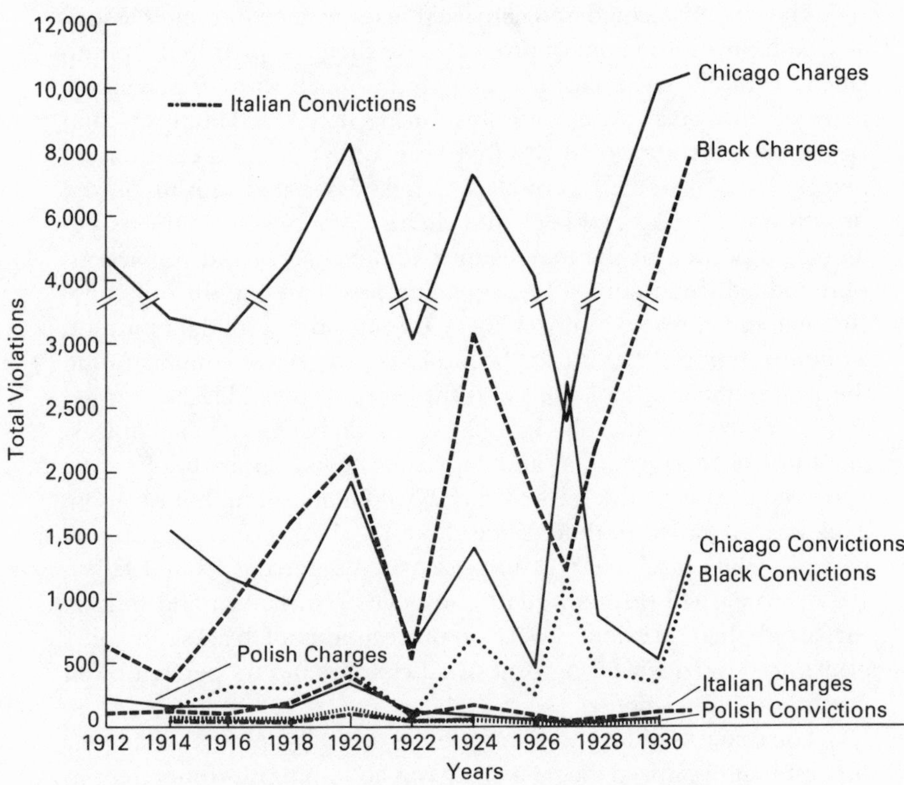

Figure 6.9 Gambling Offenses, 1912–1931

about one-third of all offenses from 1915 to 1920, and then dropped sharply until the time of the Dever administration. From 1924 through 1928 blacks were charged with about 45 percent and convicted of about 52 percent of the gambling offenses for the entire city, but in 1931 the proportions rose to 75 and 88.3 percent, respectively. In 1931, for example, 87 percent of the 306 locations that were raided for gambling charges held only blacks and were located in the poorest black neighborhoods. Standardizing these rates shows that the Italian and Polish figures approximate their size in the population, while the black index of overrepresentation rose to six or more. Standardization of the gambling offenses between census years eliminates the critical variations between 1920 and 1930. Black charges and convictions closely follow the city's pattern, while the Polish and Italian pattern of offenses was completely flat (Pinderhughes 1977b:347, 360; Reckless 1933:15).

The city prosecuted and convicted black women of crimes associated with prostitution out of proportion to their numbers in the population. Typically the police charged black women with 40 percent or more of the streetwalking offenses during both the Thompson and Dever administrations. In the first year after Cermak's election, 71 percent of such women were black. Blacks associated with organized prostitution (owners, workers, and clients in houses) were not as significant a portion of the total against whom charges and convictions were lodged (see figure 6.10), equalling less than one-fifth of those charged and convicted until midway through the second Thompson administration in 1920. At the beginning of the Dever administration the total number of violations and the percentages of blacks charged and convicted rose sharply. In 1924 and 1926 blacks equalled at least one-third of those charged and convicted; this dropped briefly on a percentage basis at the start of the third Thompson administration. This was a relative decline, since the total charges increased by 65 percent, while black charges increased by 42 percent from 1926 to 1927. From 1928 through 1930, the police returned to and quickly surpassed their previous levels of prosecutions of blacks. In 1931 blacks accounted for 55 percent of all charges and 68 percent of all prostitution convictions.

The remarks of Mayor Thompson in the epigraph to this chapter suggest that organized illegal activity was an important component in the city's life, economy, and politics. The Volstead Act, in effect from 1919 until 1933, forbade alcohol consumption. Private clubs sprang up to slake Chicago's acute thirst for alcohol, gambling, and prostitution. Chicago was a particularly resilient market for bootleg liquor, since large numbers of German, Polish, Italian, and other eastern European immigrants considered it part of their adopted "pursuit of happiness" to be able to consume alcohol, especially on Sunday, their day of rest.[25]

Did the police enforce the law more rigorously against blacks, or were blacks more frequently involved in gambling, prostitution, and disorderly conduct? Although Polish and Italian involvement in crime differed sharply, their violation rates were very similar. Blacks were also involved in illegal activities, but their levels of arrests, charges, and convictions differed sharply from both the Polish and Italians. Two factors explain these anomalies: the strength of the ethnically based organization of illegal criminal activities and the level at which most of the ethnic or racial groups were employed. The stronger the

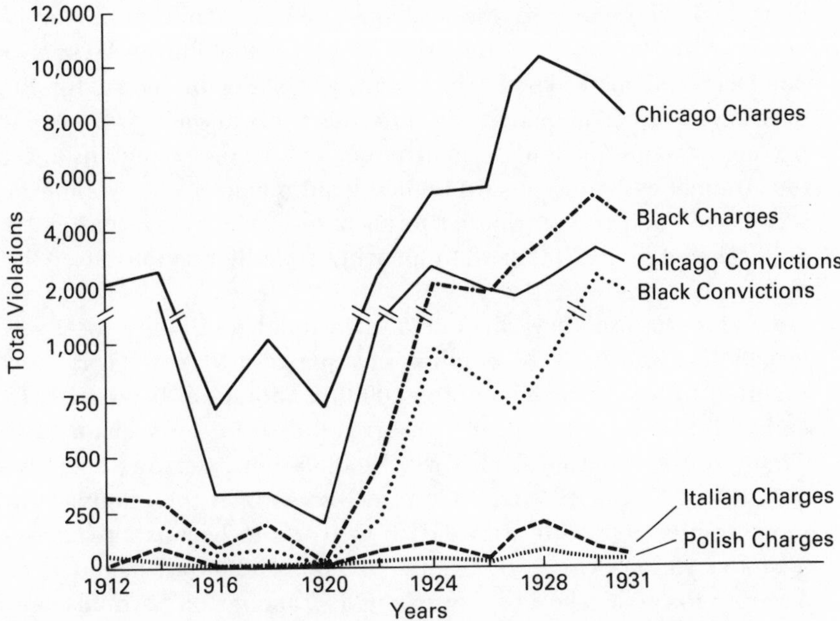

Note: Polish and Italian convictions were insignificant, 60 or less in each of these years.

Figure 6.10 Houses of Prostitution, 1912–1931

illegal organization, the more effectively it freed its work force from the danger of arrests and prosecution. Although powerful alliances between the underworld and public officials minimized their susceptibility to arrests, the foot soldiers of the highly visible gambling dens and houses of prostitution were more vulnerable to punishment than middle- and upper-level officials of the organization. Blacks filled the lower levels of organized crime, while Italians focused on the more protected production and management sectors.

Public Policy and the Politics of Crime

Criminals and Politics

Chicago's political and governmental institutions, including the police, were highly susceptible to influence by legitimate as well as illegitimate business. The underworld was represented in several ways in politics. Just as there were specialists in crime and politics, there were also intermediaries whose task it was to make connections between them. This offered the possibility of multiple roles for some individuals whose private responsibilities were hidden from the casual observer. In the first case, the criminal simply took his problem to a politician and made known his financial abilities in return for his needs. Such an arrangement was intermittent, with neither party expecting or wanting a long-term arrangement. In the second instance, the criminal wished to ensure he had good relations with whomever was elected and so contributed to all parties. He had no particular political preferences other than assuring friendly relations after the election.[26]

Criminals also knew that one of the candidates in most races was usually less hostile to the conduct of criminal activities. Torrio was reported to have contributed $250,000 to Thompson between 1918 and 1923; he even carried a membership card in the William Hale Thompson Republican Club (Lyle 1960:85–90; Peterson 1952:137; Wendt and Kogan 1953:232, 268). At other times the criminal was more comfortable with a candidate with whom he was already acquainted. In some cases, the criminal nominated his own candidate or associate for political office. For example, Capone and Serritella supported William Pacelli's candidacy over Albert Prignano for the twentieth ward alderman in 1929 (the twentieth was one of the wards that the city had created out of the old Italian nineteenth ward).[27] Tim Murphy and John Oberta symbolized the perfect union between politician and criminal: John "Dingbat" Oberta entered politics as a candidate for state senator and alderman with the strong support of Joe Saltis and Tim Murphy, a former state legislator and gang leader; Oberta was unsuccessful in his early attempts, but was elected ward committeeman in the primary of 1928 (*Chicago Tribune,* Jan. 9, 1929; Lashley 1929:1007–21; Nelli 1970a:224–25; Pasley 1930:338–41; Wendt and Kogan 1943:328–29).[28]

The greater the investment of the criminal in the outcome, the more likely he and his organization were to engage in electoral politics. After Capone was invited into Cicero in 1924, his men campaigned actively to support a political ticket that would give him the leeway to operate his gambling and prostitution houses freely. On election day Capone's workers were out in force, kidnapping election workers, raiding polling places, and "voting" for others. The violence was so widespread that Edmund Jarecki, one of the top elected Polish officials of the time and the county judge who supervised the Cook County election machinery, dispatched police to Cicero to end the disorder. The election ended in a gun battle between the two groups. Although Capone's brother Frank was killed, his ticket won and Cicero became a wide-open town.[29] Capone made similar inroads in Burnham, Stickney, and a number of other suburban towns to the south of Chicago. The Dever administration and the increased use of automobiles in the 1920s made outlying roadhouses and organization-controlled areas convenient as well as necessary to illegitimate business.

The 1927 Chicago mayoral campaign was also particularly important to Capone and other gangsters because it offered the opportunity for them to move back into the city and to reopen, without police harassment, their profitable illegal operations. Capone was reported to have contributed between $100,000 and $250,000 to Thompson's 1927 campaign for mayor (Peterson 1952:137; Wendt and Kogan 1953:268). Jack Zuta contributed $50,000 to the campaign and "held Card No. 772 in the William Hale Thompson Republican Club" (Wendt and Kogan 1953:269).[30] Thompson appointed Capone's lieutenant, Daniel Serritella, as inspector of weights and measures after the election (Nelli 1970a:225).

Gangsters supported wet (antiprohibition) candidates such as Thompson openly and lavishly, but they campaigned for other political factions as well. O'Banion, for example, generally supported the Deneen Republicans and organized the forty-second and forty-third wards for elections. The Gennas were directors in the Italian Republican Club, while their political ally, Joseph Esposito, was murdered in the Pineapple Primary in 1928 because he was the Deneen candidate for committeeman of the twentieth ward (Lyle 1960:93; see also Lashley 1929:1014; Nelli 1970a:226; Pasley 1930; Wendt and Kogan 1953: 303).[31]

Perhaps the most telling of the multitudes of crime and politics stories of early twentieth-century Chicago was the changing balance of the relationship between first ward aldermen Kenna and Coughlin and the crime syndicate. Aldermen Kenna and Coughlin dealt with Colosimo's successor, John Torrio, and with *his* successor, Al Capone. By the early 1920s, however, Capone and Torrio interacted with Kenna and Coughlin; as the syndicate grew more wealthy and powerful, Kenna's and Coughlin's influence dwindled. Capone cemented the alliance by exchanging personnel; he made Kenna's right-hand man, Dennis Cooney, his lieutenant in charge of brothels. Capone did not mince words, however; he told Coughlin at his headquarters at the Metropole Hotel, in what can only be assumed to be a paraphrase of the actual conversation:

> "Alderman, you was a good pal of Big Jim's [Colosimo]. You stood in wid Torrio. Well, they gone now an' we runnin' things, an' we don't want no trouble wid you. Let it git aroun'. I'm telling you cause I like you." The Alderman, sweating through his extra suit of underwear, nodded rapidly and was ushered from the sanctum. For days afterward, he told all who would listen, "My God, what could I say? S'pose he had said he was goin' to take over th' organization. What could we do then? We're lucky to get as good a break as we did" (Wendt and Kogan 1943:344–45).

When Daniel Serritella was elected Republican committeeman in 1927, Capone controlled both first ward committeemen. The organizational heir of the man whom Kenna and Coughlin had personally brought into the machine now commanded them.[32]

Within the world of criminal activities, black owners of gambling casinos allied with the appropriate politicians. Club owners Edward Green and Teenan Jones subsidized a number of black politicians, including State Representative Sheadrick B. Turner, alderman DePriest and R. R. Anderson, as well as Democrat Maclay Hoyne, candidate for state's attorney in 1912. George Jones established political arrangements with black Republicans such as Oscar DePriest and Louis B. Anderson. Daniel Jackson was a gambling casino owner, politician, and ally of both Thompson and Capone. Truman Gibson reported that William Dawson's requirement for supporting the Democratic party was that whites allow blacks to operate policy freely (interview, 1975). But neither black nor white politicians successfully protected blacks involved in illegal activities from prosecution. In fact, black politicians were often subject to investigation and indictment for their own illegal activity.

Blacks were highly committed to the Thompson Republicans. Did the variation in political administrations significantly affect black arrests and prosecution? Figure 6.11 is a diagram of the four types of political administrations: reform and non-reform Democrat, reform and non-reform Republican. Blacks supported Republicans almost exclusively, especially the non-reform Thompson Republicans. Thus although blacks were well organized politically and made significant electoral contributions to the Thompson administration, their almost exclusive commitment to one faction of one party coupled with Demo-

		Posture Toward Illegitimate Business	
		Reform	Nonreform
Partisanship	Democratic	HOSTILE TO CRIME	HOSTILE TO BLACKS
	Republican		LENIENT

Figure 6.11 Political Leniency Toward Blacks and Crime

crats' and reform Republicans' aversion to black voters reduced the opportunities for partisan-based police protection for blacks. Poles and Irish split their support across parties, thereby allowing accommodation regardless of party.

This explains the high levels of prosecutions and convictions in black areas for gambling and prostitution during the Dever administration and the first years of the Cermak administration, as shown in figures 6.9 and 6.10 and reported in great detail in the *Chicago Defender* in the fall of 1931 (Aug. 29, Sept. 8, Oct. 24, Nov. 28, and Dec. 5; John Leonard East, interview, Jan. 1974). It does not, however, explain the rapid increases in black prosecutions and convictions during all three Thompson administrations. While violations lodged against blacks dropped in the first year of the third Thompson administration (though black rates dropped about the same as the other groups), in the later years these rose rapidly. From time to time Thompson appointed reform-oriented police chiefs, such as Charles Fitzmorris in 1920, after which charges and convictions rose rapidly. Even under the Thompson administration, blacks were susceptible to discretionary application of police power. When city officials needed to emphasize political reform, raids in the black belt were neither economically nor politically costly for Democratic or Republican administrations. Moreover, blacks were not well enough organized economically to protect themselves from erratic prosecution.

Figure 6.12 summarizes the overall impact of crime upon the respective communities; it represents the black, Italian, and Polish prosecutions and convictions as a percentage of their respective populations. On a statistical basis approximately 20 percent of the black population had direct encounters with the police during this period,

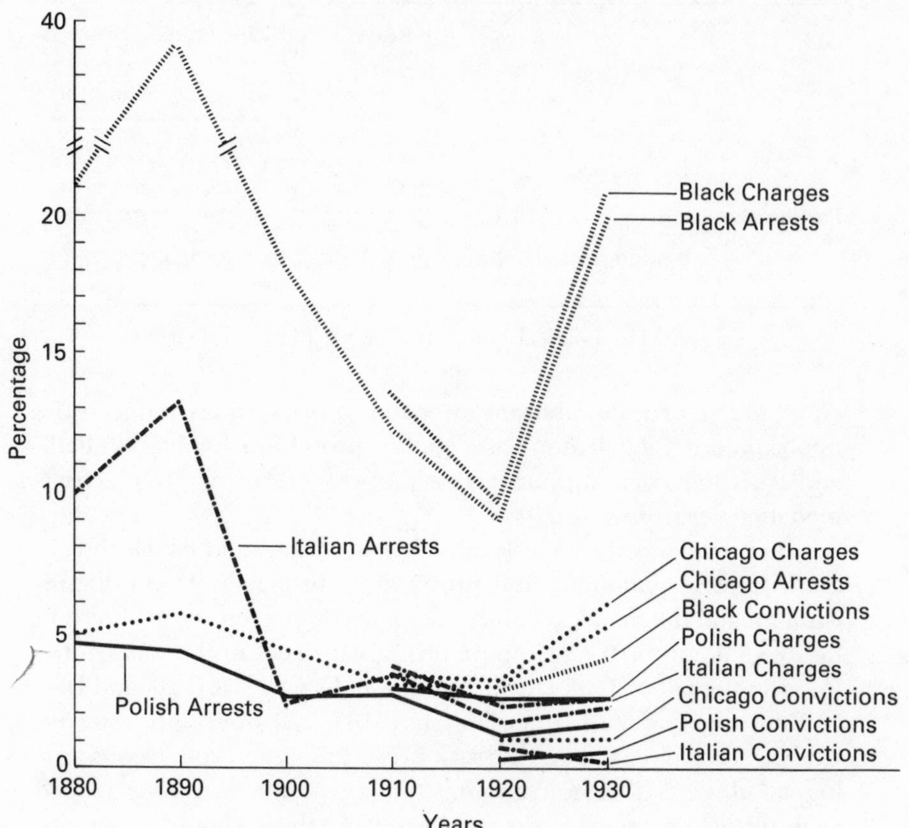

Figure 6.12 Arrests, Charges, and Convictions as Percentages of the Population, 1880–1931

while fewer than three percent of the Polish and Italian population interacted with law officers on a recorded basis. The type of crime, the geographic location, social structure, and economic organization of crime exerted powerfully different effects upon the black, Italian, and Polish communities' involvement in crime and vulnerability to punishment.

Police and Government

The police department was under the direct political control of the mayor. This was signified by the location of the police commissioner's office in city hall rather than in police headquarters. The commissioner and senior officers served at the pleasure of the mayor.

A rapid succession of individuals held office until the creation of the Democratic machine in 1931. At the bottom, "policemen had to learn which criminals, for political reasons, could not be seriously pursued. . . . An arrest was futile [if] the criminal would escape conviction through contacts in the State's Attorney's office or from among judges and other court personnel" (Haller 1970:650).[33]

The city's police were linked to organized crime at every level, and the administrative structure of the police force was confused and highly disorganized. Reform pressures emanating from the business community emphasized administrative efficiency and protection from crimes against persons and property rather than campaigns against liquor, vice, and gambling violations. The Dever administration offered a fleeting opportunity for reforms aimed at administrative efficiency and vice, but the subsequent gang wars and the third Thompson administration undermined this ineffectual start. Even during the Dever administration, Police Commissioner Morgan Collins "was not entirely successful in controlling the police," since he ordered that "police flivvers were not to be used to escort beer trucks" (Haller 1970:655).

The Chicago Crime Commission was formed in 1919 by the Chicago Association of Commerce. The commission and the Citizens Police Committee, formed in 1929, emphasized administrative reform and increased personnel. Cermak named a new police commissioner, James Allman, who implemented all the administrative reforms proposed by the various studies of the 1920s but ignored the issues of corruption and political control.

The police were particularly eager to raid black gambling houses and to arrest blacks on little or no evidence. The Chicago Commission on Race Relations took voluminous testimony from judges of the Chicago municipal courts on the subject during its investigation of the 1919 riot. Judge Scanlon reported, "I don't think the police are quite as careful with reference to the rights of the colored man as with the white man." A number of judges identified racial distinctions made by jurors and lawyers in the processing and outcomes of trials (Chicago Commission on Race Relations 1922:351–53, chap. 7).

In the streets the police exercised considerable discretion in arrests, which is strongly reflected in the figures for disorderly conduct (see figure 6.13). The statistics reflect the overall increase in reported violations over time. Blacks went from 7 percent of those arrested for that offense in 1911 to a high of 26 percent in 1929. Convictions ran a

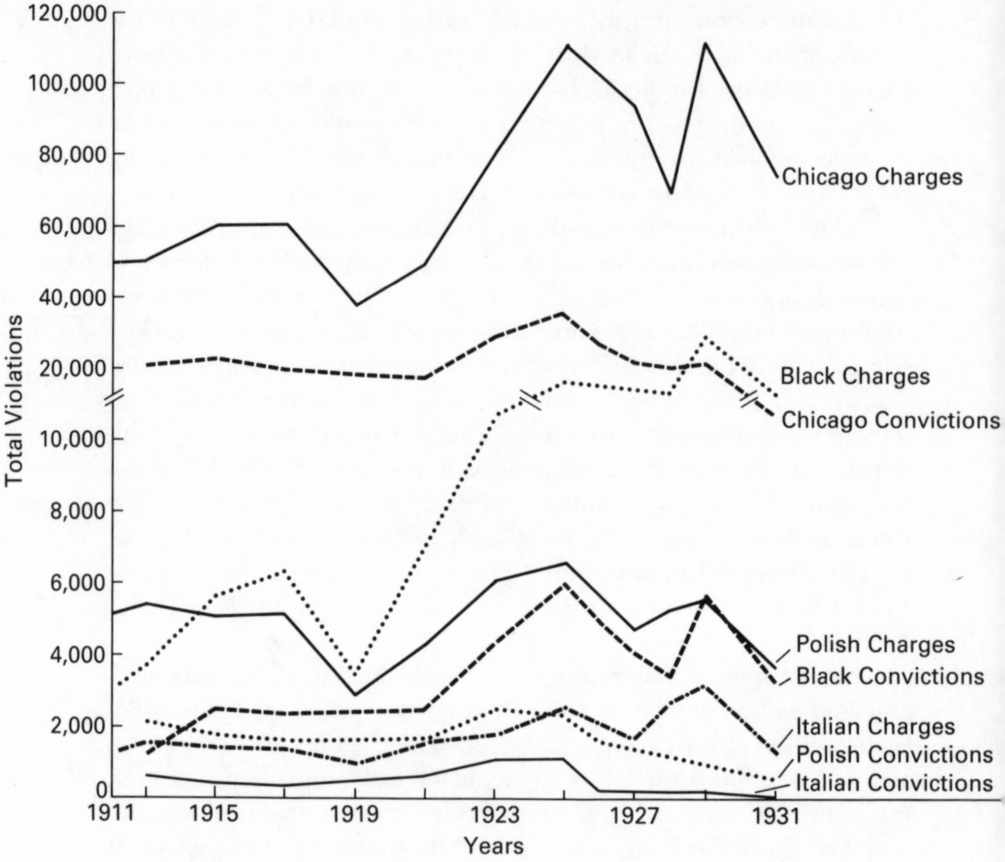

Figure 6.13 Disorderly Conduct: Charges and Convictions, 1911–1931

little below this level. The change in misdemeanor charges against blacks accounted proportionately for more of the increases and less of the declines than for the city as a whole, as shown in figure 6.13.

Police personnel greatly influenced the kind and character of interaction at the moment of arrest. Gosnell noted that the force was 98 percent white between 1910 and 1920. Black officers were usually assigned in predominantly black districts, but blacks still encountered white officers more than black ones. Reckless noted the conclusion of the Chicago Commission on Race Relations that: "Police officers share in the general public opinion that Negroes 'are more criminal than whites,' and also feel that there is little risk of trouble in arresting Negroes, while greater care must be exercised in arresting whites"

(Reckless 1933:28–29). During the 1919 riot, the police arrested and the state's attorney prosecuted blacks until the grand jury balked. Four-fifths of the police forces were concentrated in black areas, although they prevented neither the death of blacks nor disorder (Reckless 1933:235–39).

Politicians and Crime

How did black, Italian, and Polish public officials influence criminal justice policy? The public understanding and the one proposed by Merton was that politicians and representatives of illegitimate business created a web of protection against criminal prosecution; failing that, politicians rescued their hapless clients from the confusing, complicated judicial system.

Thompson appointed Dan Jackson, an undertaker and head of policy and gambling operations on the south side, to succeed the independent-minded Ed Wright as second ward committeeman. Gosnell noted that many black politicians were associated with gambling and prostitution houses and other underworld activities because they were important sources of otherwise scarce black campaign revenue. Gosnell described Daniel Jackson as a gambling king who "protect[ed] the ordinary Negro against police brutality and against interference in his petty vice" (Gosnell 1967:133). Although politics were important for Jackson's economic survival, he was not an aggressive force in shaping politics on the south side, preferring to let others direct him. To a Thompson query about his choice for Madden's successor to the U.S. Congress, Jackson said, "I'm with you, Mr. Mayor" (Gosnell 1967:192). John Leonard East reported that Jackson did not want the congressional seat, later won by DePriest, because he did not want to be in Washington.[34] East also reported that Jackson agreed to take the Commerce Commission appointment only if East would sit in for him at meetings (John Leonard East, interview, Jan. 11, 1974).

Blacks employed in organized crime or subject to police interaction were on the whole much more frequently prosecuted, though not necessarily convicted, than Italians. Though the two groups had organized systems of protection, the black system was clearly the weaker. The Italian system was relatively strong; on the whole Italians were subject to arrest as an exception rather than the rule. Because the black system was weak, blacks were subject to arrest as the rule rather than the exception. Black politicians then intervened to protect their client on an individual basis, but they had no impact on the striking pattern of arrests and charges. Moreover, black politicians were themselves frequently victims of prosecution. Black politicians were limited by their ties to Thompson Republicans, by their own or their colleagues' lack of economic organization in crime. At best, in the Thompson years, they used conventional machine politics incentives; DePriest, Jackson, Anderson, and others exerted selective influence for specific individuals, but they did not challenge the discriminatory implementation of policies on a collective basis. When Thompson took himself out of the 1923 mayoral campaign, Oscar DePriest threw his support to William Dever, but black arrests and prosecutions increased after his election.

These same individuals were completely powerless under the Cermak administration. As Cermak reorganized police assignments, broke the existing patronage arrangements between police and blacks involved in illegitimate business, and sent the newly reassigned officers on raid after raid in the black belt, Republican politicians had no political or economic recourse. The police raids centered on the black belt, and Cermak relentlessly publicized their operations. The *Chicago Defender* and other blacks charged that the raids were prejudicial. Cermak sought to weaken Capone's control of economic activities in the black belt and to pry blacks loose from their Thompson Republican-Capone alliance. Since Capone and black voters were strong Republicans, continued operation of illegal activities provided Thompson or any other Republican challenger with a critical source of economic and political support. Democrats who wished to win political office over Cermak needed only to look to blacks for electoral support and to the underworld for economic support. Until this alliance was dissolved and recreated under Democratic control, Cermak's monopoly was threatened.

Blacks challenged the Cermak campaign against crime in December 1931, but they used their traditional nonelectorally created organizations and strategies. The NAACP, the *Chicago Defender,* and 1,000 people protested the raids. The protests challenged the mayor's and police's actions based on racial groups. The *Defender* reported, "Citizens Aroused by Police Brutality; Demand Action" (Nov. 28, 1931). The Ritz Cafe lost its license and was closed in August. A "notorious black and tan resort" (an integrated club), the Ritz was owned by a black, former Thompson precinct captain from the second ward. The *Defender* reported that this was the only black-owned club in the city and that similar raids on integrated clubs had last been made in the

Dever administration (Aug. 29, 1931). A teacher, an auto salesman, and a doctor, among others, were stopped and searched or questioned because they looked "suspicious." When one of those in question asked the reasons for the action, the police replied "they were working on orders out of the mayor's office." When asked if the order applied throughout the city, the police replied, "Nope, . . . only in the black belt" (*Chicago Defender,* Oct. 10, 1931). The *Defender* warned against "the hope of Mayor Cermak and his advisors to build a Democratic party on the south side through the brutality of the police department, augmented by the weakness of those who are supposed to represent him in this section of the city."

Blacks protested the raids on the grounds that they were confined to black areas and focused on black-owned, integrated rather than white-owned, segregated clubs. In effect, they rejected accommodation with externally imposed collective status and demanded a noncollective policy. "Certain policemen . . . vent their personal prejudice against people of color. . . . 'Breaking up policy' [is] a subterfuge to humiliate respectable citizens who opposed the Democratic party" (*Chicago Defender,* Nov. 28, 1931). Dr. Herbert Turner of the NAACP and attorney Earl Dickerson (long time Democrat and subsequent second-ward Democratic alderman) and other private citizens met with the mayor to protest the series of raids. In order to capture Cermak's attention and to address a policy issue with collective import in both the public and racial policy areas (see charts on public policy orientations and racial policy orientations, chapters 3 and 5), blacks used nonelectoral organizational and individual leaders and mass public protest.

Conclusions

How much influence over criminal justice policy did blacks, Italians, and Poles exercise? Were blacks more heavily involved in crime than other groups, or did the police arrest and prosecute them more frequently? The inability of black politicians or underworld leaders (in some cases, of course, they were the same people) to reduce the high levels of black arrests, charges, and convictions symbolizes their physical exclusion by whites, their limited participation in the more desirable sectors of Chicago's economy, and the contempt with which whites viewed them. This, in turn, led to whites' moral, physical, and psychological association of blacks with corruption and vice. The lack of involvement of Poles and the involvement and low rates of charges and convictions among Italians suggests their greater economic and political freedom as well as their overall acceptance by the native white population. In contrast, blacks were limited from full participation in many legitimate economic occupations or were accepted only during periods of labor scarcity. They were excluded from every neighborhood but those in which gambling and prostitution were allowed to operate freely. Even in these least prestigious businesses, blacks were limited to control of the least profitable sectors and to employment in the low-paying, service level occupations.

In effect, all of the pressures in the legitimate and illegitimate sectors exerted relentless repression on blacks, forcing them into occupations, locations, and social interaction that provoked frequent encounters with the criminal justice system. Because of the restrictions on their economic and other activities, political representatives exerted only marginal counterpressures and protection on black underworld activities. Individuals might be extracted from the interstices of the criminal justice system, but the structure of the economic system and the pressure of the political system made blacks the most frequent targets of reform campaigns and least able to protect themselves from them.

Chicago was a city whose citizens viewed repetitive and even serious violations of the law with bemusement and mild misapprobation. Several types of criminal activity in the city were usually reproduced in every area of the city. On a block-by-block and neighborhood-by-neighborhood level, adolescent groups fought over territory and status. Over larger areas, their older brothers and fathers might have been members of the senior division of a gang or an athletic club, which was an important source of ethnic and geographic identity for its membership but which also increased their collective political and economic leverage. Members of these clubs might also belong to organizations devoted to crime as a business. These were, consequently, in constant conflict with neighboring groups or with the larger syndicate, which might be attempting to expand its territory through and at the expense of the smaller, locally organized groups.[35]

Crime was an openly acknowledged fact of life in Chicago. This is best captured in the changing relationship between organized crime, which had achieved an effective monopoly on operations around 1929 or 1930, and the political machine led by Cermak. After Thompson's election in 1927, the city acquired the reputation for being the world center of unlicensed criminal activity. Community groups, the business community, and the press were afraid the publicity would depress the expected revenues for the 1934 World's Fair and had begun talking about the need for a "World's Fair Mayor."[36] Anton J. Cermak's campaign against Thompson was carefully balanced to appeal to these reform sentiments. In any other election Cermak might have been the object of severe criticism for his underworld connections, but the Thompson-Capone association gave Cermak the reform advantage. Cermak's desire for a complete monopoly over the party organization prompted his black-belt reform campaign; when Capone was in federal prison Cermak named his own representative as leader of the syndicate. This required the removal of Capone's agent, Frank Nitti, who had been appointed in his absence.[37] Cermak's personal bodyguard, Sergeant Harry Lang of the detective squad, seriously wounded the unarmed Nitti in the neck and chest while he was under arrest and being held by a police officer in December 1932. In retaliation, "Nitti threatened to make disclosures that would wreck the Democratic party," but he was dissuaded; his case was continued and eventually dismissed. Lang, on the other hand, was tried and "found guilty of assault with a deadly weapon. The verdict was reversed but the sergeant was not retried. He was dismissed from the force" (Lyle 1960:264–66; Peterson 1952:162).

Meanwhile, Ted Newberry, a former ally of the Morans, moved into the Capone organization after the St. Valentine's Day Massacre and began maneuvering to take control of northside gambling operations. Peterson reported that Lang's action was coordinated with "Newberry's effort to control the north side gambling with the backing of the Cermak administration" (1952:161–62). Lang wounded Nitti on December 19, 1932; Newberry was killed on January 7, 1933, and on February 15, 1933, Anton Cermak was wounded as he stood in an open car next to Franklin D. Roosevelt in Miami. Cermak eventually died from the wounds. Cermak's biographer did not entirely discount the possibility that Cermak was involved in underworld dealings; Gottfried suggested Cermak was probably trying to break up the syndicate and quoted Carter Harrison to the effect that Cermak was too conservative to be mixed up in murder. Neither Judge John Lyle nor Frank Loesch of the Chicago Crime Commission believed Cermak's death was the accidental result of a bullet intended for Roosevelt. The Sicilian assassin, Giuseppi Zangara, who later died in the electric chair for the murder, was used by the members of the Capone organization precisely because they knew his general hatred of all public officials and the question of his personal sanity would cloud the issue of motivation (Gottfried 1962:318–24). Two bullets were found on Cermak's person, which suggests that Zangara's aim was not misdirected.[38] Both Lyle and Loesch were concerned enough about their personal safety to conceal their theories until Loesch's death in 1944 and the publication of Lyle's autobiography in 1960 (*Chicago Daily News,* Aug. 1, 1944; Lyle 1960:267).

Society was much more sensitive to violations of social norms and values by blacks than for any other group. Irish, Italians, blacks, Poles, Bohemians, and white Americans drank, gambled, and prostituted themselves in Chicago; blacks were punished. As the politicians campaigned on, the police and courts arrested, prosecuted, and convicted blacks out of all proportion to their presence in the population. Whites and blacks committed crimes; blacks were punished for them.

7

Educators, Machinists, and Reformers: The Politics of Race and Class

That the school machinery of Chicago is largely defective is not a matter for surprise.

—*Report of the Educational Commission of the City of Chicago, 1899*

The impact of black, Italian, and Polish citizens on the formation of educational policy is the subject of this chapter. How did the school system distribute its resources; in what way were the funds spent; what was the school system's employment policy; who was hired; what was the pupil teacher ratio; in what condition were the buildings in different neighborhoods maintained; what books were ordered and from whom for classroom use; who won the contracts to supply heating fuel to the school system and were employees of the school system patronage or civil service? All of these issues affected classroom instruction as greater or lesser proportions of the tax money available were invested in supporting the in-classroom interaction between teacher and child.

The political machine focused on the tangible rather than the substantive aspects of the educational system. Education was of value to the machine only to the extent that its operations added material benefits and incentives to the political system. Ethnic and racial groups, though part of this system of machine politics, had alternate non-material goals for the school system and sought to integrate those goals into the educational agenda.

The number of children enrolled in Chicago schools rose from 301,172 in 1910 to 441,682 in 1938. Most of the population felt the bite of taxation when the yearly property tax bill arrived from the county assessor's office, out of which school operations were financed. The vast majority of the population had some contact with the school system, whether as child, parent, teacher, janitor, principal, administrator, or contractor (Chicago Board of Education 1909–45:147; Herrick 1971:249).

According to pluralist theory, assimilation is an effect of continued participation in political and social life, and the educational system has a powerful role in facilitating ethnic and racial upward mobility and in increasing economic and social heterogeneity. The system communicates a uniform, or at least similar, set of facts and values; it hires or rejects members from the newly arrived ethnic groups and from among teachers and administrators; and it teaches immigrant children their place in the new environment. If any urban organization affects political and social integration, it is certainly the school system. The classroom is not only the first universal experience of public or group life that children encounter but it also figures in the lives of the largest portion of the city's population. The educational system is a contact point through which children experience complex social relations, accept the authority of persons outside the family, and find parentally taught culture, language, and values reinforced or challenged.

Yet the system also involves many of the complex issues described above. The pattern of educational policymaking, data on educational expenditures, employment patterns, and physical maintenance, particularly if these vary by race or ethnicity, provide important clues on the type of information communicated to students about ethnic group social and political status. Gross discrepancies in expenditures, personnel administration, or plant quality among the three groups are reflected in the educational values conveyed in the classroom. Because of its broad and profound impact on the social and cultural environment and on the economic and political systems, the schools are the most inclusive and far-reaching governmental apparatus in the city (Grimshaw 1979:chap. 1; Katznelson et al. 1981).

The Formation of Educational Policy; or What Happened to Reform in Chicago

The major economic interest groups in the Chicago school system included: the teachers, whose employment was directly dependent on educational policy; the politicians, who wished to tap the enormous numbers of personnel of the schools for their patronage army; and the businessmen, who sought low expenditures and workers equipped to join the city's industrial labor force. Racial and ethnic groups had their own economic interests in the educational system, although their interests were not necessarily exclusively economic. They sought descriptive representation as teachers, administrators, and maintenance staff. They focused on questions of educational policy, such as whether their children attended segregated or integrated schools, whether the city's educational requirements threatened their (usually Polish) children's attendance at parochial schools, and whether the physical plant at their children's school was well maintained.

These issues differ radically; economic issues involve tangible, selective benefits that machines supply best and most willingly. Business concerns about educational preparation and black and white parents' concerns about segregation involve collective issues that establish the rules of the game, the norms and values of the society. Given the pattern of operation for political machines and the overall tendency for economically powerful interests to dominate policymaking, as described by Downs (1967) and McConnell (1966), I compare the relative capacity of economic interest groups and of ethnic and racial groups to influence economic and collective dimensions of early twentieth century Chicago school politics in this chapter.

Extraordinary controversies burst forth over educational policy during the first decades of the twentieth century. Politicians, teachers, and businessmen fought to mold the educational system to their own purposes. Politicians attempted to strengthen their hold on one of the city's largest sources of patronage. Between 1910 and 1938 educational expenditures rose from $9.53 million to $73.31 million annually. "The especial political value of school jobs [contracts and other financial resources] is therefore obvious: they can be distributed among every district and to virtually every socioeconomic and cultural/ethnic group in the city" (Grimshaw 1979:29). The business community discouraged excessive spending and supported a business-oriented educational curriculum. The teachers mixed their radical labor goals, concern for an educational curriculum independent of business concerns, and a school administration freed of political control, with the practicalities of jobs and the independence of the school system (Bureau of the Census 1910:137, 230; Herrick 1971:179).

Politicians

After 1872 the school system was formally independent of the city government, but the mayor appointed members of the board of education, which gave the incumbent considerable discretion over educational policy and the uses to which the schools were put. The city council set overall spending levels while the board of education made specific decisions. Mayors Busse, who served from 1907 to 1911, and Thompson sought to remove board members unresponsive to their concerns. Busse demanded the resignation of a number of the reform-oriented members of the board, and when some refused to comply he summarily removed the recalcitrants. They took their case to the Illinois Supreme Court, which ruled in 1908 that they could not be unseated at the mayor's will.[1]

An even more complicated conflict developed during Mayor Thompson's first term. The board of education voted to prohibit teacher membership in unions, but the Chicago Federation of Teachers won a court injunction against the board, which retaliated by firing sixty-eight teachers, principals, and district superintendents (including many representatives from the federation) in May 1916 (*Chicago Daily News Almanac* 1916:645). When the board's decision was upheld by the state supreme court, the teachers successfully lobbied for tenure protection (and, in effect, recognition of their union), which was incorporated by the legislature into the Otis Law. The Otis Law guaranteed tenure for the teachers, reduced the board from twenty-one to eleven members, and established a four-year contract for the superintendent. This law struck deeply into the system of machine politics by strengthening the independence of the teachers, the board, and the superintendent.

Mayor Thompson retained his power to appoint board members, but technical complications slowed his first efforts to politicize the board. The state supreme court ruled that the city council's incomplete confirmation of the new board invalidated it and they reinstated the previous board of twenty-one. The 1916 twenty-one-member board, most of whom had preceded Thompson's election as mayor to the board and who were reinstated by the court, appointed Charles Chadsey to the superintendency in 1919. As former superintendent of schools in Detroit, he favored a strongly reformist program. He proposed increasing the power of the central administrator, extending civil service status to nonteaching personnel, and electing the school board. When the state supreme court certified the Chadsey board's legality, Thompson ran for reelection in 1919, based on an attack on this board and on Chadsey's incumbency. When Thompson won, the third Thompson board of eleven locked Chadsey out of his office and appointed Peter Mortenson, a former superintendent of the Parental School, to head the system. During the conflict the court found nine members of the Thompson board in contempt for their actions against Chadsey, fined them, and ordered them to serve several days in jail, which they did. Chadsey took his case to court and won approval of his right to a four-year term. Chadsey, having made his point, resigned, after the board removed all authority given him by the Otis Law (Counts 1971:52–54; Herrick 1971:137–39).[2]

After Mortenson's appointment the Thompson board quickly took political advantage of its position. The board's attorney, William Bither, who had served a short jail sentence because he had collaborated in the Chadsey case, and other board members engaged in profitable and illegal deals, including the acquisition of property for the site of the new Wendell Phillips High School (Herrick 1971:140–43; Stuart 1936:158–61; Wendt and Kogan 1953:201). In 1922 State's Attorney Robert Crowe indicted Fred Lundin (Thompson's patronage chief), former board president Edwin S. Davis, Albert Severinhaus (former vice-president of the board), William Bither, and twenty others for stealing over $1 million from the school treasury through fake contracts and false and inflated bids for school supplies. This scandal forced Thompson from the 1923 mayoral race and allowed Robert Leuder, who was supported by State's Attorney Robert Crowe, to win the Republican nomination. Lundin and his associates reportedly demanded campaign contributions from all who did business with the schools. "Incidentals cost the board in 1921, $8,714,065—a sum greater than the entire cost, twenty years ago, of the whole public school system" (Counts 1971:263). In spite of this sharp rise in expenses and other evidence, the jurors managed to acquit the defendents. Other members of the board were indicted in 1922, but they also escaped conviction (*Chicago Daily Tribune*, Sept. 9, 1922, cited in Counts 1971:263; Counts 1971:260–61; Wendt and Kogan 1953: 174–76, 208–13).[3]

The schools received a slight respite during the Dever administration. William McAndrew was appointed superintendent by Mayor Dever in 1924 as part of his reform administration. McAndrew antagonized most of the major interests involved in school politics in Chicago with his reform program and gave Thompson, a juicy campaign issue. Upon Thompson's reelection as mayor in 1927, the board dismissed McAndrew (Counts 1971:276–80; Herrick 1971:169; Stuart 1936:293).[4]

Counts reported that Thompson wanted "to make the school textbooks of this city serve the purpose of political scoundrels; in short, to make the public schools a private asset" (Counts 1971:9).

McAndrew's departure marked the beginning of the full politicization of the schools. In March 1927 an appellate court decision required that school janitors and firemen be chosen by the Chicago civil service commission; in practice, aldermen and precinct captains controlled these appointments through the civil service commission. This decision opened approximately three thousand patronage jobs to selective political use and to promises of future employment, since the court decision was made just before Thompson's April election (Herrick 1931:90–91, table I, 1930 figures).[5]

By August 1927 the board of education ordered that clerks' positions in the schools, which certified teachers had held since 1909, were now to be filled with temporary civil service appointees, who were not required to pass civil service exams. In short order Thompson had a patronage army at his disposal. As the total amount of patronage increased, access to it was gained only through proper political channels. A candidate for a janitor's job took the civil service exam, but aldermanic contact and approval were also required before the individual was hired (Herrick 1971:164–65).

The school board declared the schools closed shops so that the janitors had to become members of the union run by Nate DeLue, an executor of Jack Zuta's will and an accountant or recordkeeper for the Capone and Moran underworld organizations. DeLue was appointed an inspector in the labor bureau at the board of education and was swiftly promoted to assistant business manager in 1928 and head of the bureau in 1929. The Thompson administration oversaw the development of this complex system for building workers to his requirements on a selective basis, while generating increasing sources of revenue.[6]

In 1931 the board of education commissioned Columbia University's George Strayer to study the Chicago school system. The Strayer report dealt gingerly with questions of janitorial patronage, stating "there is a very decided and outspoken opinion on the part of many of the employees that there are other sources [which the report did not specify] to which they must look for the security of their position" (Strayer 1932, vol. 4:189). The union assured the board of education's civil service commission of the applicant's membership and payment of the forty dollar entrance fee. A janitor might be fired at any time, because the union retained the option of expelling its members during a six-month probationary period. Herrick suggested that DeLue and the aldermen from the respective wards shared in the forefeited initiation fees (1931:63).[7]

Partitioning the operations and responsibilities of the patronage system among as many separate but interlocking individuals and groups as possible increased the number of citizens with obligations to the machine at the middle and grass-roots level and increased the possibilities for profit and the total number of people eligible for patronage. The aldermen avoided direct liability, since the union guarded the barriers to entry.

After 1917 the teachers were protected by tenure, although they still had to survive a three-year probationary period, but political considerations influenced appointments from time to time. In 1926 (during the Dever reforms) Wallace Caldwell, the president of the board, advised the teachers who worked as clerks to contact their aldermen or precinct captains and to submit a letter from them to the board president's office (Herrick 1931:50). Thompson lost his bid for reelection in 1931 despite his control of this group of selectively employed workers, but the Cermak administration incorporated his system of selectively distributed patronage employment into the machine. The Cermak and Kelly administrations organized the use of patronage even more effectively. They directed their energies toward an extension of political jurisdiction over any available economic enterprise.

In June 1936 three publishing houses, Allyn and Bacon, Ginn and Company, and Harcourt, Brace, terminated their affairs with the Chicago Board of Education charging that it had not yet paid $2 million on books billed before January 1, 1924. The city's severe economic situation might have been a valid explanation, except that, as *Daily News* reported, some companies were getting paid "while others wait years without getting what is due them or any part of it." The *Daily News* subsequently reported that Billy Skidmore, a bondsman, Democratic party official, "millionaire junkman," pickpocket chief, and gambling boss, had been making collections on textbooks series (*Chicago Daily News,* June 5, 1936, cited in Herrick 1971:228; see also Peterson 1952:160, 165–66, 181).[8]

Thompson began to transform the school system into an institution for selective manipulation of workers during the relatively prosperous 1920s. This system was operated directly from the mayor's and board president's offices:

> After the new Chicago Teachers Union had tried for a year to meet with Superintendent Johnson, it managed with the active help and presence of John Fitzpatrick (president of the Chicago Federation of Labor) to get an interview with the President of the Board James B.

McCahey. When the union president protested against Johnson's treatment of the union, McCahey said, "Don't pay any attention to him; if you want something, you've got to come to me." Johnson sat in the corner and said nothing (Herrick 1971:268; see also Cronin 1973:149).

The arrival of the depression at the same time as the formation of the Democratic machine cemented the patronage system firmly in place. Where there might have been the possibility of defection, rebellion, or disloyalty to the Democratic political machine, the threat of unemployment was enough to dispel any such thoughts among supporters and to encourage those who were not yet involved to sign up. In effect, the Thompson and Cermak administrations "reformed" the school system by taking it out of politics. While the schools were subject to patronage use, the selective manipulation of school employees removed any debate over substantive, intangible, or collective issues from the public agenda. The teachers were politically isolated and unable to force consideration of policy issues. Although Thompson and Cermak did not submit the reforms that the business community wanted, they helped lower overall expenditures by concentrating their attention and rewards on business employees.

Over the years the mishandling of the school system began to have an effect on the system's standing with accrediting institutions. A series of investigations, reports, and warnings began in the 1930s. In 1934 the North Central Association of Schools and Colleges denied accreditation to ten new high schools; in 1935 the association warned several older high schools of their standing with the association, and in 1938 the association warned all the high schools about overcrowding. In May 1945 a seventy-page study of the National Education Association made specific recommendations about improvements in the administration of the schools. The following January, Superintendent William Johnson was expelled from the National Education Association for unprofessional conduct.

In March 1946 the North Central Association of Schools and Colleges released its annual report, which notified the board of education that "further accreditation of Chicago high schools would be dependent upon the centering of responsibilities in the office of the superintendent of schools and upon the provision for a politically independent Board of Education" (Herrick 1971:273). Mayor Kelly was forced to appoint a blue-ribbon commission to study the problems of the system, the board, and the superintendent. The commission recommended across-the-board resignations from the senior educational officers in the city and reorganization of the board to establish its independence from the political control of the mayor (Herrick 1971:271–77).

The Teachers

From its founding the Chicago Federation of Teachers (CFT) was pitted against the growing politicization of the schools and against attempts on the part of the business community to influence the level of educational expenditures and organization in the schools. In the 1920s the organization was characterized as having "strongly radical leanings" and accepting "its orders from Moscow" (Counts 1971:100). In fact, the teachers supported reform when it advanced their financial or political interests.[9]

The federation fought the board of education head-on in the 1890s, when the board announced that there was no money to increase the teachers' salaries. The union appealed to the political and judicial system and won a new assessment, producing taxes of $2.3 million, but the federal court accepted business criticism and lowered them to $600,000 (Herrick 1971:100–102).[10]

In 1897 the union defeated a school reorganization plan in the Illinois legislature that would have strengthened the superintendent's and weakened the union's powers. In 1919 the legislature approved, with CFT support, the Otis educational reform because of the conflict over union membership. While the teachers approved of the creation of tenure, they disliked the greatly enlarged powers of the office of superintendent. The teachers tacitly supported Thompson's opposition to the reform board and to Chadsey's reform superintendency. Superintendent Mortenson, although amenable to political uses of the schools, won their support for his recognition of the teachers' councils and "the largest salary increase they had received in half a century" (Cronin 1971:76; Grimshaw 1979:29–33).

The Dever administration was committed to reform in a number of policy areas, including education. Dever appointed William McAndrew, a reformer, superintendent of schools. McAndrew abolished the Chicago Federation of Teachers' treasured teachers' councils and created a new, more heterogeneous school council on which the teachers had only one representative, and he also emphasized efficiency and hierarchical control by administrators (Grimshaw 1979:29–35). He quickly lost the teachers's support as a result of these policies.

The next significant conflict between the teachers and the board was precipitated by the depression. In 1914–15 the board ceased expending cash on hand and issued tax anticipation warrants to local banks until the taxes were collected. As enrollments increased, expenditures outran receipts. By 1927 the property tax assessments were increased to cover the school board's debts. City property was still greatly undervalued, but the continuing decline in revenues prompted increasing pressure for public disclosure of the property tax lists. The county assessors and the board of tax review attempted to block this in May 1928 by declaring the 1927 assessment incomplete. The 1928 tax bills had not yet been mailed, and the school board was already spending its 1928 budget. The portion of the budget spent on servicing the schools' debts increased rapidly, from 1.8 percent of the total annual expenditures in 1922 to approximately 13.6 percent in 1932.

The Illinois general assembly passed a new assessment and published the taxpayer lists, which showed the average rate of assessment to be 31 percent of total value instead of the 60 percent described by the assessors, or the 100 percent required by Illinois law. Small homes were assessed at much higher rates than large, while Loop properties were devalued in the new assessment by $300 million and accounted for less than four percent of the city's total. The 1930 taxes collected could not match the city's $23 million deficit. The board budgeted an additional $21 million from the reassessment for the 1929–30 fiscal year. The percentage of students in school was rising at the same time that the percentage of students staying in school through the upper grades was increasing (Strayer 1932, vol. 1:140, table 8).[11]

Rising unemployment caused by the depression began to complicate an already difficult situation. Tax payments from the overdue taxes for 1928 and 1929 slowed as unemployment increased, and income for the entire city government spiralled downward as the depression worsened. City banks became more and more reluctant to buy any more tax ancitipation warrants as defaults on mortgages increased and after Samuel Insull's empire, Midwest Securities, collapsed, leaving most city banks with millions of dollars of worthless securities. Insull's biographer described the bankers' response to Insull's faltering position in 1930 and 1931: "The Chicago banks were in no condition to save Insull or even Chicago: They had to save themselves" (MacDonald 1962:295).

Thus while the general assembly planned a revision in the state tax system, the city government and the school board operated at a deficit. The teachers' pay began to arrive one to two months late, beginning in December 1929. On December 31, 1931, County Judge Edmund Jarecki ruled the 1928 and 1929 assessment rolls invalid. He was later reversed by the state supreme court, but Jarecki's decision encouraged tax strikers and made collection even more difficult (Herrick 1971:197). From September 1930 through March 1931, they were paid in cash, but for several years afterward they were not paid or were paid in scrip (which were largely worthless) or tax warrants (which could be used for little other than to pay taxes). In addition, teachers' salaries had been cut by 23.5 percent. In aggregate, the board owed the teachers $42 million for one year, not including interest.

In the summer of 1933 the new school board, appointed by Mayor Kelly after Cermak's assassination, dealt with this situation by making drastic cuts in the educational programs with strong business support; the board eliminated the ten-year-old junior high school program, the physical education and athletic programs, doubled administrative responsibilities for district officials, and cut the number of school teachers by 10 percent. Mass public protests blocked some of the program cuts, but the new board, without notifying Superintendent Bogan of their intentions, "had on their own, cut deeper into the services to children than had any other urban Board of Education in the country . . . [but] had reduced no patronage jobs" (Herrick 1971:213). The board rehired the teachers at their 1922 salary schedule. This was an "ironic accompaniment," since at the time the teachers were receiving no pay at all (Vieg 1939:203–4).

As part of depression economy measures, the city dismissed 1,400 teachers but hired 700 political appointees from the same source of funds. Herrick reported that the sanitary district, consisting solely of political appointees, suffered the fewest cuts, while the number of South Park employees was reduced only temporarily. Property tax rates increased the most for heavily politicized city or county bureaucrats during this period (Grimshaw 1979:36; Herrick 1971:212). Park district employees had been paid up to date by February 1934; the pay for Cook County employees was two and one-half months in arrears, three months in arrears for the city of Chicago, and six months in arrears for the teachers (Vieg 1939).

Among the groups of city employees, the teachers resisted efforts to bring them under political control longest. They were the strong supporters of educational reform, but their anticapitalist labor orientation and their concern with retaining control over educational policy made them on some occasions reform opponents of the politicians, on others allies of the Thompsonites, and during the Cermak administration the opponents of both the politicians and business community. The teachers paid dearly for this resistance by bearing the full brunt of the economic depression. Repayment of back salaries to teachers was much slower than to any other employee group, especially political appointees. Because teachers were disloyal to the political machine, the organization found little gain in paying them ahead of political appointees. The teachers fought for increased educational expenditures, while the city's businessmen emphasized fiscal austerity and administrative efficiency. The political interests rationalized the conflict by cutting nonpolitical appointees. With neither economic nor political clout, the teachers lost.[12]

The Businessmen

The business community also paid close attention to the educational system. Business concerns focused on the financial costs of the schools and on increased efficiency. As the number of students attending high school increased after 1910, the Commercial Club and other industrial organizations proposed that the common high school curriculum be divided into general and vocational programs. The Cooley Bill, the result of recommendations by former Chicago superintendent Edwin J. Cooley, which was introduced in the Illinois legislature, addressed these issues (Herrick 1971:117–20; see also Counts 1971: chap. 8).

Businessmen called for scientific management of the schools, and educators responded by incorporating financial and administrative efficiency in their decision-making criteria. Samuel Bowles and Herbert Gintis argued that the needs of the economy shape the eventual construction of the educational curriculum. Herrick also argued that business interests and curricular proposals are related. Foundations, educators, and large companies, therefore, attempt to synchronize the human products of the American educational system with the requirements of the economic system. The patterns of behavior and the types of relations that are taught in schools help prepare students for their roles in factories. Under their regime a worker needs only to learn to tolerate long hours of tedious labor, while a manager or owner should learn how to prepare for the unexpected, to think independently. As increasing numbers of students stayed in school, businessmen and educators committed to scientific efficiency felt it inappropriate that high schools had been "Miltonized, Chaucerized, Vergilized, Schillered, physicked and chemicaled" and that they placed too much emphasis on "culture" and a "gentleman's education," for the masses (Callahan 1962:50).[13]

When Cooley suggested a two-track system of vocational and classical education, the Commercial Club and the National Association of Manufacturers agreed and proposed a two-tier system of schools after the sixth grade, for general, preferably compulsory, vocational education and for a classical program. The teachers, organized labor, and some educational groups opposed a separate curriculum and argued that business wanted to develop a source of cheap labor at the expense of the state. The Commercial Club's position was that "the increase of socialism can be minimized by a vocational training which will increase the intelligence and future earning power of our children. . . . There will always be a difference in individual character and ability. . . . No social plan can be maintained that goes contrary to these basic truths" (*Commerce,* Nov. 21, 1913:28, quoted in Counts 1971:142). The Teachers Federation strongly opposed the Cooley plan, which was defeated in the general assembly in 1913, 1915, and 1917. The Chicago Federation of Labor "accused business of trying to get cheap, submissive labor without the educational background American citizens should have, calling it the most direct of all the open-shop, anti-union drives ever made" (Herrick 1971:119).[14]

In 1924 Superintendent McAndrew introduced a number of reforms; the teachers and labor unions interpreted his program, such as the introduction of junior high schools, as a disguised version of the Cooley Bill. Their fears increased when McAndrew announced that he had been brought to Chicago "to loose the hold that certain outside agencies and the city hall had on the school system" (*Chicago Daily Tribune,* May 16, 1927, quoted in Counts 1971:247). McAndrew also introduced the platoon system, or Gary Plan, so called because it had originated in Gary, Indiana, under the superintendency of William E. Wirt. The plan increased the daily use of schools and the number of students handled by the schools each day. In light of their reforms,

Dever and McAndrew quickly lost the support of the teachers and of organized labor in favor of Thompson in the 1927 mayoral campaign.[15]

Grimshaw argues that other factors besides ideological commitment motivated the teachers. The junior high school plan weakened the union's constituency base, which was lodged in the elementary schools. "By creating a junior high school, which included the seventh and eighth grades, the federation's primary source of membership was reduced by 25 percent. To make matters worse, McAndrew instituted a special qualifying examination for the junior high school teaching positions" (Grimshaw 1979:35–36). Since the heart of the union's membership was older, drawn directly from high school rather than college, their careers were undermined by the reorganization.

The business reform goals of superintendent McAndrew conflicted with both patronage politics and teacher self-rule. The conflicts between reformers and politicians arose not so much because the latter were necessarily opposed to the systematic use of schools by the business sector, but because that use might interfere with their ability to control the schools. The triangular pattern of conflict on the citywide level meant that the politicians during Thompson's administration, interests such as teachers and labor, and the business reform interests under Dever and McAndrew played each against the other from time to time as the situation required, but none remained permanent allies.[16]

Educational reform came very late to Chicago because the interests that successfully implemented reform in other cities failed to resolve their differences. First, the politicians devoted themselves to the plunder of the schools for economic and political profit, and the public expected a certain degree of corruption in its officials, but they were careful to let those involved know when they had violated even these lenient boundaries. Thompson withdrew his mayoral candidacy in 1923 for these reasons. The formation of the Democratic machine eliminated the possibility of internal dissent about the uses to which the school system was put. Second, the Chicago teachers were the first in the country to form an organized teachers union, in March 1897; their struggle to increase salaries drew sympathetic support, and they had organized 50 percent of the teachers within three years. Their public expressions of interest in school policy emphasized their commitment to educational quality, which, by their definition, meant higher pay and control over policy decisions. Few other cities had organized teachers unions so early. Under Margaret Haley's leadership, the union joined the American Federation of Labor in 1902. This was unusual, since most people, particularly status-conscious teachers, thought of unionization as too unprofessional and base, even lower class.

In 1916 the Chicago union became a founding member of one of the two major national teachers organizations, the American Federation of Teachers. "The AFT was organized in Chicago when the Chicago Teachers Federation joined with the Chicago Federation of Women Teachers, the Chicago Federation of Men Teachers, and a teachers local in Gary, Indiana, to secure a charter as an affiliate of the American Federation of Labor" (Doherty and Oberer 1967:23). Groups from New York, Scranton, Oklahoma, and Washington, D.C., also joined simultaneously (see Eaton 1975). Unlike the National Education Association, which emphasized professional and educational improvements, the CFT concentrated on conditions of employment, curricular reform, Taylorist efficiency, and hierarchical administrative reforms.[17]

Chicago was one of the few large cities that escaped educational reform in the early twentieth century. The city's teachers blocked reform in 1897, and both the politicians and the teachers foiled implementation of the 1919 Otis Bill. Although Mayor Dever's reform administration slowed the political exploitation of the schools for a few years, the Republicans fell upon the schools in 1927 with an appetite stimulated by a four-year-long fast from patronage. The coalescence of the machine in 1931 ensured the organized manipulation of the schools for patronage for another fifteen years. Politicians used the schools as a source of patronage and over time they tightened their grip on the educational bureaucracy.

Business reformers and labor-educational reformers fought each other in the policy debates in public or through conflict with conservative school superintendents, such as John Shoop, Charles Chadsey, and William McAndrew, and educational reform failed at the legislative or implementation phase until it was forced upon the city by external authorities in the late 1940s.

Descriptive Representation in Employment

How representative of Chicago's heterogeneous population were the employees of the school system? Precisely what criteria were used to select employees, and how were decisions on political employment made and enforced? The school administration was divided into the education and business departments. Appointments were made from a pool of inexperienced teachers who had graduated from the Chicago Normal College or experienced teachers who held accredited normal training and had passed an exam administered in Chicago. A surplus of normal school graduates in the early 1930s produced a three-year waiting list; graduates from the normal college and college graduates with or without teaching experience obtained certificates as substitute teachers. Herrick did not specify which office initiated appointments, although her account suggests that the central administrative offices ordinarily assigned teachers to the schools (1971).

As illustrated in table 7.1, black teachers, including substitutes and clerks, amounted to only 2.91 percent of the total teacher population in Chicago. In the education department the supply of black teachers was not especially large, although Herrick reported that experienced teachers were drawn from the "better segregated southern city schools" in Washington, Baltimore, and St. Louis by Chicago's higher salaries. Demand was also weak; many principals refused to accept black teachers, and at times even school children objected to them: "When a colored substitute was sent from the Farren [to Burke], the children struck and refused to come back in the afternoon, and their parents supported them" (Bureau of the Census 1918:526).[18]

The central administration assigned black teachers only when the individual was acceptable to the school in question. If it was unsure of an applicant's race, it simply avoided the appointment if the home address was in a black neighborhood. On the whole, the possibility of a "qualified black candidate" being appointed was much less than was the case for whites, since teaching certificates were "never granted to Negroes unless a specific request is made either for one of the individuals or for a Negro teacher" (Gosnell 1967:282–83; see also Herrick 1931:chap. 2).

In all cases principals held final veto power; consequently, the process was highly decentralized, and racial discrimination was allowed at the discretion of the neighborhood school. Herrick, Gosnell, and the Chicago Commission on Race Relations described principals who found fault with or rejected a black teacher. Even if the teacher was finally assigned, he or she often had to face personal rebuffs or

Table 7.1
Black Employees of the Chicago Board of Education, June 1930

Education Department	Total Number of Blacks	Blacks as a Percent of all Employees in Category	Blacks in Category as Percent of Total Black Employees
Principals	1	.2	
Teachers	308	2.9	26.7
Substitutes	150	6.0	13.0
Truant Officers	6	5.0	.5
Playground Workers	21	11.0	1.8
Community Center Directors	6	20.0	.5
Health Officers			
M.D.'s	5	4.0	.5
Nurses	12	13.0	1.0
Lunchroom Workers			
Penny Lunch	10	3.0	8.6
School Clerks	12	3.0	1.0
Subtotal	531		45.9

Business Department	Total Number of Blacks	Blacks as a Percent of all Employees in Category	Blacks in Category as Percent of Total Black Employees
Clerks in Offices	7	2.3	.60
Firemen	15	3.0	1.30
Janitors	420	35.0	36.40
Janitresses	182	35.0	15.80
Plasterers } 3	2	.9	—
Truckdrivers } 3	1		
Subtotal	627		54.38
Total	1158	5.38	100.00

Source: Herrick 1931: table 1, pp. 90–91.

on-the-job segregation (Chicago Commission on Race Relations 1922:247–48; Gosnell 1967; Herrick 1931).[19]

In the 1930s Maudelle Bousfield, the only black principal in the city, headed one of the smallest, oldest, and least equipped schools.[20] Other blacks who had passed the principal's exam were required to wait a long time for appointment. As table 7.2 shows, black teachers tended to concentrate in the black areas of Morgan Park, the Old Ghetto along Roosevelt Road, the Lake Street neighborhood, and the inner South Side, but an all-black school was no guarantee of the racial composition of the teaching staff. Of fourteen schools that were predominantly black in 1930, only seven had a majority black teaching staff (Herrick 1971:13–15, 21).

In schools adjoining black neighborhoods where racial boundaries were changing, a black teacher was seen as a challenge to the maintenance of white privileges. Schools that were mixed or in transition, from 15 to 75 percent black, had few black teachers, since principals felt they should not risk racial conflict by placing black teachers in charge of white students. "Schools in the area where there was greatest violence during the race riot of 1919 had no Negro teachers, although the population was 40 percent colored" (Gosnell 1967:290). "They are most successful in the foreign districts on the West Side. The European people do not seem to resent the presence of a colored teacher" (Chicago Commission on Race Relations 1922:248).[21]

Table 7.2
Black Teachers and Pupils in Black Neighborhoods

	Percentage of Black Children			Percentage of Black Teachers		
	1920	1930	1934	1920	1930	1934
Drake	24	100	100	—	20	23
Felsenthal	20	100	100	—	2	3
Willard	13	100	100	—	34	49
Forrestville	38	100	100	—	52	55
Emerson	75	88	98	—	69	62
Moseley	70	100	100	—	100	38
Colman	92	100	100	—	80	85
Doolittle	85	100	100	6	80	85
Douglas	93	100	100	—	20	65
Farren	92	88	98	—	17	16
Fuller	90	100	100	—	—	7
Hayes	80	100	100	—	84	75
Keith	90	100	100	50	80	71
Raymond	93	100	100	15	42	57

Sources: Chicago Commission on Race Relations 1922:247–48; Gosnell 1967:288; Herrick 1931: table 2, pp. 92–94.

The ultimate responsibility for the appointment of teachers resided with each principal. If the principal or community was hostile to blacks, the individual teacher had no recourse but to hope for an appointment at another school. On infrequent occasions political influence helped, but no such pattern of teacher appointment was found in any of the studies consulted.

The fact that black teachers experienced difficulty in securing school assignments is shown in table 7.1, where they were represented twice as frequently among the substitutes as among the teachers, based on the total employees in each category. Black teachers in predominantly black areas equalled only about 33.8 percent of the teachers (Herrick 1931:94), which was partly accounted for by the fact that there was no increase in teachers to match the rapidly expanding black population. The number of pupils per class was allowed to increase, rather than the number of teachers, so that by the mid-1930s over thirty elementary schools on the black south side were on double shifts reaching 50–60 pupils each (Herrick 1971:16–17, 223, 237, 270).[22]

Political considerations exercised relatively little influence in the education department. Black teachers and the one black principal, Maudelle Bousfield, felt their appointments were not political, although Herrick found a small number of teachers and teacher-clerks who were relatives or acquaintances of black politicians (Herrick 1931:50, 55). In 1926 board president Caldwell directed the teacher-clerks to secure a letter of recommendation from their ward representatives. Some of the black candidates who submitted letters for such jobs, but who made no offers of money or political support, also received no jobs.[23] Black politicians' influence was confined by racial barriers, by administrative jurisdiction, and by the fact that only certain types of political influence were acceptable. They were most successful in placing black constituents in political jobs that did not offend the sensibilities of white Chicagoans, while jobs which violated the existing status rankings were only infrequently available.

In the business department the city's civil service commission conducted and marked exams, but the board of education established a commission of its own during McAndrew's administration. Since the commission was composed of the president and two members of the board of education, the commission facilitated the application of political standards instead of job-related criteria. Some employees took exams that were graded, while others were appointed from lists of temporary employees, which were renewed every sixty days. Blacks tended to be concentrated in the lower civil service grades. At the board of education 54 percent or 627 of the blacks were business department employees, compared with only 14.8 percent of total board employees; only 18 (1.7 percent) of the 1,025 firemen, school engineers, electricians, machinists, bricklayers, and other skilled workers were black, while blacks equalled 602 or 34.2 percent of the 1,760 unskilled workers. Blacks held patronage positions in the school system in proportion to their numbers in the population, but these replicated the hierarchical social relations they encountered in the private sector. Moreover, the high-paying skilled tasks in the business department were dominated by whites.

It is not clear from historical accounts whether regular civil service or temporary appointment procedures were required for particular jobs or whether there was a standard procedure for any single category. In all probability procedures varied according to the political requirements of the day. Political criteria were employed more frequently in the Thompson administration's business department. Since blacks with janitorial ambitions faced the same complex set of interlocking arrangements that stretched from the ward organization through the janitor's union and the civil service commission, their positions were hardly improved by the political support of Republican administrations or by the intervention of black political officials. "[T]his particular share of the reward for Thompson's support received from Negro politicians had some long and very tough strings tied to it." Of twenty-three separate employees' organizations, only the business department unions had 100 percent membership. Herrick noted that "at least 800 jobs have been apparently under the control of DePriest, Anderson, Jackson, Cronson" (1931:62, 69, 109–10).[24] If Herrick is correct, this equals more than two-thirds of the black employees in the school system (see table 7.1).

Herrick reported that alderman Jackson "stated blandly . . . just how many janitresses from his ward would be passed in the next examination" (Herrick 1971:174). Her earlier study, on which this quote was based, contradicts this assertion and suggests that affairs were somewhat more flexible:

> [Jackson] said he didn't know the exact number [of janitors appointed from his ward], as he didn't know how many had paid the union. Of course, he had sent the union a list of those who had done good work for him, but they had to pay their fees before they got a job. The

janitresses were not all appointed, but he knew that Mrs. Grady, the union president, had finished certifying one hundred sixty-two women, because the hundred sixty-second was in his ward. "Oh yes," he added blandly, "they all take the civil service examination" although it seemed to be the least significant link in the chain (Herrick 1931: 53–54).

Educational Expenditures

In order to examine the city's educational expenditures, areas of heavy black, Italian, and Polish concentration were identified and schools selected to compare expenditures. Increased political participation and integration by the three groups should have increased their influence in the formation of educational policy. The review of Chicago's educational history suggests that political and business considerations dominated policy more often than reformist, black, or ethnic issues. An analysis of school expenses shows that small businessmen and politicians profited from inflated school contracts, but even with considerable graft and corruption, the school system's total budget was low, governed by business concern for fiscal austerity. Based on expenditures per capita and per enrolled pupil and on average daily attendance, Chicago's total budget usually ranked well below most other cities of comparable size. Figure 7.1 shows the expenditures per pupil for Chicago for the early twentieth century. These are simple per-pupil figures; the comparative measure used contributes significantly to the resulting level of expenditures.[25]

Educational expenditures rise according to the level of education provided within the system; the costs of high school, junior college, and college instruction, which are included in the rates per pupil in figure 7.1, disproportionately increase the level of expenditures for the entire system, although the numbers of students attending these upper levels constitute a much smaller portion of the student population. Expenditures for each high school pupil in Chicago averaged $40–$75 more than the average per elementary pupil (Strayer 1932: 155, 159). Most of my analysis of expenditures within Chicago focuses on elementary students. Partitioning expenses into educational and non educational categories will allow an evaluation of the impact of political control upon the budget. Table 7.3 shows the standard recommendation for proportional distribution of school expenditures and the distribution of expenditures across these same categories for

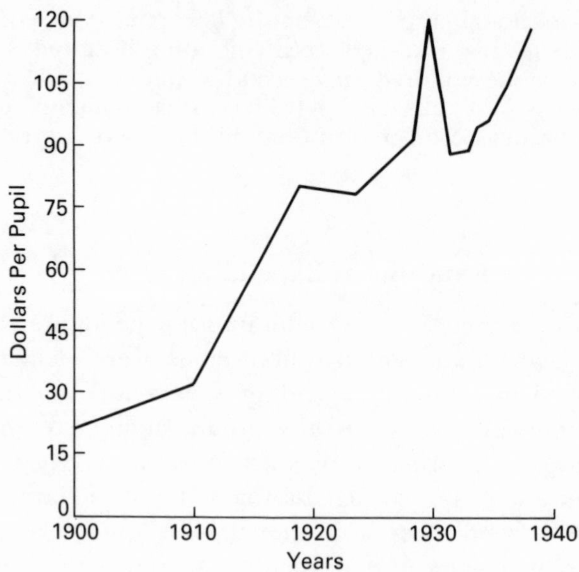

Figure 7.1 Educational Expenditures in Chicago, 1897–1938

Chicago from 1921 to 1932. Chicago spent the recommended proportions for instruction from 1923 to 1926, during the Dever-McAndrew years, but fell below before and after.

In 1931 on a city-by-city comparison, New York spent considerably more per pupil in every category except plant operation and maintenance on both a dollar and a percentage basis. Chicago spent nearly twice the dollar amount per pupil as New York ($15.65 versus $8.74) for plant operation. For total instructional expenses Chicago spent only 38 percent as much as New York; for operations and maintenance Chicago spend 82 and 63 percent of the New York budget. The city ranked high in other areas: per-pupil costs of the construction of school buildings exceeded those in New York by 31.5 percent. Costs were also higher for heating and ventilating equipment, for plumbing, gas, and sewer installation, and for electrical work and fixtures (Strayer 1932, vol. 1:150).[26] Vieg (1939) compared Chicago's educational expenses with several other cities and found that most, including Gary, Indiana, spent more per pupil on instruction than Chicago did. In brief, the data overwhelmingly support historical reports that school operations, where political appointments were highest, were protected, while instructional expenses were

Table 7.3
Recommended Levels of Expenditure

Practice or Standard	General Control	Instruction	Operation	Maintenance	Coordinate Acts & Auxiliary Agencies	Fixed Charges
65 cities over 100,000 population[a]	3.2%	77.5%	8.7%	3.0%	3.0%	3.8%
Moehlman[b]	5.0	75.0	12.0	5.0	2.0	1.0
Toothaker[c]	4.0	74.0	11.0	4.0	5.0	2.0
Year[d]			Chicago			
1921	4.491%	71.841%	13.767%	6.415%	3.085%	.401%
1922	4.210	72.813	11.305	8.172	3.385	.115
1923	3.561	76.275	10.630	5.127	3.347	1.060
1924	3.566	76.278	9.896	4.486	3.501	1.823
1925	3.765	76.409	9.523	4.886	3.171	1.946
1926	4.047	75.861	10.040	4.640	3.609	1.803
1927	4.202	73.612	10.661	6.064	3.583	1.878
1928	4.418	70.106	13.788	5.999	3.576	2.113
1929	4.104	71.970	14.119	4.781	3.741	1.285
1930	3.951	69.546	12.967	7.500	3.516	2.520
1931	3.951	72.107	12.881	4.997	3.469	2.595
1932 Budget	3.793	68.133	13.452	7.327	3.416	3.879

a. Adapted from "Budget as an Instrument for Economy" 1933: table 3.
b. Moehlman 1927:482–83.
c. Toothaker 1923:47–48.
d. Strayer 1932:table 11, 1, p. 149. The percentages given for 1932 are based on appropriations, not expenditures, for this year.

slashed. In 1932 the city spent only 68.13 percent on instruction, the lowest level for the years for which we have information.

The emphasis on instruction is apparent when pupil-personnel and personnel-teacher ratios are examined. Principals, school nurses, and clerks were typically in substantially greater supply relative to janitors and attendance officers in cities of over 100,000 population. In Chicago, schools hired a greater proportion of janitors and attendance officers than other cities (see table 7.4). Chicago schools hired lower numbers of all types of employees except janitors and attendance officers, where it came closest to the average for cities of over 100,000. Personnel statistics thus parallel the expenditure data for the city: the system was underfunded on the whole, but noninstructional personnel fared best. Teacher-pupil ratios averaged 1:41, at the upper limit of approved class size ("Teachers' Salaries and Teacher Load," 1933:89, table 8, teachers' salaries for cities of over 100,000).

The expenditure data confirm the extreme politicization and low expenditures reported earlier. If business interests had less influence, the total expenditures would have been higher. If the political interests had been ineffective in their attempts at politicization, expenditures for patronage employees would have been lower, and the distribution of funds within the budget would have been higher for instruction. With varying success, economic interests integrated their own considerations into the educational system: they established a ceiling on expenses and lowered land values and tax rates on business properties. They also sought to shape the character of education by influencing the kinds of information presented to students and by ordering the educational system hierarchically in order to reinforce and legitimate the existing racial, social, and economic divisions in society.

If competing, though not always conflicting, interests, such as the Commercial Club of Chicago, politicians, and William McAndrew, set the boundaries within which educational policy developed for the city, what were the racial and ethnic educational expenses like in this already dismal picture? The politicians shifted priorities from educational goals to facilitate and enlarge the instrumental uses of the system.[27] Examining educational expenditures in the three communities will help determine whether blacks, Italians, or Poles were sufficiently powerful to improve the local pattern.

There are four possible variations in level and distribution of expenditures; the combination of low overall expenditures and high

Table 7.4
Chicago Pupil-Personnel Ratios

Teacher Personnel Ratios			Personnel Pupil Ratios			
Teachers Per:	1932–33 Average 100,000+ Cities[a]	1930 Chicago[b]	Pupils Per:	Chicago[c]	Practice[d]	Standard[e]
Janitor	15:1	11:1		451:1	414:1	250:1 ADA
Attendance Officer	148:1	108:1		4,400:1	6,432:1	3,000:1
School Nurse	138:1	147:1		6,016:1	2,318:1 ADA	1,500:1
Principal	21:1	38:1		—	—	—

a. Based on *NEA Research Bulletin,* "An Efficient Staff: A Prerequisite," 1933:62, table 1.

b. Based on Herrick June 1930 information (1931:90, table 1).

c. Chicago statistics based on Herrick for categories of employees (1931:90, table 1). Enrollment figures from *Chicago Daily News Almanac* 1931:800.

d. Standard practices for cities over 100,000.

e. Based on standards proposed by a number of educational authorities; see "An Efficient Staff: A Prerequisite for Economy," "Constructive Economy in Education," in *Research Bulletin of the National Education Association* 11 (Sept. 1933), p. 62, table 2.

noninstructional expenses is the least optimal possibility. If there were no significant differences in expenditures in black, Italian, and Polish schools from the city average, then a disproportionate amount of money was spent in noninstructional areas. The city might have spent little in black areas but concentrated those expenditures in instruction. If the city spent more in the areas in question, black and ethnic schools could still have only mixed results if the proportion of instructional expenses remained low. Only if the city developed higher amounts of revenue and invested a high proportion of its budget on instruction would it be concluded that they placed a high priority on educational benefits of the classroom environment. If black, Italian, or Polish schools received fewer funds, especially for instruction, than the Chicago average, they were in very serious difficulty.

The schools examined for this study were selected by identifying areas in which blacks, Italian, and Polish populations were heavily concentrated;[28] the black areas, as expected, were much more concentrated by race than the Italian or Polish areas (Chicago Commission on Race Relations 1922: 242, table 10). Although 15 to 20 percent of Polish minors attended parochial schools, most were enrolled in public schools. When they attended school at all, Italians were much more likely to enroll in public schools.[29] The survey attempted to add five new schools in each new census year to respond to the expansion in community areas, although this was not always possible. Budgetary information for each school was recorded after 1910 in order to determine if there were changes in the level and distribution of expenditures as the schools became more heavily attended by the respective groups. The period of the study stretched for thirty budget years, from 1910 through 1940, with approximately 77 schools and several line items examined for every other budget year. The expenditures were standardized by basing them on the numbers of students enrolled and on the percentage that each of the line items contributed to the total budget.

In the effort to distinguish black, Italian, and Polish efforts on educational policy, the simplest means of summarizing the information for all of the schools was to average expenditures for schools dominated by a particular nationality into one rate per year. The total expenditures per pupil by nationality are presented in figure 7.2. The results are intriguing and much more complex than original predictions. The major discovery is that there are striking similarities in the time series, and there are no dramatic differences in the levels of

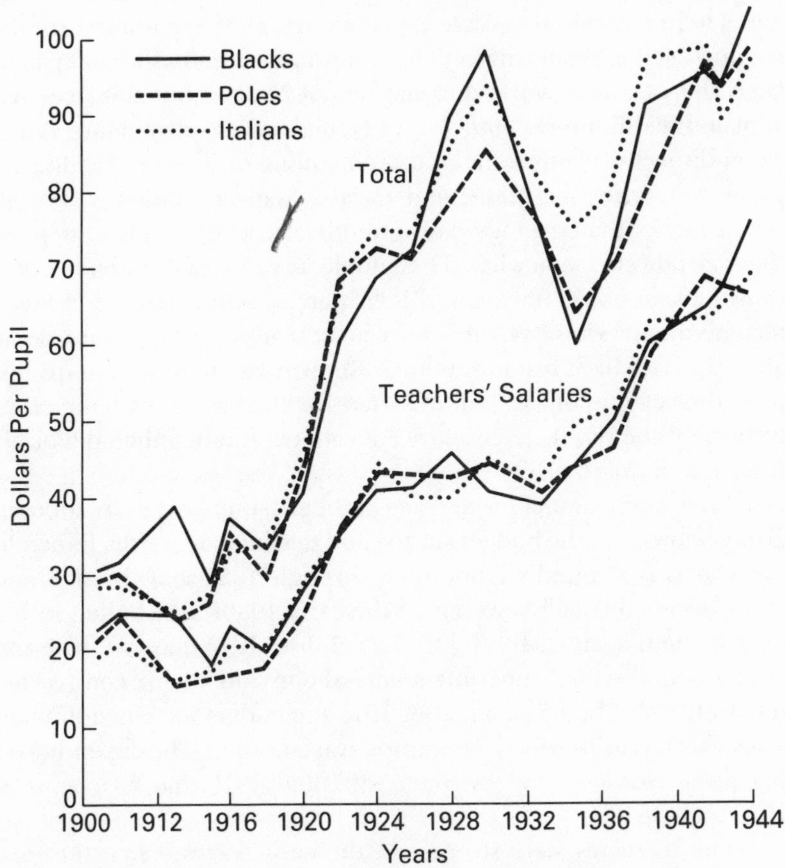

Figure 7.2 Expenditures per Pupil in Selected Black, Italian, and Polish Elementary Schools

expenditures for the three groups, especially when they are compared with the city's rates. From time to time the black or the Italian schools stand out above or the Poles fall below the others, but no one group revealed a consistently different pattern of educational expenditures throughout the period. Per-pupil expenditures in the schools in these areas were all lower than the city average.

There are several possible explanations. The expenditures for the city included a greater percentage for administration than may have been the case for each individual school budget, but this does not explain the differences entirely.[30] The high school-elementary gap in expenditures explains some of the remaining difference. Finally, the pupil figures for the ethnic and racial schools are based on enrollments rather than average daily attendance, which tends to depress the expenditures somewhat. The sample, because of its intended concentration in black, Italian, and Polish areas, selects schools in lower income areas. These possibilities can be considered in more detail after the data have been examined. Returns for all three groups display a lower rate of expenditure than for the city as a whole; other sections of the city received more educational funding than did black, Italian, and Polish areas.

An examination of the average of the per-pupil expenses for each group shows that the budget surged and declined unevenly. Expenditures increased rapidly from 1918 through 1922 and in 1928 and 1930, declined equally severely in the early 1930s, concluding with a recovery in the late 1940s (figure 7.2). Before 1915 mayors Busse and Harrison and school superintendents Shoop and Young constructed relatively stable budgets, but after 1915 the budget increased dramatically every year in which Thompson was in office. The expenditures per pupil rose only $11 between 1897 and 1910, but $47 between 1910 and 1920.

The increases were steepest in the early 1920s, when the total budget increased by 132 to 150 percent in 1922 and 1924, to $44.35 and $66.70 per enrolled pupil. Part of this increase can be attributed to post-World War I inflation, but inflation leveled off at the end of the Thompson administration. The last year in which Thompson was in office showed average expenses at their highest point, which the budget did not reach again until 1940, ten years later. Chicago's entanglement of assessment problems, taxpayer strikes, and the depression forced 14 percent of the city's families onto relief by 1934 and led the new Democratic administration to make sharp budget cuts.

The school budget was reduced by 15 percent for two successive years, pushing expenditure rates back to the 1922 averages. Herrick (1971) reported that the school budget did not recover from these cuts until the late 1930s, and the data confirm this.

It is possible to partition the increases in spending levels according to the type and the proportion of each expenditure. The increase in teachers' salaries did not keep pace with the increases for the entire budget. When dollars-per-pupil for teachers' salaries are plotted against the total expenses, the gap widens from 1920 to 1934 as the level of expenditures increased. This is even more clearly demonstrated when teachers' salaries are considered as a percentage of the total budget (figure 7.3). Here the results are similar when Chicago's total budget is compared with the groups' total budgets, but teachers' salaries in the black, Italian, and Polish areas as a percentage of the total budget were significantly lower than the average for the city. Since the Chicago system ranked well below recommended proportions, it is an important finding that the schools in this sample fared much worse. From 1909 through 1944, with nineteen observation years, there were only a few years when the instructional expenses even approximated 75.5 percent of the experts' recommended level. There are no years after Thompson's first election until 1934 when the recommended level was reached (Wirth and Furez 1938:4).[31]

Part of the difficulty in interpreting the data is the result of combining the changes in level of expenditures with the differing proportions of expenditures for a variety of categories. Thus for teaching costs to have remained as significant a proportion of the school budget in 1920 as they had been in 1913, they would have to have kept pace with total school costs. Even though teachers' incomes rose significantly between 1918 and 1924, during Chadsey's superintendency total expenditures grew at a faster pace, as is shown in both figures 7.2 and 7.3. In 1922 teachers' salary increases contributed only about one-third of the total budgetary increase, while newly listed expenditure categories, such as plant maintenance, contributed 25 percent and plant operation about 9 percent. Other items that absorbed the increase included high school construction (suspended during the war), principals' salaries, and the recently approved free textbook requirement;[32] postwar inflation also made up some of the difference between total increases and teachers' salaries. The school budget included all of these costs as well as hidden costs, such as the inflated price of school land purchases or maintenance contracts.[33]

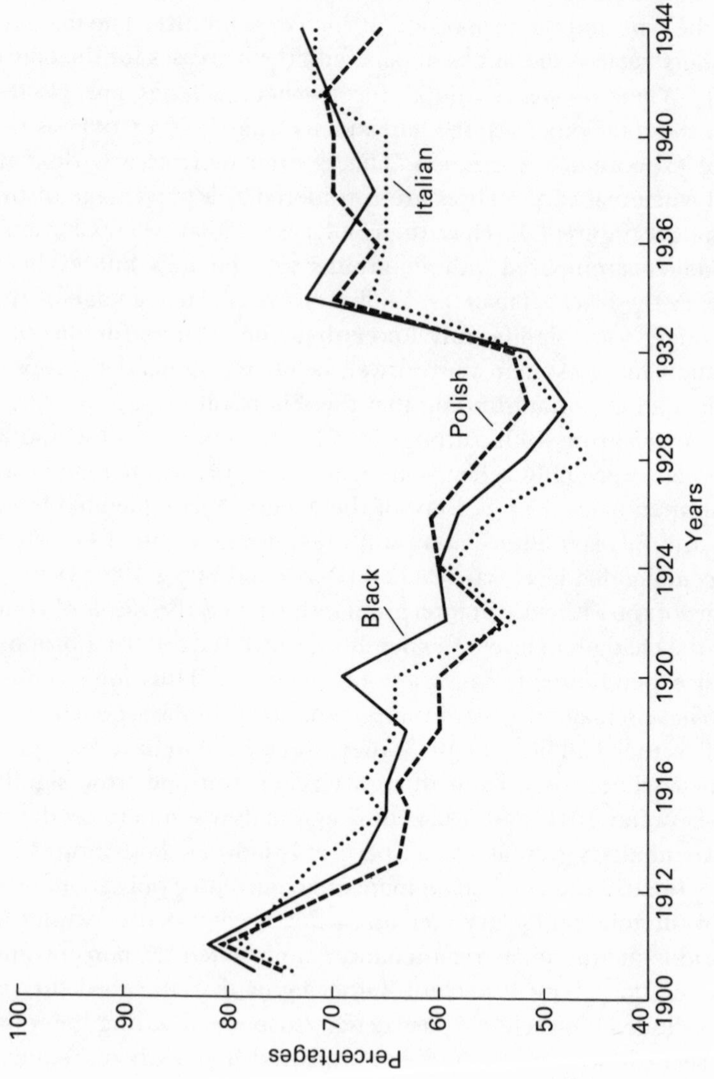

Figure 7.3 Teachers' Salaries as a Percentage of Total Expenditures

While teachers' salaries fell below the average proportion of the Chicago budget, maintenance and plant operations in black, Italian, and Polish areas were generally well above the recommended levels. The city may have invested more money in operating and maintaining these particular schools than it did on average, because they were old, but in 1931 the Strayer report found that fully two-thirds of Chicago's schools needed substantial renovation and improvement (Strayer 1932:19).

The Dever administration exerted a perceptible influence on the budget. Operating and maintenance expenditures for teachers' salaries reversed the previous twelve-year trend and stabilized temporarily. After the four-year Dever hiatus, teachers' salaries resumed their downward slide as a proportion of total expenditures. Plant maintenance and operations increased 162 and 204 percent in 1928 alone, thereby accounting for most of that year's budget increases.

At the onset of the depression the board cut deeply into the school budget, but the statistics used in this study do not explain all of the decrease. Figures 7.2 and 7.3 show that total expenditures decreased by nearly 25 percent, while teachers' salaries declined only slightly, both on a dollar and percentage basis. This is in direct contradiction to all historical accounts, which reported that the teachers' pay was reduced and delayed. The board of education operated on a record of expenditures or the total dollar amounts expanded until the 1930 budget year. After 1930, because of worsening fiscal and tax crises, the board reported only appropriations rather than actual expenditures. The reductions were obviously never officially acknowledged.[34]

In light of historical accounts that formal cuts were made by reducing income and paying the teachers on a delayed schedule, it is probable that salaries were reduced even more than these figures report. The proportion of teachers' salaries in the budget began to increase slightly in 1932 and then dramatically in 1934, so that for the first time in years the sample schools were all within 10 percent of the recommended proportions. In fact, the increase in the percentage of teacher's salaries was not the result of a dollar increase in salaries but an artifact of the substantial decreases in total expenditures.

Second, the board reported appropriations, but expenditures fell considerably below their original predictions. On a dollar basis, operating costs remained relatively stable, but their portion of the budget increased substantially. They declined only 4 percent from

1928 to 1934, while the total budget contracted by 35 percent from 1928 to 1934 (see figures 7.4 and 7.5). Even though the budget was cut by 6.4 percent, the percentage cost of maintaining the schools increased by 37.2 percent from 1931 to 1932. This increase did not show up in the schools in the sample, because plant maintenance expenses were cut sharply in 1932 and 1934. On the whole, the data confirm that a rise in expenses occurred as the schools were used for political purposes. When McAndrew was in office, although instructional salaries remained stable, operating expenses fell to a lower portion of the budget and total expenses stabilized.[35]

Expenditures in Black, Italian, and Polish Schools

Two hypotheses predict school expenditures in racial and ethnic schools: (1) that educational expenditures varied by racial status, and (2) that in the absence of racial or ethnic differentiation based on group status, educational expenditures were correlated with group loyalty by political administration. For example, in the first case, Polish schools might have ranked above Italian and well above black schools. In the second case, Polish expenditures might have declined after Thompson's election and risen after Cermak's, since he received only mixed support in these areas. Black schools might have received substantial decreases after Cermak's election. The data confirm these hypotheses.

On total expenditures, the city spent slightly more on black schools in the early years of the Thompson administration, but from 1918 to 1920 Italian schools ranked slightly higher. During the Dever administration Polish schools recovered slightly. Black and Italian rates rose well above the Polish schools during the second Thompson administration in 1928, but after the Democratic mayoral victory in 1931, black schools fell back to 1922 levels. Toward the end of the 1930s the city narrowed the gap, until black expenditures surpassed the other groups in 1944.

On teachers' salaries, the city spent only 46.8 percent in 1928 in Italian schools, when only two years before McAndrew's administration had spent 55.6 percent when the recommended levels were at least seventy percent. Black rates declined to as low as 47.8 percent in 1930. Because the total budget declined so sharply in the early 1930s, teachers' salaries constituted a significantly lower portion of the budget, though the graph shows a slight dollar rise. From 1936 on, the

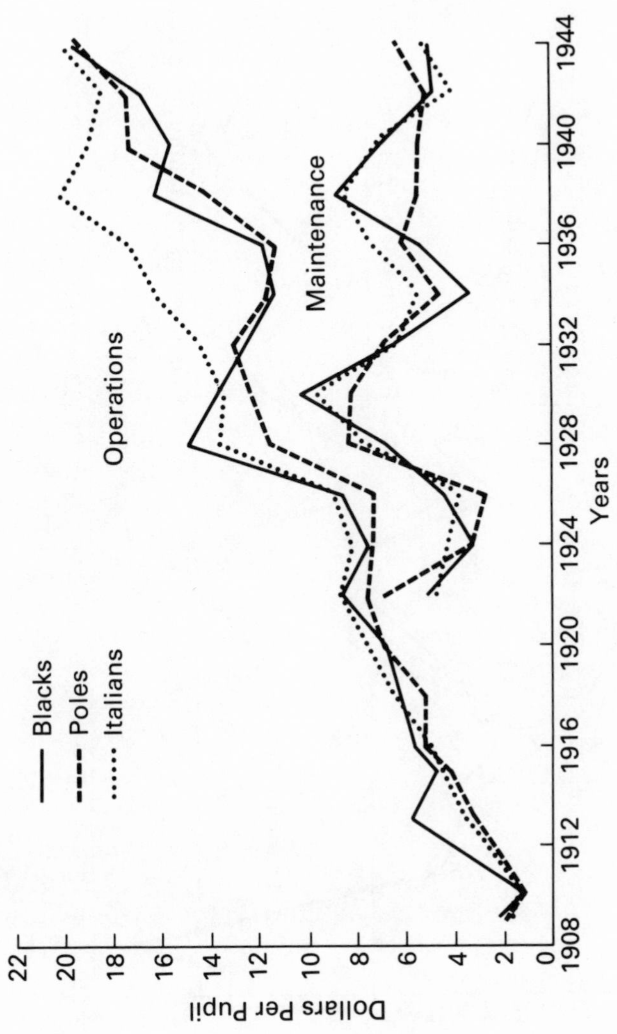

Figure 7.4 Expenditures for Operations and Maintenance

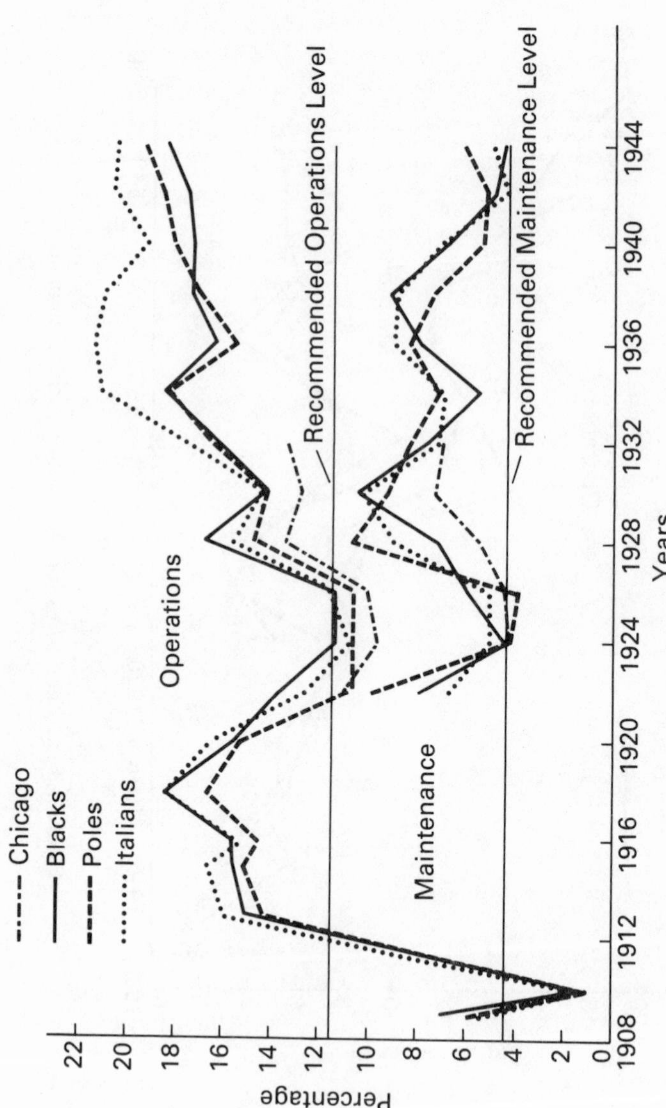

Figure 7.5 Operations and Maintenance as a Percentage of Total Expenditures

salary increase paralleled but did not close the gap with the total budget.

If teachers' salaries did not increase in proportion to the total budget, what accounts for the sharp rise in expenditures? All school expenditures increased dramatically during the period of the study, but expenses for operations and maintenance outdistanced all other categories. Salaries for noninstructional employees were located under operating costs, and it was in this category that most patronage employees were classified. While teachers' salaries remained constant, the increasing costs for operations' employees made up most of the difference. When black or Italian schools stood out above the others, it was often due to the increase in operating costs. Where the Polish schools fell below black and Italian schools, it was because they did not keep pace in these political areas. During the depression Italian expenses decreased less than black or Polish for two reasons: Italian teachers' salaries decreased and operating costs rose dramatically, from $13.40 per pupil in 1930 to $16.09 in 1934; black school costs declined from $13.86 to $11.27, and the Polish schools fell from $12.25 to $11.79 (see figure 7.6).

The Strayer report described citywide budget reductions in 1932: 23.9 percent for coordinate activites such as transportation, 10.1 percent for administration, 6.4 percent for all current expenses, 5.5 percent for auxiliary agencies, but only a 2.3 percent reduction for plant operation. Maintenance was cut by 50 percent from 1930 to 1934, but by 1938 it had risen almost to its 1930 level, while operations had equalled or surpassed its 1928 peak. In other words, budget items used to finance patronage operations were reduced the least. Even with reductions, both of these items remained almost continually above their recommended budget percentages. They fell to the recommended levels only in the Dever administration, when expenditures stabilized. The city first calculated maintenance expenses separately in 1922, at a level well above that recommended; the McAndrew administration cut this item in 1924 and 1926, but Thompson patronage pushed it upward during 1930 and 1938 (Strayer 1932, vol. 1:204).

What do these findings reveal about school politics? First, although Chicago's expenditures were relatively low, black and ethnic schools ranked even further below the city's. The data suggests that the schools, especially in Italian areas, were organized for political advantage, with maintenance and operations expenditures well above

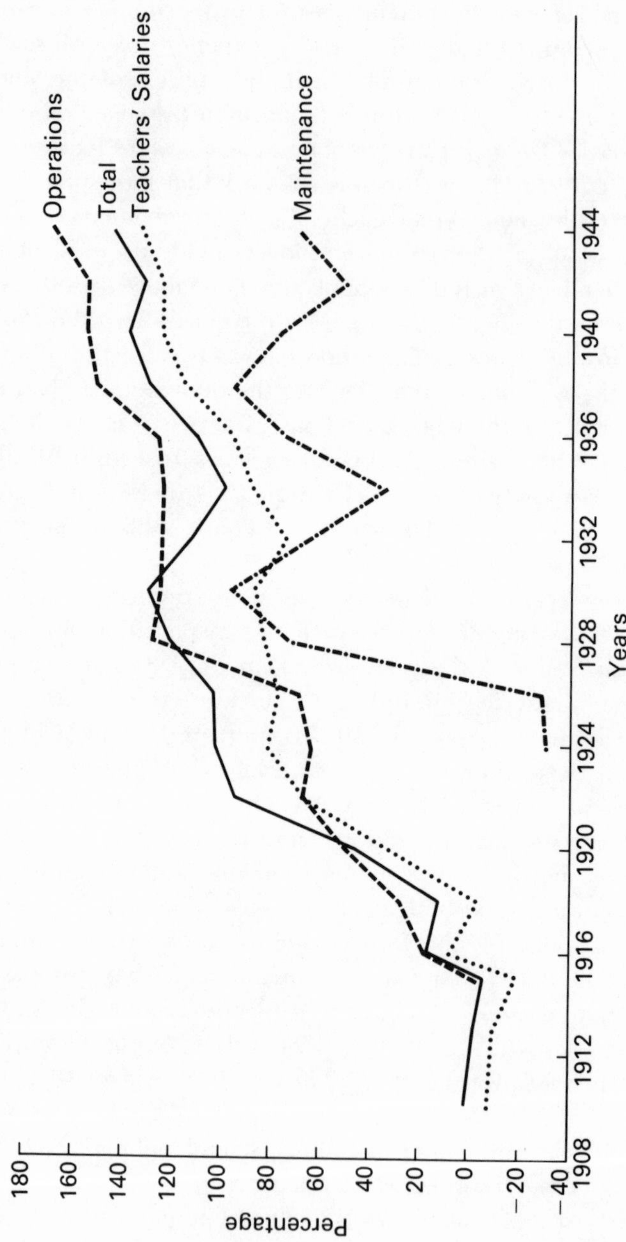

Figure 7.6 Percentage Increases in Educational Expenditures in Black, Italian, and Polish Schools

recommended levels. Teachers' salaries were stable during the depression, which created the incorrect impression that they constituted a larger portion of the budget.

Conditions of the Physical Plant

The Strayer report (1932) showed how widely school building conditions varied. Predominantly black schools were underequipped. In 1920 only one-third of the schools in black areas had bathrooms, and two-thirds had been built before 1900. Herrick reported that "electric lighting was promised for all schools as soon as possible" in 1922 (1971:141). The Strayer report recommended substantial reno-

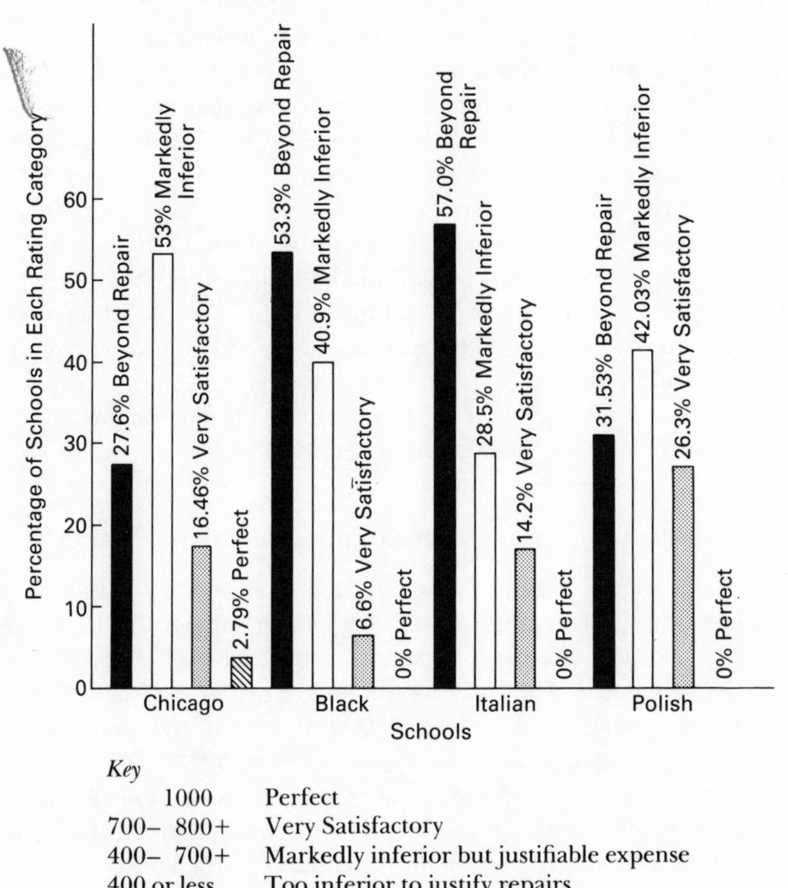

Figure 7.7 Strayer Ratings of Chicago Schools by Group, 1932

vation, improvements, and additions for a full two-thirds of the schools.

The Strayer report rated physical conditions of all the schools in the city, which provides additional data on the same schools for which there is expenditure data. Figure 7.7 shows the distribution of ratings for the city and for the black, Italian, and Polish areas. Over 50 percent were too inferior (400 or below) to justify the expense of repairs. Only 32 and 27 percent of the Polish and Chicago schools scored as low, but the report recommended that more than half of the Italian and black schools "under normal economic conditions . . . should be abandoned just as rapidly as new buildings could be erected to carry the pupil-load now housed in them" (Strayer 1932, vol. 4:19). Economic conditions were not "normal" for another fifteen to twenty years. Twenty-five percent of the Polish and 15 percent of the Italian and Chicago schools were ranked very satisfactory, while only 5 percent of black schools scored so high. This constitutes the least optimal scenario of the four possibilities considered (Chicago Commission on Race Relations 1922:243, table 11, Herrick 1971:141; Strayer 1932, vol. 4:17–20).

Three of the four high schools in this study (Fenger, Morgan Park, and Schurz) scored poorly, but the black high school, Phillips, scored lowest, slightly above "abandon all hope" at 420. Schurz High School, which was attended by large numbers of Poles, scored poorly also. Overall conditions in the school plant were considerably worse in the black and Italian areas of the city than in Polish neighborhoods or in the rest of the city (see Herrick 1931:14–15).[36]

Substantive Issues: Blacks and Educational Policy

Michael Homel studied black influence on educational policy in Chicago from 1910 through 1941. This section and figure 7.8 summarize and evaluate the three types of issues and twelve major cases discussed (Homel 1976), based on the theoretical framework of racial policy and public policy orientations formulated and described in chapters 3 and 5.

First, all the issues raised racial rather than economic questions. Black groups focused on issues of racial discrimination or conditions of black schools when they might have attacked the board of education on its citywide spending policies. Since racial status was an issue with which blacks still had to deal, it was easier to generate broad public support with a racial rather than an economic focus, which logically could have led to attempts to form coalitions with other white ethnic groups.

Second, elected politicians were rarely involved in educational issues. Homel cited ambiguous evidence on their influence over patronage appointments, but except for overcrowding in black schools they stayed away from public involvement in school politics. The NAACP, a large, noneconomic, heterogeneous, broad-based organization, was most active, although the Chicago Council of Negro Organizations, local parent-teacher associations, and other issue-specific groups led the public criticism of school board policies. Homel's study showed that the NAACP was involved exclusively in issues of racial status raised through integration questions. Although the Chicago Council of Negro Organizations helped appoint a black representative to the board of education, descriptive representation was also a status issue. Homel reported that this was consistent with the council's original goal, as the organization was funded as a moderate (that is, anticommunist or procapitalist) counterpart to the National Negro Congress, which was dominated by Marxists.

Nonelectoral organizations and leaders were much more likely to become involved in these issues because they involved debate over racial segregation. To redress or discuss such grievances forced consideration of collective status and the intangible rules of the game. This was politically dangerous for machine politicians, since it loosened their hold over their constituents and threatened the stability of their own positions (Homel 1976:190–91).

Thirdly, the twelve issues fell into two general categories: questions on racial status, which separated neatly into issues of descriptive representation and segregation of pupils, and questions on the physical conditions of black schools. On a simple basis the issues seem to divide into James Q. Wilson's status and welfare issues, but they represent a more complex theoretical framework. Homel reported that blacks pressed for descriptive representation (an integrationist position) on the board of education after Thompson's election in 1915, but Midian O. Bousfield (physician, insurance executive, and husband of the only black principal in Chicago, Maudelle Bousfield) was not appointed until 1939. Those who expected Bousfield to articulate substantive policy and to assume an integrationist position using protest tactics were disappointed when he used bargaining strategies and took an accommodationist position on most issues.

Type of Educational Issue	Issue Originator	Outcome
I. Representation (Descriptive)		
a. Board of Education Member	Chicago Council of Negro Organizations	Midian Bousfield appointed 1939 with bipartisan support
b. Teachers, school employees	Politicians	Appointment through machine
II. Segregation Protest		
a. 1912 Hyde Park Improvement Association Pro-Segregation Statement		High-ranking school officials disavow
b. 1916 Wendell Phillips High School segregated social hour which had been integrated		Superintendent Young ends social hour altogether
c. 1918 Loeb proposed segregated schools	NAACP	Mayor Thompson decries Loeb proposal
d. 1926 Shoop district lines follow black areas rather than "natural boundary"; whites allowed to transfer to another "white" school; blacks refused. NAACP filed court suit	NAACP, community Leaders	Judge Kerner ruled no grounds because no proof of intent to discriminate by board
e. 1934 Morgan Park High School; board created separate black and white feeders	NAACP, Urban League, Black State Legislator, Morgan Park Community Groups	Mayor Kelly overruled school board and ordered blacks to Morgan Park High School
f. Overcrowding issue; Dickerson recommended district changes, permissive transfers, end to restrictive housing covenants as solution	Alderman Earl B. Dickerson, White Citizens Schools Committee, PTAs	Unresolved

Type of Educational Issue	Issue Originator	Outcome
III. School Conditions		
a. 1936 Lilydale complaints about poor condition of portables; when board was unresponsive, black parents made them unusable, picketed school and disrupted school board meetings	Lilydale Citizens' Committee	Board responded after direct action and protest demonstrations
b. 1930's calls for new black high school. After several years of requests, DuSable built using federal public works funds in 1935		Board responded when federal funds available
c. Protests over classroom conditions; Colman 1938 fire; Hayes 1936, 70 students contracted trenchmouth	PTAs, etc.	Board responded to crises, not earlier protests
d. Overcrowding; no new schools from 1930 to 1940, but school population grew by 49.7%. Groups recommended more schools and portables; Grant and Bousfield recommended more schools	PTAs, Alderman Ben Grant, Maudelle Bousfield	Unresolved

Source: Homel 1976.

Figure 7.8 Blacks and Educational Policy

The school segregation conflicts arose when the board, school principal, or board member formally articulated a prosegregation or clearly discriminatory (de jure) policy. As the black population was concentrated in predominantly black areas by housing market discrimination, the school board drew district lines that followed rather than crossed racial boundaries, creating de facto discrimination. According to Homel, black groups focused on the de jure rather than the de facto cases. For example, the 1926 Shoop and 1934 Morgan Park cases involved two de jure segregation cases. Alderman Earl Dickerson challenged the general philosophy of school district policy, arguing that the issue of overcrowding was a direct result of the board's discriminatory policy that segregated blacks into school districts too small to reasonably accommodate them. In two other cases the Hyde Park Improvement Association and Max Loeb proposed segregated schools. Finally, the principal of Wendell Phillips instituted segregated social hours in 1916 after several years of integration. In summary, the black community assumed a defensively integrationist posture, since it attacked the de jure cases rather than de facto discrimination (Homel 1976:182).

The third type of issue dealt with the material conditions of the schools, in effect, welfare questions. Although these questions incorporated economic elements, the racial aspects dominated the economic in their political articulation, and it is for this reason that their racial character is emphasized. In general, black schools were in very poor condition; when combined with the rapid growth in the number of black school children (by 49.7 percent from 1930 to 1940) and the failure to build new schools during that time, it is clear why four of the twelve issues involve the question of school conditions.

A member of the new Democratic machine, Alderman Benjamin Grant, and principal Maudelle Bousfield, in classic welfare fashion and in direct contrast to Alderman Earl Dickerson, recommended an increase in material items (more schools and portable classrooms) without touching on the more general, collective, and redistributive issues involved. They supported an accommodationist educational policy.

DuSable High School was built after requests for change. Parents at Colman and Hayes had also pressed for physical rehabilitation, but no action was taken until a fire and an outbreak of trenchmouth affected seventy students. One of the most interesting cases occurred in 1936 at the Lilydale Community School (on the far south side), where parents complained about the school's and its portables' poor condition. Although the board promised improvements, none were made. By fall, after arson and other vandalism made the portables unusable, the parents picketed the school and threatened to disrupt school board meetings. The parents ignored the issue of integration and the broader issue of total expenditures, but they used direct action and protest to address existing conditions, what James Q. Wilson described as a welfare issue. Wilson argued that welfare issues were promoted through bargaining strategy, but this is an instance of protest advancing demands for increased resources, that is, for welfare policy.

Finally, the outcomes fall into an interesting pattern. In eight of the eleven cases, a simple evaluation shows positive responses by officials. Bousfield and other teachers were appointed, Mayor Thompson and school officials disavowed any implementation of segregation, and Mayor Kelly overruled the school board on the Morgan Park case. The board built a new high school, repaired the Lilydale portables, and dealt favorably with Colman and Hayes. The favorable outcomes are not as unusual as the events themselves or the conditions of protest that helped determine the outcome. In all the cases, either the situations had been allowed to develop into crises or black public opposition was so unanimous that school or public officials were forced to act.

Midian Bousfield was appointed to the school board after the concept of a black appointment received bipartisan support in the 1939 mayoral election. The first Pole had been named to the board in 1894 and the first Italian in 1927.[37] This, more than any other single example, suggests the importance of racial hierarchy and its consequences in the lives of individual blacks and in the status of the group as a whole. Both the Democratic and Republican parties publicly supported a black appointment before either one acted.

The rulings of school officials and Mayor Thompson's disavowal of de jure segregation were costless in light of the much more significant and simultaneous development of de facto segregation. In the most appealing victory, Mayor Kelly overruled the school board, but this was early in the new machine era (1934), when the Democrats were still courting black voters. Most importantly, black groups were united in unanimous opposition to the policy. The NAACP, Urban League, a black state legislator, and the local Morgan Park black groups opposed the policy. Moreover, Morgan Park was located far to the south of the black belt. A pro-integration ruling there did not threaten to unleash the torrent of racial conflict that would have occurred on the western and especially on the southern boundaries of the near south side.

On school conditions the board responded to crises, specifically the fire at Colman in 1938 and the trenchmouth outbreak at Hayes in 1936. It built the new DuSable High School, but only when the federal government made public works funds available.[38] It moved to repair the Lilydale portables when the parents' willingness to engage in direct action and protest demonstrations precipitated a political crisis for the board.

What of the issues on which the black community was defeated or in which the outcome was uncertain? The overcrowding issue remained unresolved. The board simply ignored the protests and continued its policies of drawing school district lines along racial boundaries. The two clear defeats occurred in the cases of the 1916 Phillips social hour controversy and the 1926 Shoop school district line. Superintendent Ella Flagg Young ruled that the segregated school hours should end. That is, she did not reinstate integrated social hours; she simply eliminated them altogether, thereby strengthening segregation. In the Shoop case the NAACP filed a "mandamus petition in Cook County Circuit Court demanding a boundary shift" (Homel 1976:187). The Shoop district lines were drawn around the black neighborhood, even though some of the blacks lived closer to another school: to attend Shoop some students had to cross the dangerous railroad tracks. Whites were exempted; blacks were not. Judge Otto Kerner ruled "that the NAACP legal force had failed to prove that racial segregation was the intent of school personnel" (Homel 1976: 185).

In summary, blacks were successful in both descriptive representation cases (although after a long struggle and unanimous political support in the city), in three of the four cases involving material issues, but successful in only three of the six involving segregation or collective issues. Blacks were able to influence educational policies only when the issues fit the machine's requirements. Issues that involved tangible goods and services and selective recognition received more favorable hearings than collective issues. Questions of redistribution were not even raised.

Conclusion

One puzzling question remains. If racial discrimination permeated the Chicago environment and the school system so thoroughly in the early decades of the twentieth century, why were expenditures so similar in black and white schools? First, black, Italian, and Polish schools had lower total expenses and proportionally lower expenditures than the city as a whole. In this specific area, why had racially discriminatory spending practices not developed?

The most important component of educational expenses was teachers' salaries. At the time the teaching force was 98 percent white. Even though there were a number of black schools, black teachers remained a very small portion of the teaching population because of grass-roots resistance to their employment. Thus as long as the number of black teachers remained small, there was no basis for internal racial differentiation of salary expenditures.

As early as the 1920s the Riot Commission reported on the critical evaluations of white teachers for their black charges. As long as depression-enforced economies held down the expansion of the school system, white teachers had little alternative but to remain in black areas. When World War II ended the depression and gave birth to the baby boom, school systems all over the country expanded rapidly. In 1952 Howard Becker reported that teachers attempted to transfer from lower-status black schools to upper-status white schools. For the teachers lower-class included "all Negroes," whom they found "difficult to teach, uncontrollable and violent in the sphere of discipline, and morally unacceptable on all scores, from physical cleanliness to the spheres of sex and 'ambition to get ahead'" (Becker 1952:471). Becker reported that most of the sixty teachers interviewed stayed in the black lower-income schools only a short while (Chicago Commission on Race Relations 1922:247–50).

Harold Baron's 1971 report of Chicago's school expenditures for the Chicago Urban League showed that there was considerable difference in expenditure patterns according to race and income groups. The Chicago average was $324, but black schools spent only $264 while the white schools spent $341. The rates varied because classroom size differed by both race and income. Overcrowding was greater in lower-income white schools, but the level of overcrowding was relatively consistent in all black areas, regardless of income. Ninety percent of double shifts were concentrated in black schools.[39]

Richard Berk and Alice Hartman confirmed Baron's study. White school expenditures ranked at the top, black at the bottom of all schools. When Berk and Hartman examined teachers' salaries, they found "predominantly nonwhite districts receive allotments higher than the overall means . . . [but] average instructional salary expenditures favor predominantly white schools." Students in "predominantly white schools received on the average $40 [9.2 percent] more than students in predominantly nonwhite schools" (Berk and Hartman 1972:55, table 2).

Educational expenditures were undifferentiated by race before World War II for several reasons. The constraints imposed by the depression limited expansion of the system and, therefore, prevented migration away from less desirable teaching assignments in black schools. As the number of schools increased rapidly in the 1950s and 1960s, teacher mobility assumed a pattern that reflected racial hierarchy. White teachers with more experience and education took priority in winning the most desirable teaching asignments in white schools. All black teachers and white teachers with less attractive credentials were more likely to be assigned to black schools at the bottom of the status and racial hierarchy. As this pattern developed, Baron suggested, it became more difficult to attract enough teachers to black areas or to lower-income white areas to minimize classroom overcrowding, thereby resulting in lower teacher expenditures in black areas.

Race was, therefore, a critically important factor in educational expenditures, although it did not appear to be a distinguishing element before 1945 because the data reflected a closed system. The schools were generally closed to black professional employment, and the entire system was closed to expansion. The prewar system was highly differentiated along status lines. It can be compared to the contrasting systems of race relations in southern urban centers based on agricultural or nonindustrial (traditional) versus industrial (modern) economies. Whites dominated in both systems, but the form of domination was quite different.[40]

The "traditional" closed system required perfect or near-perfect dominance (Dorn 1979), with whites holding all high-status positions and authority. In this system whites coexisted in close but clearly superordinate proximity to blacks. In the modern system racial hierarchy remained, but it had become a system of imperfect dominance; white and black spatial differentiation increased. In the postwar expanding system in Chicago, status rankings were important but racial dominance was no longer perfect; racial hierarchy was thus elaborated and differentiated as both black and white teachers worked in schools, but white teachers with seniority moved into predominantly white schools leaving blacks and whites with less seniority and lower pay in black areas. Most intimate, proximate interaction between black students and white teachers ended in the schools. Under the second set of circumstances, expenditure differences appeared.

The impact of economic, ethnic, and racial groups on educational institutions is now clear. School system expenditure outputs for black schools were approximately equal to Polish and Italian schools, but the overall impact was nevertheless inequitable. The black, Italian, and Polish neighborhood schools operated with even fewer resources than the already poorly supplied schools in the rest of the city. Yet the racial and ethnic expenditure patterns varied sufficiently by political administration for them to have been of more than passing importance. Black schools received the most funds during the third Thompson administration, but they fell rapidly when the Democrats took power. When this occurred, it was because of the use of operations employees for patronage purposes rather than because of greater expenditures for classroom instruction. Thompson invented the use of noninstructional employees for his personal patronage army, but the Cermak and Kelly administrations institutionalized the policy. The business community successfully imposed its concern for fiscal austerity upon the board of education.

Until World War II, discrimination was enforced through restraints on employment and discriminatory school districting policies. In light of the rather powerful restraints on racial equal opportunity, the political uses of and the economic restraints imposed on the schools added economic and educational discrimination to the racial discrimination blacks already faced. "The question of who benefits from public services is answered at least as much by decisions about what types of services will be provided as by decisions regarding the distribution of existing services" (Rich 1979:241–42).

8

Race and Ethnicity in America

> The Negro is a sort of seventh son, born with a veil, and gifted with second-sight in this American world,—a world which yields . . . no true self-consciousness, but only lets him see himself through the revelation of the other world. It is a peculiar sensation, this double-consciousness, this sense of always looking at one's self through the eyes of others.
>
> —W. E. B. DuBois

The Chicago machine disintegrated with stunning speed after Mayor Richard J. Daley's death in 1976, as evidenced by Jane Byrne's successful challenge to the machine in the mayoral race of 1979 and Harold Washington's election to office in 1983. It is time to summarize the analyses offered in the preceding chapters, to apply the models developed for Chicago politics from 1910 to 1940 to events of the past decade to show why pluralist theory fails to explain and misinterprets the characteristics of black political behavior. Finally, in this chapter I show how the Chicago political environment changed so that the black community was able to mount a successful campaign for mayor, and why this made Harold Washington's first year in office difficult.

Black, Italian, and Polish Politics Using the Political Participation Model

In chapter 4, I outlined the political participation model, which identifies the variables that predict a group's success in winning city-wide political leadership. Three categories of variables include: external, which arise from outside the group's behavior; demographic; and internal variables, which have developed from the group's own specific history. Three external variables—geographic concentration, partisan competition, and political structure—indicate how factors external to the group locate it politically. In Chicago racial discrimination against blacks in the real estate and banking industries created the highest geographic residential concentration in the city. In early twentieth century Chicago, over ninety percent of blacks lived in highly concentrated, extremely homogeneous neighborhoods; Poles lived in concentrated areas with fifty percent of their total group in homogeneous neighborhoods, while Italians were scattered throughout the city in small pockets.

From 1940 to 1980 a few Polish neighborhoods survived, but most of the Polish population was dispersed throughout the city and suburbs. The only Italian neighborhood was displaced by the construction of the campus of the University of Illinois at Chicago in the 1950s, scattering Italians throughout the city and suburbs even more widely than in previous decades. Meanwhile, black neighborhoods continued to expand in extremely homogeneous fashion. By the process called "invasion and succession," the black areas moved southward toward the city's southern boundaries and by the 1950s expanded westward from the Loop. Blacks lived in many areas of the city by the late twentieth century, and black-white segregation was not perfect, but the concentration of blacks in black neighborhoods remained one of the highest in the country.[1] As an area's population became predominantly black, its voting patterns and its political leadership shifted appreciably. By the late 1970s sixteen wards were predominantly black, and black aldermen and committeemen represented all but two of these (the committeeman of the ninth and the alderman and committeeman of the twenty-seventh). The significance of a predominantly black voting district was recognized by black and white political actors in the early 1980s when a series of redistricting suits affecting city council, the state legislative, and congressional districts were filed to expand the number of black districts (Grimshaw 1980:28–29; Preston 1982a:179–80).

From a relatively small but significant and highly loyal group in the 1920s and 1930s, by the 1970s and early 1980s the black population had grown to over forty percent of the city's total and was clearly the single largest racial or ethnic voting group within the city, equalling 400,000 registered voters for the 1977 special mayoral primary election and 600,000 registrants out of approximately 665,000 blacks of voting age for the 1983 mayoral primary. Although a large voting bloc, blacks had extremely poor turnout rates in the 1960s and 1970s. While there were issues of great importance, such as discrimination in employment, housing, and schools, the machine's structure prevented these issues from reaching the political agenda by close control over substantive issues, by attending to party and governmental personnel, or by stripping power from black leaders such as Ralph Metcalfe, who broke with the machine to place racial issues on the political agenda (Alkalimat and Gills 1984:88; Kleppner 1983:70; Preston 1982b:95).

Partisan competition represents the degree to which political parties competed for racial and ethnic group voters. Although only one faction of the Republican party sought black votes in the period of the study and the local Democratic party actively pursued black votes only after 1930, at no time did both parties compete for the black voter. This contrasted dramatically with most other groups in the city whether past or present; the Irish, the Poles, and other groups usually divided their votes and their political candidates among the many factions in the Democratic and Republican parties before 1931. Although the two parties were in fact divided into five different factions, only blacks and Italians were almost entirely pursued by only one party.

Partisan competition also refers to the degree of competition between and among parties in the city. From a high degree of electoral competition in 1910, partisan conflict dwindled to insignificant proportions by 1940 and has remained at that level. With the exception of the 1983 mayoral election in which Bernard Epton won the votes of dissident anti-Washington Democrats, genuine partisan competition has not returned to Chicago, but political competition certainly has.

Political structure refers to the organization of elections. District rather than at-large elections typically increase ethnic and racial descriptive representation on city councils. This proved true in Chicago, as the second and third wards elected two black alderman to the city council in the 1920s and early 1930s. With the rise of the machine, however, black representation on the city council stagnated at two aldermen until the 1950s when two new black aldermen were added to the city council. Two additional black aldermen were also elected in the 1960s, and ten new blacks were added to ward leadership in the 1970s. Oscar DePriest (1929–35), Arthur Mitchell (1935–43), William Dawson (1943–70), and Ralph Metcalfe (1971–78) in succession represented the first congressional district as the only black congressman from Chicago, until George Collins was elected to the sixth district in 1970 to fill an unexpired term (McWorter et al. 1984:19).

The second set of variables is demographic. The size of a group, its proportion to the city's total, and its proportion within the voting-age population of citizens contribute significantly to blacks' political influence. In early twentieth century Chicago, the relatively small proportion of the total black population was mitigated by the disproportionately large size of its voting-age population, all of which was native to the United States thereby establishing its citizenship. Poles constituted a much larger percentage of Chicago's overall population in the early twentieth century, but they equalled a smaller sector of the voting-age population, and a relatively minor proportion were citizens eligible to vote. Italians faced the disadvantages of both blacks and Poles with the advantages of neither, being small both in real numbers and in numbers of voters.

From 1940 through the early 1980s, the black population reached a more normal age distribution profile, and the Poles became citizens and natives, with most adults eligible to vote. However, Poles expanded only by natural increase after foreign immigration was ended in the early 1920s, while the black population of Chicago grew both by reproduction and by continued migration from the south. By the 1980s blacks equalled 39.8 percent of the city's population, and 35.5 percent of its voting-age population (Alkalimat and Gills 1984:60; Pinderhughes 1984:87).

A second important demographic variable is the city's ethnic and racial heterogeneity. In chapters 3 and 4, I showed how blacks exerted a disproportionate influence in Chicago's electoral politics because of the city's numerous European ethnic groups, which constantly competed for electoral power before 1931. In a city with fewer groups in search of political and economic power and with less complex partisan and factional competition, black voters would have found themselves either ignored or perhaps coerced into political alliances, as eventually happened when the machine eliminated ethnic competition. By the 1980s, strong national identification had evolved into a sense of race.

Internal variables include leadership institutions, political socialization, partisan identification, and political issues. In the Polish community of Chicago, the Catholic church assumed the definitive leadership role; a cornucopia of Polish organizations were developed by, linked to, or opposed to the church. The church was much less prominent among the Italians, whose fraternal organizations based on family and personal contacts formed the basis for unions and other economic activities.

Churches, civil rights organizations, and fraternal groups structured black political, social, and economic life in the first decades of the century. One of the striking aspects that characterized Harold Washington's recent mayoral campaign and that distinguished it from the earlier era was the dazzling array, specialization, and cooperation of the black organizations, which laid the groundwork for and which developed and ran his campaign. McWorter, Gills, and Bailey described them as outsider and insider groups that created a series of alliances within and among black organizations and then developed links to white authority structures and organizations in order to legitimize the campaign for the postelection period. Black nationalists of cultural and political dimension, black prointegrationist civil rights leaders, black capitalists, black Marxists, black politicians (independents at first, and after the primary, most of the machine-linked politicians), the black press, and Jesse Jackson served in a variety of ways during the campaign (McWorter et al. 1984:5).

Ironically the complexity and specialization of these coalitions allude to James Q. Wilson's analysis of black organizations in Chicago in the 1960s, when he observed that they focused too much on race. He prescribed increased specialization into civic-oriented associations in order for them to successfully integrate themselves into and to affect the formation of public policy (Wilson 1960a:282–89). Instead, racial organizations developed whose focus was more specialized than either the NAACP or the Urban League. In addition blacks moved upward through public sector organizations such as trade unions, the school board, community organizations, and the police; but rather than focusing entirely on institutionally defined policy, they brought a highly explicit and vocal expression of their concern with racial policy to their mainstream responsibilities.[2]

Organizational specialization therefore occurred, but in combination with a focus on racial issues that resulted in the creation of an alternate, highly integrated (within itself) black interest group structure bridging the public and private sectors, with some ties to white economic and interest groups and in support of Harold Washington's campaign for mayor. This institutional effort united for an election campaign, which was to say the least unusual. I will discuss the sources of this unusual unity later in this chapter.

Three additional internal variables include political socialization, partisan identification, and political issues. The three groups underwent radically different forms of political socialization, although the bulk of each group's population entered life in agricultural environments far removed from the politically complex sectors of society. Most of Chicago's black population by 1920 had been born and grown to maturity in the rural south, subject to severe segregation, discrimination, violence, and the cooptation of all political rights. The move to a more liberal setting created both strong efficacy, as reflected in the high levels of black political participation early in the century, as well as a palpable sense of the continuing reality and the very real dangers in which racial discrimination expressed itself in the city. Once the machine formed, creating a stabilized racial and ethnic political hierarchy, black expectations of successful competition declined and, along with them, electoral participation, until in the late 1970s and early 1980s the machine weakened and with its decline came opportunities for political changes. The 1979–83 years are a critical electoral period for Chicago's blacks, as turnout increased and substantive issues reached a crisis. On the other hand, neither Polish or Italian immigrants had been socialized into politics in their native lands. In the United States, where they first voted and participated in self-government, they faced some discouragement but no organized nationwide, or even citywide, dejure or de facto discrimination.

Partisan identification distinguished the groups more clearly. Poles tended to lean toward the Democratic party even before the 1931 local critical election, but the Republican party attracted a share of the group's support to a sufficient degree to make the first Polish campaigns for office in the late nineteenth century unsuccessful. By the twentieth century, the Italians identified with the Republican party, but this was masked by Democratic control of the one major concentration of Italian voters throughout the early 1920s. After Cermak's election in 1931, Italians, like blacks, gradually shifted their allegiance to the Democratic party. The vast majority of black voters identified with the Republican party through the early 1930s. When the Democrats took permanent control of the city in 1931, the proportion of blacks voting for Democratic mayoral candidates increased, but the narrow votes suggested some resistence on the part of black voters and perhaps continuing Republican identification, at least at the local level, through the early 1950s. Grimshaw, for example, contrasts the differing level of Democratic support among blacks voting for mayor (low) and president (high) in the 1940s and early 1950s, which suggests an incomplete transformation in identification with the local Democratic party based on coercive incentives. By the mid 1950s, however, black voters moved decisively into the Democratic party at the local as well as the national levels (see chap. 3 of this volume for a discussion of Andersen's [1979] work on black voter shifts; see also Grimshaw 1980:15–17).

A group's posture toward the political regime rests on the political and economic issues that critically affect it. Although discrimination affected the Poles and Italians, they were nonetheless active in important sectors of Chicago's legitimate and illegitimate economy, as were the Italians, or the discrimination was too inconsistent to severely limit their movement into the economy or politics, as was the case with the Poles. Because the discrimination was not absolute, both were unlikely to place issues of ethnic discrimination on the political agenda.

Blacks as a group were subordinated in their search for jobs and housing (as shown in chapter 2), in political life (as described in chapters 3 and 4), in criminal justice and education (as I have shown in chapters 6 and 7), and they were also subjected to physical violence when racial tensions grew too great. Racial status so pervaded the Chicago environment that it affected every sector of the economy and the polity. Racial status was in and of itself a political issue and was raised in the pre-machine era by the most successful black and white candidates who sought to represent black voters. Before the machine, politicians used race to address or to repel black voters. The machine era subordinated and submerged race as a political issue in general and ignored its effects on public policy in particular, in favor of a concentration on technical concerns with the delivery of tangible, selective incentives. This pattern of subordination over many decades resulted in an increasing desensitization of white politicians to the significance of race, to its ability to empower and to motivate black voters. Daley was one of the few living politicians old enough to remember the race riots of 1919 and the powerful influence of black voters in the late 1920s. The Daley, Bilandic, and Byrne administrations created racial issues of descriptive and substantive character and allowed them to accumulate to an explosive level.

Preston summarized some of these long-standing issues from the Daley and Bilandic administrations, which in combination with Bilandic's mistakes led to his defeat by Byrne in 1979. They:

> included Daley's attempt to punish Metcalfe by slating cabinet member Erwin A. France to run against Metcalfe in the primary; the issues of police brutality and the shooting death of Black Panther leader Fred Hampton by police assigned to State's attorney Edward V. Hanrahan; the total disrespect shown [black] Alderman Wilson Frost (thirty-fourth ward) when, as president pro tem of the city council, he

was passed over as acting mayor after Daley's death; and the disregard and disrespect shown the black community with the slating of Bennett Stewart for Metcalfe's seat in Congress (Preston 1982b:106).

Descriptive issues are perhaps more significant at certain times than substantive because they alienate the upper and middle classes of a subordinated group, the sector most able to organize and to take some action if sufficiently aroused. Because Daley's machine had concentrated on limited and tangible benefits for black areas, the growing black middle class in Chicago drifted away from the machine and toward independent candidates by the 1970s (Grimshaw 1982; Peterson 1976; Preston 1982b). The middle class sought group recognition as heads of city bureaucracies and government boards and failed to find it in the public sector in Chicago. Confirmation of some of these changes occured in the 1975 primary election for mayor when William Singer, black State Senator Richard Newhouse, and former State's Attorney Edward Hanrahan challenged Daley's nomination. While Newhouse won only 7.9 percent, Singer 29.3 percent, and Hanrahan 5 percent of the vote, "in 1971 [Daley] won by pluralities of more than 5000 votes in eleven of the fourteen wards that had been at least 66.7% black in 1970. Four years later he [received no] such pluralities in any of these wards" (Zikmund 1982:42).

After this challenge to Daley's leadership, the party offered thirty-fourth ward alderman Wilson Frost the city council's most powerful position, chairman of the Finance Committee. The chairman of this committee formally becomes president pro tem of the city council on the death of the mayor but the party and city council leaders collaborated to block Frost from this post and from the position as acting mayor after Daley's death, naming alderman Michael Bilandic of Daley's eleventh ward to lead the city.

Jane Byrne won election with strong black, Polish, and lakeshore liberal support, but turned inland in search of support from white ethnic neighborhoods once she was in office. Black citizens expected descriptive representation on the city's governing boards, but Byrne continued to name whites to the school board, to the public housing and transit authority boards, as well as to head the school system and police department. In the process she repeatedly reminded blacks of their subordinate positions within the machine and of her belief in the superiority of the white electorate over black voters in the city.

The End of the Machine

Political Leadership, Organization, and Incentives

Important, even radical shifts occurred in all of the aforementioned variables between the end of the period of this study and the early 1980s, but before summarizing those, the changes in that most important element in the Chicago environment, the machine itself, should be analyzed. One of the most important aspects of the organization of politics in the city was the character of its leaders. This section begins with an analysis of the impact changes in leadership have had on the machine.

The Chicago machine was created by Anton Cermak but assumed its most powerful form under the administration of the late Richard J. Daley. Each of these men understood the immense economic, ethnic, and racial complexities of their cities and wove them into a political organization to govern and to manage these potential sources of conflict. When Cermak entered politics early in this century, he faced a disorganized system of competitive machine politics, one in which disparate, usually ethnically-linked, political factions manipulated selective incentives for partisan gain. When he died of an assassin's wounds in 1933, he left a political machine firmly controlled by the Democratic party, a centralized hierarchical monopoly that regulated selective incentives, economic conflict, and ethnic and racial groups so completely that its basic structure dominated Chicago and Illinois politics for the half century from 1931 through the early 1980s.

When Richard Daley won the mayor's race in 1955, he had already assumed chairmanship of the party (in 1953). He was a talented leader who took control of the machine after a short-lived, machine-directed era of "reform" under Mayor Martin Kennelly. Kennelly was nominated by the Cook County Central Committee of the Democratic party to head the city after Kelly's administration, when corruption grew so great that it outpaced even Chicago's normal levels. Kennelly cleaned up the city's image slightly, but the party selected him because he could add respectability but little genuine authority to his task. The ward committeemen ran the city as a coalition during the Kennelly years; power had become relatively decentralized and corruption had increased significantly.

Len O'Connor reports that there are three major positions of power in Chicago: mayor, chair of the city council finance committee, and the chair of the Cook County Democratic party's central committee. Richard J. Daley became the first man to join the mayor's office and chair of the party's central committee in a powerful political marriage. Cermak had shared control with Pat Nash, while Kelly held the position briefly in the 1940s. Daley, first elected to the leadership of the party in 1953, had promised to give it up if he won the mayor's post, but control of both the administrative and political apparatus of the city strengthened his hold over the city and in turn over the party (Rakove 1975:92). Alderman Paddy Bauler described Daley on the night of his election to mayor in 1955, as "the dog with the big nuts" who would run Chicago and who would tolerate no subleaders, black or white, within his organization (O'Connor 1975:124).

Daley was a successful leader of the machine because, like Cermak, he devoted his passions to politics and left the weaknesses of the flesh to those he ruled. Even in his early years Ben Adamowski reported, "Most of the time he kept to himself, stayed in his hotel room, and worked hard. In Springfield, you could tell real fast which men were there for girls, games, and graft. He wasn't." This is not to sanctify Daley; Adamowski continued, "He made it through sheer luck and by attaching himself to one guy after another and stepping over them" (Royko 1971:45). Like Cermak, Daley brought an understanding of the Chicago political environment, of its individual human beings, as well as of their racial, ethnic, and economic identities, and of the complex relations formed by them to the mayor's office. As Alkalimat and Gills report, "He was a formidable opponent who could scream four-letter words on national television, order police to shoot to kill looters during riots, and force prominent civil rights leaders to give him the Black Power handshake" (Alkalimat and Gills 1984:64). He also had the ability to subordinate idiosyncratic responses to political events into a consistent pattern of rewards and punishments, which strengthened the machine without necessarily concentrating on his ego.

We can understand the impact of both Cermak and Daley by an examination of the machine on black politics and of its effect on black political leadership in the city between 1940 and 1980. Black politics presents an intriguing history during the machine era. Whether blacks were ever anything but restless under machine rule may have been obscured by the image of William Dawson as a powerful "submachine" ruler in the city. Blacks' political position within the city was of a significantly different character than Poles' or Italians' for a variety of reasons (see discussion in chap. 3 of this volume; see also Wilson 1960a:50).

First, they held a clearly subordinate position to whites in the city. William Dawson, alderman, committeeman, congressman, Republican, and later Democrat, headed what James Q. Wilson designated as the Negro "submachine." Wilson compared the character of Dawson's rule with Adam Clayton Powell's in New York City; Dawson closely fitted his leadership style to the politics of the Chicago machine. He eschewed all flamboyant displays of political power and any suggestions of direct political competition with whites in both Chicago and Washington. Most importantly, he concentrated on delivering selective benefits to his constituents and on avoiding any discussion of substantive issues involving racial discrimination. This extended to the point of shunning sensitive public policy committee assignments in the House of Representatives, choosing to concentrate his rise to seniority through the less visible and substantively less controversial Government Operations Committee. Powell on the other hand chose to serve on the Education and Labor Committee, a pivotal and highly controversial location that frequently involved racial issues (Wilson 1960a:350–51).

According to Wilson's theory, Dawson created the black machine, subordinated it to the citywide political machine in the 1930s, and in the process became a powerful if not independent ally of the city's white leaders. In chapter 3, I showed that Dawson attained power because he consolidated political resources in the black community by joining with the Dickerson Democrats. In effect Dawson created a black monopoly. Dawson was also credited with dumping Kennelly and with helping Daley win the mayor's race in 1955 (Grimshaw 1980:21).

Grimshaw has recently offered a revisionist interpretation of these events, arguing that Dawson was much less independent than heretofore supposed. The concept of a powerful Dawson submachine presumed the central organization sought to heighten black electoral participation, and to decentralize organizational and substantive decision making. As Grimshaw comments: "The choice the machine's central leadership very likely faced, then, was *not* one of merely determining how best to maximize the machine's electoral effectiveness. Rather, it had to determine how best to maintain itself at the head of the machine, while generating a level of productivity from the membership *sufficient* for maintaining the machine's dominance" (Grimshaw 1980:7, emphasis added).

Grimshaw contends that the concept of a submachine within a larger machine is first of all a contradiction in terms unless one accepts the concept of moderate organizational decentralization. Machines require hierarchical decision-making structures in which loyalty inheres while a submachine necessarily implies decentralization in organizational and substantive authority, as well as the potential for serious internal conflict. During the late 1940s and early 1950s there was certainly room for this kind of decentralization. The members of the party's central committee, for example, after convincing Mayor Kelly that his stand in favor of open housing had hurt the party's chances in the 1946 elections and would damage his campaign for mayor in 1947, chose Martin Kennelly to run. As Jake Arvey said, Kennelly was "a man of high integrity . . . [but] unfortunately he was inept. The council ran him" (Rakove 1979:13).

There was indeed enough slack for Dawson to have been the kind of leader Wilson describes, but Grimshaw marshalls evidence to the contrary. Dawson removed the committeeman of the third ward in 1952, Christopher Wimbish, but the central committee replaced him with Ralph Metcalfe (the late congressman), an outsider to Dawson's organization and a Daley protégé, over Dawson's objections (Grimshaw 1980:11–12).

Claude Holman and Metcalfe represent two examples of attempts by black officials to use race as a substantive issue during the machine era. Holman, according to Grimshaw, surprised his black and white political colleagues when he violated Dawson's policy of avoiding collective issues and cosponsored an open housing bill with an independent alderman. Dawson, as in the earlier situation with Wimbish, sought to remove Holman from his positions as alderman and committeeman but was blocked by the central committee with Daley's support. As soon as his new position was clarified, Holman dropped his quest for housing reform. He had simply used the threat of race, a substantive issue in this case, to win a stronger position within the organization (Grimshaw 1980:13). In the struggle, Dawson's position was seriously weakened.

In another example, Ralph Metcalfe, in the early 1970s, found that even his black friends who were upper-middle-class professionals (but who were indistinguishable from other blacks to the Chicago police) were subject to police brutality. It provoked him into confronting the issue of racial discrimination by the city government and, therefore, by the machine. Metcalfe was not only a committeeman but by 1971 a respected member of Congress, having been elected after Dawson's resignation in 1970. He was not in search of greater status within the organization, as Holman had been, and held his ground on the issue of race. Daley's response was radically different. He stripped Metcalfe of his patronage, but Metcalfe held onto his congressional seat and his role as committeeman of the third ward. His lack of selective incentives combined with his previous failure to use racial appeals inevitably weakened his position, however (*Chicago Tribune,* Oct. 11, 1978).

When Grimshaw analyzed the electoral support garnered by the Dawson submachine, black voters turned out and displayed only moderate loyalty to the Democratic party until Richard Daley's first election in 1955, after which their loyalty and turnout for the Democratic party was quite high for a time (Grimshaw 1980:26). Grimshaw explains this pattern by the fact that a peculiar set of circumstances shaped voter behavior. The wards which Dawson headed also served as home to the local illegitimate industry known as "policy," a betting game that the public sector has legalized and coopted through state-run lotteries in recent years. Dawson was attacked by local reform and blue ribbon leaders, who accused him and other party leaders who had slated Richard Daley of corruption in dumping Martin Kennelly. The attack was posed in a form that explicitly raised the issue of race in a Chicago election, which gave black voters an unusual opportunity. With Dawson the target of what seemed to be racist attacks, blacks rallied to defend him and also Daley, by turning out in large numbers and with great loyalty for the Democratic ticket. Assuming that policy employed some people in the second and third wards and that many people bet on a daily or weekly basis, one could also argue that Kennelly's promised reforms threatened the economic and tangible goods of a sector of the black population. So the event can be interpreted as having both selective economic and racial dimensions. "In the preceding 1951 mayoral general election, Black voters had given the Democratic candidate an average plurality of 931 votes per ward. Daley received an average plurality of nearly 12,000 votes per Black ward [in 1955]" (Grimshaw 1980:22).[3]

Grimshaw's argument is a fascinating one because it suggests that selective incentives do not always generate strong electoral support and that the relatively mediocre levels of participation that characterized black political participation in Chicago in the late 1960s and early 1970s may well have been the rule rather than the exception. Turnout increased as a result not of the routine skill of the Dawson submachine but of an unusual event, a substantive issue with racially controversial and economic implications.

Mayor Daley reorganized and strengthened the machine, and he reaffirmed its maintenance of racial political hierarchy. Although he won office with Dawson's support, once in power he sought to maximize his authority over the entire city. He blocked Dawson's later efforts to strip fourth-ward committeeman Claude Holman of his patronage in 1958 and "established the precedent whereby all of the Black committeemen could begin, if they were not already doing so, dealing directly with the central leadership of the party, in particular, Richard Daley." Dawson led in name only (Grimshaw 1980:23).

Grimshaw's argument confirms the analysis of the consequences of the formation of the machine for black politics offered earlier in this book, and of the factors that explain the disintegration of the machine in recent years. When the political machine focused on selective benefits it necessarily excluded important substantive concerns of the black population from its political agenda. The consequences of that exclusion were low electoral participation and turnout, because racial issues have motivated Chicago's black voters much more effectively than singularly selective ones. Selective issues with a racial component motivate black voters more than purely selective issues. The fact that the city operated under a powerful centralized machine precluded Dawson's use of racially focused, collective incentives.

Thus where Cermak invented his own organization from the bits and pieces of ethnic and economic groups in the city, Daley remade the one he found. He brought it to its preeminent status by strengthening and dominating the black electoral organization, by combining control of party patronage and government of the city, and by bringing in an ally as chairman of the city council finance committee.

Neither of Daley's immediate successors, Bilandic or Byrne, managed the city bureaucracy very successfully and neither controlled patronage. George Dunne, a near north side forty-second ward alderman and ward committeeman, chaired the central committee of the Democratic party after Daley's death and has presided over the county commission since 1969. Once patronage distribution turned erratic, fought over by warring north and south side Irish, and Bilandic and Byrne aggravated the already difficult political situation by frequent public reassertion of racial hierarchy, not only black middle-class voters turned restive, but working-class black voters grew restless as well. Neither Bilandic nor Byrne had the leadership skills to bully blacks back into their subordinate positions or to create a new, somewhat more liberal balance of power. And completely apart from black voters, neither had the legitimacy to rule the increasingly restless white ethnic groups. Without strong disciplined leadership to manage economic, organizational, and group competition, the machine quickly disintegrated into the type of politics with which Chicago had grown familiar in the first three decades of the century. As early as 1979, independent black candidates defeated three incumbent aldermen, and two former regular Democrats whom the machine had dumped won office (Preston 1982b:107).

In contrast to Daley, mayors Bilandic, Byrne, and Washington have held or hold office without controlling the chair of the city council finance committee or party chair. Mayors Bilandic and Byrne had working relationships with the head of the party (after Daley's death, George Dunne) and with the chairman of the finance committee, Wilson Frost. Mayor Washington is now engaged in open warfare with both Edward Vrdolyak, head of the party, and Edward Burke, chairman of the finance committee (Edward Burke, interview, June 1983; Wilson Frost, interview, June 1983; O'Connor 1975:38–46).

The value of a talented political leader such as Daley and the contrast between him and those who have followed him have become all too quickly apparent. Bilandic had too little appetite for political life; he became an alderman only after years of encouragement by Daley (Rakove 1979:398) and, most importantly, he had not developed the meticulous store of knowledge of the operations and internal connections within the machine—the political instinct—that helped give Daley his power. Bilandic, for example, chose to move to the lakeshore after taking office, as Cermak, Kelly, and Kennelly had done before him, but as Daley never did.

Michael Bilandic's distance from the city's administrative operations allowed for a breakdown in the organization's basic system of rewards and punishments. When Bilandic's leadership failed in a number of administrative maintenance areas, the blizzard of 1979 became a surrogate for these issues. Failure to keep the streets clear of snow, combined with lack of mass transit service in black areas, galvanized black voters. Basic and very elementary selective incentives though these were, Bilandic's delivery failures violated black citizens' expectations of their rewards for participation in the machine.

Jane Byrne ran and won the mayor's post as a charismatic candidate on a reform platform. Once in office, she made a number of mistakes, which cost her a second term. First, she quickly abandoned her reform platform. Her major base of support in the 1979 election had been drawn from the predominantly black wards, but she aimed all her political overtures after the election at the declining numbers of white ethnic voters in the city. Fifteen of the twenty-nine wards with a majority or plurality for Byrne were black. She won all seven north shore/reform wards, only two of the eleven white ethnic wards, and none of the machine wards (Zikmund 1982:50). Second, unlike Daley, she was unpredictable and idiosyncratic in her attempts to reward or punish her competitors, in a way that discouraged political loyalty and undermined the long-term survival of the machine. She acted so inconsistently that her potential allies felt early in her administration that they could either no longer rely on a guaranteed source of rewards from her or that they would be better off risking a challenge and supporting Richard M. Daley, the prince of the city and state's attorney, who challenged Byrne in the 1983 Democratic primary for mayor.

Probably most important is that Bilandic's and Byrne's administrations discouraged party unity and loyalty. Bilandic was too weak and viscerally uninvolved a politician to dominate or even mediate city government, city council, party, and racial-ethnic conflicts simultaneously. Byrne had the psychic energy and involvement, but her unpatterned responses to machine officials encouraged incipient factionalism and political disunity. She opposed Daley as state's attorney in 1980 and George Dunne as candidate for Cook County board president (Alkalimat and Gills 1984:92). The breakdowns in the Bilandic and Byrne administrations, however, were only the final addition to a series of problems that had been building throughout the Daley era.

Of the three groups on which this study focuses, only the blacks and Poles were of sufficient size to claim mayoral leadership in the post-Daley era. One of the clear characteristics of politics in Chicago even through the present is that political leadership is a group process, one in which the race or ethnicity of the candidate is critically important in shaping the electorate's response. By the 1960s and 1970s the Italians constituted too small and too dispersed a group to contend for electoral leadership of the city. Poles as early as 1955 and blacks in the 1970s challenged the Irish and the machine for leadership. Ben Adamowski ran as an independent Democratic candidate for mayor in the 1955 contest in which he placed third, winning 15 percent of the vote, far behind Daley and Kennelly (O'Connor 1975: 113). In 1963 Adamowski ran again as the Republican nominee for mayor against Daley and won 44 percent of the vote. "Adamowski was strong in Polish wards, but not all Polish wards went to Adamowski. . . . Where the machine was weaker, Polish identity probably had some impact. But across the city as a whole, loyalty to the machine and traditional identity with the Democratic party won out" (Zikmund 1982:40).

Without an Irish surrogate (Bilandic) or even an Irish woman (Byrne) as an effective ruler, contention for alternative political leadership began. In the 1977 Democratic primary, Alderman Roman Pucinski of the forty-first ward and State Senator Harold Washington challenged the machine's candidate, Michael Bilandic. Bilandic "won with a smaller proportion of the votes than at any time since Daley's first contest for mayor in 1955" and Washington fared better than any previous black candidate (Zikmund 1982:43). Zikmund argues that Pucinski, who won 32.7 percent of the vote, was more of a neighborhood or regional candidate and fared very poorly south of the Loop. Pucinski considered running again in the Democratic primary of 1983, but desisted when it became clear he would only guarantee Washington's chances for the Democratic nomination by splitting the white vote between himself, Daley, and Byrne.

Political Ideology

The final political change that the results of the 1983 elections reflect is that of black political philosophy. Racial discrimination existed in Chicago before 1931. It did not mysteriously disappear between 1931 and 1979. What made the black population more responsive to racial appeals in the late 1970s than it had been previously?

In the 1979 elections, black political activists discovered the motility of unregistered black voters in ward and citywide elections. Using collective/racial appeals, they generated successful voter registration, effected a high turnout, and defeated several machine candidates. The combination of declining selective benefits, increasing intraparty competition, and increasing attempts at reasserting racial political hierarchy pushed the black population in Chicago to the stage of Doug McAdam's cognitive liberation, a realization of the possibility of and the means to political reform (McAdam 1982:48).

Reaching that stage required the black population to focus on racial discrimination, which the city's mayors had cooperated in facilitating. In a number of policy areas and in issue after issue Daley laid the groundwork, and then Bilandic and Byrne denied the black population increased descriptive representation and aggravated them through the poor formulation and implementation of substantive policy affecting blacks. The constant reassertion of racial hierarchy, of the legitimacy of blacks' subordination under whites, provoked blacks of a variety of class backgrounds and ideological positions to a very rare event in philosophical behavior patterns—almost universal agreement among all blacks (one of the possible combinations in the model described in chapter 5) on the necessity for black political leadership in the most important political office in the city, the mayor. Once blacks reached "cognitive liberation," in which they aggressively focused on the issues of racial discrimination in city politics, they behaved as blacks had not done since prior to the creation of the machine in 1931. They focused on their collective racial identity as a result of their heightened awareness of racial discrimination facilitated by the Daley, Byrne, and Bilandic administrations, and they voted according to that group identity in order to elect Harold Washington as mayor (McAdam 1982:51). This unity appeared only as the success of black independent candidates for alderman and ward committeemen in the late 1970s and early 1980s, as a series of polls (from late 1980 through early 1982) showed high agreement on an appropriate black candidate for mayor, as black organizations successfully filed suits to liberalize voter registration, and as Ed Gardner of the Soft-Sheen Cosmetics Company, a major black hair products producer, funded publicity for voter registration drives (McWorter et al. 1984:23, 27).

The effect of these changes is captured in this quote from Mc Worter, Gills, and Bailey:

> The two other city-wide organizations did as much as the Task Force, although they all worked together so closely, that an average volunteer often was not clear what group they were *working under*. Everybody seemed just to know what they were *working for:* the election of Chicago's first Black Mayor, Harold Washington. One organization was Chicago Black United Communities (CBUC), headed by Lu Palmer [also a columnist for the *Chicago Defender* and a radio commentator],

> and the other was PUSH [People United to Save Humanity] headed by Reverend Jesse Jackson. These two were headquartered in the First Congressional District represented by Harold Washington. . . . Each organization had powerful personalities who had been frequently at odds, between each other and with Washington. However in this context, there was a contagious rapproachment spreading because the possibility of a Black mayor was something all of them wanted. The nationalists began to unite with Jesse Jackson. Lu Palmer and Jesse made up and Lu began to speak on the PUSH Saturday morning radio broadcasts, reformers began to speak on the PUSH Saturday morning radio broadcasts, reformers began working with the nationalists, etc. The *historical moment created this militant Black unity* of "outsiders" and this unity *helped the movement have a magical quality people could believe in* (McWorter et al. 1984:8–9; latter emphasis added).

How can this "historical moment of magical quality" be explained? In chapter 5, I described the ideological complexities of black political philosophy based on the two intersecting dimensions of racial-political and of economic status. The political environment ordinarily provokes considerable disagreement on the choices black citizens and political activists make about their racial and economic goals, as well as on the strategies they use, resulting in the variety of political positions scattered along the two dimensional continua described in chapter 5. On rare occasions at the national level or in local situations, the political environment reaches a stage where these conventional lines of dissonance fade, and black leaders, nonelected as well as elected, subordinate their disagreements because they agree on what they are working for. The entire range of black organizations and individuals ordinarily arrayed in conflict or at least in distinction from each other along the racial and economic dimensions of black political philosophy reached a moment of agreement and unity in Chicago in the early 1980s. All could see significant benefits from the election of a black mayor in general and from the election of Harold Washington in particular.

Several things make this seemingly simple event so unusual. It is rare for such a wide array of organizations to agree with each other on a candidate. Black nationalists and Marxists do not always agree that electoral politics is a relevant or rewarding strategy for achieving their goals. Significant sectors of the black electorate have remained impervious to political mobilization for several decades. Black businessmen have typically remained aloof from political activities. On occasions when unifications of the entire black political spectrum have occurred, such as the National Negro Congress and the National Black Political Assembly, it has not been tied so closely to an electoral event. It was highly unusual for black politicians to unite behind a black candidate for office using explicit racial appeals.[4]

Most of Chicago's black organizations, as well as blacks working in public or private sector institutions, recognized that their status as individuals and as a group would be significantly altered by Washington's election as mayor because it would help destroy the basic elements of racial hierarchy and collectivism in Chicago. How completely or successfully the election would actually accomplish this was of course uncertain, but there was general agreement among blacks of all economic, social, and educational levels that it would make a difference. Because the common denominator that limited economic advancement among blacks regardless of their economic position was race, their own status would be subordinate to whites until they challenged the existing racial hierarchy and elected a black mayor with a substantive program of reform.

Doug McAdam's discussion of cognitive liberation describes the development of social movements as "a transformation of consciousness within a significant segment of the aggrieved population"; to reach it "people must collectively define their situations as unjust and subject to change through group action" (McAdam 1982:51). The size of Chicago's black population had grown large enough, and with sufficient turnout and loyalty a black candidate might win the mayor's office. To win, however, blacks needed the appropriate candidate, and a coalition of organizations set out in a series of polls by local organizations and newspapers to choose one. Harold Washington ranked at or near the top of several polls (McWorter et al. 1984:23). This same coalition of black organizations successfully registered and turned out a large number of black voters to the polls for the primary and for the general election. Once a group of activists was convinced that there were sufficient electoral resources and that Harold Washington was the best possible candidate for mayor, the "historical moment" took on the "magical quality" described by McWorter, Gills, and Bailey. Blacks broke through their half-century expectations that the machine was invincible and worked directly and effectively to change their status.

From Political Machine to Machine Politics

The political participation model includes the variables geographic concentration, partisan competition, political structure, the size of the group, ethnic and racial heterogeneity, leadership institutions, political socialization, partisan identification, and political issues. These as well as factors affecting machine strength and the model of black political philosophy discussed in chapters 3, 4, and 5 predict Polish and black electoral success.

A series of factors thus explain the changes from the political machine of Richard J. Daley to the competing coalitions that the Chicago Democratic party has now become. Daley's death, poor leadership by mayors Bilandic and Byrne, combined with increasing hunger for political status among white party politicians held in check by Daley's long rule, made individuals' efforts to carve out their own domains irresistible. Daley was obviously as skilled at distributing rewards in the 1950s as Bilandic and Byrne were at mishandling them in the 1970s. The city's demographics, Byrne's and Bilandic's awkward administrative styles, and the growing decentralization of city power and party patronage severely reduced the political stability of the system. Byrne and Bilandic made mistakes, such as his handling of the snowstorm of 1979 and her rejection of Manfred Byrd as superintendent of schools; they also violated some of the underlying norms and values of the Chicago machine. No snow removal and declining descriptive representation are poor payment in exchange for racial subordination. As black neighborhoods watched their snow-covered streets freeze solid in the winter of 1979 and blacks lose appointments to positions in city government, blacks of all classes and educational levels realized that the coerced fifty-year-old political compromise with the machine was no longer worth the denial of selective, tangible rewards. Moreover, party leaders had not produced a fourth generation of Irish or other white ethnic machine leaders whom blacks could support; the Irish had held the reins alone too long. Under such political circumstances, the group that held the demographic advantage of size, extreme partisan loyalty, high turnout, and substantive dissatisfaction stood a chance of defeating the machine.

Poles had grown restive under two and one-half decades of Irish Democratic machine rule by the early 1950s, but their efforts at winning the mayor's position fell short in a series of attempts. They challenged Irish leadership, but the relatively dispersed patterns of Polish neighborhood settlement, the result of low ethnic and economic discrimination against them earlier in the twentieth century, resulted in a physically dispersed Polish electoral vote. There was little partisan competition among the Poles because of the strength of their identification with and support for the Democratic party in the 1950s and the 1960s. By the mid-twentieth century, Polish adults constituted perhaps 200,000 votes, the largest European ethnic voting bloc in the city. The absence of political issues strongly associated with Polish concerns combined to define the limits of Polish success at the ballot box to Adamowski's two races and to Pucinski's efforts (Zikmund 1982:37).

Blacks, on the other hand, held all of the "advantages." Because of continuing discrimination, they lived in homogeneous neighborhoods, which by the 1970s produced the single largest bloc of votes on the city council as a potential support for a black mayor. The black population had grown large enough, if united, to dominate although not to control the electorate. They strongly identified with the Democratic party, and in the 1983 mayor's race they did not divide among themselves over a candidate. Strong self-conscious ethnic heterogeneity had subsided in the decades since 1940 into a stronger racial identity. Once Washington won the Democratic nomination the Poles, Irish, and others became "white." Only Hispanic voters and a small number of whites (including Jews) along the lake shore added the votes to create an electoral majority. In fact, Hispanic voters are currently in a position to play the role once held by blacks, since they have the ability to create the majority when the rest of the electorate is narrowly divided. Black organizations demonstrated considerable unity, resourcefulness, and agressiveness in developing the black electorate, identifying a candidate, and funding and managing a campaign. Finally, the previous Democratic administrations had created a wealth of issues upon which the black electorate based their opposition to further white and machine rule.

Thus the violent and powerfully hypnotic general election campaign of 1983 took shape because white voters in Chicago faced an election in which a black candidate competed openly with a white man, Bernard Epton (a Republican and a Jew), and challenged the racial hierarchy that had long been maintained by the machine. Rakove quoted fourteenth-ward alderman and committeeman Edward Burke in the late 1970s: "There is a latent anti-Semitism in Chicago and a large population that will never vote for a Jew. They would vote for anybody before a Jew" (Rakove 1979:144). Whites reacted strongly during the election campaign because they realized that they had lost their dominant political position in Chicago politics. The top political official in the city would in all probability no longer be white; they wanted to maintain their racial privilege in politics as well as in their ordinary lives. They produced buttons with watermelons and with the words "Chicongo Polease"; their campaigns rallied to the words of a song "Bye, Bye Blackbird," which had been played by the Democrats during the 1927 mayoral campaign when a Republican, William Hale Thompson, last won that office in the twentieth century with the support of 80 percent of the black voters, who were Republicans at the time (Allswang 1971:147).

In the fifty years that the machine operated there had been few elections in which the voters so openly expressed racism because the machine carefully regulated racial and ethnic competition in the city. With Mayor Daley died the power and the personality capable of that regulation. Byrne and Bilandic cooperatively heaped fuel on the dissatisfaction that had smoldered for decades. When the Chicago political monopoly disintegrated, blacks and white ethnics were freed to compete for political office as they had not done in fifty years.

The Washington Administration: The End of Machine Politics?

Creating an electoral coalition and creating a governing coalition involve quite different considerations. Where Washington won nearly all the black vote and 20 percent of the white vote in the general election (or 51.6 percent of the total vote), in the city council he held only twenty-one certain votes from the wards dominated by the black electorate. There are fifty wards in the city of Chicago, whose representatives are elected in nonpartisan contests. The remnants of the old machine and the white-dominated wards controlled approximately the same number of seats immediately after the election as Washington, with nine ward representatives uncertain as to their allegiance. Here leadership and personal judgment played an important role in significantly limiting Washington's eventual freedom of action during the first two years of his administration.

Washington evidently expected that election to the mayor's office would guarantee him the kind of power relationships that Richard

Daley held, because he made no efforts to woo this critical group of city council representatives in order to strengthen his position within the city council (Robert T. Starks, interview, June 1983). As a result, this group of nine eventually joined with the remnants of the old machine, the white wards who did solicit their support, to form a twenty-nine vote majority in the council. Once that occurred, the white coalition held two of the three most important positions in Chicago politics: the city finance committee and the control of the party. As a consequence, Washington's position in the city was fundamentally weakened and he faced a stalemate. Burke's and Vrdolyak's control of the city council and Vrdolyak's leadership of the Cook County central committee of the Democratic party, which began in 1982, allowed them to appoint committee chairs (they reduced the number of black chairs from eight to three, replacing Wilson Frost as head of the finance committee with Burke), to control the council's rules and to control the agenda in such a way that Washington's substantive concerns about race had to be subordinated to conflict over procedural and organizational issues. That is, procedure and organization became substantive. While Washington appealed quite successfully to black voters during his campaign using racial appeals on the elimination of racial hierarchy, such goals lost their significance in the postelectoral arena of the city council.

Once Washington was in a politically weakened position, he appealed to other parties, such as the courts, to reestablish his power, but he lost in each instance. In a few cases, such as the truce on June 9, 1983, both sides agreed to cooperate in order to win urban development action grants from the Department of Housing and Urban Development. In another, Washington strengthened his position relative to the twenty-nine city council representatives in June of 1983 through bargaining, when he committed himself and the city to a specific budget level stating he would not lay off government workers, thereby forcing the responsibility for cutbacks onto Burke and Vrdolyak (Love 1984: 12).

Vrdolyak and Burke wished to "avoid restoring the $22 million in taxes [which the Byrne administration and the city council had cut]. The Vrdolyak plan included furloughs for 12,000 city workers, two days a month until the end of the year to save $14 million." In the process Alderman Pucinski proposed adding "8000 laborers and tradesmen to those workers who can be laid off only by reverse seniority." Washington opposed this because it "would lock in employees hired through patronage . . . permanently in place" (Love 1984:19–20).

This struggle, therefore, centered simultaneously over funds and control of city workers. Washington won his tax restorations because he created a situation in which the blame for the layoffs rested in a last clear opportunity for his opponents, which forced Vrdolyak and Burke to concede and all parties into a compromise. Washington and the city council restored $11.9 million in taxes and laid off 700 people. Bargaining occurred in this instance, but only because it did not directly involve a racial policy issue. When such an issue arises, both Washington and Vrdolyak tend to fall into hard, uncompromising stances.

As the third mayor of Chicago after Daley, Harold Washington faces an intriguing test. As the city's first black mayor, his electoral coalition consists of the black population and he directs his policy appeals at that group. While he must be attentive to that group, his race and his formal appeals to race in the campaign free him not to be seen, for the most part, as reasserting racial hierarchy, even if his decisions or appointments are not always as his black supporters would like. More importantly, because of the city council stalemate, he will have concentrated on procedural rather than on substantive conflicts. Thus his focus, assuming that his appointments are descriptively representative of the black population, must be on winning substantive rewards (which of course have some tangible dimension) that affect the collective status of his black supporters.

The return to a decentralized, competitive party system will and already has produced the political complexities similar to those described in chapters 3 and 4 of this book. Now that the city council and city politics are deeply divided, all other arenas have fallen into serious conflicts as well. Manfred Byrd, a black man, lost the school superintendency to Ruth Love, a black woman from Oakland, during Byrne's administration. Since Washington's election, the school board has acted to end Ruth Love's contract, with the expectation that it will replace her with the long deferred Manfred Byrd. Burke and Vrdolyak have risen to Love's defense so that each faction now has a black candidate for the superintendency. Both the police department and the schools were highly aroused and divided during the elections. The first Slavic police chief, Brzeczak, publicly endorsed Byrne and resigned shortly after Washington's election. The death of the machine has opened the city to racial and ethnic political competition, but competition also heightens political conflict over the formation and administration of public policy (*Chicago Tribune,* Feb. 25, 1983; *Chicago Reader,* Aug. 10, 1984, vol. 13, no. 45).

Washington also faces a most difficult and serious aspect of staying in office, and the most contradictory one. With only 51.6 percent of the vote in the 1983 mayoral general election, in order to retain his position as mayor Washington must maintain his strength among blacks, and he must broaden his electoral support among white and Hispanic voters. To win increased white support he must somehow also appeal to, or at least not alienate, their economic interests. Here his creative leadership abilities are critically important. How well he succeeds in balancing collective issues, tangible interests, racial and ethnic politics, and party and governmental politics will be apparent in the upcoming aldermanic elections and in the next mayoral elections.

Pluralism as a Theoretical Framework for Racial and Ethnic Politics

The legislative and administrative victories of the civil rights movement in recent decades have helped clarify the even greater problems of the economic and political status of the black population that remain to be solved. Passage of the Civil Rights Act of 1964, the Voting Rights Act of 1965, the Open Housing Act of 1968, along with the creation of the Equal Employment Opportunity Commission, the establishment of affirmative action by executive order, and its limited recognition by the Supreme Court have yet had little appreciable impact on housing and educational segregation and inequalities in the north, on depression-level unemployment, and on high crime rates within black communities.

The absence of any substantial body of research that addresses these paradoxes in American black politics has been frequently noted. While there are many studies of black politics by political scientists, the bulk have been published after 1970 and few address the issue of black political integration. Sociologists and historians have devoted more detailed attention to the issue of race than political scientists. Those studies which have examined the participation of blacks in American politics have evaluated black leadership, organization, and issue conceptualiation critically.[5]

Students of black politics have frequently noted the low levels of black voting (Campbell et al. 1960), have emphasized the absence of middle class bases of political organization (Kilson 1971b), have cited their failures at developing specialized political organizations and narrowly focused policies that can be integrated into the pluralist incremental framework (Dahl 1961; Greenstone and Peterson 1976; Wilson 1960a), and have studied religious-political leaders and imagery (Hamilton 1972; Mathews and Prothro 1966; Wilson 1960a). Political scientists recommend that black groups partition racial issues into low intensity, bargainable, incremental concerns and develop a specialized leadership class that is capable of incremental rather than crisis-oriented, millenarian political formulations and mobilization.

The analytical framework against which black politics compares so poorly and which the pluralists hold up as a model for urban blacks is derivative of the social welfare state formed during the depression of the 1930s. The Roosevelt administration established the principle of public protection of the "private" economic activities of banking, housing production, labor, or of economically vulnerable states such as old age, unemployment, and others. In the postwar era, as more areas of economic activity were regulated by the federal government, more and more precise interest group arenas of legislators, administrative agencies, and representative of selective economic interests sprang up to govern each narrow issue arena (Lowi 1979; McConnell 1966; Truman 1951).

Within each of these arenas, what was proposed as public rule of the private sector was implemented as private government. All groups with an interest in the particular arena became contributors to the creation, if not of the legislation, of administrative guidelines for implementation of the law. Once these arenas had been created, the effective designation of interested parties defined the "interest group universe." As Lowi (1979) has argued, the issue of authority was ignored in favor of partitioning the rule of law to all who aggressively articulated their interest. Since no governmental authority made authoritative decisions, and parties to the policymaking process were allegedly equal, decision making became a complex process of bargaining and of the creation and transmission of the impression of strength. Since one's status as a citizen and as an economic actor was assumed and was not an issue for concern, each party in the arena received some incremental benefit through the policy settlement. No actor, according to the theory, received all he or she wanted. Though there were rulers, there were *many* rulers, with decision making arrived at democratically.[6]

At the national level, of course, blacks faced several centuries of presumptive political and economic exclusion rather than inclusion. Since the national government attacked electoral discrimination with the support of a bipartisan coalition only in the 1960s and fell short of a full-scale reform of economic discrimination, black representation in these national interest group arenas created continuously since the 1930s (when blacks were still excluded) is problematic. It is either missing or weak because blacks are not present in great numbers in these economic areas, or it appears in the form of weaker, less prosperous organized representatives.

While this summary is an abbreviated and simplified presentation of pluralist theory, it captures its major points: the presumption of citizenship rights and economic participation, and of political and economic demands that are of equivalent significance; and flowing from these, rationalized bureaucracy, bargainable issues, and incremental decision making.

At the metropolitan level, pluralists emphasized discrete, nonrepetitive arenas. Their character was more likely to be based on political and ethnic rather than on economic or class interests. Two generations of political scientists assumed that no simple class-based organization or stratification system explained the participation or formulation of positions of political groups that had an interest in these matters. Dahl, Truman, Verba and Almond (1965), and Wilson assumed that no one elite existed that influenced policy across a broad range of issue areas. Instead, multiple or plural elites existed that were linked to the issue area by interest, which influenced political decisions in each of those areas.

Postwar pluralist political scientists challenged earlier scholars who had argued forcefully for cohesive economic elites (Hunter 1953; Lynd and Lynd 1929; Vidich and Bensman 1968) which dominated all aspects of metropolitan life. In the 1950s and 1960s, these postwar political scientists found only small groups of unrelated political activists, rather than political and economic elites, making decisions and reshaping policy. In the 1970s and 1980s, scholars such as Greenstone and Peterson and Eisinger found unspecialized organization by black political activists or little fundamental resistence by white elites to black control.[7]

One of the striking elements noted by students of black political participation is the genuinely slow progress of blacks into political office in northern cities and in national politics. In the late 1960s and 1970s there were striking advances in the election of black mayors and of other political officials and in the appointment of blacks to administrative positions in national Democratic administrations, but black unemployment rates, income levels, and poverty indicators remained at depression levels. Political organizations and black politicians continued to decry the status of the black population as a whole and the responses of the larger society to black political concerns. While there were an increasing number of black interest and lobbying groups, many were incubated by federal programs rather than generated by independently existing economic groups subject to government regulations. A number of studies described the racially restrictive character of southern politics (Bunche 1973; Cleghorn and Watters 1967; Key 1949; Ladd 1969; Mathews and Prothro 1966; Wirt 1970), but with the exception of Harold Gosnell and Martin Kilson few have examined the origins of black politics in northern urban areas before World War II.

While Gosnell concluded that race affected blacks' political status, Wilson presumed that "the ghetto has a life and a logic of its own, apart from whatever whites might do to create and maintain the outer walls of it" (Wilson 1960a:7). Wilson found that blacks had few specialized political organizations, had inadequately formulated political goals, that they were unable to choose between status and welfare issues, and that they had serious leadership problems. Wilson presumed rather than proved that an external factor motivated by racism was unimportant and that there were not independent variables which influenced black politics in Chicago. At the same time, Dahl's conclusions radiated a similar kind of confidence about New Haven: "ethnic influences must decline and socio-economic factors must correspondingly increase" (Dahl 1961:59).

In short, the process of assimilation that Dahl assumed was already taking place and that Wilson prescribed simply required the integration of blacks into the existing pattern of political interaction. Blacks would, according to Dahl, Wilson, and other pluralists, have to come to see the political issues which were important to them from a more specialized perspective. In effect they would gradually no longer see the world with the "double consciousness" described by W. E. B.

DuBois in the quote which introduced this chapter (DuBois 1961:16–17).

The pluralists presumed the certainty of black political integration, but for this to be possible there can be no major impediments to racial, political, social, and economic integration into the larger society. Certainly impediments to integration existed in the south and the pluralists' work applied principally to the urban north. The criticism in this work has applied to their presumptions of political integration in the north. Where the pluralists assume few impediments exist, this study has shown that there was substantial discrimination in the north as well as in the south.

The labor and housing markets in Chicago were sharply distinguished between blacks and whites. Blacks were employed only when there were too few whites for large industries to fill their available positions. Blacks lived only where whites could no longer restrain the spillover from the overcrowded black belt. Politically the formation of the machine restricted political competition for black votes; blacks joined the political machine and accepted tangible, selective goods instead of more valued adjustments in collective racial status. While blacks scored well on descriptive representation within black neighborhoods, none represented the city as a whole. As a consequence of the particularistic economic and political environment, distinctive racial and ethnic patterns developed and persisted.

As a consequence of racial discrimination, the structure of black political beliefs also sharply distinguished itself from whites. Blacks concentrated their political loyalties within one party and showed extreme sensitivity to indications of racism among political officials. Crime data provided an opportunity to examine an area that was most sharply distinguished along racial lines, both in the statistics themselves and in the interactions between the police and blacks, Italians and Poles, within the black community, and between blacks and organized crime. Educational data showed a distinct pattern of economic differentiation. Political and economic interests cooperated to reduce overall educational expenditures and to direct them to their own economic benefit. Black school expenditures, though low, approximately equalled Italian and Polish expenditures because the depression limited the expansion of teaching personnel and their migration away from less desirable assignments in black neighborhoods.

Racial criteria affected the structure of black political organizations, the orientation and level of black voting, the relative patterns of black ideological orientation, and the character of black political leadership. The society's emphasis on race in the economic, social, and political areas forces blacks to elevate their "racial" interests above their economic interests, although the two are not totally independent. Blacks are not just another ethnic group as Dahl, Glazer, Kilson, and more recently Sowell and others would have because the limits to their participation in the polity and economy are of a nature and character beyond anything that immigrant groups have faced.[8]

Even second generation pluralists such as Greenstone, Peterson, Wolfinger, Eisinger, and the early Parenti, all of whom certainly recognize the importance of northern racism, minimize racially based impediments to political participation. They discuss constitutionalism, pluralist bargaining, and orientations, structures, and other nondiscriminatory requirements. Greenstone and Peterson, for example, argue that participation requires that rulers shall be selected by citizens who participate in free, uncontrolled democratic elections (1976:14). Pluralist bargaining requires that rulers make no more than incremental changes in the pattern of public policy and then only after consulting the interests that have a legitimate stake in the matter. Policies must be rationalized in the sense that only universalistic or achievement categories are used to distinguish among citizens. And the fundamental requirement of constitutionalism is that policies do not injure basic freedoms of speech, religion, privacy, and assembly.

Pluralists also presume these criteria apply in an undifferentiated fashion when they analyze black political participation. If one assumes American political institutions are ideologically and operationally egalitarian, then black politics is rather curious and difficult to comprehend. However, in the Chicago described in this study, the "internal life and logic of the ghetto" makes sense because it is directly related to the racially circumscribed external life of the city. In an attempt to fit racially influenced politics into a pluralist framework, for example, Paul Peterson analyzed ideological bargaining by the Chicago school board over which desegregation plan the board would implement. The board eventually committed itself to integrating the school system at minimal levels in order to preserve the white population of the city: "Chicago will become a predominantly Negro city unless dramatic action is taken soon. We propose . . . that Negro enrollments in the schools in the changing sections of the city be limited and fixed immediately" (Peterson 1976:174).

Meaningful bargaining requires several factors. The issues must be bargainable, the subjects must be narrowed or partitioned to the point that the fundamental issue is not in question, and the parties must be equal. If the parties bargain about social status or political recognition, or if one of the parties seeks to inhibit entry of new individuals into competition, then the incremental nature of the bargaining process becomes an impediment to the entry or full recognition of one of the parties. The bargaining process is fundamentally unequal. If the parties are unequal, bargaining only reinforces their existing inequality. This is not a minor or insignificant point; the *incremental* nature of bargaining or of the political process in general (both generally characteristic of pluralist politics) becomes an impediment to full political participation. Events such as those described by Peterson helped aggravate black hostility to such political inequality.[9]

The board's approach to integration revealed that the racial issue had not been reduced to a bargainable level. Integration of the black population still elicited such a hostile response from whites in the 1960s and 1970s that the board conceded the impossibility of integrating all black students. It did seek, however, to stabilize racial change by creating a fire break, a border zone of "integrated schools," to calm white fears and discourage white flight. This was a "we had to desegregate some portions of the city in order to preserve other segregated portions of the city" argument. In fact if it could have been avoided, the board would not have integrated the schools at all. The board felt compelled to act because of the federal government's encouragement rather than because of local black pressure. The board members were rightly engaged in bargaining, not over marginal, substantively insignificant changes in the desegregation plan, but over which desegregation plan was politically palatable to the relevant white neighborhoods.

Since I began this study, significant changes have occurred in numerous American cities of the north and south with varying proportions of black population. Los Angeles, Birmingham, Atlanta, New Orleans, Pasadena, Detroit, and Chicago are only a few of the cities in which black mayors have been elected. Since this study concentrated on city politics long before blacks began to lead cities, should not black leadership, a violation of the norms of hierarchy, significantly and permanently alter racial politics in a city. This is the subject for another book.

Speculatively, a change in leadership, though important, is not in and of itself sufficient. A black official is a change in the descriptive character of a city's leaders but is no guarantee of a substantive change in public policy. Unless the character of decision making also changes, the fundamental character of racial politics remains stable. While he found significant interactional changes, Eisinger concludes almost as much in *The Politics of Displacement,* in which he compared the issue of Irish succession to office in nineteenth century Boston with the transition from white to black in late twentieth century Atlanta and Detroit. Eisinger focused primarily on the reactions of political and economic elites and found relatively little conflict and racial tension: "The adjustment of white elites to the new configuration of power was at all times peaceful and notably free of rancor" (Eisinger 1980:148).

A broader focus, including blacks and middle-class well as working-class whites, would no doubt have shown a wider range of reactions. In Chicago, for example, it is clear that the upper classes and business community seek only to protect the city's economic stability. They will show and have already shown concern only if Harold Washington demonstrates he cannot govern authoritatively enough to maximize political and therefore economic stability. Two important points are that upper-class whites in Chicago did not and have not held the political reins for some time. Further research should show that transitions of the kind examined by Eisinger vary according to several factors: whether the shift is both racial and economic, simply racial, or simply economic. The transition is difficult where change is most radical (both racial and economic) or where a group has the most to lose, such as the case of working-class whites in Chicago or Boston, and less so where only one element is involved or where blacks do not fully displace whites in status. In cities such as Atlanta, where whites held socioeconomic *and* political power, the transition was evidently less difficult because whites, that is upper-class whites, lost power only in one of the latter areas. In Detroit, upper-class whites had not governed and adjusted their interactions from working-class whites to blacks. Analysis of working-class whites' reactions in Detroit and Atlanta to the transition would, I propose, have yielded different data. In Chicago, upper-class whites have already shown their readiness to work with Mayor Washington, but that reaction has not been apparent among the newly displaced white ethnics whose social status in the city had been established by their relative location above blacks on the city's political hierarchy. The political change leaves them no alternative but to see themselves as direct competitiors with blacks. The Chicago transition has not been quiet.[10]

Because race is a highly evocative American social characteristic that provokes deep political and economic divisions, it is too broad and controversial a matter to be the subject of meaningful trading, or bargaining. It does not, in short, fit a pluralist analytical framework. When political institutions handle racial issues, conventional rules go awry, individuals react irrationally, and constitutional rules are violated. Incremental frameworks adjudicate explosive, conflictual issues poorly. Thus black historical experiences can not be explained by pluralist analysis nor will externally imposed racial status be eroded by incremental bargaining or decision making.

Appendix

A Note on Ward and Precinct Selections

For black wards I used ward totals, since these tended to be heavily black, as indicated by the census (see Pinderhughes 1977b:table 73).

For Italian wards I used wards identified by Nelli (1970a) as having a high percentage of Italian voters (see also Pinderhughes 1977b: table 73).

For Polish wards I used wards and precincts identified by Kantowicz as having a high percentage of Polish voters. He used the official registration lists for wards and precincts from the Board of Election Commissioners. He inspected voter registration lists and counted Polish names; when in doubt as to the identity of a voter he excluded it. He chose only precincts in which Polish names composed at least sixty percent of the voters on the list; in most cases the percentage was as high as 90 to 95 percent. The Polish vote was therefore "recognized as the vote of only those Poles who were highly concentrated in ethnic neighborhoods" (Kantowicz 1972:534; see also Pinderhughes 1977b:tables 70, 71, and 72). In his *Polish-American Politics* Kantowicz cautions, "In the earlier part of the study . . . these few precincts contain a sizable proportion of all Poles registered . . . [but] as the study progresses chronologically, . . . the Polish vote figures are less reliable. . . . But, fortunately, the Polish vote is so monolithically Democratic in the 1930s that it seems unlikely any nuances have been overlooked by this relatively less reliable sample" (Kantowicz 1975: 224).

Crime Statistics

Statistics are from the Department of Police *Annual Reports,* City of Chicago, 1878–1931, Chicago Municipal Reference Library. These statistics include some inaccuracies. Merriam reported that the foreign-stock population was likely to be undercounted, while blacks were much more likely to be identified correctly (Merriam 1915:chap. 2, sec. 3). The Chicago Commission on Race Relations reported: "Reports from the Immigrants Protective League show that the foreigners arrested are often given wrong racial designations. On the other hand the classification of Negroes, even of half blood, is never in doubt" (1922:329).

Catholic Education

When we compare public and private school attendance, assuming parochial schools equalled a significant portion of the private, students attending private schools equalled about one-third of public school attendance. Poles were much more likely to join a national Catholic parish than were Italians. By combining census data on national populations with Marvin Shafter's study and the school census of Chicago, I constructed a rough estimate of Polish and Italian parochial school attendance. The school census showed that the Italian and Polish population under age twenty-one equalled about 50 percent and 40 percent, respectively, of their total populations in the city in 1910 and 1912 (see Pinderhughes 1977b:table 85). In 1914 and 1916 wards with significant Italian and Polish populations showed total school attendance above their respective minor populations in the ward, but private school attendance well below that of the Polish and Italian populations under age seventeen.

The percentage of Polish attendance was four to six times that of the Italians. The highest rates of private school attendance were in those wards where there were large numbers of Poles. The school census of 1916 showed more students in private than in public school in the seventeenth ward, an area that was heavily settled by Polish immigrants and that included the first Polish Catholic church in Chicago, St. Stanislaus. Where there was a high rate of private school attendance in Italian wards, it was coincidental with residence by large numbers of Polish minors, as in the fourth and seventeenth wards. Thus the figures suggest that Poles attended parochial schools much more frequently than Italians. Parish schools like St. Stanislaus enrolled 3,000 to 4,000 students at its peak in the early 1900s.[1] After 1920 the number of children in attendance at St. Stanislaus fell below 3,000 (Ficht 1952). Cost and distance discouraged those who did not attend parochial school, and by the early 1930s "the number of children in parochial school fell between 15% and 20% during the period of depression owing to many parents being unable to pay the school tuition" (Wargin 1948:119–20).[2] These statistics suggest that the Italians did not have the same commitment to Catholic education that the Poles did. The nineteenth ward, the largest settlement of Italians in the city, was also the ward with some of the lowest figures for private school attendance in the city. If this was the case in areas with a heavy concentration of Italians, it was even less likely that smaller settlements would develop strong Italian Catholic schools.

Nelli suggests that southern Italians viewed schooling as wasted earnings and withdrew their children from school as soon as possible. Even those Italians who wanted their children to learn Italian and to receive religious training were reluctant about paying tuition. Those Italian school children who were enrolled in parochial schools were placed there because of behavior problems, which parents expected the nuns to resolve (Nelli 1970a:66–67).

Thus we can say that the conduct of the parochial schools did not have as significant an effect on the Italian or black school-age population of Chicago as it did on the Polish, since about one-third of Polish minors were attending parochial schools. Nevertheless, the public school system was the major institution in the education of Polish and Italian communities, and so we can proceed to an analysis of the schools' operation in those areas.

As percentages of their total population in the city, the private school attendance equalled about 20 percent of the Italian and 15 percent of the Polish population, which is surprising since we would have expected attendance to be much higher in the Polish areas.

Methodology

The schools were selected by identifying wards in which blacks, Italians, and Poles were concentrated in each census year (see table A.1 for list of selected schools). The 1910 and 1920 censuses were relatively easy in this regard, since racial and nationality information was compiled by wards. In 1930 listings were compiled only by census tracts and community areas. The 1940 listings were made by ward, but only by race, with no specific listings by nationality. Thus I used earlier information combined with descriptive historical sources for 1930 and 1940. These included historical studies of various communities, such as Nelli (1970a) and Kantowicz (1975). Having chosen the areas of heavy concentration by outlining them on maps (which also noted changing ward boundaries), I then decided what types of areas I would use for the schools—high, medium, or low density. All areas with low density of the selected population groups were eliminated, although the standards varied by community and by census year because of variations in the size of the groups.[3]

All of the areas with high population were included. Because of the different sizes of the groups, it was necessary to set a minimum population of 3,000 per group per ward, which generated fifteen Polish, seven black, and six Italian wards. Because of differences in housing policy, the black areas were more likely to be exclusively black than were Polish or Italian areas. Thus the schools in the areas chosen

Table A.1
Schools in Survey

Black	Italian	Polish
Drake	Curtis Elementary	Curtis High School
Moseley	Dante	Burr
Haven	Dore	Drummond
Colman	Curtis High School	Everett
Phillips High School	Goodrich	Fulton
Fuller	Healy	Hamline
Forrestville	Jackson	Healy
Farren	Jenner	Holden
Felsenthal	Manierre	Libby
Willard	Morse	Monroe
Emerson	Pullman	Poe
Hayes	Schiller	Pullman
Van Vlissingen	Adams	Mark Sheridan
Morgan Park High School	Medill High School	Sherman
Morgan Park Elementary	Brenan	Ward
Shoop	Farnsworth	Avondale
Haines	Leyden	Schurz High School
DuSable High School	Locke	Beaubian
Dore	Foreman High School	Linne
Esmond	Medill Elementary	Fenger High School
Medill	Steinmetz High	Hibbard High School
Brownell	Fenger	Archer Avenue
Burke	Riis	Clearing
		Funston
		Hibbard Elementary
		Kelvyn Park Elementary
		Reilly
		Sawyer
		Scammon
		Barry
		Bennett
		Farnsworth
		Pasteur
		Dever
		Steinmetz High School
		Gage Park High School

were more likely to be mostly black than were schools in Polish and Italian wards.[4]

I then used the 1909–10 Chicago *Directory of Public Schools* to select a core of ten schools in each heavily populated area. To take into account the changing community boundaries, I next consulted the 1920–21 school directory and attempted to add at least five new schools from those that might have been built within the existing boundaries in the ten-year interval and from schools that were in newly settled areas. The same procedure was applied in 1930 and 1940, although it was less productive because it was necessary to use descriptive representation rather than quantitative information. I also consulted contemporary maps from 1910 to 1940 from the Department of Development and Planning, City of Chicago.[5] The maps showed areas of settlement at ten-year intervals; the information was described as estimated and based on descriptive rather than statistical data. The addition of new schools after each census was difficult and sometimes impossible for black and Italian areas because there was less expansion of their residential area; there were fewer schools for these two groups.

I recorded budgetary information for each school, when it was listed, from the beginning of the sample period in order to determine if there were changes in the level and distribution of expenditures as the schools became more heavily attended by the respective groups. The period of the study stretched for thirty budget years, from 1910 to 1940, and there were approximately fifty schools to be examined for each of these years. Each of the budget years included about ten line items, of which I recorded seven. I quickly decided to reduce by half the thousands of recordings required by the study, by recording budgets for every other year rather than for every year.[6]

I used two measures to standardize the expenditures: (a) the number of students enrolled in each school. More accurate figures, such as average daily attendance, were not consistently available for each school. In rare instances, enrollment figures were unavailable for individual school years, in which case I substituted the previous year's figures for the missing year, assuming that there would probably have been few radical changes over the period of a single year; and (b) the percentage that each of the line items contributed to the total budget for each school, so that we might compare these on a school-by-school and a group-by-group basis. The averages were calculated with the core schools and then recalculated with the non-core schools to see whether there was a significant difference between expenditures.

After all this, the computer runs were made using the variables of schools, nationality, and year in the following combinations: (1) all

Table A.2
School Selections Arranged According to Years

Years by School Directory Listings	Years by Census Changes			
	1909–20	1920–30	1930–38	1938–44
1909–1910 Schools	1	2	4	7
1920–21 Schools	A	3	5	8
1930–31 Schools	B	C	6	9
1938–39 Schools	D	E	F	10

schools by all years; (2) all schools by each year; (3) each school by all years; (4) each school by each year; (5) nationality (all schools designated by a particular nationality) by all years; (6) nationality by each year; (7) school by nationality by each year; and (8) school by nationality by all years. In each case these were run with a layering effect to take population and geographical changes into account.

The computer runs were made in the following sequence for the core schools: 1909–20, box 1; 1922–30, boxes 2 and 3; 1932–37, boxes 4, 5, and 6; and 1938–44, boxes 7, 8, 9, and 10 (see table A.2). This procedure allowed me to look at the schools for each group during the years when there were large numbers of Italians, Poles, and blacks around them. To see whether there were higher or lower expenditures before the schools' areas were heavily settled by each group, the non-core schools were also calculated with the core schools: 1909–20, box 1; 1909–30, boxes 1 + A, 2 + 3; 1909–37, boxes 1 + A + B, 2 + 3 + C, 4 + 5 + 6; 1909–44, boxes 1 + A + B + D, 2 + 3 + C + D, 4 + 5 + 6 + F, 7 + 8 + 9 + 10.

Notes

1. The Last Days of the Chicago Machine

1. Two days before the primary in a *New York Times* op-ed piece, Nobel prize winner Saul Bellow discussed Byrne at some length, gave a lukewarm endorsement to Daley, and more or less dismissed Washington in a paragraph (*New York Times,* Feb. 20, 1983).

2. *Chicago Sun-Times,* Feb. 24, 1983; *Chicago Tribune,* March 24, 1983.

3. *Chicago Tribune,* March 8, 15, 16, and April 6, 10, 1983.

4. The phrase "race in the race" comes from the title of an article, "Race in the Race," *Chicago Reporter* 12, no. 3 (March 1983).

5. See *Chicago Tribune,* March 28 and 29, 1983. One article pointed out that "Gov. James R. Thompson had appeared at a number of Northwest Side churches in his reelection campaign last year, with no adverse reaction" (March 28, 1983).

6. School children called his successor "Mayordaley Bilandic" and "the new Mayor Daley" (Kemp and Lineberry 1982; *Wall Street Journal,* Jan. 12, 1983).

7. For information on Daley's life, see Kennedy (1978), O'Connor (1975), and Royko (1971).

8. These terms were first cited by Paula Wilson and quoted by Michael Preston to distinguish aldermen with some degree of independence. I have chosen to use the terms to characterize the behavior of some of these same public officials at a slightly earlier time. Mavericks or dissidents, though rare, were the third category (Preston 1982b:88–117; P. Wilson 1978).

9. For information on Chew, Hubbard, and Vrdolyak, see Bogira (1982) and Rakove (1979).

10. Marguerite Ross Barnett writes, "hierarchy specifically means the existence of a principle (racism) that ranks groups consistently and pervasively *and is enforceable through social control.* Collectivism means that each individual member of a group is treated according to some principle that defines the whole. Ultimate meaning resides in the definition of the whole—the characteristics ascribed to the group as a whole. Hierarchy and collectivism define the Black structural position in the United States" (1976:20, emphasis in original).

11. For a discussion of the rejection of racial subordination, see Garrow (1978: chap. 7) and McAdam (1982: chaps. 1–3).

2. Racial and Ethnic Economic Life: The Case for a Pluralist Interpretation

1. See McConnell (1966: chap. 4) for a discussion of size of constituency.

2. For Robert Dahl's recent comments on this subject, see Dahl (1979a, 1979b).

3. See, for example, Dahl (1961:chaps. 2–7). Other sources include Kilson (1971b); Wilson (1960a); and Wolfinger (1974: chap. 3). For other variations, see Banfield (1961); Banfield and Wilson (1963: chap. 3 and pp. 234–42 for the public/private regarding concept that divided along immigrant/Anglo-Saxon lines); and Kilson (1971b).

4. In addition to Balbus and Kilson, see Greenstone and Peterson (1976: chap. 4) and Peterson (1976), who contrasts pluralist and ideological bargaining (esp. chaps. 2 and 7).

5. Europeans immigrated in order to accumulate the resources to return to their village and purchase land; some moved back and forth for years before they settled permanently in the United States. For the history and politics, see Drake and Cayton (1970: esp. chap. 13); Gosnell, (1967); Kantowicz (1975); Nelli (1970a); and Spear (1967: chaps. 6 and 10). For a detailed examination of economic, religious, journalistic, and other organizational life of the Italian and Polish communities in Chicago, see Pinderhughes (1977b: chap. 2).

6. This, of course, assumes a relatively equitable distribution by race throughout the labor force; nondiscriminatory hiring practices in the present would not obliterate the effects of past discrimination. Other factors might influence employers' hiring choices, although skills and education were not a requirement in many industrial jobs.

7. See Dorn (1979: chap. 4) for a theoretical analysis of racial discrimination and the remedial effects of equal opportunity versus affirmative action models. See also Bonacich (1976:41); Harris and Spero (1969: 108–55); Herbst (1932: chap. 3, pp. 28–37); Newell (1961:chap. 8, pp. 2–32); Northrup (1944:75–78, 141–44, 177–79); and Tuttle (1972:chap. 4).

8. See W. Wilson (1978:72) and Bonacich (1976:41) for information on black strikebreaking; see Harris and Spero (1969) pp. 262–63 for the steel industry and p. 268 for meat-packing and black strikebreaking; see also Harris (1977).

9. Compare Chicago Commission on Race Relations (1922:363, table 23), Herbst (1932: chap. 5), Tuttle (1972: chap. 4), and Harris and Spero (1969: chaps. 11–13).

10. W. Wilson (1978:82–87) and Bonacich (1976:39–44) argue more strongly in favor of capital acting to maximize the availability of cheap labor, that is, black workers.

11. The following sources include information on the exclusion of blacks by skilled crafts unions: Bonacich (1976:41–44); Greenstone (1977); Harris and Spero (1969: chaps. 4 and 5); Herbst (1932:xix–xxii); Newell (1961:237–42); Northrup (1944: chap. 2); and Tuttle (1972: chap. 4).

12. On black animosity toward unions, see Harris and Spero (1969: chaps. 4 and 7); Northrup (1944: chap. 1); Strickland (1966: chaps. 2 and 3); and Tuttle (1972: chap. 4).

13. For an application of Olson's concepts to black organizations, see Pinderhughes (1983).

14. For a discussion of such practices by the Ford Motor Company at its River Rouge plant in Detroit, see Williams (1977:170–71). See also Bonacich (1976:42) and Chicago Commission on Race Relations (1922:364).

15. See also Wells (1953: chaps. 7, 8, and 64). Wells commented that lynching was frequently an excuse to eliminate blacks who had acquired some wealth and property.

16. Strickland (1966) describes how Rosenwald attempted to influence the Urban League's policy decisions in exchange for his financial contribution. Philpott (1978:97–103) suggests these institutions. He notes that Binga and other businessmen supported the South Side Settlement House, but the depression eliminated both their business and their support (1978:219, 265, 320–21); see also Wells (1953:331).

17. The Pullman Porters often acted as an informal black communications network. In some cases they acted as distributors for the *Defender* (see Gosnell 1967:104; Ottley 1955:262–63). See Brazeal (1946: chap. 4 and p. 51) and Harris (1977:44–48) for a detailed discussion of black newspapers in Chicago and for their criticisms of the Pullman Porters and of their links with the Klan-dominated American Federation of Labor.

18. For discussions of this concept, see Dahl (1961: chap. 4); Glazer (1971:203); Glazer and Moynihan (1963:186–90); Parenti (1970:63–78); and Wolfinger (1970).

19. One of the problems in discussing ethnic groups is the highly variable nature of their enumeration. Only the foreign-born are counted in all censuses; in others, the second generation of an ethnic group may or may not be included. For the third generation, the only statistical accounting is usually by foreign tongue. Thus the concentration of Poles by 1930 might have been above 50 percent, but that is an estimate and one that Kantowicz was not willing to make. Wards 16 and 17 held the largest foreign-born Polish population in the city in 1920, but there were even larger numbers of native whites of native parentage, foreign stock non-Polish, and other foreign-borns (Bureau of the Census 1922: vol. 2:275).

20. Kantowicz notes the boundary changes of 1921, which effectively split the Polish community's vote (1975:184–88). Irish alderman John Powers also repressed potential Italian political influence by a similar division of the Italian community on the near west side in the same ward redistricting of 1921 (Nelli 1970a:123–24). Gosnell describes a similar exercise imposed upon the black community in 1931 (1967:76–78). See also Pinderhughes's comments on the consequences of the 1931 redistriciting and her discussion of the size of districts (1977b:250–54).

21. Lieberson (1963: chap. 4) and Duncan and Duncan (1957) provide in-depth studies of the processes of racial invasion, succession, and internal

differentiation from 1900 to 1950. Hirsch examines the continued pattern of racial segregation in housing in Chicago during "an era of hidden violence" in "the apparently peaceful interlude following World War II" (1983:xi, 40).

22. Taylor notes that there were unsuccessful attempts to restrict the Mexican population (1931:51–61, maps 51–52; see also Philpott 1978:141, table 7).

23. See annual reports of the Department of Health, City of Chicago, 1919–1922, table entitled "Number of Buildings for Which Permits Were Approved by Ward"; only 52,457 apartments and houses were constructed during this period.

24. Reports from the Department of Buildings, *Permit Ledger 1910–1946*, in the Chicago Municipal Reference Library, show slightly different data from the annual reports of the Department of Health, City of Chicago, 1903–1930. The latter source shows building permits by ward.

25. Several studies have speculated on Mayor Daley's involvement in attacks against blacks during the 1919 race riot. Daley was a member and later president (as of 1924) of the gang and social club known in the Bridgeport area as the Hamburgers. They were reported to have attacked blacks during the riot (O'Connor 1975:19).

26. Racial segregation in housing was not so consistently enforced in the rural south, where racial hierarchy was more firmly established. Separate accommodations in public facilities and institutions, on the other hand, were more consistently maintained in the south (see Lowi 1979: chap. 9).

27. For a significant expansion of the model, see Barnett (1983). She lists the components of hierarchy and collectivism: legal segregation, political disfranchisement, economic segregation, cultural marginalization, and psychological stigmatization.

3. From Competition to Monopoly: The Formation of the Chicago Democratic Machine

1. See Dahl (1961: chap. 4) and several examinations of Dahl's analysis in Hawkins and Lorinskas (1970, esp. discussions by Parenti and Wolfinger). See also Banfield and Wilson (1963:115–50); Gans (162:3–16); Kilson (1971b); Merton (1949:71–83); and Wilson (1960a:21–77).

2. The continuing formation and reformation of factional alliances was so frequent that Gotffried resorted to the use of initials to help his readers keep track of the Crowe-Barrett-Thompson-Brundage faction, which was active in the mid-1920s (see Gottfried 1962:191–92).

3. See Beyle (1928, compare chart 1, p. 23, and chart 2, p. 25). Merriam, Parratt, and Lepawsky (1933) found 27 governments, including 7 major ones in the city of Chicago and 419 for the county of Cook. See Lowi (1964: chap. 4) for a discussion of Tammany Hall's gradual expansion of influence throughout the city.

4. O'Connor reported that "Cermak openly hated the Irish" (1975:24). Allswang analyzed their interaction differently: the Irish "had to recognize this ambitious new man" (1977:108–9). MacDonald summarized the major

details of the political topography (1962:254–56). The *Chicago Primary of 1926* included invaluable chronological Republican factional history (Wooddy 1926:286–87).

5. Harrison was weakened by his campaign to close down the red-light district shortly before the election. Citizens of the "levee" had come out in force against Harrison (Gosnell 1967:50; Kantowicz 1975: chaps. 7 and 12).

6. At the time the Thompson-appointed school board was under indictment for misappropriation of funds (see Gottfried 1962: chap. 9, for details).

7. Gosnell notes the consistently strong opposition to prohibition in Chicago (1968:100, 144–45). Between 1919 and 1933, 62.7 percent to 81.9 percent of the electorate supported the repeal of prohibition and 92 percent of the electorate ratified the Twenty-first Amendment, which replaced it.

8. Stuart (1936) has summarized political events at the beginning of each chapter. Listings for 1930 include the murder of a *Chicago Tribune* reporter who turned out to have underworld connections, the resignation of the police chief, and an underworld shootout on State Street (1936:400).

9. Royko noted that Richard J. Daley's rise to power was punctuated by several similar events (1971: chap. 3, p. 50).

10. This was reflected by changes on the national level. For the literature on critical elections, consult Andersen (1979:1–19); Burnham (1965); Key (1955); and MacRae and Meldrum (1960).

11. Merton's language leaves some doubt as to the intended meaning of the word *function;* in the single phrase quoted here he uses the words "to perform positive functions" and "satisfying basic latent functions," thereby mixing active and passive meanings.

12. Steffens was so moved by the political responsibility of ward representatives that he went off to talk with "Filene and Brandeis and others about it" (1931:618).

13. The editors report that this was originally written in a letter from Weber to his mother.

14. Pitkin (1967) also includes "symbolic" representation, but that is less useful for our purposes. See also Peterson's application of this framework to the community action program (1970).

15. John Leonard East suggested that Dawson moved into the Democratic party reluctantly (interview, Jan. 11, 1974).

16. Dickerson suffered from the change. He served four years as second-ward alderman, from 1939 to 1942, and was replaced by Dawson loyalist William Harvey. Dawson went to Congress that year, but he also went about the work of organizing the south side. James Q. Wilson alludes to Dawson's treatment of Dickerson in *Negro Politics* (1960a:81). The work of creating a black submachine was slow, lasting at least a decade (Wilson 1960b).

4. Hierarchy and Political Ethnicity

1. This is not to say that ethnic voting does not have a symbolic element (see Edelman 1967). Glazer and Moynihan (1963) argue that assimilation has not occurred in New York City, but the bulk of the literature relies on Dahl.

Group identity in heterogeneous populations necessarily supposes concern with socioeconomic issues.

2. Dahl's *Who Governs* was published in 1961, Wolfinger's first discussion of the issue came in 1965 (reprinted 1970), and Parenti's article was published in 1967 (reprinted 1970). These works represent key explications of the theoretical debate under discussion.

3. Polish wards and precinct selections are based on Kantowicz's (1975) examination of voter registration rolls. Data on Italian voters are based on Nelli's (1970a) selections. Black voters did not have sufficiently distinctive names, nor were they identified by race in poll books. I therefore used areas of black settlement—namely wards 2 and 3—as indicators of black voting behavior. Initially these wards were predominantly black; over time the wards became more accurate representations of the black vote (see appendix).

4. For the growing literature on district and at-large elections, see Davidson (1979) and Engstrom and McDonald (1981). The Supreme Court's ruling in *Mobile* vs. *Bolden* (April 1980) held that the impact of at-large electoral systems was not an unconstitutional dilution of black voting strength (see *New York Times,* April 23, 1980). The 1982 extension of the 1965 Voting Rights Act overturned this decision (see also Davidson and Korbel 1981; Mundt and Heilig 1982).

5. Nelli and Kantowicz examined voter registration lists at the Board of Election Commissioners' warehouse for registrants with names from the respective groups. Precincts with 50–60 percent or more voters of the groups were designated Italian or Polish precincts. Italian and Polish yearbooks sometimes estimated their communities' voting power. Schiavo estimated that there were 65,000 Italian voters in Chicago in 1928 and that they increased in yearly increments of 5,000 (1928:104). The following procedure was used to estimate the voting potential of Poles and Italians. First, the number of adult foreign-born citizens was combined with the adult natives of foreign-born parents. The census did not correlate age with specific immigrant groups on a metropolitan or citywide basis, but I also estimated the minimum number of adult citizens. Because only naturalized citizens voted, I partitioned Polish and Italian foreign stock into three types of adults: naturalized foreign-born, non-naturalized foreign-born, and native-born. After excluding the non-naturalized foreign-born, I combined estimates of the naturalized foreign-born with adult native-born.

6. On blacks, see Bunche (1973); Meltzer (1965); and Wells (1970). On ethnics, see Gosnell (1928); see also Forthal (1946:81–82); Gosnell (1929); and Merriam and Gosnell (1924).

7. It is possible Kowalski and Rostenkowski retained honorary memberships in both organizations; see the biographical sketches in *Poles of Chicago, 1837–1937* (1937:199–256). Among officials of the organizations, the conflict may or may not have disappeared, since this memorial book excluded the PRCU from the chapter on Polish organizations, although it is mentioned elsewhere in the text.

8. Based on a quotation from Ralph Bunche (1929).

9. Black ministerial leadership in secular affairs has been a frequent

occurrence in black politics. Black ministers have served as intermediaries (the ministers cited most frequently are the Revs. Walter Fauntroy, Andrew Young, William Gray, and Carl McCall) or as forces external to electoral politics (such as the Revs. Martin Luther King, Jesse Jackson, members of the Southern Christian Leadership Conference, and a number of others).

10. Contemporary examples include the Frank Rizzo mayoral campaign in Philadelphia, the 1981 Andrew Young Atlanta mayoral election, Charles Robb's Virginia gubernatorial election in 1981, and the campaign on the tuition tax-credit referendum in Washington, D.C., in the fall of 1981.

11. Some Poles continued to support the Republicans. John Smulski, "respectable" in Kantowicz's terminology, stayed in the party as a member of the Deneen faction and was elected city attorney in 1903 and state treasurer in 1906. Kantowicz reports that he defeated a Polish Democrat, N. L. Piotrowski (1975:65–66). He served for a little more than a year and, except for his 1911 mayoral primary loss, never ventured into electoral politics again. Harrison, with whom Kiolbassa was associated, lost the Democratic nomination for mayor and was defeated as an independent (see also Kantowicz 1975:175).

12. The ninteenth ward succession dates are based on Rollheiser (1975, ward 25). See Nelli (1970a:172–76) for a more complete description of the Unione Siciliana.

13. The segregated vice district overlapped with black neighborhoods at the time (Branham 1977).

14. More than one representative was elected from each state legislative district using a system of cumulative voting; each voter "had three votes which could be concentrated on a single candidate or split between two or three candidates" (Gosnell 1967:65, 69). On the 1928 race, see Gosnell (1967:72).

15. Pietrowicz served from June 24, 1914, to December 22, 1915.

16. See the *Chicago Daily New Almanac,* which lists the thirty-five Republican committeemen elected in 1923 (1926:818).

5. The Philosophical Labyrinth of Race and Political Beliefs

1. See chapter 2, Reich (1981), and Tuttle (1969). The Motley family was among those whose homes and businesses were bombed between 1918 and 1920 as blacks attempted to settle in the Hyde Park section of Chicago (Tuttle 1972:171–83).

2. Of course, the racist rationales used by post-Reconstructionist historians, such as Ulrich B. Phillips and twentieth-century scholars of racial differences based on intelligence and other standardized testing, emphasize the biological aspect to these distinctions. See Dorn's description of perfect and strict dominance (1979:20–21; see also Barnett 1976:14–18).

3. For a discussion of the decline in black voting in the late 1800s and an increase in the mid-twentieth century, see Lawson (1976: chap. 1) and Key (1949:533–643). See also Black (1978); Pinderhughes (1984); and Walton (1972).

4. See also Greenberg (1970b); Marvick (1965); and White (1977).

5. See Axelrod (1972:15); Bunche (1973); Campbell (1977); see also Axelrod (1978).

6. *The Gallup Report* 185 (Feb. 1981):37; *The Gallup Poll, Public Opinion, 1935–1971,* vol. 3 (1972:1884). For a more detailed summary of these differences, see Pinderhughes (1984:72–74, 89); see also Schwartz and Schwartz (1976).

7. Aberbach and Walker have shown that blacks belong to more organizations in every category except business and the professions (1973:33, table 2.3).

8. Proponents of this view include: Clarke (1974); Curtin (1967); Elkins (1963); Fogel and Engerman (1974); Genovese (1965); Gutman (1976); Ransom and Sutch (1977); and Williams (1974).

9. For a series of articles on both sides of the discussion, see Davis (1976); DuBois (1969); Jordan (1968); Kovel (1970); Noel (1972); and Williams (1961). For a historical analysis of slavery's impact on a founding father, see Brodie (1974). For a fascinating fictional biography of Sally Hemmings, one of Jefferson's slaves, see Chase-Riboud (1979).

10. Discussions that deal with status-oriented organizations include Kluger (1975) and Lawson (1976); see also Ladd (1969:148) for a summary of the studies that include status and welfare categories. Other studies of southern politics include: Burgess (1973); Hamilton (1974); Mathews and Prothro (1966:186–90); and Myrdal (1964). See Wright (1972), Bracey, Meier, and Rudwick (1970), and Marx (1969) for analyses of black attitudes. See Bennett (1964) for historical discussions of blacks in the 1950s and 1960s.

11. Walker helped organize the General Colored Association of Boston; he also urged national unity among all blacks in the United States (see Bracey et al. 1970:30).

12. For biographical information on DuBois, see DuBois (1961, 1968, 1969) and Walden (1972). For other important black leaders see: Cronon (1969); Garvey (1969, 1970); Harlan (1972); Hill (1983); Martin (1976); Ullman (1971); and Washington (1970).

13. For historical information on black organizations, see: Cruse (1967:30); Kellogg (1967); Meier and Rudwick (1975); Robert (1943); Strickland (1966); Stuckey (1972); and Thomas (1981). For work on black organizations in recent decades, see Carson (1981); Marable (1980); Morris (1984); and Zinn (1964).

14. Cruse's *Crisis of the Negro Intellectual* (1967) has shown the perturbations of black polticial philosophy from the 1920s through the 1960s; see also Haywood (1978).

15. See Gosnell (1967: chap. 15) for a discussion of the Unemployed Councils and labor union organizing. Although the Communist party never won a majority of electoral support in the black community, the black south side included several of the very few districts that contributed more than seven percent of the vote to that party.

16. For descriptions of the conflict within the civil rights movement between leaders who wished to use bargaining rather than protest styles, see

Bennett (1965); Carmichael and Hamilton (1967); Garrow (1978); Ladd (1969:133– 232); and Zinn (1964).

17. The percentages presented here are based on extrapolation from Marx (1969); there were a total of 1,095 respondents. See Marx (1969:40– 48) for his definition of militancy.

18. Marx based his index on replies to the following issues: "refusal to fight for the United States in the event of war and giving black Americans their own country" and identification of the Muslims as the group doing the most to help Negroes and Malcolm X as the individual doing the most to help (1969:107). See Aberbach and Walker regarding support for Black Power, a much less rigorous ideological position (1973:107, 165) and on the Nation of Islam (1973:39).

19. For a psychiatric analysis of the race, see Kardiner and Ovesey (1951). For a very interesting article on the psychological problems of adjustment while in the midst of the civil rights movement, see Pouissant and Ladner (1968); see also Comer (1972) and Danigelis (1977).

20. Important sources for this debate include: Cruse (1967:171–80) and the *Black Scholar* from 1972 to 1974; see also Cronon (1969); Garvey (1969, 1970); and Moses (1972).

21. Examples of newer organizations include: National Conference of Black Political Scientists (established in 1970), National Black Economists, National Association of Black Social Workers, National Conference of Black Lawyers, Black Psychologists, Blacks in Government, Afro-American Patrolmen's League, African Heritage Studies Association, and Black FBI Officers.

22. For discussion of the National Black Political Convention, see Wilkins (1972). Examples of this interest in varied forms of black nationalism include Ahmed (1972); Hare (1973); and Walters (1973).

23. On black conservatives, see Institute for Contemporary Studies (1981); *Gallup Poll* (1972); and Marx (1969). The reverse is true for whites. James Kuklinski and T. Wayne Parent show that when racial integration and governmental intervention or strong central government were tested, whites "were as likely to oppose a strong central government as not" (1979:6).

24. Cruse (1967) reported on the repeated shifts in the party's appeals and its own confusion on the use of nationalist appeals. Gosnell described the determined campaign waged by Chicago's Red Squad in the police against the party's organizing efforts on the black south side (1967:327); see also Record (1964).

6. Crime and Punishment in Chicago

1. Ogburn and Tibbits also surveyed race and ethnicity of criminals by nine categories of activity and found widely varying rates of distribution on both variables (1930:39, table 1). In reference to the controversy about Italians and organized crime, I describe as illegitimate business the activity that involved the struggle to control markets and to organize production and distribution networks, problems which are common to most businesses; these

were made more complicated by the necessity for eluding capture by the police, avoiding being murdered by competitors, and other hazards. There are numerous accounts of these events; among them are Asbury (1928); DeMaris (1969); Dobyns (1932); Lashley (1929); Lyle (1960); Nelli (1976); Pasley (1930); Peterson (1952); Reckless (1933); and Wendt and Kogan (1943).

2. For more information, see Lashley (1929:1003). Drake and Cayton (1970:486–87) allude to the Jones brothers, although not by name; see also Committee to Investigate Crime in Interstate Commerce (1951:1409); the *Chicago Defender,* Sept. 26, 1931. The father of the Jones brothers, Rev. S. S. Jones, had been president of the National Baptist Convention (see Spear 1967:chap. 5; Robb 1929:129–200). Spear also reported that the black lodges were in decline by the early twentieth century (1967:107–10). All of the groups developed organizations with a fraternal base; however, the orientation was somewhat differently set in each case: the Italian Unione Siciliana concentrated on insurance, politics, labor activities, and alcohol production; the Hamburgers and Ragen Colts on sports, politics, and petty crime; the Phalanx Forum Club was a social "labor" group. Mayor Daley, a former Hamburger, demonstrated his understanding of the potential of neighborhood gangs in the 1960s as the Blackstone Rangers, a Woodlawn-based black gang, and the Vice Lords began to show signs of expanding into more complex diversified organizations. The Rangers received federal funding and responded by expanding and federating throughout the south and west sides of the city. As the political potential of their growth became obvious, the Police Gang Intelligence Unit clamped down on the group, the state's attorney began prosecuting its members, and the mayor moved to block the flow of funds. On the federal level, the FBI confused and obstructed the Rangers (see Dawley 1973 and Keiser 1969; both involve participant-observation, but the former seeks an academic analysis and the latter a history of the Vice Lords gang from its own perspective). The Vice Lords appeared at the Board of Election Commissioners with Minister Louis Farrakahn to register for the 1984 Illinois presidential primary.

3. Different accounts stress different leadership groups, which suggests that there were different syndicates in different types of operations. See Wendt and Kogan (1943, map of territories on p. 8). The Chicago Crime Commission seemed to oppose Capone and other criminally inclined types as much for their lack of etiquette as for their illegal activities (see Peterson 1963). Coughlin was described as a "voluble and uncouth person," and gangsters of the early 1960s were described as "for all [their] outward refinements, still [knowing] . . . only one law—the law of the jungle" (Chicago Crime Commission 1953:31, 39). See also Kobler (1971: chaps. 1 and 5); Lashley (1929: pt. 3); Nelli (1970a:149–51, State's Attorney Michael Hoyne was conducting investigations of syndicate affairs); and Wendt and Kogan (1943:237).

4. By 1928 the Unione listed 4,000 adult members in thirty-nine lodges and owned assets of $176,000 (Schiavo 1928:206). For cryptic information about the Unione, see Nelli (1969, 1970a, 1976) and Cordasco and Lagumina (1972). Sensitivity about the association between Italians and crime is appar-

ent in a number of other sources, such as Mariano (1925). Vecoli (1963) includes choice quotations about early twentieth-century Chicago attitudes towards Italians. Nelli has uncovered evidence that "Italian" organized crime seemed to have been peculiar to the American experience, since no Al Capones or John Torrios appeared in Brazil or Argentina although large numbers of Italian immigrants also settled there (1970a:137–39).

5. The Unione was important in ending Black Hand or individualized extortion in the Chicago Italian community around 1910; by the early 1920s it was also important as a fraternal organization and played an unspecified role in underworld activities in the Italian community. Pasley described it as an "alky cooking" guild (1930:49; see also Nelli 1970a:174, 224). A certain amount of alcohol had to be produced for medicinal and religious uses; see, for example, *Annual Report of the Commissioner of Prohibition* (1927). In Chicago, gangsters who did not own a brewery or who has been dispossessed might rob one, as per Torrio's unsuccessful attempt on the Sieben brewerry in 1925 (Lashley 1929: chap. 20). The Gennas had also organized a group of families from Sicily in the nineteenth ward to brew alcohol in backyard stills (Lashley 1929:962; Pasley 1930:90–95). Pasley reported that they were making $100,000 per month by 1925 (Hearings Before the Subcommittee of the Judiciary of the U.S. Senate Bill to Amend the National Prohibition Law, 1926). From the testimony of Mayor William Dever, April 22, 1926: "In one instance policemen . . . with an eye upon incoming trucks laden with liquor fell afoul of each other and opened fire as if upon the high seas in time of war" (Merriam 1929:47). Police participation in collection of protection was so routine that a police captain's assignee for that task was called a "bull dick" (Truman Gibson, Jr., interview, Aug. 17, 1975).

6. Capone helped elect a slate of city officials in Cicero in April of 1924; Pasley reported that the syndicate demanded 25–50 percent of the profits (1930:39–42).

7. O'Banion's shop, unlike Capone's second-hand furniture store, was a genuine business. Gangsters frequently placed their orders with him for the funerals of other gangsters whom they might have helped to kill. Other underworld figures also operated legitimate businesses; for example, Daniel Jackson and John Sbarbaro were both underworld undertakers (see Lashley 1929:924–31, for a list of related murders). The Gennas opposed O'Banion in the southside beer wars, in which the Saltis fought with the Spike O'Donnells and later with the Ralph Sheldon gang.

8. In one foray in the late 1920s, Capone's gangsters surrounded the police detective bureau (Pasley 1930:192–83; see also Peterson 1952, 1963). Peterson reported fifteen gangland-style killings in 1961 (1963:36). In 1975 Sam Giancana, the head of the Colosimo-originated syndicate, was murdered after he reportedly prepared to testify about his involvement in alleged plots to kill Fidel Castro (*New York Times*, April 12, 1976).

9. Policy is a lottery game, the midwestern version of "numbers."

10. Jones's departure was part of a larger drive by the Hyde Park Protective Association to maintain Hyde Park as a white community (see Gosnell 1967; Spear 1967).

11. John Leonard East described one occasion when he and Jackson went to the racetrack and Jackson spent some time in conversation with Capone (interview, Jan. 14, 1974; see also Lashley 1929: chap. 20; Peterson 1952: 140–41).

12. For a detailed description of the social and organizational characteristics of policy, see Drake and Cayton (1970:452, 481, and chap. 17); see also Peterson (1952:180, table 74 in appendix). See Special Committee to Investigate Crime in Interstate Commerce (1951:1407, 1409) for statistics on policy income.

13. Peterson reported that Benvenuti's "cordial relations" with and favors done for Capone helped the Benvenuti's Erie-Buffalo wheel to continue in independent existence. After Benvenuti's and Capone's deaths in 1945 and 1947, Capone's associates moved in to share the profits (Peterson 1952:195, 295–96).

14. In 1953 Peterson commented in a similar vein: "This myth was exploded when the books and records of the Erie-Buffalo wheel were made public. They established that the Capone gang leader Tony Accardo and his lieutenant Jake Guzik received the sum of $278,000 from this one wheel in 1949" (Chicago Crime Commission 1953:17).

15. Gosnell reported that black syndicate head Jackson's estate was probated at $75,000, but probably was worth three times as much (1967:131). On the Chicago scale, that amount was relatively small. Black underworld figures came from different backgrounds than the violent Capone and O'Banion. Jackson was a graduate of Lincoln University, while the Jones brothers were described as "well-educated, affable fellows" (Drake and Cayton 1970:487).

16. John Leonard East reported that Jackson discouraged some gangsters from trespassing in his territory (interview, 1974).

17. Maclay Hoyne indicted DePriest partly because he had supported his opponent in the state's attorney's race. Jones turned state's evidence against DePriest (Gosnell 1967:173), who was acquitted.

18. Even day-to-day operations of blacks were not always protected. The following intriguing incident was cited by Gosnell (1967:133): Daniel Jackson was robbed of $25,000 on the steps of city hall in 1928. Clearly someone knew he was making a payment (Truman Gibson, Jr., interview, 1975).

19. For a complete description of arrests, charges, and convictions by race and ethnicity from 1878 to 1931, see Pinderhughes (1977b:519–28). The reports of arrests and convictions are based on the *Report of the General Superintendent of Police to the City Council* (1878–1931). The data are not accurate indications of the rates of arrests, charges, and convictions because of the inconsistencies in the reporting procedures, the incorrect identification of European ethnics, and a variety of other problems. Moreover, the data terminate in 1931 because of the city's financial problems. However, they provide a great deal of information on the general patterns of contact between specific groups and the system of criminal justice. For that reason they are an invaluable data source.

20. Greek population figures are not reported for 1890 and 1900, so that they have an exceptionally high mean arrest rate (311.03), but that excludes

several years. They were also higher than blacks in 1910 and 1920, but dropped below them in 1930 (Pinderhughes 1977b).

21. The maps after p. 342 in *The Negro in Chicago* show the rapid expansion of the vice district from 1914 to 1916 (Chicago Commission on Race Relations 1922). One of the consistent themes in most studies of the black community during these early years was its opposition to the presence of vice (Branham n.d.:3; Chicago Commission on Race Relations 1922:211; Reckless 1933:25 and maps 9, 106, 202; Spear 1967: chap. 1).

22. In Italy, a separated, unmarried, widowed, or sexually active single woman's status was about the equivalent of a prostitute, so the community mobilized its resources toward structuring or restructuring the woman into a regularized pattern of marriage to diminish the threat she posed to the rest of the community.

23. This issue was raised by Moynihan (1965) in the mid-1960s and responded to by Billingsley (1968), who argued that black families were not necessarily nuclear but could also survive in extended form. Gutman (1976) reexamined plantation records of slave families to argue that the black family remained fairly intact during slavery. As the percentage of black females who head families has risen to more than fifty percent of all black families in the two decades since Moynihan's report was first published, the debate over black family structure has arisen again.

24. Gambling, prostitution, and disorderly conduct equalled 57.2 percent in 1913, 50.2 percent in 1917, 47.6 percent in 1923, 61.4 percent in 1927, and 53.7 percent in 1931.

25. Gosnell listed results for city referenda on prohibition. On four separate occasions Chicagoans cast 70 percent or more of their votes in opposition to prohibition (1968:145). By 1930 the estimated number of speakeasies, gambling joints, beer flats, and cigar stores ranged from 6,000 to 20,000. Pasley commented on the disparity: "the newspapers have not listed the drug stores and cigar stores peddling gin and Bourbon, and the beer flats. These I included under the general heading of speakeasies" (1930:289).

26. Gosnell reported that Mushmouth Johnson gave "$10,000 to the Democrats and $10,000 to the Republicans so that no matter who won, he'd be protected" (1967:127).

27. Prignano, a Democrat, had been anti-Thompson, and Capone wanted a friendly alderman there.

28. Landesco described an emotional community gathering at which Oberta was honored.

29. Czarnecki was a Polish election commissioner who paved the way for the Cicero chaos by striking the names of registered voters and regular election judges from the lists (Lashley 1929:1007–11).

30. Zuta had also given loans to Judge Emmanuel Elder, the son of twentieth-ward committeeman Morris Elder.

31. This was the election in which Octavius Granady, a black Deneen candidate in the twenty-fifth ward, was killed. Stuart's biography of Thompson cited a 1931 Thompson campaign booklet in which Serritella acknowledge having been called upon to stop a *Tribune* strike. As president of the

Newsboys Union, Serritella said he was powerless, but the *Tribune's* director of circulation said he wanted to meet with Capone to see what he could do. Serritella "attended" the meeting, at which Capone agreed to call off the strike (Stuart 1936:463–64).

32. It was evidently a rough life for Serritella, as he reported to the Kefauver Committee that he had seven or eight nervous breakdowns between 1938 and 1949 (Special Committee to Investigate Organized Crime 1951:665, 683).

33. This section is based on Haller (1970) unless otherwise cited.

34. Jackson in effect approved of DePriest's nomination.

35. Lashley described a testimonial dinner for Dingbat Oberta in the Back of the Yards district. Ragen Colts were also reported to have been active in "defending" the eastern areas of the south side, which adjoined the black belt, during the 1919 riot (1929:1008–10).

36. Chicago's Pineapple Primary received press coverage in European as well as American newspapers. There are multitudes of criminal-political stories encountered on the subject (see esp. Lyle 1960 and Peterson 1952).

37. Cermak had his own criminal connections; he had been president of the county board during the Dever administration when Capone and other gangsters had based their operations outside the city but within county limits (Wendt and Kogan 1943:351–52).

38. Gottfried (1962) concludes that Giuseppe Zangara was aiming at Roosevelt.

7. Educators, Machinists, and Reformers: The Politics of Race and Class

1. The board had voted an increase in teachers' salaries, which Mayor Busse opposed. The members Busse wanted to resign had been appointed by the reform-minded Mayor Dunne (Herrick 1971:109–11). The Illinois Supreme Court reinstated the seven board members whom Busse had removed. Cronin reported on changes in the school board: from 1839 to 1872 the board grew from seven to twenty members with ward-based representatives appointed by the city council; from 1872 to 1900, twenty-one members were appointed at large by the mayor; in 1897 the Harper reform proposal recommended an eleven-member board, but it was killed in the state legislature by the Chicago Federation of Teachers (CFT); in 1919 the Otis Law reformed the board with support from the CFT; an eleven-member board was appointed at large by the mayor with the consent of the city council, but the law failed in the implementation stage; in 1946 the National Education Association (NEA) Defense Committee and other organizations recommended school reform. The NEA Defense Committee recommended a new superintendent with enlarged powers and a board elected at large; the mayor's Heald Committee recommended an eleven-member board appointed by independent commission (Cronin 1973:45, 50, 76, 92–93, 110–11, 126, 149–50).

2. Lowi noted that this type of reorganization in New York in 1917 ended the dominance of the city's social elite on the board (1964: chap. 2; see also Cronin 1973:111; Grimshaw 1979:29–33; Stuart 1936:160–61).

3. Lundin's friends in boiler sales had been paid $105,000 more for boilers than another contractor had offered. Buses for handicapped children were rented at $28.50 rather than $12.50 per day. Supplies were purchased and fees were fixed for every ton of coal bought by the city, and contracts were awarded to dummy companies owned by Fred Lundin, who oversaw the whole deal (Herrick 1971:137–39; Stuart 1936:200–201). These and other scandals, such as the expert fees case and Gov. Len Small's $600,000 indebtedness to the state, weakened Thompson's candidacy for mayor in 1922, and he withdrew.

4. McAndrew originally taught at and then served as principal of Hyde Park High School in the late 1800s until his dismissal in 1891, when he refused to promote a politician's son (Herrick 1971:143). McAndrew aroused the teachers' ire by formally announcing that he would not meet with the teachers' councils, an informal twenty-year-old apparatus that ensured a certain amount of teacher input into school administration. Most of the other superintendents ignored them without controversy, but McAndrew's formal announcement aroused anger (see Counts 1971: chap. 5; Herrick 1971:150–54).

5. The 1927 decision did not introduce the janitors to this sort of patronage. They were reported to have contributed between $78,000 and $90,000 to school board members in the early 1920s. Now that the politicians held judicial permission to reorganize the janitorial service, these events beame more frequent (Counts 1971:261–62; Herrick 1971:142, 164–66).

6. "His [DeLue's] occupation was given as secretary of a distillery (during prohibition!)" (Herrick 1971:173; see also 174–75).

7. Herrick suggested but did not state unequivocally that Nate DeLue was organized crime's representative at the board as head of the janitor's union (1971:174–75).

8. In the Democratic party Billy Skidmore served as purchasing agent in 1903 and sergeant-at-arms at the Democratic national conventions of 1912 and 1916 (Peterson 1952:166; see also Lyle 1960:126).

9. For example, newspaper accounts of speeches given by federation members at a 1915 rally were headlined "Halt Plot to Make Schools Serf Factories" and "Capitalism in Assault on Public Schools" (Herrick 1971:123, see also 94, 254; Counts 1971: chap. 6; Herrick 1931:109). The federation examined property tax lists and found that the Pullman Company and public utilities, such as Chicago Edison and Chicago Telephone with franchises valued at $200 million, paid no taxes.

10. The eventual lower amount of $600,000 received by the city was based on a much lower assessment in the federal courts, which was agreed upon at the request of the utilities. The school board actually received $249,-545. As part of the remains of a large congressional grant of property to school districts in the eighteenth century, the board owned the land on which the *Chicago Daily News,* the *Chicago Tribune,* and John M. Smyth Furniture stood in the late nineteenth century. In 1889–90 the board agreed to a series of 100-year leases that required a set rental fee. The latter would be high in the short run but extraordinarily inexpensive in the long run (Herrick 1971:44; see also Counts 1971: chap. 4).

11. "Real estate in Cook County was estimated to be about one-third of the property in the county, but it paid approximately 85 percent of the property tax" (Herrick 1971:182). This conflict took place during the chaotic years of Thompson's third term (Stuart 1936:403; Wendt and Kogan 1953:314).

12. Peterson reported that teachers' salaries rose dramatically after their union finally made accommodations to the machine in the 1960s (1976: chap. 8). See also "Spasmodic Diary of a Chicago School Teacher" (1933); this anonymous article described the difficulty of making ends meet while working without pay and the author's gradual radicalization because of these conditions.

13. In other words, if it cost more money to teach children to read by concentrating on half-hour sessions rather than on ten-minute sessions three times a day, the latter was to be preferred, apart from any question as to students' concentration or reading ability (see Callahan 1962: chap. 3; see also Bowles and Gintis 1976: chap 1; Herrick 1971: 175). If Bowles and Gintis's hypothesis is correct, these patterns should have had a comparable, if not greater, influence on the black portion of the school population. Both the curriculum and classroom relationships should have reinforced rather than challenged black status. Their "statistical data applied only to non-Negro males: if inequality for white males can be documented, the proposition is merely strengthened when sexual and racial differences are taken into account" (Bowles and Gintis 1976:30). Bowles and Gintis noted in the introduction that their book was a reply to liberal reformers of the 1960s, who did not go far enough in their efforts to reduce inequality in American society. Since much of that effort centered around the status of blacks, their argument has relevance for this study. They also challenged the reaction to liberal reform by Moynihan, Glazer, and Jencks by stating that their explanation of the source of inequality does not lie either in the schools or in the internal factors of race or intelligence, but in the economic system.

14. The presidents of Yale and Dartmouth, A. T. Hadley and E. M. Hopkins, felt that continuing education should be restricted to "those who have brains and the inclination to cultivate them" (quoted in Counts 1971: 146). The federation's position is even more clearly reinforced by Herrick's historical treatment, since she and her father, who was a high school principal, participated in many of these events. In her master's thesis on black employees in the Chicago school board, little is lost of the character of the interpretations of the business community's actions or intentions, since Herrick shares their views (Herrick 1971:117–19).

15. Callahan reported that McAndrew helped lead the attack on inefficient schools (1962:51). Since Gary had only been built in 1907 by U.S. Steel, Wirt was assumed to be aligned with the steel industry. Callahan suggests that Wirt rejected that interpretation (1962:111).

16. Bowles and Gintis described the proletarianization of the teaching profession (1976: chap. 3). McAndrew introduced time checks, efficiency ratings, and performance requirements, which were the equivalent of industiralizing the schools (see Herrick 1971:158, for instances where McAndrew

revealed his alliance with business). Even the conservative *Chicago Tribune* perceived the growing correspondence between the school and the factory in an editorial on October 3, 1924: "Is Teaching Labor or Professional Service?" If rewards such as "relative freedom from detailed supervision . . . are not present," said the *Tribune,* "the teachers will naturally ally themselves with labor. . . . Schools are not steel mills. Chicago's children can be rightly taught only by voluntary cooperation of all the forces. A conquered teaching force will be worse than useless" (quoted in Herrick 1971:161).

17. See Wesley (1957), which describes how the NEA was still struggling to organize even a small minority of the profession at the time.

18. There were 29,432 black teachers in the entire country in 1910 (Herrick 1931:3, 22–23).

19. Some principals described black teachers as "cocky" to the Riot Commission (Gosnell 1967:289, 296–97).

20. The Strayer report listed the school among those on which money should not be spent (1932).

21. See also Chicago Commission on Race Relations (1922:238–71) for a long description of racial interaction in the school system (see also Herrick 1931:22–23).

22. Predominantly black schools were 85–100 percent black (see Herrick 1931: appendix).

23. Homel argued that politics sometimes played a role in the appointment of black teachers (1976:185).

24. DePriest was appointed third-ward committeeman after 1927; Anderson was second-ward alderman and committeeman; R. R. Jackson was third-ward alderman; and Cronson was fourth-ward alderman.

25. Seymour Sacks noted eight possible measures of expenditures that might be applied, including: enrolled pupils, pupils in average daily membership, pupils in average daily attendance, weighted averages of the latter two measures, size of classroom unit, size of teacher unit, number of school-age children, and number of high school graduates. The first three measures tend to increase the real level of expenditure per child, since the number of students declines (see Sacks 1972: chap. 2, esp. 22–24). For example, the number of students who enrolled in Chicago's schools for 1914 was 332,248, the average daily membership was 276,558.2, and the average daily attendance was 261,447.7 (based on the report of the superintendent for 1913–14, p. 443, from the Chicago Board of Education 1909–45:438). As the measure changes, the expenditure per pupil rises. Thus the use of enrollment figures as a basis for comparison for the data in this study means that the rate per pupil is somewhat lower than the real levels of expense. However, the rate per enrolled pupil is used in all reporting years, and this measure was chosen because of incomplete data for all other measures for all years (see Pinderhughes 1977b: appendix, for full citations for figure 7.1).

26. See Vieg (1939:160, table 17) for Chicago expenses compared with New York, Detroit, Philadelphia, Los Angeles, and Gary (see also Strayer 1939: vol. 4:71–73, tables 28 and 29, pp. 83, 89, 90).

27. In this regard Fred Lundin announced triumphantly in 1922 that the Thompsonites were at the "feedbox" of the schools and would not back away (Herrick 1971:142).

28. See appendix for detailed explanation of methodology and list of schools (table A.1).

29. For a discussion of Polish and Italian public versus private school attendance, see Pinderhughes (1977b:529–39).

30. In 1931 administrative costs contributed only $5.02 per pupil in average daily attendance (see Pinderhughes 1977b:406, table 52; see also, for example, Homel 1984:58–87). Homel's recent work (1984) reaches similar conclusions about the overall impact of school policy on black education: that the school system discriminated against blacks.

31. Educational expenses generally include all costs, such as teachers' salaries, textbook expenses, and other items. I did not record textbooks, and while I recorded principals and teacher-clerks' salaries (they were listed together), I did not include them in instructional costs. Thus my instructional costs indicator is not complete and the total costs are somewhat higher than the figures show. It is unlikely, however, that they would bring the averages up to recommended levels of expenditure; the pattern is clear and I do not believe the missing data would alter it significantly.

32. Herrick reported that the schools began providing free textbooks around 1922 (1971:178).

33. This was not included in line-item expenses in the sample schools, so it does not affect their total costs. The budget items surveyed cannot account for all of the increases in the budget. If we look at the average increase for all three groups in the years 1918–22, we can see quickly that the increases in operations and maintenance did not equal the difference between salaries and total expenditures. Thus some of the line items that were included in the total costs but were not identified or calculated separately in this study made up the difference.

34. I did not calculate principals' and teacher-clerks' salaries separately, and since some of the money saved came from elimination of administrative positions, some of the cuts came from this category. This was a result of the city's fiscal crisis, which meant that when the board composed its budget, the assessor's office was still in the process of attempting to collect back taxes for the 1928 and 1929 school years and was also considering a new tax rate for the 1930 year. We can see changes in budgeting for principals' salaries; the board changed from a yearly to a monthly rate in its records: the "teaching force['s] . . . salaries are computed by multiplying the monthly basic rate set up in this Budget by nine (the number of school months) and deducting 15%" (Proceedings of the Chicago Board of Education 1933–34:732).

35. For year-by-year percentage increases and decreases in the various expenditure categories, see Strayer (1932, vol. 1:205).

36. Just as Phillips ranked lower on quality standards than all other high schools in my survey, it ranked higher than all others in its shortage of seats. Morgan Park was one of the few high schools that had a surplus (Strayer 1932:35–36, tables 10 and 11), while other schools fell in between. On the

elementary level, more Italian and Polish schools had vacant rooms than did black schools. There were no vacancies in the black areas in 1931, while the Italian and Polish areas were mixed (see map in Strayer 1932, vol. 4:29; see also vol. 4:27, table 5).

37. Ten Poles had served on the board by 1937 (see *Poles of Chicago* 1937:124–28). Only seven blacks had served by 1968 (see Rather 1972:125).

38. Thirty years later the board used federal funds to make up the difference between black and white per-pupil expenditures (Berk and Hartman 1972).

39. Baron reported that racial protests in the early 1960s challenged the board to reduce inequalities. The board used the newly approved Elementary and Secondary Education Act and its own supplementary appropriations to target increased personnel in lower-income areas (Baron 1971).

40. Ladd contrasted Greenville, South Carolina's black population employed as manual laborers and servants with Winston-Salem's, in which blacks were employed in the tobacco mills. Greenville's blacks lived in a number of dispersed residential areas, while blacks in Winston-Salem were much more highly concentrated (1969:54–57). Lowi showed that Iron City's blacks lived in a number of highly disparate areas; as the Supreme Court declared school segregation illegal, the city implemented a "Black removal" plan that relocated all blacks literally on the wrong side of the railroad tracks (1979: chap. 9 and maps, pp. 238–45).

8. Race and Ethnicity in America

1. Chicago is frequently cited by Duncan and Duncan (1957: esp. chaps. 5–7) and others as the most segregated city in the nation.

2. See, for example, Peterson (1976), Preston (1982a, 1982b), and Mc Worter et al. (1984) for discussions of conflict on the Chicago school board over segregation policy and the role of a black official such as Warren Bacon in the conflict.

3. Other economic considerations include a publishing industry that is associated with such betting. Many people use information derived from their dreams to identify the numbers on which they should bet. A variety of dream books interpret and translate dreams into numbers. The combination of collective and economic issues should mobilize blacks and other groups of comparable status more effectively than economic issues alone (see Pinderhughes 1983 for a discussion of this point).

4. See chapter 5 for a discussion of the National Negro Congress in 1936 and the National Black Political Convention in 1972.

5. Examples include: Barker and McCorry (1976); Cole (1976); Gosnell (1968); Holden (1973); Karnig and Welch (1980); Katznelson (1976); Kilson (1971b); Morris (1975); Nelson and Meranto (1977); Walton (1972); and Wilson (1960a). Only Katznelson (1973) and Kilson (1971b) directly address the issue of political integration in the initial stages when the black population was first expanding in urban areas.

6. Two examples of such positions include Agger et al. (1966) and Sullivan et al. (1980).

7. In urban areas, these included members of immigrant groups that had arrived early in the twentieth century. While Glazer and Moynihan (1963) found them assimilating less quickly than Dahl did, they concluded that ethnics were moving into elective and appointive office at the metropolitan and state levels and that they were enthusiastic members of local decision-making arenas. For a review, reevaluation, and reconstruction of the urban politics literature, see Peterson (1981).

8. Thomas Sowell is one of the most prolific of a recent generation of black conservatives who criticize governmental intervention, such as affirmative action. These conservatives include chairman of the U.S. Civil Rights Commission, Clarence Pendleton, and another economist, Walter Williams. Sowell's many publications on this subject include *Ethnic America: A History* (1981) and an edited volume, *Essays and Data on American Ethnic Groups* (1978).

9. This parallels and is derived from Edwin Dorn's analysis of governmental reforms applied to racial status. See his discussion of the logical basis for affirmative action in *Rules and Racial Equality* (1979).

10. Eisinger masters a large volume of historical and interview material with ease in his study. Additional case studies with different variable combinations will no doubt appear very slowly.

Appendix

1. The school census of Chicago did not calculate these for the same years; thus the year in which school attendance by type of school was recorded was mutually exclusive with the years when minor population by wards and by nationality was reported. However, these school census years are within eight years of each other, so I will treat them as comparable although they are certainly not identical. The figures are derived from Ficht (1952) and Wisniewski (n.d.).

2. On the other hand, St. Hedwig's, Holy Trinity, and St. Casimir all enrolled about two thousand pupils in the early 1930s (Wargin 1948).

3. This information was compiled from: Bureau of the Census (1932: vol 2); Bureau of the Census (1943: vol 2:Illinois, p. 640); Chicago Board of Education *School Census*, respective years; *Chicago Daily News Almanac* (1915, 1917, 1931); and Schafer (1929). See also Chicago Commission on Race Relations (1922); Gosnell (1967); Herrick (1931); *Historic City: Settlement of Chicago* (1976); and Pinderhughes (1977b:529–39). I used working maps in the preparation of this volume to identify areas of heavy racial or national settlement.

4. See the Chicago Commission on Race Relations report, which showed that black school population usually outstripped the general black population of the areas (1922:242, table 10).

5. See *Historic City: Settlement of Chicago* (1976); the maps were also unable to show that the Swedish and Irish were heavily mixed. There was no information on Poles for 1910.

6. Sources: for school expenditures, Chicago Board of Education, *Proceedings* (1913–44); for pupil figures, Chicago Board of Education, "Report of the Superintendent" (1908–45).

Bibliography

Abbott, Edith. *The Tenements of Chicago, 1908–1935.* Chicago: University of Chicago Press, 1936.

Aberbach, Joel D., and Jack L. Walker. "The Meanings of Black Power: A Comparison of Black and White Interpretations of a Political Slogan." *American Political Science Review* 64 (June 1970a): 367–88.

———. "Political Trust and Racial Ideology." *American Political Science Review* 64 (Dec. 1970b): 1199–219.

———. *Race in the City, Political Trust and Public Policy in the New Urban System.* Boston: Little, Brown, 1973.

Adams, Mary Faith. "Present Housing Conditions in South Chicago, Deering and Pullman." Unpublished M.A. thesis, University of Chicago, 1926.

Agger, Robert E., Daniel Goldrich, and Bert E. Swanson. *The Rulers and the Ruled: Political Power and Impotence in American Communities.* New York: Wiley, 1966.

Ahmed, Akbar Muhammad. "The Roots of Pan-African Nationalism." *Black Scholar* 3 (May 1972): 48–55.

Alkalimat, Abdul, and Doug Gills. "Black Power vs. Racism: Harold Washington Becomes Mayor." In *The New Black Vote, Politics and Power in Four American Cities,* edited by Rod Bush, 53–180. San Francisco: Synthesis Publications, 1984.

Allswang, John M. *A House for All Peoples, Ethnic Politics in Chicago 1908–1936.* Lexington: University Press of Kentucky, 1971.

———. *Bosses, Machines and Urban Voters: An American Symbiosis.* Port Washington, NY: Kennikat Press, 1977.

Andersen, Kristi. *The Creation of a Democratic Majority, 1928–1936.* Chicago: University of Chicago Press, 1979.

Andrews, Theodore. *The Polish National Catholic Church in America and Poland.* London: S.P.C.K., 1953.

Annual Report of the Commissioner of Prohibition. Chicago, Illinois, June 1927.

Aptheker, Herbert, ed. *A Documentary History of the Negro People in the United States from Colonial Times to 1910.* New York: Citadel, 1963.

Asbury, Herbert. *Gem of the Prairie: An Informal History of the Chicago Underworld.* Garden City, NY: Garden City Publishing, 1928.

Axelrod, Robert. "Where the Votes Come From: An Analysis of Electoral Coalitions, 1952–1968." *American Political Science Review* 66 (March 1972): 11–20.

———."1976 Update." *American Political Science Review* 72 (June 1978): 622–24.

Bachrach, Peter, and Morton Baratz. "The Two Faces of Power." *American Political Science Review* 56 (Dec. 1962): 947–52.

Balbus, Isaac. "The Concept of Interest in Pluralist and Marxian Analysis." *Politics and Society* 1 (Winter 1971): 151–77.

Banfield, Edward C. *Political Influence.* Reprint. New York: Free Press, 1965.

Banfield, Edward C., and James Q. Wilson. *City Politics.* Cambridge: Harvard University Press, 1963.

———. "Public Regardingness as a Value Premise in Voting Behavior." *American Political Science Review* 58 (Dec. 1964): 876–87.

———. "Political Ethos Revisited." *American Political Science Review* 65 (Dec. 1971): 1048–62.

Barbour, Floyd, ed. *The Black Power Revolt.* Boston: Porter Sargent, 1968.

Barker, Lucius J., and Jesse J. McCorry, Jr. *Black Americans and the Political System.* Cambridge, MA: Winthrop Publishers, 1976.

Barnett, Marguerite Ross. "The Congressional Black Caucus." *Academy of Political Science Proceedings* 32 (1975): 34–50.

———. "A Theoretical Perspective on Racial Public Policy." In *Public Policy for the Black Community: Strategies and Perspectives,* edited by Marguerite Ross Barnett and James A. Hefner, 1–54. New York: Alfred Publishing, 1976.

———. "Congressional Black Caucus: Symbol, Myth and Reality." *Black Scholar* 8 (Jan. 1977): 17–26.

———. "The Congressional Black Caucus: Illusions and Realities of Power." In *The New Black Politics, the Search for Political Power* edited by Michael B. Preston, Lenneal J. Henderson, Jr., and Paul Puryear. New York: Longman, 1982.

———. "The New Federalism and the Unfinished Civil Rights Agenda." *Black Law Journal* 8 (Winter 1983): 375–86.

———, and Ndoro Vincent Vera. "Afro-American Politics and Public Policy Priorities in the 1980s." *Black Scholar* 11 (March 1980): 9–21.

Baron, Harold. "Race and Status in School Spending: Chicago, 1961–1966." *Journal of Human Resources* 6 (Winter 1971): 8–11.

Baxter, Sandra, and Marjorie Lansing. *Women and Politics: The Invisible Majority.* Ann Arbor: University of Michigan Press, 1981.

Becker, Gary. *The Economics of Discrimination.* Chicago: University of Chicago Press, 1971.

Becker, Howard. "The Career of the Chicago Public School Teachers." *American Journal of Sociology* 5 (March 1952): 470–77.

Bennett, Lerone. *The Negro Mood.* Chicago: Johnson Publishing, 1964.

———. *Confrontation: Black and White.* Chicago: Johnson Publishing, 1965.

Berk, Richard, and Alice Hartman. "Race and School Funds in Chicago, 1971." *Integrated Education* 10 (Jan.–Feb. 1972):52–57.

Berry, Mary F. *Black Resistance, White Law: A History of Constitutional Racism in America.* New York: Appleton-Century Crofts, 1971.

Beyle, Herman C. *Governmental Reporting in Chicago.* Chicago: University of Chicago Press, 1928.

Billingsley, Andrew. *Black Families in White America.* Englewood Cliffs, NJ: Prentice-Hall, 1968.

Black, Merle. "Racial Composition of Congressional Districts and Support for Federal Voting Rights in the American South." *Social Science Quarterly* 59 (Dec. 1978): 435–50.

Bogira, Steve. "Citizen Chew." *The Chicago Reader* 11, no. 26 (April 9, 1982).

Bolek, Reverend Francis, ed. *Who's Who in Polish America.* Greenville, PA: Beaver Printing, 1940.

Bonacich, Edna. "Advanced Capitalism and Black-White Relations in the United States: A Split Labor Market Interpretation." *American Sociological Review* 41 (Feb. 1976): 34–51.

Bowles, Samuel, and Herbert Gintis. *Schooling in Capitalist America: Educational Reform and the Contradictions of Economic Life.* New York: Basic Books, 1976.

Bracey, John H., August Meier, and Elliott Rudwick, eds. *Black Nationalism in America.* Indianapolis: Bobbs-Merrill, 1970.

Branham, Charles. "Oscar DePriest and the Origins of Black Politics in Chicago: The Aldermanic Years." Ms. funded by the U.S. Dept. of Health, Education and Welfare, the Welfare Administration, and the Social Security Administration. University of Chicago, n.d.

———. "Black Chicago: Accommodationist Politics Before the Great Migration." In *The Ethnic Frontier: Essays in the History of Group Survival in Chicago and the Midwest,* edited by Melvin G. Holli and Peter d'A. Jones, 211–62. Grand Rapids, MI: William B. Eerdmans, 1977.

Brazeal, Brailsford R. *The Brotherhood of Sleeping Car Porters: Its Origins and Development.* New York: Harper and Brothers, 1946.

Bright, John. *Hizzoner Big Bill Thompson: An Idyll of Chicago.* New York: Jonathan Cape and Harrison Smith, 1930.

Brodie, Fawn. *Thomas Jefferson: An Intimate History.* New York: Norton, 1974.

"The Budget as an Instrument for Economy." *Research Bulletin of the National Education Association* 11 (Sept. 1933): 66–69.

Bunche, Ralph J. "The Thompson-Negro Alliance. *Opportunity* 7 (March 1929): 78–80.

———. *The Political Status of the Negro in the Age of FDR.* Chicago: University of Chicago Press, 1973.

Bureau of the Census. U.S. Department of Commerce. *Tenth Census of the United States, 1880: Population,* vol. 1, Washington, D.C., 1883.

———. *Eleventh Census of the United States, 1890: Population,* vol. 1, Washington, D.C., 1895.

———. *Twelfth Census of the United States, 1900: Population,* pt. 2, Washington, D.C., 1902.

———. *Financial Statistics of Cities.* Washington, D.C., 1910.

———. *Thirteenth Census of the United States, 1910: Population,* vol. 2, Washington, D.C., 1913.

———. *Thirteenth Census of the United States, 1910: Population,* vol. 4, Washington, D.C., 1914.

———. *Negro Population, 1790–1915.* Washington, D.C., 1918.

———. *Fourteenth Census of the United States, 1920: Population,* vol. 3, Washington, D.C., 1922.

———. *Fifteenth Census of the United States, 1930: Population,* vol. 3, Washington, D.C., 1932.

———. *Negroes in the United States, 1920–1932.* Washington, D.C., 1935.

———. *Nativity and Parentage of Native Population, Mother Tongue,* Washington, D.C., 1943a.

———. *Sixteenth Census of the United States, 1940: Population,* vol. 2, Washington, D.C., 1943b.

———. *Seventeenth Census of the United States, 1950: Population,* vol. 2, Washington, D.C., 1952.

Burgess, M. Elaine. *Negro Leadership in a Southern City.* Chapel Hill: University of North Carolina Press, 1973.

Burgess, Ernest W., and Charles Newcomb, eds. *Census Data of the City of Chicago 1920.* Chicago: University of Chicago Press, 1931.

———. *Census Data of the City of Chicago, 1930.* Chicago: University of Chicago Press, 1933.

Burnham, Walter Dean. "The Changing Shape of the American Political Universe." *American Political Science Review* 59 (March 1965): 7–28.

———. *Critical Elections and the Mainstream of American Life.* New York: W. W. Norton, 1970.

Busyn, Helen. "The Political Career of Peter Kiolbassa." *Polish American Studies* 7 (Jan.-June 1950): 8–22.

———. "Peter Kiolbassa, Maker of Polish America." *Polish American Studies* 8 (July-Dec. 1951): 65–84.

Callahan, Raymond. *Education and the Cult of Efficiency: A Study of the Social Forces that Have Shaped the Administration of the Public Schools.* Chicago: University of Chicago Press, 1962.

Campbell, Angus, William Converse, Donald Stokes, and Warren Miller. *The American Voter.* New York: Wiley, 1960.

———. *White Attitudes Toward Black People.* Ann Arbor: Michigan Institute for Social Research, 1971.

Campbell, Bruce A. "Patterns of Change in the Partisan Loyalty of Native Southerners, 1952–1972." *Journal of Politics* 39 (Aug. 1977): 730–61

———. "Interaction of Race and Socioeconomic Status in the Development of Political Attitudes." *Social Science Quarterly* 60 (March 1980): 651–58.

Carmichael, Stokeley, and Charles V. Hamilton. *Black Power: The Politics of Liberation in America.* New York: Random House, 1967.

Carpenter, Niles. *Nationality, Color and Economic Opportunity in the City of Buffalo.* New York: University of Buffalo, 1927.

Carson, Clayborne. *In Struggle: SNCC and the Black Awakening of the 1960s.* Cambridge, MA: Harvard University Press, 1981.

Cassell, Carol A. "Change in Electoral Participation in the South." *Journal of Politics* 41 (Aug. 1979): 907–17.

Cayton, Horace R. "Negro Housing in Chicago." *Social Action* 6 (April 15, 1940): 4–39.

———, and George S. Mitchell. *Black Workers and the New Unions.* Chapel Hill: University of North Carolina Press, 1939.

"Certain Personnel Practices in the Chicago Public Schools." Washington, D.C.: National Commission for the Defense of Democracy Through Education of the National Education Association, 1945.

Chase-Riboud, Barbara. *Sally Hemmings: A Novel.* New York: Viking Press, 1979.

Chicago Board of Education. *Proceedings of the Board of Education.* Chicago, 1909–44.

———. "Report of the Superintendent." *Chicago Board of Education Annual Report.* Chicago, 1909–45.

———. *School Census.* Chicago, 1908–16.

Chicago Commission on Race Relations. *The Negro in Chicago.* Chicago: University of Chicago Press, 1922.

Chicago Crime Commission. "A Report on Chicago Crime and Criminals." 1953.

Cipriani, Lisi. *Italians in Chicago and the Selected Directory of Italians in Chicago.* Chicago: By the Author, 1933.

Clarke, John Henrik, ed. *Marcus Garvey and the Vision of Africa.* New York: Random House, 1974.

Cleghorn, Reese, and Pat Watters. *Climbing Jacob's Ladder: The Arrival of Negroes in Southern Politics.* New York: Harcourt, Brace and World, 1967.

Cole, Leonard A. *Blacks in Power: A Comparative Study of Black and White Elected Officials.* Princeton, NJ: Princeton University Press, 1976.

Comer, James P. *Beyond Black and White.* New York: Quadrangle Books, 1972.

"Compiled by Frederick Rex, Librarian." Chicago: Municipal Reference Library, 1942.

Connolly, William E. "The Challenge to Pluralist Theory." In *The Bias of Pluralism,* edited by William E. Connolly, 3–34. New York: Atherton Press, 1969.

Cordasco, Francesco, and Salvatore Lagumina, eds. *The Business of Crime: Italians in the United States: A Bibliography of Reports, Texts, Critical Studies and Related Materials.* New York: Oriole Editions, 1972.

Counts, George S. *Schools and Society in Chicago.* New York: Arno Press and the New York Times, 1971.

Covello, Leonard. *The Social Background of the Italo-American Schoolchild: A Study of the Southern Italian Family Mores and Their Effect in the School Situation in Italy and America,* edited by Francesco Cordasco. Leiden: E. J. Brill, 1967.

Cronin, Joseph M. *The Control of Urban Schools: Perspectives on the Power of Educational Reformers.* New York: Free Press, 1973.

Cronon, E. David. *Black Moses: The Story of Marcus Garvey and the Universal Negro Improvement Association.* Reprint. Madison: University of Wisconsin Press, 1969.

Cruse, Harold. *The Crisis of the Negro Intellectual.* New York: Williams Morrow, 1967.

Curtin, Phillip D., ed. *The Atlantic Slave Trade: A Census.* Madison: University of Wisconsin Press, 1969.

Curtis, Mildred. "Statistics of Arrests in Chicago in Relation to Race and Nativity." Unpublished M.A. thesis, University of Chicago, 1926.

Dahl, Robert A. *A Preface to Democratic Theory.* Chicago: University of Chicago Press, 1956.

———. *Who Governs? Democracy and Power in the American City.* New Haven, CT: Yale University Press, 1961.

———. *Pluralist Democracy in the United States: Conflict and Consent.* Chicago: Rand McNally, 1967.

———. "Pluralism Revisited." *Comparative Politics* 10 (Jan. 1978a): 191–203.

———. "Who Really Rules." *Social Science Quarterly* 60 (Jan. 1978b): 31–47.

Danigelis, Nicholas L. "A Theory of Black Political Participation in the United States." *Social Forces* 56 (Sept. 1977): 31–47.

———. "Black Political Participation in the United States: Some Recent Evidence." *American Sociological Review* 43 (Oct. 1978): 756–71.

Davidson, Chandler. "At-Large Elections and Minority Representation." *Social Science Quarterly* 60 (Sept. 1979): 336–38.

———, and George Korbel. "At-Large Elections and Minority Representation: A Re-examination of Historical and Contemporary Evidence." *Journal of Politics* 43 (Nov. 1981): 982–1005.

Davis, David Brion. *The Problem of Slavery in the Age of Revolution, 1770–1823.* Ithaca, NY: Cornell University Press, 1976.

Dawley, David. *A Nation of Lords: The Autobiography of the Vice Lords.* Garden City, NY: Anchor Press, 1973.

DeMaris, Ovid. *Captive City.* New York: Lyle Stuart, 1969.

Diamond, Irene, and Nancy Hartsock. "Beyond Interests in Politics: A Comment on Virginia Sapiro's 'When Are Interests Interesting? The Problem of Political Representation of Women.'" *American Political Science Review* 75 (Sept. 1981): 717–21.

Doherty, Robert E., and Walter E. Oberer. *Teachers, School Boards and Collective Bargaining: A Changing of the Guard.* Ithaca, NY: New York State School of Industrial and Labor Relations, Cornell University Press, 1967.

Dorn, Edwin. *Rules and Racial Equality.* New Haven, CT: Yale University Press, 1979.

Downs, Anthony. *An Economic Theory of Democracy.* New York: Little, Brown, 1967.

Drake, St. Clair, and Horace R. Cayton. *Churches and Voluntary Associations in the Chicago Negro Community.* Chicago: Works Progress Administration Project, 1940.

———. *Black Metropolis: A Study of Negro Life in a Northern City.* New York: Harcourt, Brace and World, 1970.

DuBois, W. E. B. *The Souls of Black Folk, Essays and Sketches.* Greenwich, CT: Fawcett, 1961.

———. *The Negro Church: Report of a Social Study Made Under the Direction of Atlanta University.* Atlanta: Atlanta University, 1968.

———. *The Suppression of the African Slave Trade to the United States of America, 1638–1870.* New York: Schocken, 1969.

Duncan, Otis Dudley, and Beverly Duncan. *The Negro Population of Chicago: A Study of Residential Succession.* Chicago: University of Chicago Press, 1957.

Eaton, William Edward. *The American Federation of Teachers, 1916–1961: A History of the Movement.* Carbondale: Southern Illinois University Press, 1975.

Edelman, Murray. *The Symbolic Uses of Politics.* Urbana: University of Illinois Press, 1964.

"An Efficient Staff: A Prerequisite for Economy." *Research Bulletin of the National Education Association* 11 (Sept. 1933): 61–65.

Eisinger, Peter K. *The Politics of Displacement: Racial and Ethnic Transition in Three American Cities.* New York: Academic Press, 1980.

Elkins, Stanley M. *Slavery: A Problem in American Institutional and Intellectual Life.* New York: Grosset and Dunlap, 1963.

Engstrom, Richard L., and Michael D. McDonald. "The Election of Blacks to City Councils: Clarifying the Impact of Electoral Arrangements on the Seats/Population Relationship." *American Political Science Review* 75 (June 1981): 344–54.

Essien-Udom, E. U. *Black Nationalism: A Search for an Identity in America.* Chicago: University of Chicago Press, 1962.

Federal Emergency Relief Administration. *Unemployment Relief Census.* Washington, D.C., October 1933.

Feldman, Herman. *Racial Factors in American Industry.* New York: Harper and Brothers, 1931.

Ficht, Sr. Mary Inviolata. "Noble Street in Chicago." Unpublished M.A. thesis, DePaul University, 1952.

Fogel, Robert W., and Stanley L. Engerman. *Time on the Cross: The Economics of American Negro Slavery.* Boston: Little, Brown, 1974.

Forthal, Sonya. *Cogwheels of Democracy: A Study of the Precinct Captain.* New York: William-Frederick Press, 1946.

The Gallup Poll, Public Opinion, 1935–1971. New York: Random House, 1972.

The Gallup Report 185 (Feb. 1981).

Gans, Herbert J. *The Urban Villagers: Group and Class in the Life of Italian-Americans.* New York: Free Press of Glencoe, 1962.

Garfinkel, Herbert. *When Negroes March: The March on Washington Movement in the Organizational Politics for FEPC.* New York: Atheneum, 1969.

Garrow, David. *Protest at Selma: Martin Luther King, Jr., and the Voting Rights Act of 1965.* New Haven, CT: Yale University Press, 1978.

Garvey, Amy Jacques, ed. *Philosophy and Opinions of Marcus Garvey.* New York: Atheneum, 1969.

———. *Garvey and Garveyism.* London: Collier Books, 1970.

Genovese, Eugene D. *The Political Economy of Slavery: Studies in the Economy and Society of the Slave South.* New York: Random House, 1965.

Gerth, H. H., and C. Wright Mills, eds. *From Max Weber: Essays in Sociology.* New York: Oxford University Press, 1946.

Glazer, Nathan. "Blacks and Ethnic Groups: The Difference and the Political Difference It Makes." In *Key Issues in the Afro-American Experience,* vol. 2, edited by Nathan Huggins, Martin Kilson, and Daniel Fox, 178–211. New York: Harcourt, Brace and Jovanich, 1971.

———, and Daniel P. Moynihan. *Beyond the Melting Pot: The Negroes, Puerto Ricans, Jews, Italians and Irish of New York City.* Cambridge, MA: MIT Press, 1963.

Gordon, Milton. "Models of Pluralism: The New American Dilemma." *Annals of the American Academy of Political and Social Science* 454 (March 1981): 178–88.

Gordon, Rita Werner, "The Change in the Political Alignment of Chicago's Negroes During the New Deal." *Journal of American History* 56 (Dec. 1969): 584–603.

Gosnell, Harold F. "Non-Naturalization: A Study in Political Assimilation." *American Journal of Sociology* 33 (May 1928): 830–39.

———. "Characteristics of the Non-Naturalized." *American Journal of Sociology* 34 (March 1929): 845–47.

———. *Negro Politicians: The Rise of Negro Politics in Chicago.* Chicago: University of Chicago Press, 1967.

———. *Machine Politics: Chicago Model.* Chicago: University of Chicago Press, 1968.

Gosnell Papers. Chicago Historical Society. Chicago, Illinois.

Gottfried, Alex. *Boss Cermak of Chicago.* Seattle: University of Washington Press, 1962.

Gove, Samuel K., and Louis H. Masotti, eds. *After Daley.* Urbana: University of Illinois Press, 1982.

Greenberg, Edward S. "Children and Government: A Comparison Across Racial Lines." *Midwest Journal of Political Science* 14 (May 1970a): 249–76.

———. "Orientation of Black and White Children to Political Authority Figures." *Social Science Quarterly* 51 (Dec. 1970b): 561–71.

Greenberg, Stanley. *Race and State in Capitalist Development: Comparative Perspectives.* New Haven, CT: Yale University Press, 1980.

Greenstone, J. David. "Party Pressure on Organized Labor in Three Cities." In *The Electoral Process,* edited by M. Kent Jennings and L. Harmon Ziegler, 55–80. Englewood Cliffs, NJ: Prentice-Hall, 1966.

———. *Labor in American Politics.* Chicago: University of Chicago Press, 1977.

———, and Paul E. Peterson. *Race and Authority in Urban Politics: Community Participation and the War on Poverty.* Chicago: University of Chicago Press, 1976.

Grimshaw, William J. *Union Rule in the Schools: Big City Politics in Transformation.* Lexington Books, 1979.

———. *Black Politics in Chicago: The Quest for Leadership, 1939–1979.* Chicago: Loyola University of Chicago, 1980.

———. "The Daley Legacy: A Declining Politics of Party, Race and Public Unions." In *After Daley: Chicago Politics in Transition,* edited by Samuel K. Gove and Louis H. Masotti, 57–87. Urbana: University of Illinois Press, 1982.

Guterbock, Thomas H. *Machine Politics in Transition: Party and Community in Chicago.* Chicago: University of Chicago Press, 1980.

Gutman, Herbert. *The Black Family in Slavery and Freedom, 1750–1925.* New York: Pantheon Books, 1976.

Haley, Alex. *The Autobiography of Malcolm X.* Reprint. New York: Grove Press, 1966.

Haller, Mark. "Police Reform in Chicago, 1905–1935." *American Behavioral Scientist* 13 (May-July 1970): 649–66.

Hamilton, Charles V. *The Black Preacher in America.* New York: William Morrow, 1972.

———. *The Bench and the Ballot: Southern Federal Judges and Black Voters.* New York: Oxford University Press, 1974.

———. "Public Policy and Some Political Consequences." In *Public Policy for the Black Community Strategies and Perspectives,* edited by Marguerite Ross Barnett and James A. Hefner, 237–56. New York: Alfred Publishing, 1976.

———. "New Elites and Pluralism." In *The Power to Govern,* edited by Richard M. Pious. *Proceedings of the Academy of Political Science* 34 (1981): 167–73.

Hare, Nathan. "The Revolutionary Role of the Black Bourgeoisie." *Black Scholar* 4 (Jan. 1973): 32–35.

Harlan, Louis R. *Booker T. Washington: The Making of a Black Leader, 1856–1901.* New York: Oxford University Press, 1972.

Harper, William R., chair. *Report of the Educational Commission of the City of Chicago.* Chicago: The Lakeside Press, 1899.

Harris, Abram L., and Sterling Spero. *The Black Worker: The Negro and the Labor Movement.* New York: Atheneum, 1969.

Harris, William H. *Keeping the Faith: A. Philip Randolph, Milton P. Webster and the Brotherhood of Sleeping Car Porters, 1925–37.* Urbana: University of Illinois Press, 1977.

Hawkins, Brett W., and Robert A. Lorinskas, eds. *The Ethnic Factor in American Politics.* Columbus, OH: Charles E. Merrill, 1970.

Haywood, Harry. *Black Bolshevik: Autobiography of an Afro-American Communist.* Chicago: Liberator Press, 1978.

Hearings Before the Subcommittee of the Judiciary of the U.S. Senate. Bill to Amend the National Prohibition Law. 69th Congress, 1st sess., April 5–24, 1926.

Helper, Rose. *Racial Policies and Practices of Real Estate Brokers.* Minneapolis: University of Minnesota Press, 1969.

Henderson, Elmer W. "A Study of the Major Factors Involved in the Change in Party Alignment of Negroes in Chicago." Unpublished M.A. thesis, University of Chicago, 1939.

Henry, Charles. "Race or Class: The Post-Liberal Dilemma." In *Race, Class and Urban Politics,* edited by Linda F. Williams and Dianne M. Pinderhughes. Chatham, NJ: Chatham House Publisher, 1987.

Herbst, Alma. *The Negro in the Slaughtering and Meat-Packing Industry in Chicago.* Boston: Houghton Mifflin, 1932.

Herrick, Mary J. "Negro Employees of the Chicago Board of Education."

Unpublished M.A. thesis, Dept of Political Science, University of Chicago, 1931.

———. *The Chicago Schools: A Social and Political History*. Beverly Hills, CA: Sage, 1971.

Higginbotham, A. Leon. *In the Matter of Color: Race and the American Legal Process: The Colonial Period.* Reprint. New York: Oxford University Press, 1980.

Hill, Robert A., ed. *The Marcus Garvey and the Universal Negro Improvement Association Papers.* Berkeley: University of California Press, 1983.

Hirsch, Arnold. "Race and Housing: Violence and Communal Protest in Chicago, 1940–1960." In *The Ethnic Frontier, Essays in the History of Group Survival in Chicago and the Midwest,* edited by Melvin G. Holli and Peter d'A. Jones, 331–68. Grand Rapids, MI: William B. Eerdmans, 1973.

———. *Making the Second Ghetto: Race and Housing in Chicago, 1940–1960.* New York: Cambridge University Press, 1983.

Historic City: The Settlement of Chicago. Chicago, 1976.

Holden, Mathew, Jr. *The Politics of the Black Nation.* New York: Chandler, 1973.

Homel, Michael W. "The Politics of Public Education in Black Chicago, 1910–1941." *Journal of Negro Education* 45 (Spring 1976): 179–91.

———. *Down From Equality Black Chicagoans and the Public Schools, 1920–1941.* Urbana: University of Illinois Press, 1984.

Houghteling, Leila. *The Income and Standard of Living of Unskilled Laborers in Chicago.* Chicago: University of Chicago Press, 1927.

Hughes, Edward J., comp. *Democratic Party Year Book.* 1934–35a, 1936–37a, 1938–39a, 1940–41a.

———. *Republican Party Year Book.* 1934–35b, 1936–37b, 1938–39b, 1940–41b.

Hughes, Elizabeth. "Living Conditions for Small Wage Earners in Chicago." Department of Public Welfare, City of Chicago, 1925.

Hull House Maps and Papers: A Presentation of Nationalities and Wages in a Congested District in Chicago. New York: Thomas Y. Crowell, 1895.

Hunter, Floyd. *Community Power Structure: A Study of Decision Makers.* Chapel Hill: University of North Carolina Press, 1953.

Institute for Contemporary Studies. *The Fairmont Papers.* San Francisco, 1981.

Jennings, Jerry T. *Voting and Registration in the Election of November 1982.* Current Population Reports, U.S. Department of Commerce, Bureau of the Census, Washington, D.C.: November 1983.

Jordan, Winthrop. *White Over Black: American Attitudes Toward the Negro, 1550–1812.* Chapel Hill: University of North Carolina Press, 1968.

Kain, John, ed. *Race and Poverty: The Economics of Discrimination.* Englewood Cliffs, NJ: Prentice Hall, 1969.

Kantowicz, Edward. "American Politics in Polonia's Capital, 1888–1930." Unpublished Ph.D. dissertation, University of Chicago, 1972.

———. *Polish American Politics in Chicago, 1880–1940.* Chicago: University of Chicago Press, 1975.

Kardiner, Abram, and Lionel Ovesey. *The Mark of Oppression: A Psycho-social Study of the American Negro.* New York: W. W. Norton, 1951.

Kariel, Henry S. "Pluralism." In *International Encyclopedia of the Social Sciences,* edited by David L. Sills, 164–69. New York: Macmillian and Free Press, 1968.

Karnig, Albert K., and Susan Welch. *Black Representatives and Urban Policy.* Chicago: University of Chicago Press, 1980.

Katznelson, Ira. *Black Men, White Cities: Race, Politics and Migration in the United States, 1900–1930, Britain, 1948–1968.* Chicago: University of Chicago Press, 1976.

———, Kathleen Gille, and Margaret Weir. "Public Schooling and Working Class Formation: The Case of the United States." Paper presented to the American Political Science Association, Sept. 1981; published in *American Journal of Education* 90 (Feb. 1982): 111–43.

Keech, William. *The Impact of Negro Voting: The Role of the Vote in the Quest for Equality.* Chicago: Rand McNally, 1968.

Keiser, R. Lincoln. *The Vice Lords: Warriors of the Streets.* New York: Holt, Rinehart and Winston, 1969.

Kellogg, Charles Flint. *NAACP: A History of the National Association for the Advancement of Colored People, 1909–1920.* Baltimore: Johns Hopkins University Press, 1967.

Kelso, William Alston. *American Democratic Theory: Pluralism and Its Critics.* Westport, CT: Greenwood Press, 1978.

Kemp, Kathleen, and Robert Lineberry. "The Last of the Great Urban Machines and the Last of the Great Urban Mayors? Chicago Politics, 1955–77." In *After Daley, Chicago Politics in Transition,* edited by Samuel K. Gove and Louis H. Masotti, 1–26. Urbana: University of Illinois Press, 1982.

Kennedy, Eugene C. *Himself!: The Life and Times of Mayor Richard J. Daley.* New York: Viking Press, 1978.

Key, V. O. *Southern Politics in State and Nation.* New York: Random House, 1949.

———. "A Theory of Critical Elections." *Journal of Politics* 17 (Feb. 1955): 3–18.

Kilson, Martin. "Black Politics, A New Power." *Dissent* 18 (Aug. 1971a): 333–45.

———. "Political Differentiation in the Negro Ghetto." In *Key Issues in the Afro-American Experience,* vol. 2, edited by Nathan Huggins, Martin Kilson, and Daniel Fox, 167–91. New York: Harcourt, Brace, Jovanovich, 1971b.

Kleppner, Paul. *Chicago Elects a Black Mayor: An Historical Analysis of the 1983 Election.* Chicago: American Jewish Committee and Northern Illinois University, 1983.

Kluger, Richard. *Simple Justice: The History of Brown v. Board of Education and Black America's Struggle for Equality.* New York: Vintage Books, 1975.

Kobler, John. *Capone: The Life and World of Al Capone.* Greenwich, CT: Fawcett, 1971.

Kovel, Joel. *White Racism: A Psychohistory.* New York: Penguin, 1970.

Kuklinski, James, and T. Wayne Parent. "Race and Big Government: An Exploration into the Sources of Racial Policy Attitudes and a Comment on Some of the SRC Race Items." Paper presented at the 1979 American Political Science Association, reprinted in *Washington Post,* Nov. 4, 1981.

Kuziniewski, Anthony. "Bootstraps and Book Learning." *Polish American Studies* 31 (Autumn 1975): 5–26.

Ladd, Everett Carl. *Negro Political Leadership in the South.* New York: Atheneum, 1969.

Lashley, Arthur V., dir. *The Illinois Crime Survey.* Chicago: Illinois Association for Criminal Justice, 1929.

Lawson, Stephen F. *Black Ballots: Voting Rights in the South, 1944–1969.* New York: Columbia University Press, 1976.

Lieberson, Stanley. *Ethnic Patterns in American Cities.* New York: Free Press of Glencoe, 1963.

Lincoln, C. Eric. *The Black Muslims in America.* 2d ed. Boston: Beacon Press, 1973.

Lindblom, Charles E. "Another State of Mind." Presidential Address, American Political Science Association, 1981, published in *American Political Science Review* 76 (March 1982): 9–21.

Long, Herman H., and Charles S. Johnson. *People vs. Property: Race Covenants in Housing.* Nashville, TN: Fisk University Press, 1947.

Love, Marsha. "Two Strategies of Bargaining in Chicago Politics: 1983." Ms. in possession of the author, Jan. 1984.

Lowi, Theodore J. "American Business, Public Policy, Case Studies and Political Theory," *World Politics* 16 (July 1964a): 677–715.

———. *At the Pleasure of the Mayor: Patronage and Power in New York City, 1898–1958.* New York: Free Press of Glencoe, 1964b.

———. *The End of Liberalism: Ideology, Policy and the Crisis of Public Authority.* New York: W. W. Norton, 1979.

Lyle, John. *The Dry and Lawless Years.* Englewood Cliffs, NJ: Prentice-Hall, 1960.

Lynd, Robert S., and Helen M. Lynd. *Middletown: A Study in Contemporary American Culture.* New York: Harcourt Brace, 1929.

MacDonald, Forrest. *Insull.* Chicago: University of Chicago Press, 1962.

MacPherson, C B. *The Real World of Democracy.* Oxford: Oxford University Press, 1966.

MacRae, Duncan, Jr., and J. A. Meldrum. "Critical Elections in Illinois, 1888–1958." *American Political Science Review* 54 (Sept. 1960): 669–83.

Madaj, Reverend Miecieslaus. "The Polish Immigrant, the American Catholic Hierarchy and Father Wenceslaus Kruszka." *Polish American Studies* 25 (Jan.-June 1969): 16–29.

Manley, John F. "Neo-Pluralism: A Class Analysis of Pluralism I and Pluralism II." *American Political Science Review* 77 (June 1983): 368–89.

Marable, Manning. "Black Nationalism in the 1970s: Through the Prism of Race and Class." *The Socialist Review* (March-June 1980): 57–108.

Mariano, John H. *The Italian Immigrant and Our Courts.* Boston: Christopher, 1925.

Martin, John Frederick. *Civil Rights and the Crisis of Liberalism: The Democratic Party, 1945–1976.* Boulder, CO: Westview, 1979.

Martin, Robert. "Racial Invasion." *Opportunity* 19 (Nov. 1941): 324–28.

Martin, Tony. *Race First: The Ideology and Organizational Struggles of Marcus Garvey and the Universal Negro Improvement Association.* Westport, CT: Greenwood, 1976.

Marvick, Dwaine. "The Political Socialization of the American Negro." *The Annals* 361 (Sept. 1965): 112–27.

Marx, Gary T. *Protest and Prejudice: A Study of Belief in the Black Community.* New York: Harper and Row, 1969.

Mathews, Donald R. *U.S. Senators and Their World.* Chapel Hill: University of North Carolina Press, 1960.

———, and James W. Prothro. *Negroes and the New Southern Politics.* New York: Harcourt, Brace and World, 1966.

McAdam, Doug. *Political Process and the Development of Black Insurgency, 1930–1970.* Chicago: University of Chicago Press, 1982.

McConnell, Grant. *Private Power and American Democracy.* New York: Vintage Books, 1966.

McFarland, Andrew S. *Power and Leadership in Pluralist Systems.* Stanford: Stanford University Press, 1969.

McWorter, Gerald, Doug Gills, and Ron Bailey. "Black Power Politics As Social Movement: Dialectics of Leadership in the Campaign to Elect Harold Washington." Urbana: Afro-American Studies and Research, University of Illinois, March 1984.

Meier, August, and Elliott Rudwick. *CORE: A Study in the Civil Rights Movement, 1942–1968.* Urbana: University of Illinois Press, 1975.

Meltzer, Milton, ed. *In Their Own Words: A History of the American Negro, 1865–1916.* New York: Thomas Y. Crowell, 1965.

Charles Merriam Papers. University of Chicago Special Collections. Chicago, Illinois.

Merriam, Charles Edward. *Chicago: A More Intimate View of Urban Politics.* New York: Macmillan, 1929.

———, chair. "Report of the City Council Committee on Crime of the City of Chicago." Chicago, March 22, 1915.

———, and Harold Gosnell. *Non-Voting: Causes and Methods of Control.* Chicago: University of Chicago Press, 1924.

———, Spencer D. Parratt, and Albert Lepawsky. *The Government of the Metropolitan Region of Chicago.* Chicago: University of Chicago Press, 1933.

Merton, Robert. *Social Theory and Social Structure.* Glencoe, IL: Free Press, 1949.

———. "The Latent Functions of the Machine." In *Urban Government: A Reader in Politics and Government,* edited by Edward Banfield, 180–90. Glencoe: Free Press, 1961.

Moehlman, Arthur B. *Public School Finance.* Chicago: Rand McNally, 1927.

Montay, Sr. Mary Innocenta. "History of Catholic Secondary Education in the Archdiocese of Chicago." Unpublished Ph.D. dissertation, Catholic University, 1953.

Morris, Aldon. *The Origins of the Civil Rights Movement: Black Communities Organizing for Change.* New York: Free Press, 1984.

Morris, Lorenzo, and Charles Henry. *The Chit'lin Controversy, Race and Public Policy in America.* Washington, D.C.: University Press of America, 1978.

Morris, Milton D. *The Politics of Black America.* New York: Harper and Row, 1975.

Morse, Steven. "The Voting Rights Act." Ms. in possession of the author, Aug. 1981.

Moses, Wilson J. "A Reappraisal of the Garvey Movement." *Black Scholar* 4 (Dec. 1972): 38–49.

Moynihan, Daniel P. *The Negro Family: The Case for National Action.* Washington, D.C.: Government Printing Office, 1965.

Mundt, Robert J., and Peggy Heilig. "District Representation: Demands and Effects in the Urban South." *Journal of Politics* 44 (Nov. 1982): 1035–48.

Myrdal, Gunnar. *An American Dilemma: The Negro Problem and Modern Democracy.* New York: McGraw-Hill, 1964.

National Commission for the Defense of Democracy Through Education of the National Education Association. "Certain Personnel Practices in the Chicago Public Schools." Washington, D.C., 1945.

Nelli, Humbert S. "Italians and Crime in Chicago, 1890–1920." *American Journal of Sociology* 74 (Jan. 1969): 373–91.

———. *The Italians in Chicago, 1880–1930: A Study in Ethnic Mobility.* New York: Oxford University Press, 1970a.

———. "John Powers and the Italians: Politics in a Chicago Ward, 1896–1921." *Journal of American History* 57 (June 1970b): 67–84.

———. *The Business of Crime: Italians and Syndicate Crime in the United States.* New York: Oxford University Press, 1976.

Nelson, William E., and Philip J. Meranto. *Electing Black Mayors: Political Action in the Black Community.* Columbus: Ohio State University Press, 1977.

Newell, Barbara Warne. *Chicago and the Labor Movement: Metropolitan Unionism in the 1930s.* Urbana: University of Illinois Press, 1961.

Nie, Norman, Sidney Verba, and John Petrocik. *The Changing American Voter.* Cambridge, MA: Harvard University Press, 1976.

Noel, David L., ed. *The Origins of American Slavery and Racism.* Columbus, OH: Charles E. Merrill, 1972.

Northrup, Herbert R. *Organized Labor and the Negro.* New York: Harper and Brothers, 1944.

O'Connor, Len. *Clout: Mayor Daley and His City.* New York: Avon Books, 1975.

Ogburn, William, and Clark Tibbits. A Memorandum on the Nativity of Certain Criminal Classes, July 30, 1930. In the Charles Merriam Papers, University of Chicago Special Collections. Chicago, Illinois.

Olson, Mancur. *The Logic of Collective Action Public Goods and the Theory of Groups.* Reprint. New York: Schocken Books, 1968.

———. "Evaluating Performance in the Public Sector." In *The Measurement of Economic and Social Performance,* edited by Milton Moss, 355–83. New

York: National Bureau of Economic Research, Columbia University Press, 1973.

Osofsky, Gilbert. *Harlem: The Making of a Ghetto: New York, 1890–1930.* New York: Harper and Row, 1966.

Ottley, Roi. *The Lonely Warrior: The Life and Times of Robert S. Abbott.* Chicago: Henry Regnery, 1955.

Parenti, Michael. "Ethnic Politics and the Persistence of Ethnic Identification." *American Political Science Review* 61 (Sept. 1967): 717–26. Reprinted in *The Ethnic Factor in American Politics,* edited by Brett W. Hawkins and Robert A. Lorinskas, 63–78. Columbus, OH: Charles E. Merrill, 1970.

Park, Robert E. *The Immigrant Press and Its Control.* New York: Harper and Brothers, 1922.

Parot, Joseph John. *Polish Catholics in Chicago, 1850–1920: A Religious History.* DeKalb, IL: Northern Illinois University Press, 1981.

Parsons, Talcott. *The Social System.* Glencoe, IL: Free Press, 1951.

Pasley, Fred. *Al Capone: The Biography of a Self-Made Man.* New York: I. Washburn, 1930.

Peterson, Paul E. "Forms of Representation: Participation of the Poor in the Community Action Program." *American Political Science Review* 64 (June 1970): 491–507.

———. *School Politics, Chicago Style.* Chicago: University of Chicago Press, 1976.

———. *City Limits.* Chicago: University of Chicago Press, 1981.

Peterson, Virgil. *Barbarians in Our Midst: A History of Chicago Crime and Politics.* Boston: Little, Brown, 1952.

———. "Chicago: Shades of Capone." *Annals of the American Academy of Political and Social Science* 347 (May 1963): 30–40.

Philpott, Thomas Lee. "The House and the Neighborhood: Housing Reform and Neighborhood Work in Chicago, 1880–1930." Unpublished Ph.D. dissertation, University of Chicago, 1974.

———. *The Slum and the Ghetto: Neighborhood Deterioration and Middle Class Reform, Chicago, 1880–1930.* New York: Oxford University Press, 1978.

Pinderhughes, Dianne. "A Retrospective Examination: The Failure of Black Power." *Journal of Afro-American Issues* 5 (Summer 1977a): 255–63.

———. "Interpretations of Racial and Ethnic Participation in American Politics: The Case of Black, Italian and Polish Communities in Chicago, 1910–1940." Unpublished Ph.D. dissertation, University of Chicago, 1977b.

———. "Collective Goods and Black Interest Groups." *Review of Black Political Economy* 12 (Winter 1983): 219–36.

———. "The Black Vote, the Sleeping Giant." In *The State of Black America, 1984,* 69–94. New York: National Urban League, Jan. 1984.

———. "Legal Strategies for Voting Rights: Political Science and the Law." *Harvard Law Journal* 28, no. 2 (1985): 515–40.

Pitkin, Hanna F. *The Concept of Representation.* Berkeley: University of California Press, 1967.

Poles of Chicago, 1837–1937: A History of One Century of Polish Contribution to the City of Chicago, Illinois. Chicago: Polish Pageant, 1937.

Pouissant, Alvin F., and Joyce Ladner. "Black Power: A Failure for Integration Within the Civil Rights Movement." *Archives of General Psychiatry* 18 (April 1968): 385–91.

Powell, Adam Clayton, Jr. *Marching Blacks: An Interpretative History of the Rise of the Black Common Man.* New York: Dial Press, 1945.

———. *Adam by Adam: The Autobiography of Adam Clayton Powell, Jr.* New York: Dial Press, 1971.

Powell, Adam Clayton, Sr. *Against the Tide: An Autobiography.* New York: R. R. Smith, 1938.

Preston, Michael B. "Black Politics and Public Policy in Chicago: Self-Interest Versus Constituent Representation." In *The New Black Politics: The Search for Political Power,* edited by Michael B. Preston, Lenneal J. Henderson, Jr., and Paul Puryear, 159–86. New York: Longman, 1982a.

———. "Black Politics in the Post-Daley era." In *After Daley: Chicago Politics in Transition,* edited by Samuel K. Gove and Louis H. Masotti, 88–117. Urbana: University of Illinois Press, 1982b.

Przudzik, Msgr. Joseph. "Schism in America." *Polish American Studies* 4 (Aug.-Sept. 1947): 39–43.

Quaintance, Esther Crockett. "Rents and Housing Conditions in the Italian District of the Lower North Side of Chicago, 1924." Unpublished M.A. thesis, University of Chicago, 1925.

"Race in the Race." *The Chicago Reporter* 12, no. 3 (March 1983).

Rainwater, Lee. "Crucible of Identity: The Negro Lower-Class Family." *Daedalus* (Winter 1966): 206–7.

Rakove, Milton. *Don't Make No Waves, Don't Back No Losers: An Insider's Analysis of the Daley Machine.* Bloomington: Indiana University Press, 1975.

———. *We Don't Want Nobody Nobody Sent: An Oral History of the Daley Years.* Bloomington: Indiana University Press, 1979.

———. "Jane Bryne and the New Chicago Politics." In *After Daley: Chicago Politics in Transition,* edited by Samuel K. Gove and Louis H. Masotti, 217–36. Urbana: University of Illinois Press, 1982.

Ransom, Roger L., and Richard Sutch. *One Kind of Freedom: The Economic Consequences of Emancipation.* Cambridge, Eng.: Cambridge University Press, 1977.

Rather, Ernest R., ed. *Chicago Negro Almanac and Reference Book.* Chicago: Chicago Negro Almanac and Reference Book Publishing Company, 1972.

Reckless, Walter C. *Vice in Chicago.* Chicago: University of Chicago Press, 1933.

Record, Wilson. *Race and Racialism: The NAACP and the Communist Party.* Ithaca, NY: Cornell University Press, 1964.

Reich, Michael. *Racial Inequality: A Political-Economic Analysis.* Princeton, NJ: Princeton University Press, 1981.

Report of the General Superintendent of Police to the City Council. Police Department, Chicago, 1878–1931.

Rich, Richard. "Distribution of Services: Studying the Product of Urban Policy Making." In *Urban Policy Making,* edited by Dale R. Marshall, 237–59. Beverly Hills, CA: Sage, 1979.

Robb, Frederick H., ed. *1927 Intercollegian Wonder Book or the Negro in Chicago, 1779–1927.* Chicago: Washington Intercollegiate Club, 1927.

Robert, Jack I. *History of the National Association for the Advancement of Colored People.* Boston: Meador, 1943.

Rollheiser, Sandra. "List of Chicago Aldermen by Ward." Chicago: Municipal Reference Library, April 1975.

Sacks, Seymour. *City Schools/Suburban Schools, A History of Fiscal Conflict.* Syracuse, NY: Syracuse University Press, 1972.

Salamon, Lester M., and Stephen Van Evera. "Fear, Apathy and Discrimination: A Test of Three Explanations of Political Participation." *American Political Science Review* 67 (Dec. 1973): 1288–1306.

Schafer, Marvin. "The Catholic Church in Chicago, Its Growth and Administration." Unpublished Ph.D. thesis, University of Chicago, 1929.

Schiavo, Giovanni. *The Italians in Chicago: A Study in Americanization.* Chicago: Italian American Publishing, 1928.

———. *What Crime Statistics Show About the Italians.* New York: Italian Historical Society, 1932.

Schwartz, Sandra Kenyon, and David C. Schwartz. "Convergence and Divergence in Political Orientations Between Blacks and Whites: 1960–1973." *Journal of Social Issues* 32 (1976): 153–68.

Scott, James. "Corruption, Machine Politics and Political Change." *American Political Science Review* 63 (Fall 1969): 1142–59.

Sexton, Patricia Cayo. *Education and Income: Inequalities of Opportunity in Our Public Schools.* New York: Viking Press, 1971.

Shingles, Richard D. "Black Consciousness and Political Participation: The Missing Link." *American Political Science Review* 75 (March 1981): 76–91.

Skogan, Wesley G. *Chicago Since 1840: A Time-Series Handbook.* Urbana, IL: Institute of Government and Public Affairs, 1976.

Smith, Robert. "On Studying Black Leadership in America: A Review Essay." Unpublished manuscript, Howard University, 1981.

Sowell, Thomas, ed. *Essays and Data on American Ethnic Groups.* Washington, D.C.: The Urban Institute, 1978.

———. *Ethnic America: A History.* New York: Basic Books, 1981.

"Spasmodic Diary of a Chicago School Teacher." *Atlantic Monthly* 152 (Nov. 1933): 513–26.

Spear, Allan. *Black Chicago: The Making of a Negro Ghetto, 1890–1920.* Chicago: University of Chicago Press, 1967.

Special Committee to Investigate Crime in Interstate Commerce. U.S. Congress. *Senate Hearing on the Investigation of Organized Crime in Interstate Commerce,* 81st Congress, 2d sess. Washington, D.C., 1951.

Steffens, Lincoln. *The Autobiography of Lincoln Steffens.* New York: Harcourt, Brace, 1931.

Strayer, George D. *Report of the Survey of the Schools of Chicago, Illinois.* New York: Columbia University Teachers College, 1932.

Stratton, William J., comp. *Democratic Party Year Book,* 1930a, 1932a.

———. *Republican Party Year Book,* 1930b, 1932b.

Strickland, Arvarh. *The History of the Chicago Urban League.* Urbana: University of Illinois Press, 1966.

Stuart, William H. *The Twenty Incredible Years, As "Heard and Seen" By William H. Stuart.* Chicago: Donohue, 1936.

Stuckey, Sterling. *The Ideological Origins of Black Nationalism.* Boston: Beacon Press, 1972.

Sullivan, Denis G., Robert T. Nakamura, and Richard F. Winters. *How America is Ruled.* New York: Wiley, 1980.

Taylor, Paul S. *Mexican Labor in the United States.* Berkeley: University of California Press, 1931.

"Teachers' Salaries and Teacher Load." *Research Bulletin of the National Education Association* 11 (Sept. 1933): 88–90.

Thomas, Richard. "Survival and Progress in Detroit: Black Bourgeois Style." Paper presented at the Association for the Study of Afro-American Life and History, Philadelphia, Nov. 1981.

Thomas, William I., and Florian Znaniecki. *The Polish Peasant in Europe and America: Monograph of an Immigrant Group.* 5 vols. Boston: Richard G. Badger, Gorham Press, 1918.

Thompson, Daniel C. *The Negro Leadership Class.* Englewood Cliffs, NJ: Prentice Hall, 1963.

Thrasher, Frederick M. *The Gang: A Study of 1,313 Gangs in Chicago.* Chicago: University of Chicago Press, 1936.

Thurner, Arthur. "Polish American Politics in Chicago, 1890–1930." *Polish American Studies* 28 (Spring 1971): 20–21.

———. "Review of Edward R. Kantowicz, *Polish American Politics in Chicago, 1880–1930.*" *Polish American Studies* 32 (Autumn 1975): 64–70.

Toothaker, O. H. "A Basis Standard for the School Budget." *American School Board Journal* 67 (Sept. 1923): 47–48.

Travis, Toni-Michelle C. "Racial and Class Consciousness Among Black Political Activists in Boston." Unpublished Ph.D. dissertation, University of Chicago, 1983.

Truman, David. *The Governmental Process: Political Interests and Public Opinion.* New York: Knopf, 1951.

Tuttle, William M., Jr. "Labor Conflict and Racial Violence: The Black Worker in Chicago, 1894–1919." *Labor History* 10 (Summer 1969): 408–32.

———. *Race Riot: Chicago in the Red Summer of 1919.* Reprint. New York: Atheneum, 1972.

Ullman, Victor. *Martin R. Delaney: The Beginnings of Black Nationalism.* Boston: Beacon Press, 1971.

U.S. Congress. Senate Special Committee to Investigate Crime in Interstate Commerce. *Investigation of Organized Crime in Interstate Commerce.* 2d sess., Washington, D.C., 1951.

Vecoli, Rudolph. "Chicago's Italians Prior to World War I: A Study of their

Social and Economic Adjustment." Unpublished Ph.D. dissertation, University of Wisconsin, 1963.

———. "Contadini in Chicago: A Critique of *The Uprooted.*" *Journal of American History* 51 (Dec. 1964): 402–17.

Verba, Sidney, and Gabriel A. Almond. *The Civic Culture, Political Attitudes and Democracy in Five Nations, An Analytic Study.* Boston: Little, Brown, 1965.

Verba, Sidney, and Norman Nie. *Participation in America.* New York: Harper and Row, 1972.

Vidich, Arthur J., and Joseph Bensman. *Small Town in Mass Society: Class, Power and Religion in a Rural Community.* Princeton, NJ: Princeton University Press, 1968.

Vieg, John A. *The Government of Education in Metropolitan Chicago.* Chicago: University of Chicago Press, 1939.

Walden, Daniel, ed. *W. E. B. DuBois: The Crisis Writings.* Greenwich, CT: Fawcett, 1972.

Walters, Ronald. "African-American Nationalism." *Black World* 22 (Oct. 1973): 9–27.

Walton, Hanes. *Black Politics: A Theoretical and Structural Analysis.* Philadelphia: J. B. Lippincott, 1972.

Wargin, Sr. Lucille, C. R. "The Polish Immigrant in the American Community, 1880–1930." Unpublished M.A. thesis, DePaul University, 1948.

Washington, Booker T. *Up From Slavery: An Autobiography.* New York: Bantam Pathfinder Editions, 1970.

Wells, Ida B. *Crusade for Justice: The Autobiography of Ida B. Wells,* ed., Alfreda Wells Duster. New York: Bobbs-Merrill, 1970.

Wendt, Lloyd, and Herman Kogan. *Lords of the Levee: The Story of Bathouse John and Hinky Dink.* New York: Bobbs-Merrill, 1943.

———. *Big Bill of Chicago.* New York: Bobbs-Merrill, 1953.

White, Philip V. "Political Socialization and Political Obfuscation: Black Americans in the 1960s." Paper presented at the Midwest Political Science Association, Chicago, 1977.

Wildavsky, Aaron B. *Leadership in a Small Town.* Totowa, NJ: Bedminister Press, 1964.

Wilkins, Roy. "The NAACP and the Black Political Convention," *The Crisis* 79 (1972): 229–31.

Williams, Chancellor. *The Destruction of Black Civilization: Great Issues of a Race From 4500 B.C. to 2000 A.D.* Chicago: Third World Press, 1974.

Williams, Eric. *Capitalism and Slavery.* New York: Russell and Russell, 1961.

Williams, Linda Faye. "Race, Class and Politics: The Impact of American Political Economy on Black Detroit." Unpublished Ph.D. dissertation, University of Chicago, 1977.

Wilson, James Q. *Negro Politics: The Search for Leadership.* New York: Free Press, 1960a.

———. "Two Negro Politicians." *Midwest Journal of Political Science* 4 (Nov. 1960b): 346–69.

———. *Political Organizations.* New York: Basic Books, 1973.

Wilson, Paula. "Black Aldermen Search For New Power in the Post-Daley Era." *The Chicago Reporter* 7 (Jan. 1978): 1–8.

Wilson, Ronald. "African-American Nationalism." *Black World* 22 (Oct. 1973): 9–27.

Wilson, William J. *The Declining Significance of Race: Blacks and Changing American Institutions.* Chicago: University of Chicago Press, 1978.

Wirt, Frederick M. *Politics of Southern Equality: Law and Social Change in a Mississippi County.* Chicago: Aldine, 1970.

Wirth, Louis, and Margaret Furez. *Local Community Fact Book.* Chicago: Chicago Recreation Commission, 1938.

Wisniewski, Reverend Joseph A., C. R. "Saint Stanislaus Kostka Parish in Chicago: Its Spiritual, Educational and Cultural Legacy to the 600,000 Americans of Polish Extraction, 1869–1908." Unpublished M.A. thesis, DePaul University, 1965.

Wolfinger, Raymond E. "The Development and Persistence of Ethnic Voting." *American Political Science Review* 59 (Dec. 1965): 896–908. Reprinted in *The Ethnic Factor in American Politics,* edited by Brett W. Hawkins and Robert Lorinskas, 101–23. Columbus, OH: Charles E. Merrill, 1970.

———. "Why Political Machines Have Not Withered Away and Other Revisionist Thoughts," *Journal of Politics* 34 (May 1972): 365–98.

———. *The Politics of Progress.* Englewood Cliffs, NJ: Prentice-Hall, 1974.

Wooddy, Carroll Hill. *The Chicago Primary of 1926: A Study in Election Methods.* Chicago: University of Chicago Press, 1926.

Woodson, Carter G. *The History of the Negro Church.* Washington, D.C.: Associated Publishers, 1921.

Works Progress Administration Files. Carter G. Woodson Regional Library Center, Chicago Public Library, Chicago.

Wright, Nathan, ed. *What Black Politicians Are Saying.* New York: Hawthorn Books, 1972.

Wytrwal, Joseph A. *America's Polish Heritage: A Social History of the Poles in America.* Detroit: Endurance Press, 1961.

Zikmund, Joseph II. "Mayoral Voting and Ethnic Politics in the Daley-Bilandic-Byrne Era." In *After Daley: Chicago Politics in Transition,* edited by Samuel K. Gove and Louis Masotti, 27–56. Urbana: University of Illinois Press, 1982.

Zinn, Howard. *SNNC: The New Abolitionists.* Boston: Beacon Press, 1964.

Zuziniewski, Anthony. "The Polish National Catholic Church." *Polish American Studies* 31 (Spring 1974): 30–34.

Index

A Note on the Author

Dianne M. Pinderhughes is assistant professor in the political science and Afro-American studies faculties of the University of Illinois at Urbana-Champaign. She received her master's and doctoral degrees in political science from the University of Chicago. She spent a year on a Ford Foundation postdoctoral fellowship at the Center for Afro-American Studies at the University of California at Los Angeles, where she completed work on this book.